ECOLOGY, THE SHAPING ENQUIRY

ECOLOGY, THE SHAPING ENQUIRY

A course given at the
Institute of Contemporary Arts

EDITED BY
Jonathan Benthall

LONGMAN

LONGMAN GROUP LIMITED
London

Associated companies, branches and representatives throughout the world

First published 1972

ISBN 0 582 12659 2 cased
0 582 12660 6 paper

Printed in Great Britain by
T. & A. Constable Ltd, Hopetoun Street, Edinburgh

CONTENTS

Culture and Nature

PART TWO: CONTEMPORARY ISSUES

SOURCES OF LINE DRAWINGS

Chapter 4
Fig. 2 is copied from J. P. M. Pannell: *Techniques of Industrial Archaeology*, David and Charles, 1966
Fig. 3 is from Agricola's *De Re Metallica*, 1546
Fig. 5 is from C. Thomlinson: *Cyclopaedia of Useful Arts and Manufactures*, published in the early 1850s
Fig. 6 is from Sheridan Muspratt: *Chemistry as applied and relating to Arts and Manufactures*, 1860
Fig. 7 is from C. Thomlinson: *Illustrations of Useful Arts, Manufactures, and Trades*, *c.* 1850
Fig. 8 is from *Knight's Cyclopaedia of the Industry of All Ages*, 1851
Figs 1 and 4 are from the author's collection

Chapter 7
Figs 1-4 are drawn by Miss M. E. Ogilvie, Department of Anatomy, University of Otago, New Zealand

Chapter 10
Fig. 1 is reproduced by permission of General Engineering Co. (Radcliffe) Ltd, Manchester

Chapter 12
Figs 1 and 2 are © E. M. Nicholson 1970

What have they done to the earth?
What have they done to our fair sister?
Ravaged and plundered
And ripped her and bit her
Stuck her with knives
In the side of the dawn and
Tied her with fences
And dragged her down.

From 'When the Music's Over'
by The Doors

INTRODUCTION

JONATHAN BENTHALL

Generations have trod, have trod, have trod;
And all is seared with trade; bleared, smeared with toil
And wears man's smudge and shares man's smell: the soil
Is bare now, nor can foot feel, being shod.

And for all this, nature is never spent;
There lives the dearest freshness deep down things . . .

Gerard Manley Hopkins,
'God's Grandeur'

THE Institute of Contemporary Arts winter lecture courses are now becoming an annual tradition. 'Ecology, The Shaping Enquiry' was the second in the series, held in 1970-71, following a course on Linguistics the previous season.

The ICA, not being constrained by academic curricula or departmental structures, can approach a subject such as ecology from a broad inter-disciplinary perspective. The implications of ecology are immense and this lecture course certainly does not claim to be complete. But it is unusually wide-ranging and in some aspects of the subject, such as that aspect covered by Mary Douglas, it has broken new ground.

The term ecology has been bandied about indiscriminately, and speculation about the world ecological crisis has often been rather hysterical. There has been a backlash. For instance, some now claim that the ecology movement is, or was, a mere fashion whipped up by journalists. It is also pointed out that many scientists interpret the available data fairly optimistically, and that science and technology may find ways that we cannot foresee to cope with environmental problems. Certain aspects of the total problem, particularly the issue of over-population, have provoked passionate controversy.

No one can claim to have the answer to these problems. This lecture course is an attempt to let in some air and prevent any one aspect of the subject being isolated from the whole. But certain principles were clear to us when we planned the course, and have helped to give it coherence.

First, the ecology movement is not a flash in the pan but a real change in consciousness, of the widest cultural relevance. It is only recently that scientists have given much priority to biological processes at a super-organismic level. Until recently, schoolchildren were taught to classify and dissect nature. The ecological approach teaches us to construe and articulate nature. (Ecology might be called the syntax of nature.)

Second, the cause of ecology and conservation is now a major political issue – in the United States and Japan even more than in the British Isles. Crucial political questions such as economic growth, industrial colonialism, population control and the freedom of the consumer are bound up with the debate about ecology. The available facts about the state of the biosphere can be used to support either repressive authoritarian policies, or revolutionary libertarian policies, or any ideological nuance in between. It is possible that new political alignments will emerge from the ecology movement, and especially from its emphasis on the unity and indivisibility of 'Spaceship Earth'. The political and economic problems raised can only be tackled internationally.

Third, ecology is no longer merely a subsection of biology but also an annexe of the social sciences and the humanities. Man's relationships with animals, plants and inanimate nature reflect, and interact with, his social structures and the symbolic world of his imagination. Artists have traditionally been inspired by the natural environment as much as by their fellow-men, and it is no accident that many artists and poets are interested in ecology today. Christianity, and many of the other great religions, have proposed detailed orderings of man's relationships with the living world and the inanimate world. But nowadays most of us in the West live by a hotchpotch of humanist and utilitarian moral beliefs. How *can* we make up our minds about the optimum use of material resources – when most of us have no idea what, if anything, makes life worth living at all? Any 'human ecology' worthy of the name must take account of the full needs and resources of man in nature, including his psychological or spiritual needs.

The contributors to this volume differ greatly from each other in method and style, and we have made no attempt to impose homogeneity. Part One is devoted, by and large, to Theory, and Part Two to Practice. It will be apparent from a glance at the titles of the papers that the term 'ecology' has been interpreted very broadly. When ecology was defined merely as a branch of biology, a discussion of the 'practical' aspects of ecology would presumably have been devoted mainly to techniques of field-work. In this volume, the only papers that deal with such techniques – Raymond Vaissière's and Mary Marples's – appear in Part One, which contains historical material also. The 'practical' half of the volume is devoted to various aspects of the world's *present* social and environmental crisis and its possible remedies.

Part One, 'Theory' is divided into three sections: *Chronological*, *Model Ecosystems*, and *Culture and Nature*.

The *Chronological* section begins with a discussion by **N. W. Pirie** of 'The Biosphere Without Man'. This is necessarily the most theoretical of all the contributions to this volume, and one which the non-scientific reader may find a little daunting in parts. He reviews with subtlety and erudition various competing theories about the origin of life on earth, and various definitions of 'life' that have been offered. The chemical cycles in our biosphere are also introduced in this paper. **Hans Kalmus's** paper, 'Living Together Without Man' covers the basic principles of ecology in somewhat more detail, emphasizing the richness of interactions among plants, animals and their habitats, and incorporating also some material from recent studies of animal behaviour. Among the modes of organic interaction outlined by Kalmus are *commensalism, parasitism, predation, symbiosis, pollination and mimicry*. He concludes that it is not the existence of life which man is increasingly threatening by proliferation, expansion and industrial activity but the 'infinite richness and diversity of the organic world'.

This is followed by 'The Impact of Man on Nature', where **C. D. Darlington** traces the process by which men acquired a monopoly of the world's resources and exploited it through successive technical innovations. Among the subjects he covers are man's colonisation of the earth; the development of settled farming; environmental disasters such as those in Mesopotamia and the Indus; the destruction of forests; and the growth of infectious diseases. Darlington traces a pattern whereby repeatedly man has used his inventions for short-term advantage at the expense of the long-term future; but 'in some groups among some peoples there are always likely to be a few who can see far enough ahead to warn the rest'. **Archie Clow's** paper 'The Influence of Technology on Environment' is concerned mainly with the last two millennia and concentrates on the British Isles, since it was there that, during the later part of the eighteenth century, anxiety about population and pollution first began to be seriously felt. As Clow shows, our present-day concern over the environmental effects of the chemical and extractive industries, and over the running-down of scarce resources, has a long historical background.

Peter Self's paper 'The City and its Environment' explores some theories and beliefs about cities and their environment. He criticises both the Chicago School of Social Geography – which applied a botanical model to land-use in cities – and also the view that the city is a tension-point of excessive population growth. If anything can be learnt by applying ecological principles to urban studies, it is, Self argues, that we are concerned with the relations between men and their *total* environment. A synoptic approach to urban problems, drawing on many branches of the social sciences, is therefore called for. The problems of the city are problems of social adjustment and political management. Self closes with a review of various theories of future cities; after considering the opposing views of Jane Jacobs and Melvin Webber, he examines the concept of the city region as the most fruitful and realistic theory available to us.

The second section, *Model Ecosystems,* is designed to give some impression (without which the volume would be incomplete) of the diversity of ecological systems and of the range of procedures needed to explore them. **Raymond Vaissière's** paper 'A Model Marine Ecosystem: 24 Hours in the Life of a Rock-Pool' is representative of a biology equipped with the tools of cybernetics and information theory. Vaissière considers how a hypothetical rock-pool and its inhabitants are affected by the flow of tides, and sun-rise and nightfall, in a cycle of twenty-four hours. He outlines the techniques whereby flows of physical energy through the ecosystem can be tracked, quantified and mathematically simulated; and those whereby the composition of the different communities of organisms in the pool can be analysed.

Mary Marples's 'The Human Skin as an Ecosystem' is very different. The 'flora' and 'fauna' inhabiting our skin provide an unusual illustration of ecological interaction. Though these organisms are very small or invisible, their propinquity to ourselves gives them a special interest, and many readers will be surprised by some of the facts that Marples's paper discloses. It may also stimulate philosophical speculation about the ethics and aesthetics of man's relationship with the animal kingdom.

The third section, *Culture and Nature*, ranges outside the field of natural science to explore some of the cultural implications of ecology. **Mary Douglas** in 'Environments at Risk' contributes some insights from ethnology and particularly from the Durkheimian tradition of sociology. Without questioning the truth and objectivity of scientific facts, Professor Douglas draws attention to the process whereby first the experts – with emotional investments in their respective systems of discourse – select and interpret these facts, and then the layman – 'whose horizon is his back yard' – selects from the available interpretations. 'How to be credible? This perennial problem of religious creed is now a worry for ecology.' Her paper discusses how risks and dangers are perceived and handled by various societies; how movements such as the ecology movement succeed in changing opinion; how 'nature' – like time, money and God – is used as a verbal weapon of social control; how different societies tend to blame different classes of people for putting their environment at risk; and how perhaps we may learn to use our self-awareness to confront our present dangers more wisely. Though her closing prescriptions appear to be almost immiscible, the diagnosis is searching and provocative.

Raymond Williams, the cultural historian and social critic, closes the first part of the book with a survey of how the word 'nature' has been used since classical times, through the middle ages and the eighteenth and nineteenth centuries, up till the present day. 'The idea of nature contains, though often unnoticed, an extraordinary amount of human history.' Williams has some harsh words for some contemporary conservation enthusiasts who spend week-ends in the country 'and then go back, spiritually refreshed, to invest in the smoke and the spoil'. His arguments relate interestingly to Mary Douglas's.

In part two of the book, 'Contemporary Issues', the titles of each lecture are more self-explanatory, except for **Steven Rose's** 'The Real Significance of CBW', where CBW stands for Chemical and Biological Warfare.

Two special points, however, may be made. First, **Michael Allaby's** lecture on Food condemns the present use of artificial fertilisers and pesticides vehemently, and we thought it fair to include in this volume a comment on his arguments by **Dr C. D. Sutton**, a leading agriculturalist who works for a British fertiliser company. Secondly, **E. Eric Pochin's** lecture 'Man's Exposure to Radiation', which emphasises the importance of statistical risk analysis, could be read not only as a quantitative study of the particular problem of radiation but also as a provisional working model for the examination and control of other pollutants and potential hazards.

The volume closes with **Barry Commoner's** 'The Social Use and Misuse of Technology'. Though this paper does not claim to be a complete analysis of the problem – for instance, it deals largely with North America – Dr Commoner points the way forward more constructively, perhaps, than do those who inflate a single aspect of the environmental crisis – such as over-population – as if it were the chief determinant. The social use of technology is clearly one of the kernel issues that will preoccupy us in the 1970s.

After reading about the contemporary issues of ecology, the reader may well be confused and puzzled by the mixture of facts, theories and value-judgments that have been offered him. He may feel that the most pressing need is for political lobbying, and direct action by the citizen. Many of the audience who listened to the lectures at the ICA came away with this conclusion, and a group of them – in collaboration with 'Friends of the Earth' – organised a demonstration in which they re-cycled thousands of non-returnable glass bottles by dumping them at the head office of Schweppes in London. This was but a pale counterpart of the more damaging acts of 'ecotage' that have been tried out in the United States.

Direct action, and lobbying through orthodox political channels, are both healthy signs of practical progress in the ecology movement. But other readers of this book will want to return to the searching theoretical speculations about Culture and Nature by Mary Douglas and Raymond Williams, who draw on two great traditions of enquiry: social anthropology and the study of literary culture.

Williams writes: 'It will be a sign that we are beginning to think in some necessary ways when we can conceive [of economics and ecology] becoming, as they ought to become, a single discipline'. Clearly the idea of interdisciplinary studies has a long way to develop before this conception becomes anything like a reality. Clearly there are dangers in dismantling the barriers between disciplines when this is done unintelligently, since the result is intellectual anarchy. In this lecture-series the ICA has attempted to point the way towards new and vital syntheses, as we shall continue to do in future.

PART I
THEORY

Chronological

1

THE BIOSPHERE WITHOUT MAN

N. W. PIRIE

THE past changes that living organisms have made in the character and composition of the surface layers of the earth are vastly greater than the recent effects of manhandling with which these papers are mainly concerned. Like other scientists, geochemists and cosmologists are addicted to making confident but contradictory statements; and there is no reason to think that the last word has been spoken and that our opinions about the character and composition of the probiotic environment (i.e. the environment before life emerged) will not be as fluid in future as they have been in the past; but there are a few fully relevant facts from which very probable deductions can be drawn.

1. The present-day plant cover could make the amount of oxygen now present in the atmosphere in two to three thousand years. The presence of oxygen now tells us, therefore, nothing about the distant past.
2. The inert gases (those which form no chemical compounds) are, as Goldschmidt pointed out,[1] very much rarer than their cosmic abundance would lead one to expect; the heavier members of the group (krypton and xenon) would be held by gravitational attraction in present-day conditions.
3. The iron in plutonic rock is predominantly in the ferrous state whereas that in sediments is predominantly ferric. Furthermore, there are many substances (e.g. sulphides) in plutonic rock that would, like ferrous iron, have reacted with any free oxygen. And hydrogen is the most abundant substance in the universe.

Many different conclusions can be, and have been, drawn from these facts. The earth may have originated by the accretion of cold cosmic detritus, by the condensation of a wisp of solar material, or in some other way. Regardless of its origin it is likely that it started without an atmosphere (otherwise the inert gases should not be so rare) and built one up by modifying volcanic and other exhalations. Some authorities argue, partly on the basis of spectroscopic evidence about the atmospheres of the giant planets Jupiter and Saturn, that the original atmosphere consisted mainly of hydrogen, methane, ammonia and water vapour. Others argue in favour of an atmosphere of hydrogen, carbon monoxide, carbon dioxide, nitrogen and water vapour. Each group is dogmatic; biologists may well suspend judgement. All seem to be agreed, however, about the absence of primordial oxygen. The evidence was surveyed recently by Cloud.[2]

Oxygen could have been formed by the non-biological photodissociation of carbon dioxide or water, but there is disagreement about the concentration that would thereby be built up, because oxygen, or ozone derived from it, would have screened all but the upper levels of the atmosphere from solar ultra-violet light and so would have limited the extent of the photodissociation. Furthermore, the ferrous iron and sulphides exposed during the weathering of rock at the surface would combine with oxygen as it was formed. The quantities are interesting. The atmosphere now contains 12×10^{20} g of oxygen. This figure may be more immediately comprehensible if expressed as 235 g per sq cm of the earth's surface ($5{\cdot}12 \times 10^{18}$ sq cm). There is disagreement about the amount of 'fossil' oxygen that was consumed in making sulphate and ferric iron. The former may have consumed 940 g per sq cm; estimates for the latter quantity range from 250 to 600. It is, however, reasonable to conclude that significantly more oxygen has passed through the atmosphere than is now present in it. The total of past and present oxygen may have been 1800 g per sq cm.

If most of the oxygen that has passed through the atmosphere was formed photosynthetically from carbon dioxide, there should, as Dumas & Boussingault and Herbert Spencer pointed out, be an equivalence between oxygen and the carbon now present in reduced forms, such as coal and oil, of presumed biological origin. At one time the amount of carbon seemed disconcertingly small; recently, with the recognition of the importance of carbonaceous material in sediments, it seems to be too large. This carbon is unevenly distributed, but the estimated 3×10^{21} g of it would give about 600 g per sq cm and that would, if produced photosynthetically, correspond to nearly 2000 g of oxygen. Some estimates demand twice that quantity. The discrepancy can be interpreted in various ways: kerogen and other carbon compounds in rock may not all have been made by photosynthesis; if made by photosynthesis part of the carbon may have started in the more reduced forms of methane or carbon monoxide thus producing less concomitant oxygen; more oxygen than is allowed for in current estimates may have come from the dissociation of water with loss of hydrogen into space; the estimate quoted may not be as firmly based as is assumed; and so on.

Although initially free from oxygen, it is reasonable to assume that the atmosphere contained some by −3 G* years, for there are oxidised sediments as old or older than that. That is to say, the appearance of oxygen in the atmosphere and the appearance of first organisms of which we have a record seem to have been approximately simultaneous. The oxygen pressure in the atmosphere at any date before the Jurassic period is entirely uncertain. It can be plausibly argued that the sea became oxygenated before the atmosphere, and that its universal oxygenation was preceded by a phase in which there were oxygen-rich enclaves, and that plants and animals had to wait for oxygen to diffuse out of the sea before they colonised the land. The position in the Devonian is curious. The vast Devonian deposits containing ferric iron suggest abundant oxygen, and the large size of late Devonian and Carboniferous insects suggests, assuming that as in present-day insects their respiration depended on tracheal diffusion, that the oxygen pressure was then greater than it is now. Otherwise they would have had difficulty in maintaining a rate of energy production necessary for an activity such as flight. There is no geological evidence for a proliferation of vegetation, and deposition of reduced carbon compounds, on a scale that would account for a rate of photosynthetic oxygen production so very much greater than the present rate.

Atmospheric carbon dioxide raises other serious problems. There is now sixty-seven times as much in the oceans as in the atmosphere. The equilibrium between ocean and atmosphere is attained quickly, in geological terms, but depends on the alkalinity of the ocean and this has probably not remained constant. Arrhenius postulated intense volcanic activity in the Carboniferous as a means for producing extra carbon dioxide and consequently the enhanced growth of vegetation to which he attributed the laying down of coal. It has

* G = 1,000 million.

to be remembered, however, that deposition of peat (and hence of lignite and coal) is a measure neither of the standing crop nor the rate of photosynthesis but of the imbalance between photosynthesis and microbial destruction of what has been photosynthesised. There

Geological Time-Chart

Period	*Series and epoch*	*Distinctive records of life*	*1000 years*
		CENOZOIC ERA	
Quaternary	Recent	Modern man	11
	Pleistocene	Early man	1,000
Tertiary	Pliocene	Large carnivores	
	Miocene	Whales, apes, grazing forms	
	Oligocene	Large browsing mammals	
	Eocene	Rise of flowering plants	
	Paleocene	First placental mammals	70,000
		MESOZOIC ERA	
Cretaceous		Extinction of dinosaurs	130,000
Jurassic		Dinosaurs' zenith, primitive birds, first small mammals	160,000
Triassic		Appearance of dinosaurs	200,000
		PALEOZOIC ERA	
Permian		Reptiles developed, conifers abundant	235,000
Carboniferous		First reptiles, coal forests; sharks abundant	285,000
Devonian		Amphibians appeared, fishes abundant	320,000
Silurian		Earliest land plants and animals	350,000
Ordovician		First primitive fishes	400,000
Cambrian		Marine invertebrates	500,000
		PRE-CAMBRIAN TIME	
		Few fossils	3,500,000-4,000,000

can be no certainty about the nature of the factors that might have led to widespread microbial inefficiency in Carboniferous times. Microbial activity, i.e. rotting and decay, is now producing much more carbon dioxide than industry, and Goldschmidt estimated that industry is now producing two hundred times as much as volcanoes. It seems unlikely therefore that, during any biologically relevant phase of earth's evolution, there was volcanic activity on a scale that would have increased atmospheric carbon dioxide significantly. Furthermore, the dust resulting from such activity would have diminished photosynthesis more than the extra carbon dioxide would have increased it. If the concentration of atmospheric carbon dioxide was, at one time, greater than it is now, it would seem reasonable to postulate a change in the volume or composition of the ocean rather than an increase in volcanicity.

Gaseous nitrogen is so inert that it is not likely, even if present, to have played a significant part in the metabolism of the original organisms. For consistency, however, its origin is worthy of brief consideration. The rarity of neon and argon, which resemble nitrogen in molecular weight and so are likely to have been held to a similar extent by gravitation, suggests that any initial nitrogen was lost along with the inert gases at an early stage in atmospheric evolution. Analogy with the giant planets leads many authorities to postulate a primitive atmosphere rich in ammonia but this idea is vigorously disputed by Abelson[3]. Ammonia does, however, occur in volcanic gases and there is about 0·005 per cent of it in most plutonic rock. This contains twenty times as much nitrogen as there is in the atmosphere now. It is therefore reasonable to postulate the presence of some ammonia in the primitive atmosphere and to regard present-day atmospheric nitrogen as a secondary product of biological activity or photo-oxidation. Cyanides and cyanogen have been recognized in comets and other extraterrestrial sites, but the now familiar deduction from the rarity of the inert gases suggests that they would not have been prominent components of the original atmosphere.

In summary: it can be regarded as certain that the primitive atmosphere did not contain oxygen, but there is no certainty as yet about its composition nor about the pressure of oxygen in it at any period before the last few hundred million years.

Towards the end of last century, Darwin, Huxley, Tyndall and others assumed that organic matter would have been present before the appearance of life on earth. It was well known that hydrocarbons were formed when iron that contained carbon was dissolved in acid, and that an extensive range of substances, including polymers such as tars and azulmic acid, formed in aged solutions of ammonium cyanide. There has recently been a great resurgence of interest in reactions of this type. It is a pity that those who do this work direct their attention primarily to the small and familiar organic molecules that are easy to recognise on a chromatogram. If this work should turn out to have any bearing on the problems of the origins or nature of life, it is likely that it will be the larger molecules and polymers that are most significant. Haldane[4] and Oparin pointed out that solar ultra-violet light would promote further syntheses and that, in the absence of organisms, the organic matter would accumulate so that the first organisms could have been heterotrophic, metabolising preformed organic matter. This idea is now widely accepted. The idea does, however, deserve rather more careful scrutiny than it usually gets.

The suggestion is often made that the first organisms, supplied with organic matter in an environment without free oxygen, would have got the energy they needed by fermentation. That is to say, by catalysing the breakdown of a molecule (such as glucose in conventional alcoholic fermentation) that is stable in the absence of the catalyst. But *stable* is a quantitative term. The molecules with which the original proto-organisms, or *eobionts*, would have been confronted must, *ex hypothesi*, have been sufficiently stable to persist, presumably in solution, for a few million years on earth's surface. Though the organic matter may have been complex, it seems likely that all but the part most recently formed would already have undergone those reactions of which it was capable and attained a state that was stable in that environment. Organisms today exist because they can make use of an actual or potential energy flux and it is hard to visualise an eobiont that did not exist in a similar way. Light is the most obvious energy flux that would have been available. Present-day anaerobic photosynthetic bacteria, although vastly more complex in their capacities, are probably the nearest analogues for eobionts. It is interesting to note, however, that they do not make oxygen as a product of their photosynthesis. Furthermore, photosynthesis is not concerned always with the reduction of carbon dioxide; for example, some algae use light to supply the energy needed for the assimilation of acetate.

Until there was oxygen in the atmosphere there could have been no ozone. Ozone absorbs ultra-violet light strongly so that in its absence more of the sun's ultra-violet light would have reached ground level; this is the essence of the suggestion that there was extensive probiotic synthesis of organic matter. Ultra-violet light, at the postulated intensity, is lethal to present-day organisms and it is therefore often argued that eobionts would not have developed on the surface but only when submerged under several metres of water. There seems to be little force in this argument, because sensitivity to light depends on the presence in an organism of molecules that absorb light, become activated in consequence, and are then unable to get rid of the activation energy by any useful, or at any rate non-destructive, process. There is no reason to assume that the original catalytic systems would be damaged in this way. The assumption is tantamount to saying that eobionts behaved like sun-lit cattle that have eaten buckwheat and so become sensitised to light. Experience of the opportunism of organisms, and presumably of proto-organisms, suggests that a few million years of selection under ultra-violet light would have produced eobionts that were suitably adapted. They may have used the light for photosynthesis, or been opaque and so screened from it, or transparent at the relevant wavelengths so that the energy was not absorbed. The last possibility would exclude the use of most of the aromatic and heterocyclic compounds that now dominate biochemistry. As will be argued later, this is not a fundamental objection; for, in thinking about the origins of life, it is fallacious to make the unnecessary assumption that the early forms resembled present-day forms closely. There is absolutely no reason to assume that the original catalytic systems would have been damaged by such radiation as they could not use.

An alternative to the idea that eobionts were able to use light to bring about reactions among molecules that were sufficiently stable in one another's presence to have been able to coexist for millions of years, would be to invoke the use of activated molecules diffusing from the illuminated surface. According to this picture the eobiont would itself be protected from light, perhaps by submersion, but would depend on free radicals, or hydrogen peroxide, produced on illuminated mineral or other catalytic surfaces. In essence the only difference between these hypotheses is that in the former the surface that is using light to create a chemical disequilibrium, on which further action depends, is juxtaposed to the system using the energy, whereas in the latter they are separated to an arbitrary degree. The stage of vital evolution with which we are concerned presumably preceded the development of a cell wall. In an unencompassed catalytic system this spatial difference is not definable and may not be significant. Of all the possible types of energy flux that have been suggested – radioactivity, winds, electric fields, tides, heat flow from inside the earth, and pre-existing chemical disequilibrium – light seems much the most likely to have been important initially: just as it is today.

There is much uncertainty about the composition of the original terrestrial atmosphere, the intensity and quality of solar radiation at ground level, the consequent temperature of the surface, and the nature of the rock that made up the initial surface: speculation is therefore almost untrammelled about the nature of the organic matter that could have accumulated on the surface of the probiotic earth. Within very broad limits, if a chemical system should some time be discovered that, on prolonged incubation in the laboratory, unequivocally integrated itself into the life-like structures that have been claimed, the fact that the substances involved are not part of the conventional biological canon could not be given as a reason for refusing to accept that system as a stage in, or as an analogue for, *biopoesis* (or the initial creation of life).

Sceptical, or uncommitted, statements such as those in the last paragraph are often regarded with some impatience because no organism is known that does not contain protein and every known effective biocatalyst, or enzyme, contains protein also. From these facts the deduction is often drawn that life is a phenomenon inseparable from proteins and that a theory of biopoesis must start by describing the manner in which the necessary proteins came into being. These deductions are not as valid as they seem. Not only do all organisms contain protein, they all contain such substances as fat, carbohydrate and nucleic acid as well. The mere presence of protein is of no more necessary significance than the presence of the other components. There may seem to be a little more validity in the enzyme argument until it is realised that not even a tentative explanation has been hazarded about the features that give certain proteins their enzymic activity. By suitable chemical treatment an enzyme can be robbed of its catalytic activity, and the nature of the change it has undergone is often known. But the precise nature of the three-dimensional configuration that gives enzyme activity to some proteins is not known. Consequently, the fundamental quality needed for enzyme activity is not known; nor are the reasons why this quality is found in proteins and not in other types of macromolecule. Until these things are known, there can be no basis for a rationally based search for enzyme-like activity in other types of chemical structure. Unsystematic search has already uncovered enzyme-like properties elsewhere, for example in rare-earth oxides and the cyclodextrins.

It seems reasonable therefore to postulate a probiotic terrestrial environment containing a complex mixture of molecules, some of a type familiar in biochemistry, and some derived from them by random polymerisation. The word 'random' acquires overtones of meaning. A random event, *pace* the quantum physicists, is simply one that we do not choose to investigate at the moment. At one time there was little support for the suggestion that certain forms of polymerisation would occur preferentially during an apparently random process, and that factors such as stability, and the congruence (or fit) of one part of a megamolecule with another, would influence the composition of the final mixture and might well be correlated with catalytic ability.

The idea that definite sequences, structures and orientations could arise by processes other than the stepwise addition of components to a chain, in the manner familiar to organic chemists, gains support from recent developments in the chemistry of commercially important polymers. Zeigler and Natta find that eutactic polymers, that is to say, polymers in which the components are stereochemically ordered rather than arranged at random, are formed under the influence of certain catalysts. They find that different catalysts promote different types of ordering. The polymers that Fox and his colleagues make by heating mixtures of amino acids are also not random.

This stage of development, with a world supplied with materials that actual or postulated organisms could use, is a long way from the stage at which organisms exist. Though the nature of the gap between the two phases could not in the past be stated, even in the tentative and vague manner in which it is stated here, it has been discussed throughout recorded history. The main possibilities are outlined in the table.

Theory 1 sidesteps the problem, 2 puts it outside science, 5 has had many adherents, but since the time of Leeuwenhoek and Boyle has been gradually eroded. Most scientists now accept 3 or 4. Either presupposes some form of prevital evolution. The idea of evolution in the phase before there were organisms raises many conceptual and metaphysical difficulties. One illusion can be quickly disposed of. There is no need to think of 'chemical evolution' in terms of molecular size progressing through millennia from atoms to polymers. Polymers form as readily as, or even more readily than, monomers, and such primacy as the latter may have would be a matter of hours only. Before considering the meaning that can be given to the concept of evolution among catalysts, or in probiotic biochemistry, the nature of evolution at its other extreme may be categorised. Paleontology is a record of the evolution of morphological complexity only: it tells us nothing whatever about the evolution of biochemical capacity. Indeed, to judge from what can be inferred from the biochemical

Biopoetic Theories

Number of biopoeses	*General character*
1 None	Life has always pervaded space and an apparent origin is simply a transfer from place to place
2 One	Creation by divine intervention
3 One	Evolution on earth by the action of inevitable normal processes
4 Several	Repeated coordination of eobionts or subvital units
5 Innumerable	Classical and medieval idea that life appeared whenever there was a suitable environment

differences between surviving species, the evolution of increasingly effective structures can permit a considerable degree of biochemical degeneracy and loss of capacity. This is an aspect of evolution on which stress was laid by Lwoff[5] twenty-five years ago and his comments retain much of their force. Having followed the conventional phylogenetic tree back to its root, or roots, we reach a set of morphologically simple autotrophs able to make from inorganic materials the whole range of amino acids and vitamins that morphologically more intricate organisms have to get from their foodstuffs. In so far as biochemical competence is definable therefore, the autotrophs are more competent and complex than we are.

The essence of Natural Selection is that the amount of matter organised in the form of successful systems should increase at the expense of that organised in the form of the less successful. It can therefore operate only when there is a shortage of something, e.g. enzyme precursors, substrates or attachment sites. If the picture of an early phase of synthesis with an increasing amount of organic matter on the terrestrial surface is correct, there would be no initial competition. Those reactions that were possible would take place, with no more than the usual chemical lag, under the influence, it is postulated, of light. Oparin and others have discussed the type of process that could have been involved later, and the applicability of such concepts as Evolution and Natural Selection to nonvital systems has been critically examined; but nothing very coherent has emerged and no one has arranged an *in vitro* system (i.e. in laboratory vessels) that manifests the postulated phenomena. My own quodlibet, now twenty years old, still seems as good as any other

A suitable mineral surface, kept moist with a solution of the components of the primitive ocean and atmosphere, will absorb light and may promote a reaction whose product dissolves the active element from a mineral. This process is in a strict sense auto-catalytic and would be favoured by agents which improve illumination or confine the product to the neighbourhood of the mineral. The accidental simultaneous presence of another catalytic system using the same element and making a sponge or an oil from the materials to hand would be such a favourable influence. A sponge would help to hold the products of the action together and an oil would dispel dust and debris and so permit better access of light. Such a conjunction would spread and pieces of it scattered on to suitable surfaces would start new focuses. Even two actions, linked thus, show the beginnings of organisation; more would be added if they accidentally occurred in the neighbourhood and favoured those already present. Each action proceeds independently, but each is favoured by the others. When a system exists in an environment so unsuitable that it must carry out several chemical actions that are dependent on one another something like a cell is necessary. Catalysts have to be held together so that the product of one can get to the next and this can be done either by integrating them into a supermolecule or by having them all in a semi-permeable bag. The advantages that flow from juxtaposition have given survival value to the complexity of biological organisation with which we are familiar.

During the probiotic phase it is reasonable to imagine that a diverse group of chemical processes took place, many of which may have no counterparts in present-day biochemistry. These, in the metaphorical sense of the last two paragraphs, would compete and a few would achieve dominance. As in human affairs, the factors leading to dominance may have been in part accidental. But once a system had become associated with, and supported by, an advanced morphology it would become relatively invulnerable to competition from possibly more efficient and flexible biochemical systems not so supported. Thus, turning again to human affairs, a powerful political or military system can disseminate over a great area its often inferior grammatical, artistic or weights-and-measures habits, and extinguish preferable ones used by communities with a less powerful social morphology. Once morphological ascendancy has been achieved by an organism or group of organisms the possibilities of biochemical innovation become small – *le bien est l'ennemi du mieux.* The dominant group is then saddled with a biochemistry that is not necessarily the only one – it may not even be the ideal one.

If there is substance in that suggestion, the present-day uniformity in the biochemistry of all the organisms investigated in detail may show no more than that this is a reasonably efficient way in which an organism can work and that it successfully ousted the others two to three G years ago. In much the same way, paper has tended to oust stone, clay and wax as a vehicle for writing. Although organisms now have this uniform biochemistry, our aesthetic requirements for an organism depend very much more on its arrangement, organisation and activity than on its chemical composition. Similarly, as has been abundantly clear from the time of Pasteur, the mere bringing together of a group of conventional biomolecules does not lead to the emergence of an organism. This is the essence of the Vitalist case that an organism involves more than conventional biochemistry and that it is misguided to regard an organism as a system containing 'nothing but' molecules of determinable composition. The extra component that is needed may, however, be nothing more than organisation. Penrose and Jacobson have made mechanical models that illustrate the phenomenon clearly. A set of them can coexist indefinitely in one state, but if a single unit is given a new organisation (and this could in principle happen accidentally), the new form of organisation spreads through the whole set. These models may be more satisfying to some people than the traditional crystal or flame analogies for replication. More fancifully: it is obvious that a poem or a joke consists of 'nothing but' words; it is the organisation of the words that enables them to replicate in a suitable environment. The replication of a flame depends on something being done that allows part of the system to surmount an energy barrier. In the replication of a crystal, joke, or organism, the barrier is one of arrangement or organisation.

Evolution depends on selection, but it is not always certain from which direction the selection comes. There is already good evidence that chemical structures often exist first and uses, or new uses, are found for them later. An organism does not have a built-in urge to do something and then wait, synthesising things at random, until it happens to synthesise something suitable for doing that thing with. Rather, when a substance or structure appears by accident, the environment selects the eobiont or organism with this feature by offering a niche that it fills peculiarly well. This inversion gets over the difficulty of the uselessness of each first step in evolution. It probably was useless but, at the same time, harmless and, Micawber-like, could wait for a function to turn up.

Until the eighteenth century, life was seldom thought of as a philosophical entity and the idea that a unifying principle underlay all forms of life was not widely accepted until the end of last century. Many unsuccessful attempts were then made to particularise the principle in terms of such qualities as adaptability, cellular structure and size, chemical composition, growth, irritability, metabolism, motility, and reproduction. The more thoughtful biologists could, however, always show that there were systems, which everyone agreed to call living, that lacked at least one of these particular characters or activities, and systems which no one wished to call living that possessed some of them. Reproduction is the most widely cited character but it is neither a necessary nor a sufficient character: individual organisms can be sterile but still living, whereas flames, magnets, crystals, etc., show a form of reproduction. The other members of the conventional lists found in old-fashioned textbooks can be disposed of even more easily. It may be that some individuals of a species must at some period of their existence manifest some at least of the qualities listed if the species as a whole is to survive. That proposition lacks the rigidity that is desirable in a useful definition, but it suggests that it might be possible to define a living *species* even if it is not possible to define a living *organism*. We are therefore left in the unsatisfactory position that aesthetic and undefined considerations bring about nearly universal agreement on the status of all the systems that have been investigated so far, but they do not enable us to state the basis of this agreement. Few now agree with John Hunter's conclusion that life is a property, analogous to magnetism, that can be 'superadded' to a system.

Conclusions about the nature, origins, and antiquity of life could come from the production of life-like systems in the laboratory, from the study of structures in ancient rocks, from arguments based on the apparent universality of certain biochemical processes in present-day organisms, or from attempts to project biochemical trends backwards through the phylogenetic sequence. Claims for the creation in the laboratory of organisms such as bacteria and Crosse's 'acarids' were at one time common, but Pasteur and Tyndall, systematising the methods of Carter (1730), Appert (1810) and other early experimenters on food preservation, effectively demolished all of them. There has recently been some renewal of interest in the question. Bahadur and Perti claim that suitable sterile solutions will, under the influence of sunlight, organise themselves into particles with sizes in the bacterial range and with some life-like attributes. Kalinenko gets similar structures as a result of electrolysis. These claims have received independent support but not on a sufficient scale to warrant acceptance. In the light of the controversy over spontaneous generation during the nineteenth century, scepticism is fully justified; but it should not degenerate into dogmatism. The claims deserve fuller investigation because, even if they have no direct bearing on the nature and origins of life, they may supply interesting information about the integrative potentialities of simple systems.

Geological evidence on the antiquity of life takes two forms. Chemical analysis of some minerals suggests that segregations took place that are most plausibly interpreted biologically, and microfossils that it would be capricious not to accept as the remains of algae have been found in rocks that are two to three G years old. These structures are so similar to existing algae that there is little reason to question the conclusion that they are genuine fossils of organisms similar to those with which we are now familiar. Some even have present-day counterparts. The ammoniacal smell of the urinal in Harlech Castle reminded some visiting scientists of the probable composition of the pre-Cambrian atmosphere. They took a soil sample and from it cultured a hitherto unknown bacterium that closely resembles bacterial traces found in the ancient rock of southern Ontario. There is no evidence for organisms older than three G years, but only a fairly elaborate organism would be likely to leave a fossil record of its presence. Softer organisms or organisms with a less typically 'biological' shape may therefore be older than this.

Present-day organisms differentiate between isotopes – notably those of carbon, oxygen and sulphur. Thus the 12C/13C ratio tends to be greater in plant tissues than in the carbon dioxide of the atmosphere or ocean; it is therefore tempting when samples of xerogen, or graphitic flakes, are found that are deficient in 13C, to argue that they are of biological origin. Complications arise in argument along these lines because the carbon isotope ratio in present-day organisms is not constant throughout the organism; it is not even constant at different positions in a molecule containing several carbon atoms. Similarly, the oxygen isotope ratio depends on the temperature at which organisms live, and the sulphur isotope ratio, in deposits of presumed biological origin, shows striking variation. It would seem hazardous therefore to conclude that a structure is of biological origin on isotope evidence alone.

Mendeleeff, Moissan and others argued at the end of last century that oil was partly formed by non-biological processes. There was little support for this idea until it was recently restated by Kropotkin and Robinson. If oil has a dual origin, its presence is clearly useless as evidence of early biological activity. For similar reasons, the presence of amino acids and other 'organic' molecules in a rock is not conclusive because these substances can also appear as a result of non-biological processes. Organic molecules such as formaldehyde, formic acid, cyanides and methanol have even been found in space. If, however, an optically active substance were to be isolated from an ancient rock, the evidence for its biological origin would be very much stronger because of the extreme improbability of a non-biological stereoisomeric separation. Optical activity has as yet been demonstrated only with material that seems from other evidence to have a biological origin. Evidence on the antiquity of organisms depends at present on morphology rather than chemistry.

Looking backwards along the presumed course of phylogeny, a trend can be discerned that is compatible with the idea that life today involves the more successful aspects of an initially more catholic approach to the chemical possibilities, and that many other possibilities have been eliminated by selection. Two points must be kept firmly in mind during this exercise. However simple they may appear, present-day primitive organisms have, like their more sophisticated neighbours, existed in a dangerous environment for hundreds of millions of years and there is no reason to assume that they also have not undergone some biochemical evolution. The fossil record is a poor indicator of the biochemical processes that may at one time have operated. Details of fossil plant structure are often so similar to the details of cognate structures in existing plants, and the marks of muscle insertions on fossil bones are so similar to those on present-day bones, that it is reasonable to assume that the basic principles of photosynthesis and muscular contraction have not altered. But there is no satisfactory explanation of such major events as the extinction of the dinosaurs. It is tempting to think that this may have been the consequence of a change in plant biochemistry to which herbivorous dinosaurs did not have time to adapt. Furthermore, biochemical details as a rule leave no record at all. For example, if the tunicates had become extinct, there is nothing in their abundant fossil record that would show that vanadium plays an important part in their metabolism.

The idea of evolutionary progress is essentially an aesthetic appreciation of morphology and is coloured by anthropomorphism. Sometimes, as with the human hand, we are so sure of the function, and have such satisfactory criteria of performance, that it is not unreasonable to argue that the hand is a better instrument than anything serving the same purpose that existed at another time or exists now in another organism. As a rule, however, aesthetic morphological argument depends on such imprecise and coloured words as *uncouth* and *clumsy*. In part this arises from our familiarity with reconstructions of the earlier phases of evolution that seem to have been painted by disciples of 'Douanier' Rousseau or some other unsophisticated painter; if the Carboniferous scene had been painted by Constable it would seem much less primitive. Similarly, casual observation of present-day organisms such as the molluscs and some marine invertebrates gives the impression of a simple construction, but this impression is immediately dispelled when closer observation reveals their beautiful intricacy. Going further, electronmicrograms of tissues from organisms near the bottom of the presumed evolutionary tree show organisation within the cells as intricate as, and very similar to, that found at the top of the tree. It may be that this arises because there has been an evolution of intracellular organisation even when, as with such species as *Lingula*, there is little evidence for evolution of cellular arrangement during many millions of years. This intracellular evolution is extremely unlikely because the similarities are between structures that would, on this hypothesis, have been evolving independently. The hypothesis of parallel evolution is sometimes justified by the argument that the structure of the eye has evolved along somewhat similar lines in vertebrates, and some molluscs; it is plausibly argued that this happens because the geometrical requirements for vision are universal. The cogency of this argument cannot be assessed until we know how intracellular organisation is adapted to the biochemical requirements of the cell, and whether cells could, in principle, function with a different sub-cellular organisation. This is the contemporary form of the perennial problem: does the observed amount of biological uniformity arise because of common descent and the stereotyping of one among alternative methods that would in principle have been possible, or does it arise because no alternative methods could function as effectively in this environment?

The relevance of these generalities to the present discussion is that they justify the assumption that gross biochemical differences will not be found between present-day organisms of different types. Any gross differences that may at one time have existed between eobionts were probably eliminated by Natural Selection one to two G years ago. It is, nevertheless, useful to look for minor differences to see whether any systematic trend can be recognised. The range of organisms worthy of study is extensive and there is, unfortunately, little information about many of the species that would be most relevant to the discussion: these are the surviving species that, morphologically, resemble ancient species closely. Apparent simplicity of structure is irrelevant; this is just as likely to be a secondary adaptation to a sheltered (sometimes parasitic) life as to be a primitive characteristic. Furthermore, the viruses, though they are often referred to as intermediate stages in the evolution of life and as the present-day analogues of eobionts, are totally irrelevant. Their multiplication depends on the misdirection of the metabolism of a susceptible host so that the virus mode of existence could not have existed before there were hosts.

Versatility is an outstanding feature of microbial biochemistry. Although all those that have been studied use enzymes containing protein, and use substances such as adenosine triphosphate in their energy exchange processes, they often use them to bring about reactions that are unknown or unusual in many-celled organisms. Some, for example, attach halogens to carbon compounds with a readiness that is unmatched except among the sponges and molluscs; vertebrates retain a shadow of this capacity in making thyroxine and related iodine-containing substances. It may be argued that the restricted use of iodine has been forced on land vertebrates because there are so few regions where iodine is so plentiful as to have made its extensive use possible; this argument would not apply to chlorine which some microorganisms use even more readily. Also, microorganisms can tolerate the presence of, or even use, hydrocarbons, phenols and other substances that are toxic to most many-celled organisms; and some can tolerate biochemical changes such as the replacement of sulphur by selenium. This versatility is in part a consequence of their short generation time and small size; these allow immense opportunities for selection to be compressed into restricted time and space. Nevertheless, it is legitimate to think that considerable lack of rigid specificity may have characterised the catalytic mechanisms of primitive organisms and may have been in part retained by microorganisms.

Some of the most striking examples of primitive versatility appear in the use of unusual elements. Thus it is the more primitive among present-day plants that accumulate aluminium extensively, it is a group of radiolarians (*Acantharia*) rather than any higher animal that makes structural use of strontium sulphate, and it is in the tunicates that vanadium, niobium, and possibly titanium, appear to form part of the oxygen transporting system. It is interesting to note that those tunicate species that seem, on morphological grounds, to be the most advanced have given up the use of the more exotic elements and use iron instead. There is no reason to think that iron is intrinsically superior; but it is commoner. None of these examples can be taken as evidence for primitive versatility – but they are compatible with that concept.

Bizarre as some of the metabolic activities of ancient groups such as the insects may seem, metabolic potentialities may be being underestimated because most species depend on others to supply their nourishment. They would gain nothing by developing systems of metabolism able to handle materials that were not being produced. This is the biochemical equivalent of Plotinus' comment:

No one walks upon an alien soil,

and Blake's:

Everything that lives
Lives not alone, nor of itself.

Interdependence is not however total. Some bacteria and most flowering plants are autotrophic, that is to say, given a supply of energy (e.g. light), they can flourish on simple substances of the type found in volcanic exhalations. Those heterotrophs that have been studied use several of the intermediates used by other organisms. Versatility seems not to be complete. Nevertheless, an industrial chemist would be foolhardy if he assumed that a new unrottable fabric or plastic would retain that quality indefinitely.

Plants modified the original environment by producing oxygen which made animal life possible. When they rot they produce acids that increase the rate at which rock disintegrates. Their roots help to hold the products of disintegration in place and retain water so that disintegration is still further helped. Animals, funguses and bacteria prevent the accumulation of plant residues: without the destruction that they bring about, the carbon dioxide in the atmosphere, and the various elements essential for life, would soon be sequestrated in a layer of unrotted plant-matter so that higher plants of the dominant present-day types would be unable to survive. This cycle of use and return to the environment is characteristic of the biosphere without man. There is, of course, some loss of essential elements in the water that drains into rivers and thence to the sea, but this loss is made good by fresh material leached from rock, and the rock itself is slowly renewed by mountain building. Primitive people did not greatly disturb this pattern. Plants and animals were eaten near where they were found and the products were excreted there. Industrialised communities upset the cycles not just because of the much greater scale of their operations, but also because of the extent to which elements are moved. Food is transported great distances and water-borne sewage hurries the products to sea. Our influence on the environment need not, however, be wholly harmful. We know the elements that are being withdrawn from the soil, and industrial chemistry offers the means for replacing them. Furthermore, plants and animals cannot flourish in some parts of the world because of shortages of elements such as copper, zinc and cobalt in the soil. These can be added. The biosphere with man could, with skill and forethought, be more productive than the biosphere without.

NOTES

1. V. M. GOLDSCHMIDT (1964) *Geochemistry*, Oxford.
2. P. E. CLOUD (1968) 'Atmospheric and hydrospheric evolution on the primitive Earth', *Science*, **160**, 729.
3. P. H. ABELSON (1966) 'Chemical events on the primitive Earth', *Proc. Nat. Acad. Sci.* (*Wash.*), **55**, 1365.
4. J. B. S. HALDANE (1929) 'The origin of life', *Rationalist Annual*, 3.
5. A. LWOFF (1943) *L'Evolution physiologique: études des pertes de fonctions chez les microorganismes*, Paris.

BIBLIOGRAPHY

FOR FURTHER READING

Ann. New York Acad. Sci., **69** (1957).

H. P. BANKS ed. (1970) *Biological Reviews*, **45**.

I. A. BERGER (1963) *Organic Geochemistry*, Headington.

S. W. FOX ed. (1965) *The Origins of Prebiological Systems*, London.

J. KEOSIAN (1964) *The Origin of Life*, New York (paperback).

J. MARQUAND (1968) *Life: Its Nature, Origins and Distribution*, Edinburgh (paperback). (Includes the latest on the Harlech Castle organisms, p. 16.)

New Biology, **16** (1954), Harmondsworth.

N. W. PIRIE (1968) 'The development of Haldane's outlook on the nature and origins of life' in *Haldane and Modern Biology*, ed. K. R. Dronamraju, Baltimore. (An account of Haldane's many contributions to the discussion.)

Proc. Roy. Soc. (*B*), **171**, (1968).

B. Z. SIEGEL AND S. M. SIEGEL (1970) 'Biology of the Precambrian *Kakabekia*: new observations on living *K. barghoorniana*', *Proc. Nat. Acad. Sci.* (*Wash.*), **67**, 1005.

R. L. M. SYNGE ed. (1959) *The Origin of Life on Earth*, Headington.

2

LIVING TOGETHER WITHOUT MAN

HANS KALMUS

RECENT anxieties concerning the ill-effects of industrial man's activities have widened the circle of people interested in ecology and its application to some comprehensive 'geohygiene'. Part of the problems are inorganic, and some of those, for instance current views on cosmogeny and geochemistry as well as the presumed probiotic situation on our planet, have been described in the previous paper. The chemical basis of life and its possible origin, and the chemical and nutritional cycles in the biosphere, were also discussed in general terms.

My task is to put flesh on to these bones and to convey some idea of the rich variety of interactions between the organisms – plants and animals – in aquatic and terrestrial habitats, as they existed before the domination of man and to some degree still exist. This largely amounts to a description of the principles of ecology as it was taught some twenty years ago, with some recent additions from the study of animal sociology and behaviour.

The science of ecology – of the 'household of nature' – is a fairly recent branch of biology, though many of the basic concepts are quite commonplace and of great antiquity. For instance the idea that certain animals occur in particular habitats: deer in woods, fish in ponds, seals near the seashore, etc.; or that plants of particular species occur in 'associations' like deciduous forests, alpine meadows, arctic bogs.

PALEO-ECOLOGY

Strictly speaking: living without man means living before man and this lecture should thus mainly deal with paleo-ecology, that is biological interactions in the floras and faunas of the geological past. But that would be going too far: imaginative reconstructions of what life was like in a forest of the Carboniferous age or in the shallows of the Jurassic sea would not greatly contribute to the main theme of the series, though speculations concerning just such conditions were formerly taken seriously (Abel 1912). The main topic will be an enumeration of some typical habitats, as they exist now, which are as yet not greatly disturbed by man; certain aspects of Tertiary and Pleistocene life, in so far as they exerted noticeable effects on present-day situations, will also be discussed.

The fossil record shows that terrestrial, marine and freshwater habitats have existed for hundreds of millions of years, though their localisation and borders as well as the species of plants and animals living in them have continually changed. One characteristic of the various 'biocenoses' as they existed before the advent of the agricultural revolution was that they were and still are – if not absolutely, at least relatively – separate. Though a grizzly bear may have occasionally caught trout, the inhabitants of a stream had little contact with or effect on the inhabitants of the surrounding woods (taiga) and *vice versa*. Salmon and eel migrated in their appropriate ways from fresh water to the seas, but the vast majority of fish were either marine or freshwater inhabitants. Few organisms (species) were able to exploit the resources of more than two of the three main habitat types – possibly certain omnivorous sea-gulls or scavenging wasps. But man has done so since prehistoric time. Relics of human communities which must have mainly lived on shellfish (oysters), on freshwater fish or on mammals and birds are scattered all over the globe; vegetable diets must also have occurred. This nutritional versatility of primitive man is one of the prerequisites for his later biological success in penetrating into ever wider and larger parts of the biosphere, and one of the roots of our present ecological predicaments: the progressive occupation of the apices of the resource pyramids of many habitats. Man eats more ungulates, birds and eggs, than any species of carnivorous predator, and possibly more fish than all sharks and pikes.

There is, however, another aspect of this situation. By increasing the interactions between habitats which were formerly separated (either geographically or ecologically) man is unifying the various households on earth. It will then make increasing sense to develop 'holecology' – the consideration of the entire biosphere as a single habitat and all life on this planet as a biocenosis, with man as the dominant and to some extent unifying species. The implications of some of the insights thus gained for policies concerning human populations, food production and technological developments, and many other less tangible subjects, transcend the realm of science and will be considered later on in this book.

TYPES OF ORGANIC INTERACTION

Turning to a more detailed but still fairly general description of certain basic types of organismic interaction within particular habitats, one can distinguish between independent and dependent coexistence between species found in the same locality. Independence (commensalism) is the rule in the many plant associations. The primary producers of biological material, the green plants – be they the trees, shrubs or annuals in a wood or the various algae in the plankton – draw on the same resources of light and chemicals available at a time. Their main interactions are intraspecific and interspecific competition. On the other hand herbivorous animals and certain parasitic plants, which feed on those primary producers, as well as predatory animals (carnivores) feeding on the herbivores, interact in a great variety of ways with their food sources and with each other. They thus form extremely complex systems, which by 'feed-back control' (literally!), and sometimes even by anticipatory mechanisms, can maintain relatively stable or at least only slowly developing situations, which are popularly described as the 'balance of nature'. I shall not dwell on the mystical connotations of this concept; but may perhaps be permitted to point out that our present attempts at conservation may be considered as an anticipatory regulatory mechanism through the human agency which is destined to operate within the total biosphere.

Stratigraphic geology has shown that, during the past, different biotic conditions have prevailed at many points on the earth's surface, though a complete succession of past habitats is rarely found anywhere. Nevertheless it is clear that land may have emerged from the sea, which was in turn flooded by fresh water or covered with ice or lava, etc. The nature and rate of these changes varied a great deal. Most were gradual, climatic; some were catastrophic, volcanic. They continued through the historical past up to the present and their study preoccupies a great number of ecologists and has yielded many insights relevant to evolutionary theory. Local changes in habitat are mostly part of more widely occurring changes, but may be controlled by the properties of the habitat itself, for instance its size. A small 'periodic' puddle will produce within a few weeks a rapid and definite succession of algae, protozoa and small invertebrates, only to dry up in summer. A cow-dropping produces within a month a definite succession of fungus species and arthropods, before drying up; a small cadaver a succession of bacteria and insects, etc. As opposed to such microhabitats, macrohabitats such as extensive temperate or tropical woodlands or coral reefs develop very much more slowly and may sometimes achieve a 'final', almost stable situation, which the ecologists call a 'climax'. The destruction of any climax by whatever agency is particularly objectionable, because once destroyed it cannot be recreated and because some of the plant and animal species which form part of it can not survive in other habitats.

CLIMAX AND SUCCESSION

Popular ideas of nature conservation often focus on the wild life of tropical Africa, which in its abundance of mammalian and avian species can be considered as a relic of a type of climax which was prevalent in Europe and other now temperate places during the Tertiary age. Similarly, the abundance of plant species in Eastern Asia is also a result of long established climax conditions. But undisturbed temperate woodlands and even the depths of the ocean are also stabilised final phases of ecological development. What then are the characteristics of a climax and the conditions for its existence? To understand this it is best to begin at the other end of the succession and observe the settling of virgin localities which had been devoid or denuded of life: for instance, a lake, newly created by a dam, or – more leisurely – a terrestrial rocky area left bare for many centuries by the retreat of ice. The first settlers on such rocks are lichens, growing on patches determined by wind direction and exposure to sunlight; these are followed by mosses in the cracks harbouring sooner or later some small arthropods. Grasses or other small flowering plants follow with their corresponding invertebrate and vertebrate fauna, finally shrub sand perhaps trees. At this stage we may find horizontal zonation – and with the most advanced flora in the centre vertical stratification. Also in the centre are found a considerable diversification of ecological niches and a corresponding increase in the numbers of plant and animal species.

On a large scale and over a longer time-scale a similar process of diversification has presumably occurred during each inter-glacial period, further progressing to primary tropical forests, with their several canopies of foliage, harbouring maybe hundreds of plant species, each niche inhabited by a quite separate and distinct insect and bird fauna.

The abundance of species coupled with relatively small numbers of individuals of each species in these climax societies contrasts strongly with the relative paucity of species represented by enormous numbers in more recently established secondary woods or cultivated areas called by the German's '*Kultur steppe*'. It also contrasts with the comparative monotony of the Arctic tundra.

Various kinds of climax have been distinguished by different ecologists, but there is no unanimity as to the principles of such classification. An interesting subclass may, however, be mentioned; the dysclimax, a state of affairs resulting from repeated catastrophes. An example resulting from human practices would be an English lawn, which may for decades or centuries remain more or less unchanged through being perpetually interfered with. The successions of plant associations in the woods of Northern Canada, which from various causes are regularly destroyed by huge forest fires, also approach some form of dysclimax, as does the regularly burnt savannah in West Africa. The late summer plankton of large temperate lakes may also be counted under this heading.

We have just mentioned fire as one of the agents of ecological catastrophe; others are volcanic eruptions, storms, flood, overgrazing, overpopulation, epidemics or sometimes the immigration of a new species. Though often very dramatic, the resulting habitat destruction is usually geographically confined: tidal waves may travel over vast areas of sea, like that caused by the explosion of Santorin (Thera) some 2500 years ago, which probably destroyed the Minoan civilisation; or the eruption of Krakatoa in 1853, which charged the higher atmosphere of the earth with dust and produced spectacular sunsets for years. However, even these impressive events have not been biologically very serious. Larger catastrophes – other than slow climatic changes – in the geological past have been postulated to explain major floristic and faunistic changes, but their reality is doubtful. Later papers in this book will deal with possible future, and in particular man-produced, catastrophes, their magnitude and reversibility.

LOSS OF SPECIES

If the flora and fauna of a destroyed habitat – for instance an island, an isolated valley or a lake – contain unique species, these are lost, as they cannot immigrate or be imported from anywhere else. Habitat destruction is at present probably a greater hazard to many species than deliberate extermination – except perhaps for some of the largest animals. Whether this has been so in the past is not certain. Nobody knows with any certainty why so many species – the majority – have been exterminated during geological time. The myth that the dinosaurs died out because they were too large and too slow seems to be quite generally believed.

CLASSIFICATIONS OF INTERACTIONS

Returning to the living, it is worth stating that the number of possible interactions between the organisms forming a biocenosis is always considerable and sometimes – for instance in a mature climax – astronomical; it is therefore rarely possible to arrive at a complete qualitative – and even less a complete quantitative – description (model) of what goes on. This makes specific, detailed predictions difficult, and in particular predictions of the consequence of a new factor, such as the introduction of a foreign species – like the prickly pear into Australia, or parasitic wasps into Canadian forests – or the elimination of an established one – for instance, the temporary disappearance of rabbits in England through myxomatosis. Nevertheless, more general expectations concerning the future stability of a biocenosis, or the *succession* to be expected in a habitat, can often be formulated with some confidence. It is also possible to estimate with some accuracy the relative role a particular species plays in its community in respect of particular energy and chemical cycles. The predominantly commensal and competitive relationship between the green plants of any habitat has already been mentioned. It remains to describe some complex and less easily defined relations between organisms.

INTRASPECIFIC RELATIONS

In doing so it is useful to distinguish between the interactions between individuals – mostly animals – belonging to one species and interactions between members of different species. Most organisms are for most of their life solitary: some lower organisms among the algae or corals are colonial and only a few insects and vertebrates are social. For instance, among many thousand species of bees only several dozen are social. On the other hand really solitary ants or termites are unknown. The numbers of individuals in animal associations vary a great deal.

A coral reef may be made up of 10^{14} polyps, possibly all descended from one pelagic larva; and it may live on for tens of thousands of years. Colonies of many ant or certain termite species may be composed of several million individuals, but may only live for a few years. A colony of honey bees numbers up to 100,000. Aggregations – that is, loose associations, rather than closely knit societies – of sea birds, caribou, lemming or fur seals may number many thousands of individuals. Primate groups, including those of prehistoric men, were, and are, considerably smaller – from several dozen to perhaps some hundreds. The study of the social structures and behaviour of animals has fascinated people at all times – from primitive man observing bees, bisons or shoals of fish, to the modern research worker and journalist. The interactions between pairs, parents and offspring, generations, castes, have been studied in detail in many of these groups, as has the division of labour, cooperation, colony foundation and occasionally group conflict. Several dozen books and hundreds of papers devoted to the subject are published every year.

PRIMATE SOCIETIES

Of the animal communities, those of the primates are in some ways most relevant for comparisons with human societies. In primate studies two contradictory tendencies can be observed: on the one hand there is an ever-increasing interest in monkeys and apes, but on the other hand the demand for these animals for zoos, medical research and the pharmaceutical industry is such that many species are threatened with rapid extinction. Observations on monkeys and apes in the wild are beset with considerable difficulties and in spite of admirable work by for instance Goodall (1968) on the chimpanzee and Schaller (1963) on the gorilla, most observation on the communal life of primates is of necessity done on captive groups, more or less confined in space and living in artificial conditions. In most zoological gardens, primates are kept singly or in small numbers in much too cramped quarters for any conclusions concerning their natural interactions to be drawn. The psychotic-savage or autistic behaviour of caged adult chimpanzees, gorillas or mandrils in particular is certainly atypical. At the other extreme, monkey colonies living idyllically under extreme care and sheltered from the dangers in which they presumably live in the wild are – while pleasant to behold – equally unrepresentative of original conditions. Organised intergroup conflicts, for instance, so typical of primitive human societies, can hardly ever be observed in either condition. The application of behavioural primate studies to human affairs is in any case rather dubious: man has been genetically separated from his nearest relatives for at least 50,000 generations, which is a long time for divergent social behaviour to develop. It is, however, likely that the common ancestors of man and the other hominids already lived in extended family groups, in which complex interactions and hierarchies could develop towards specifically human social relations.

Most of the descriptions in the literature on primate behaviour have a strong anthropomorphic flavour as they, of necessity, must borrow their concepts from our insights into the working of human societies. Occasionally a paper may err in the opposite direction, being ridiculously hypercritical of common-sense approaches.

INTERSPECIFIC RELATIONS

Interspecific relations are so numerous that only a few of the more complex, even seemingly bizarre, interactions between individuals belonging to different plant and/or animal species can be described. In this field too many concepts and attitudes are borrowed from human relationships or man-animal relations; and natural history sometimes gets anecdotal. But in this field reality quite often greatly surpasses imagination. Applying a little comparative thought a great deal could be learned from role theory, the theory of games and economic models.

One may begin with a short discussion of the concepts of commensalism, symbiosis, parasitism, mimicry and other related notions. As mentioned before, the various tree species in a wood are considered mainly commensal, drawing on the same soil, air and light but showing few interactions apart from being competitive. None the less, some interactions can be observed by close inspection. It is for instance generally recognised that various species of trees have very different light requirements. In the plains of Central Europe for instance black beech seedlings (*Fagus sylvatica*), having a much lower light requirement than those of other forest trees, succeed in growing under the canopy of oak and ash, where the seedlings of these species perish from lack of illumination. In hilly regions *Picea excelsa* (pine) and in Southern Europe *Quercus ilex*, a hard-leaved oak, play very similar roles in the forest successions. Now it is a matter of definition – almost of taste – whether to consider these situations as commensalism, parasitism or symbiosis. As regards soil and carbon dioxide all the trees of each of these woods are commensal competitors. As regards humidity and wind resistance they derive mutual benefits from each other, and are in this respect symbiotic; but beech, pine and broad-leaved oak 'parasitise' the earlier species, by making use of the shade these provide. It really depends on which of these 'utilities' – soil, moisture, or shade – you consider the most important; there is nothing in biology comparable to the equivalence in physics of different kinds of energy.

There exist of course clear-cut examples of parasitism. Flowering plants devoid of chlorophyll and living on the sap of other plants like dodder (*Cuscuta*) are parasitic, as are the protozoa responsible for malaria or the liver flukes with the elaborate life cycles involving changes of hosts. There also exist numerous examples of symbiosis: lichens are composite organisms, in which fungal mycelia contain chlorophyll-bearing algae, the former providing mechanical structure and the latter providing living matter. Hermit crabs, living in deserted shells of snails, carry on these shells a kind of sea anemone (*actinia*). The sea anemones ingest food morsels from the crabs' meals and are transported to favourable conditions, while protecting the crabs by means of their poisonous tentacles.

A few of the more subtle interactions between organisms of different species deserve more detailed treatment: mainly examples in which animal behaviour plays some part, as for instance pollination or mimicry. There is no controversy concerning the major facts of pollination, but there are still some biologists who deny the reality of mimicry.

POLLINATION

Pollination is the transfer by some agency – be it the wind or an insect, snail or bird – of pollen from some flower to another flower of the same species. Where animals are concerned, only one carrier and one plant are necessary for successful pollination, though several species of insect (flies, bees, butterflies) may collect pollen from the same flower, and one insect species, e.g. honeybees, can act as pollinator for a host of flowering plants. Whatever the complexity, pollination can be regarded as a form of symbiosis; both classes of organism derive some advantage from the process: the plants are being pollinated, usually cross-pollinated, while the insects may eat or collect some of the pollen or are offered nectar, while 'working' in the flowers. The numerous mutual adaptations which have developed in these relationships have been admired and studied by naturalists for two hundred years and fresh discoveries concerning the colours, odours and mechanical arrangements of the flowers are still being made, in parallel with discoveries of special morphological features and types of behaviour, which in the animals facilitate the functioning of these symbioses. Pollination is also a good example of the diversification of habitats by the organisms which occur in it. On the one hand each species of flowering plant in a habitat provides a special and unique niche to be exploited by one or several pollinators; while on the other hand the presence of pollinating insects, which 'serve' established plant species, may enable a flowering plant, new to the habitat, to immigrate.

In pollination, as in other forms of symbiosis in dynamic equilibrium, the long-term 'interests' of the participants are common, while some of their short-term interests may be conflicting. This may result in the extinction of one or both species; but new, sometimes surprising twists can also develop.

MIMICRY

Cuckoo pint flowers (*Arum*) attract several species of flies and dung beetles by odours, reminiscent of carrion or faeces, on which these insects are wont to feed and to deposit their eggs, as well as by a surprisingly high temperature in the flowers. One species, *Arum maculatum*, in addition traps its pollinator, a small owl midge of the genus *Psychoda*, in its flowers, where they crawl about and are covered with pollen only to be released after a day. Thereafter, in search of carrion, they may be attracted and fall again into another flower of this arum lily and thus complete their role as pollen carriers. As the pollen in any arum flower matures only after the stigma has ceased to be receptive, self-pollination is prevented. During captivity the insects feed on the juices of the flowers. In other exotic species of the araceae different variations on this theme are enacted. Flowers exploit not only the search for food but can also make use of the search by insects for a mating partner. The similarity of many orchid flowers to bees, flies or even birds has found expression in their vernacular names in many languages; but it was thought that this resemblance was just coincidence. However, some recent investigations show that parts of several species of orchid flowers in fact mimic insects. In several species of *Ophrys*, for instance, the labium resembles a particular female wasp or fly. Males of these various insects are attracted by the shape, colour and possibly odour of these structures, mount them and try to copulate with them. In doing so they do not succeed in transferring their own sperm but only the plants' pollen. Other insects fare much worse. The Venus fly trap *Dionnea muscipula* attracts flies to the brightly red insides of spiny leaves, which suddenly close, trapping the insects and digesting them. One may assume that this sort of predation derives from previous habits of pollination. This story is capped by the involvement of a third class of organism, spiders, which catch insects trapped inside some other insectivorous plants – tropical pitcher plants. The jumping spiders are able to withstand the digestive juices of the plants and spin silk ladders across some of the slippery areas of the flowers.

The consideration of flowers masquerading as dummy females leads naturally to a discussion of numerous other relationships between organisms described as mimicry. This idea, that animals or plants may 'imitate' each other so as to deceive a predator, was formulated more than a hundred years ago by Bates, who found that apparently several groups of very similar individual butterflies, collected in the forests of Brazil, did on closer inspection turn out to belong to quite unrelated families. Since then a voluminous literature elaborating on this theme or trying to disprove the existence of mimicry has come into existence.

Only a few main points can be made and a few examples given. To show that individuals belonging to the different species are similar is in no way a sufficient proof that one is mimicking the other. Related species must as a consequence of their common ancestry be expected to show a number of similar features; and even unrelated forms may as a response to similar environmental conditions develop in similar ways – a situation which is called convergence. To prove the operation of mimicry it is necessary to demonstrate the interactions in nature of at least three entities of a system, consisting of one signal receiver (the one who is being deceived) and two signal emitters, one of which at least masquerades as the other. As a rule this involves individuals of three species: for instance, a bird who refuses quite palatable butterflies because he mistakes them for similarly coloured distasteful ones. Occasionally only two species may be involved: when for instance a plaice assumes the coloration of the sea bottom and thus hides from predatory fish, or – as in the case of some proverbial 'wolves in sheep's clothes' – one of the emitters (the wolf) pretends to be identical (conspecific) with the signal receiver (the sheep). On the other hand more than three species may be involved – sometimes many more – each playing roles that are quantitatively and sometimes qualitatively different. An example is the harmless, the slightly poisonous and the deadly coral snakes. Flow diagrams and numerical rules for such situations have been developed, which are of considerable theoretical interest; but as the real situations to which such models are applied are always more complex than the assumptions on which 'models' are based, most of these attempts have only a limited predictive value. We may for instance not know how many species are involved in mutual mimicry and what their interactions are in every detail. Imitation may be visual, crude or elaborate, or acoustic; tactile-chemical, behavioural, or quite frequently a combination of several of these. The signal receiver – for instance a predator – may react to a signal in a similar way to ourselves, or it may not. Thus, before one accepts any apparent similarity of different species as resulting from mimicry, one must satisfy oneself of a number of detailed interactions. In some cases this may take years.

CONCLUSION

According to one's temperament one may consider these difficulties as a reason for giving up or as a challenge. But then one might give up the study of evolution altogether. Mimicry is only a particular aspect of evolution, which has provided us with the infinite richness and diversity of the organic world. And it is this diversity and richness of life, rather than its existence, which man is increasingly threatening by proliferation, expansion and industrial activity, but which he also wants to preserve as he becomes increasingly aware of his own dominion over the other species.

O. ABEL (1912) *Grundzüge der Palaebiologie der Wirbeltiere*, Stuttgart.

J. BRAUN-BLANQUET (1932) *Plant Sociology*, London and New York.

P. R. EHRLICH AND P. H. RAVEN (1965) 'Butterflies and plants: a study in co-evolution', *Evolution*, **148**, 586-608.

H. KALMUS (1966) *Regulation and Control in Living Systems*, London, New York and Sydney.

—— (1969) 'Animal behaviour and theories of games and language', *Animal Behaviour*, **17**, 607-17.

C. B. KNIGHT (1965) *Basic Concepts of Ecology*, London and New York.

JANE VAN LAWICK-GOODALL (1968) *The behaviour of free living chimpanzees in the Gombe Stream Reserve* (*Animal Behaviour Monographs*, No. 1), London, pp. 1-311.

R. H. LOWE-MCCONNEL (1966) *Man-made Lakes*, London.

A. MACFADYEN (1963) *Animal Ecology*, London.

D. F. OWEN (1966) *Animal Ecology in Tropical Africa*, Edinburgh.

R. A. RAPPAPORT (1967) *Pigs for the Ancestors*, New Haven.

C. R. RIBBANDS (1953) *The Behaviour and Social Life of Honey Bees*, London.

C. B. SCHALLER (1963) *The Mountain Gorilla: Ecology and Behaviour*, Chicago.

N. TINBERGEN (1953) *Social Behaviour in Animals*, London (paperback).

R. H. WHITTAKER (1970) *Communities and Ecosystems*, London and New York.

W. WICKLER (1968) *Mimicry in plants and animals* (World University Library), London.

C. B. WILLIAMS (1964) *Patterns in the Balance of Nature and Related Problems in Quantitative Ecology*, London.

V. C. WYNNE-EDWARDS (1962) *Animal Dispersion in Relation to Social Behaviour*, Edinburgh and New York.

3

THE IMPACT OF MAN ON NATURE

C. D. DARLINGTON

THE SCALE OF THE PROBLEM

THE problem of man's impact on nature requires us to bring together two lines of enquiry which our forebears began for us long ago. On the one hand, thinking men in the ancient world observed, deplored, and tried to limit the damage that less-thinking men had been doing to the world around them. Their tale was taken up a few generations ago by observant naturalists like Buffon and Humboldt who saw the devastation that was being spread over the habitable world and foresaw the calamity that was being prepared for us.

On the other hand, more speculative thinkers like Lord Monboddo, Erasmus Darwin and Charles Lyell were at the same time asking themselves just how long man had been at work on this planet; they had begun putting his operations on the time-scale which we have always needed if we were to take stock of our position. Now at last we have this time-scale safely in our hands, safely in the care of the laboratories where radioactive dating can establish the sequence of events, the chronology of materials and processes.

It is only we, however, in our generation than can clinch the matter. In the nick of time perhaps we can put together the observations and test the assumptions made by enquirers on these two lines of thought. How diverse are the ideas that have to be used will be seen from the range of historical and scientific inferences that I have to use in sketching my argument.

For we have to consider what happened, how it happened and why it happened. These questions can be answered only by looking at the whole problem. We have to begin at the beginning. We have to trace the course by which a hundred thousand human beings in Africa a million years ago swelled into three hundred million people spread over most of the earth at the beginning of the Christian era.

The expansion of numbers and of the area occupied is due, we suppose, to the increase in skill, knowledge and understanding, or collectively the intelligence, of the men and women concerned. And this in turn is due to the change in the size, shape and structure of their brains and of the hands, eyes, tongues and other organs connected with them. These changes in intelligence were not continuous or uniform. They arose from diversification of the human group, from competition and conflict between the species, races and tribes into which the group divided itself.

A striking feature of these conflicts was that they ended in a single inter-fertile group confined to Africa but sharply isolated from its nearest surviving relatives, the great apes. Man (or the common ancestors of man) had killed off his closest competitors. He had acquired a monopoly of the world's resources which his successive technical inventions in due course enabled him to exploit. This was man's first impact on nature.

COLONISING THE EARTH

How did he use this monopoly? First, he colonised the earth. He early occupied Europe and Asia. Much later, armed with projectiles, he moved into America and Australia. Last of all he spread over the oceans and their islands. In these various regions he had three great separate fields of exploitation: animal, vegetable and mineral. In all three fields he developed his intelligence. He came to know, presumably to name, and certainly to depict, the things he found useful. But, whereas for a long time he merely collected the plants and the minerals, he hunted and killed the animals and sometimes destroyed them altogether, as he still does. The ones he pursued fell into two groups: those he killed for food, clothing and raw materials in general; and those he killed because they were predators and competed with him for the same victims.

If he had not been so quickly successful little harm might have been done. But competition between human tribes was the basis of their evolutionary advancement. And it must have been the short-term advantage of success in killing both food animals and predators that came to direct human evolution and made the success so overwhelming. It led to the extinction of many species of the great herbivorous mammals, first in Africa, then in America.

Of these extinctions one was notable beyond all others for its later effects on human history. The killing off of the horse in America by hunters meant that when agriculture followed hunting the horses were not there to domesticate; the process and the spread of civilisation were delayed; the stratification of society was impeded; and the Amerindian peoples were themselves exposed to easy destruction when the European colonists arrived.

The immigrant Aboriginal in Australia fortunately lacked the superlative and diverse skills of the Amerindian races and although he brought his hunting dog, the dingo, with him he did not succeed in killing off the important marsupials that he found and fed upon.

When the Europeans came in their turn they brought with them their animals, wild and domesticated: asses, goats, pigs, buffaloes, camels, cats, foxes and rabbits. All of them, in part, like the dingo, ran wild. We may say in consequence that the wild fauna of Australia is richer today than it has ever been before. And the misfortune of the Europeans' arrival has fallen not so much on the animals as on the vegetation – and the Aboriginal.

THE INVENTION OF AGRICULTURE

The climax of all man's earlier inventions came with the development of settled farming. It came some ten thousand years ago and independently in the Old World and the New. In both regions it happened between continents at the cross-roads of those human movements which followed the climatic upheaval at the end of the last ice age.

The Old World cradle or nursery of farming was the hilly border of the Fertile Crescent north of Arabia. For a long period, between 8000 and 4000 B.C., the new farming peoples hardly expanded. These peoples seem to have been accumulating experience and genetic diversity. This is the period that I have called the Silent Millennia.

This was the period during which the character of civilisation was established, the directions it was to take and the modes of man's great assault on the earth were laid down, society was stratified, spinning and weaving, pottery and the decorative and technical arts were developed. During this period the processes of agriculture were being more and more intelligently and industriously organised and the farming population must have multiplied some tenfold. How were all these things accomplished?

What had happened is fairly clear. The origin of settled farming had been made possible by an inward movement of people. The stability of food production which resulted gave rise to a second inward movement. The settlements were a magnet for all the arts and skills of the uncertain unsettled world of the hunters and collectors. The neolithic centre sucked up what it wanted from the paleolithic world outside. And it was this attraction which generated, in the course of 4000 years of dialogue, the wealth, strength and diversity at the centre.

The generation of wealth favoured not only the stratification of society but also the extension of the instinct or appetite for property which was inevitably extended from the ephemeral to the durable, from the marketable to the heritable; and with this change developed the law of property and the economic consequences of property in land and in goods, in men and in power. It was these changes which enabled the central people after four millennia of incubation, transformed in character by their success in their new activities, to spread out and colonise the whole of the habitable earth. But when they did this and made their great assault on the earth it was an assault on many fronts and we have to look at these different fronts in their different characters outside and inside agriculture.

Outside agriculture their most striking development was in the growth of mining. The demand for the best materials of all kinds and the ability of the settled peoples to pay for them meant that dispersed and sporadic collectors of flint and obsidian, lapis lazuli and amber, copper and gold were now able to establish self-supporting groups or guilds of specialist workers, miners and traders, craftsmen and artists, with trade routes all leading to the centre of agriculture; all leading to, and dependent on, what they were making the centre of civilisation.

By our present standards these operations were on a small scale. But they were the beginning of one kind of despoliation of the earth.

Inside agriculture the purposes and the results were different. The control of soil and water by terracing, by drainage and by irrigation preserved the new settlements from the effects of drought and flood and the washing away of soil. The remains of these works we can still see marvellously preserved in Persia and Anatolia, Mexico and

Peru. Their extension later across Europe and Asia from the banana plantations of the Canary Isles to the rice fields of the Philippines is still the basis at once of the cultivation of crops and the conservation of soil and water.

Meanwhile their crops show that these people developed all the arts of enriching the soil with animal and vegetable manure. Many of them had their unwritten Deuteronomies, mixtures of science and superstition, taught by forgotten sages to plant a fish with a grain of corn and feed the crop by enriching the soil. All this was the fruit of the work done and the skill and experience acquired during those early millennia. It is something we can put on the credit side of man's account with the earth.

EGYPT, MESOPOTAMIA AND THE INDUS

These things were the business of primitive tillage with pick and hoe by the villagers on the southern hillsides of Persia and Anatolia. When, however, these people were assisted by the plough and the ox they were able to tackle the richer soils at the bottoms of the valleys and in the river deltas. Then the greater problems of the control of running water had to be solved. These problems were solved by the engineers, surveyors and astronomers of Sumeria and Egypt. Calendars were devised; floods were predicted; canals were built; property and labour were organised; and the state was controlled in relation to the needs of the land for the purposes of food production.

In due course the descendants of these experts spread out over the world. But especially spreading westward by sea into Europe they were concerned, we have reason to believe, with constructing the stone circles and avenues of Britain and Brittany as well as the canals of Lombardy and Holland. They were responsible indeed for European enterprise in engineering and science. These were men who in every country and generation have been skilled in protecting nature from other men's mistakes, men who (as Marvell puts it, wisely scorning the Dutch):

> dived as desperately for each piece
> Of Earth, as if't had been of *Ambergreece*.

Their original works, however, were not all plain sailing. The governments they served took the longest view that we could expect of them but they met with quite different results in different conditions. In

Egypt they succeeded; in Mesopotamia they partly and significantly failed.

The reasons for this contrast seem to have been several but connected. In the first place the flood in Egypt came in September and spread its silt conveniently in the winter. But in Mesopotamia it came in spring and spread its silt in summer and it was – as the legend of the Flood informs us – less certain in the service it rendered. A second contrast made the first much more serious. The cities of Mesopotamia were exposed to attack; attack both from the desert and from the mountains. Time and again they were overwhelmed. And each time the delicate structure of society and the fragile organisation for the maintenance and repair of canals were liable to be broken. For these various reasons the cities of Sumeria were in the end, after a millennium, totally ruined. Cultivation and civilisation then moved together up the long valleys of the twin rivers leaving behind them (according to Jacobson and Adams) the silted waterways and salted lands which had slowly choked them.

The cities of the Indus had a similar beginning and met the same end, both being 500 years later. By the time the end came the whole region was irretrievably lost. The desert had claimed it and it lay buried under sand until Sir Mortimer Wheeler uncovered it 3500 years later.

In Mesopotamia the period from 3000 to 500 B.C. repeats this story. But each successive disaster by war and misuse becomes a little milder. Step by step the centre of government moved northwards until it was to be found in Persia. And then it was no longer a small kingdom but a great state based on the iron and the horses of the mountains, a colonial and imperial government strong enough to protect its subject peoples in the valleys from the disturbance that had always threatened them and their works when they were, so to speak, free. Meanwhile Egypt lay protected not by its men but by its deserts. Its people could maintain their system of irrigation unchanged and undamaged for another couple of millennia. Unchanged also were the people themselves.

The lesson from this contrast is of universal application. Competition, conflict, and war, as in Mesopotamia, advance the evolution and civilisation of men. But they tend to destroy the environment in which the descendants of those men have to live. To be sure their descendants in the past did not have to live there. They could move on. That is what some of them always did, leaving their devastation behind them. The damage to the environment has always in a sense damaged the people. For the enterprising ones have taken over and colonised new territory, leaving the slow-witted ones established for ever in the impoverished possession of the homelands of their ancestors.

THE FARMER AND THE FOREST

So much we may say of the most skilful use that men have made of the land they have worked. This was what happened when they were applying all their abilities, energies and foresight to pass on the benefits of what they did to their children. But there were other things they did (and still do) whose consequences were less to be foreseen and also less to be desired.

They understood, or rather the best of them understood, the land that they worked and felt that they owned. But they did not understand the wilderness, the heath, or the forest: those lands that Fraser Darling has fondly and aptly portrayed for us; those lands that belonged to no one or to everyone. Among those lands, Deuteronomy, always exact and prudent, makes a wise distinction. It is a distinction which is still always observed by the Mediterranean farmer and must therefore have governed the spread of agriculture for many millennia. The lawgiver (in Ch. 20: 20) tells the Israelites that the only trees they may cut down are those that 'do not yield food'. So it was that throughout the Mediterranean region, while forests and woods disappeared, the olive, the fig, the date and the vine, the almond, the walnut and the chestnut were preserved and propagated: save, of course, for the damage wrought by desert marauders and foreign armies.

But what happened to the general forest? Everywhere, the farmer felled trees for timber and fuel. The timber he used for building houses and ships. The fuel he burnt for heating and for baking both bread and pottery. And here the miner stepped in to demand far more for smelting and forging. In Sumeria and the Indus cities, having stripped their own woods, they went further afield. In Egypt they had to go very far afield to Nubia. All three fell a prey to those newer nations who could keep their fuel and their smiths at home. Crete being well-forested and well-harboured was made for ships and for sailors. But, since Crete was an island, a few centuries of maritime supremacy and prosperity sufficed to destroy its forests and ruin its power for ever.

The greatest threat to the forests and woods of the ancient world, however, still lay in the future. It lay in the flocks and the herds of the pastoralist.

THE HERDSMAN AND THE FOREST

The herdsman seems to have taken his livestock, his spinning and weaving and his pottery from the settled farmer. But here and there as opportunity arose and inclination agreed, he cut adrift from this early partnership. Then he often went far afield and far ahead. In the great expansion which followed the Silent Millennia he took his flocks and herds westward, to the Atlantic, southwards through Arabia and Africa and eastwards into India and Central Asia.

In every direction the resources of the world and its opportunites for the herdsman seemed unlimited. But by the end of the Bronze Age the limits were being reached and his initiative was already taking a fresh direction. Already, grazing animals had extended their pasture at the expense of the woods and the forest. And the forest itself was retreating in a drying climate. Now he began to burn the scrub and the forest in order to enlarge and refresh his pasture. The forest seemed to him an enemy but it was an enemy that could be defeated without effort and even by accident. The felling and the burning, the sheep and the goat, later, on the African side, assisted by the camel, slowly depleted the forests and woodlands of the Mediterranean region.

To achieve this result, this terrifying result, the herdsman had to wage an endless war, and a finally successful war, on one remaining enemy, the wild predators. But every success he gained against lions, leopards and wolves was a success also for wild grazing animals. So that just as the cat domestically followed the mouse across Europe so we may say that later the rabbit pastorally followed the sheep; both of these pushing back the forest and preventing its natural regeneration.

In these ways it came about that the Mediterranean forests dwindled from 500 to 50 million acres, one-tenth of the area they had covered before the agricultural revolution struck them. In India and China we cannot so well estimate the extent of what has been lost. We merely know that the causes, the scale and the timing of the disaster have all been similar. What about its consequences?

The consequences of the destruction of forest were manifold and some of them irremediable. Forests, like the sea, represent a vast reservoir of water. And they can be tapped on roughly the same scale since they yield this store of moisture to the air and provide for rain. Hence we may say that, at the end of the ice age, subtropical forests constituted a vast buffer against the sudden parching effects on the vegetable and animal world of a warmer and drier climate. Conversely temperate forests helped to drain an over-watered land and their removal, notably in Britain, left uncultivable moors behind them. Yet another consequence of deforestation was the washing away of the soil which had accumulated under the trees largely during the last ice age and was not to be replaced by any conceivable human effort.

The last consequence of deforestation may be seen where an agricultural people is endeavouring to survive in a region that is now severely depleted of wood through its use for timber and fuel. In India perhaps 300 million tons of dried cow-dung, the proper means of restoring fertility to the soil, are burnt every year to furnish the fuel which was originally furnished by the forest. This practice is equivalent to the impatient or greedy habit of those in the urban world who live on hire purchase. They are living on the future. They are taking a mortgage on posterity.

MANKIND DIVIDED

The farmer and the herdsman, carrying their crops and stock, their crafts and skills, spread over most of Europe, Asia and Africa during the fourth and third millennia B.C. Interbreeding with the native peoples they undoubtedly went some way towards bringing mankind together. Yet when all this movement was over in the Iron Age mankind found itself once more frozen up in separate and remote racial compartments. Genetically and culturally the expansion had served to unite mankind, but when the expansion ended mankind once more fell in pieces. How could this be?

First, let us notice that one link was never broken, that between the ancient east and Europe: this connection was both by land and sea and never could be interrupted. The bronze craftsmen moved into Europe on a large scale carrying their arts with them and bringing the Bronze Age to its climax in that continent. But communication of the ancient centre with the far east became intermittent. And as for the far south of Africa and India, bronze failed to make its way until iron and the iron workers had arrived. The conditions that stopped the expansion and severed the communication have now become clear.

Take first the connection with China. This was established with decisive effects several times in the third, second and first millennia B.C. But at those times the Tarim Basin was still watered from the mountains around it. The cities there discovered by Sir Aurel Stein were buried, he supposed, only during the first millennium A.D. There can be little doubt that the desert which buried them, as it has buried the Indus cities, was one which they themselves had helped to create. The grazing of the flocks and the felling of the trees had combined with a deteriorating climate to destroy them. In destroying them it had not severed but at least strangled the connection between Europe and China. And in doing so it had altered the course of history.

At the same time the same kind of change in the state of the Sahara was strangling the connections between tropical Africa and the Mediterranean. But other connections in Africa were being broken, as we can now see, not by drought but by quite other means.

THE HEYDAY OF DISEASE

One of the results of the successes of farmers and herdsmen was that their populations were now lying much thicker on the ground. Their ancestors had been protected from infectious disease by their rarity and by the isolation, at once geographical and biological, from all their neighbours which they had won for themselves. Now they became vulnerable.

Not only was man now vulnerable but so also were all the other animals he had assembled or attracted around him. These were not only cattle. Rats and mice, lice, fleas and mosquitoes and every pest and parasite, all of these in turn could prosper and multiply. New diseases could be, and were, transferred from animals and adapted themselves to the new conditions that man was now providing. All these changes proceeded with a speed in proportion to the density of the populations of the victims, human and animal; and in proportion also to the warmth and humidity of the climate. In other words they proceeded most rapidly in tropical Africa, India and South-East Asia, all of them regions which the new farmers and herdsmen were attempting to colonise.

In these countries different effects followed. In Africa the movement of cattle and cattle people colonising the country was arrested. The spread of inventions and the development of civilisation carried by these peoples (except modestly in the highlands of Abyssinia) was consequently frustrated. Bronze and the horse, the wheel and the plough all failed to break through the barrier of disease. Even the genetic remedies giving resistance to the disease of malaria, the haemoglobin defects arising in the Old World tropics, proved to be little less damaging to the men whom they protected than the disease itself.

In India the effects were again different, and indeed unique. The barrier to the spread of infectious disease was explicitly and plausibly the establishment and reinforcement by religious sanction of the system of castes which prevented contact between the clean and the unclean. Yet this system came to govern the evolution, or rather lack of evolution, of the whole society. By this indirect means it was able to impede the spread of civilisation.

So far we have looked at one half of the story. Our interpretation of it, however, is not justified until we look at the other half. Every race of mankind, exposed to these new diseases, developed its own genetic devices for acquiring resistance to them. Some of these, like the haemoglobin defects, as we saw, handicapped the peoples that acquired them. Others inevitably failed when either the people or the disease crossed their established frontier. Suddenly on a great scale after the navigations of the fifteenth century this crossing of frontiers struck mankind like a hurricane. What happened then has been exactly recorded.

When America, Australia and Polynesia were discovered by Europeans they were inhabited by peripheral and isolated populations. Their peoples lacked both the diversity and the specific resistances to disease which had been developed by the central mass of mankind among whom the great diseases of civilisation had already reached their epidemic climaxes. The results are well known: the destruction of the peripheral peoples. By man's own action the impact of man on nature had been reversed. Now we had the impact of nature on man or on some men. And because the impact in this case was sudden and recent, its cause could not be mistaken.

WHEN SUCCESS IS A FAILURE

We are lucky today in respect of what we know. We can survey the whole earth. And looking at the whole of geography we can see a cross-section of history. The early stages of exploitation, wise or unwise, stages which have almost vanished from the advanced countries, are revealed to us by the backward parts and peoples of Africa, India and Indonesia. At the same time a devastation of a different kind but no less instructive is revealed to us in the most advanced industrial societies. Among them technical exploitation is approaching its terrifying limits and showing these societies to be in their different aspects at once the most enlightened and the most dangerous of all. Showing also, I believe, that the greatest enterprise in doing the damage can be connected, socially and genetically, with the greatest skill in understanding and perhaps repairing it. For the basis of understanding and repair is in one principle: that every invention of man has made his environment more favourable for his short-term multiplication. But it has made his environment less favourable for his long-term survival.

This is not the only unexpected or paradoxical conclusion that we are forced to admit. The driving force of human evolution has been selection for competitive success in invention and also for competitive multiplication of those who succeed. It is these two forces, largely instinctive forces, which have brought the full impact of man to bear on his environment. The effects of that impact are to threaten his means of sustaining life as an individual; and to favour the diseases that threaten his life in a community. He has been brought to the point where, tightly packed in numbers and partly fixed in character, in beliefs, and in institutions, he has come near to being deprived of his initiative. He is no longer completely the master of his destiny that he once imagined himself to be.

Indeed we may be excused for putting to him an audacious suggestion. It is that he may have to reverse his initiative: to regard his virtues as vices, his successes as failures: to admit that all harm done to nature is harm done to man; and hence to scrap some part of his morals, natural or official, and of his religion, pious or political, to scrap them, strangely enough, both East and West. He may even have to allow that standards of right and wrong can never be uniformly applied to different peoples, to different classes or even to different age-groups in a world of rapidly changing structure.

This very diversity between and within societies offers us, however, our means of discovering a way out for mankind as a species. The groups and classes in which we exist are mutually dependent. In the long run we must recognise this enduring fact. And in some groups among some peoples there are always likely to be a few who can see far enough ahead to warn the rest. They will see that our values now have to be reassessed. Man depends on nature. The supply of what nature offers him is limited. He uses up nature in proportion to his numbers. But some men use up nature faster than others. Some employ nature more wisely than others, preferring the distant future to the immediate future. Some, for this reason, give more in return to nature and to mankind. What has happened in the past shows us that all these factors must influence our judgement in deciding how man will have to make his reckoning with nature in the future.

ROBERT ARDREY (1970) *The Social Contract*, London.

A. J. ARKELL (1955) *History of the Sudan*, Manchester.

I. H. BURKILL (1951) 'The greater yam in the service of man', *Adv. Sci.*, vii, 443-8.

F. FRASER DARLING (1956) 'Man's ecological dominance through domesticated animals on wild lands', in W. L. THOMAS (1956).

—— (1970) *Wilderness and Plenty* (the Reith Lectures 1969), London.

C. D. DARLINGTON (1963) *Chromosome Botany and the Origins of Cultivated Plants*, 2nd edn, London.

—— (1969a) 'The Genetics of society', *Past and Present*, **43**, 3-33.

—— (1969b) 'The silent millennia' in *Domestication and Exploitation of Plants and Animals*, ed. Ucko and Dimbleby, London.

—— (1969c) *The Evolution of Man and Society*, London.

C. J. GLACKEN (1956) 'Changing ideas in the habitable world' in W. L. THOMAS (1956).

E. GLESINGER (1960) 'The Mediterranean project', *Sc. Am.*, **203**, 86-103.

BERNHARD GRZIMEK (1967) *Four-Legged Australians* (Animals and Men, Papua), London and Sydney.

C. V. HAYNES (1966) 'Elephant hunting in North America', *Sc. Am.*, **214**, 104-12.

HENRY HODGES (1970) *Technology in the Ancient World*, London.

TH. JACOBSON AND R. M. ADAMS (1958) 'Salt and silt in ancient Mesopotamian agriculture', *Science*, **cxxviii**, 1251-8.

W. C. LOWDERMILK (1944) *Palestine: land of promise*, London.

P. S. MARTIN (1962) 'Africa and pleistocene overkill', *Nature*, **212**, 339-41.

H. MOLLER (1964) *Population Movements in Modern European History*, London and New York.

C. A. REED (1959) 'Animal Domestication in the Prehistoric Near East', *Science*, **cxxx**, 1629-39.

M. AUREL STEIN (1921) *Serindia*, I-V, Oxford.

W. L. THOMAS ed. (1956) *Man's Role in Changing the Face of the Earth*, Chicago.

P. J. UCKO AND G. W. DIMBLEBY ed. (1969) *The Domestication of Plants and Animals*, London.

4

THE INFLUENCE OF TECHNOLOGY ON ENVIRONMENT

ARCHIE CLOW

THIS essay will be confined to the British Isles. This is neither capricious nor chauvinistic. It was in Britain that, during the later part of the eighteenth century, the seeds of today's anxieties about population and pollution were sown. But the impact of technology on nature goes back far beyond the 1770s.

A proper study of the influence of technology on the environment of the British Isles would require not one chapter in a single book but a series of largish volumes.[1] The reason is simple. There is hardly a square mile of Great Britain that has not been affected in some way by technology, and the process of change has been going on for more or less 20,000 years. We fix this date, approximately, since geological studies reveal that 20,000 years ago the whole of Britain north of the Severn and Thames was glaciated and even the remaining area was ice-bound and not exactly a congenial habitat. This 'remainder' was not yet detached from continental Europe; there was no English Channel; indeed the North Sea ended somewhere about the latitude of the Humber. By roughly 20,000 B.C. the final recession of the latest Ice Age had begun (as the Pleistocene gave way to the Holocene) leaving a surface of glacial drift that overlay the particularly varied geological heritage that has played a dominant part in Britain's subsequent development as a technological nation. There being no barrier to the colonisation of this exposed glacial drift by plants and animals, the English environment as matured by time had begun to evolve. Pollen analysis reveals the succession of vegetational changes, and archeology the concomitant human influences, if and when there are any. While the direction of climatic change was, in general, towards more temperate conditions, improvement was by no means continuous. There were fluctuations in both temperature and rainfall. We cannot follow all those fluctuations here. Suffice it to note in summary that, as we leave the Paleolithic and approach the Mesolithic (*c.* 7500 B.C.), in Scotland much of the higher land was still covered with ice, but tree-sized birches grew on the lower ground, while further south, in England, much of the land was covered with pine forest and in the extreme south oak, alder, and elm were moving northwards aided by the somewhat rapid amelioration in climate. From archeology we learn that these forests had been penetrated by hunter-fishers who may have effected their colonisation by an overland route. Their numbers were small, but they did possess flint axes, and bone and antler tools and weapons. So square one of the change from a *time-made* environment to a *man-made* one had begun. Technology was on its way. Nature herself, moreover, was not standing still. About 5500 B.C. there appears to have been a break in the weather pattern which lasted at least till 3000 B.C. Warmer wetter weather enabled the oak/alder complex to advance at the expense of the established pines, and to this day this oak/alder complex has remained an important component in the southern rural environment of England. Mesolithic man, whose numbers were too small, and his technology too primitive, to have much perceptible effect on the landscape, was followed by the technologically more competent Neolithic man.

As the Atlantic Period was coming to an end (3000-2000 B.C.) man's tools and technology were becoming more effective. To hunting and fishing he had added cultivation and husbandry. Some cultivation was being undertaken which necessitated at least temporary clearance of areas of scrub or forest with tools of polished stone and antler hoes. He grew corn in small, round or oval, fields and adopted as his habitat particularly the chalk downlands in such regions as the Southern Pennines, the Yorkshire Wolds, the Cotswolds, the Mendips, the South Downs, and Salisbury Plain, in all of which areas there are still archeological remains of his activities – tombs and long barrows – and perhaps of greater technological significance, pottery (potsherds), which must have augmented the ever-growing assault on the woodlands – this time to supply the fuel necessary to fire the clay. What life was like under these conditions can be judged by the remarkable excavations at Skara Brae in the Orkneys which, although chronologically later, preserved features of this early Neolithic culture.

These early inhabitants were not to be confined indefinitely to their downland habitat. Yet another of these mysterious changes in climate took place. Rainfall dropped and as a result the downlands became too dry for primitive cultivation and at the same time the lower ground of the valleys more amenable to colonisation. So we find man moving to lower ground along the more easily cleared valleys, where pollen analysis suggests a considerable degree of human interference possibly augmented by the practice of shifting cultivation. This period too saw the return of pines to the Fenlands, the establishment of the Brecklands, and probably also the development of moors in Scotland and Ireland.

But the great change of the second millennium B.C. was the appearance of man with a knowledge of metallurgy: men who could recognise copper ore and tin ore, and convert them – again with timber as fuel – if unalloyed into copper and tin, if alloyed into bronze. The boundaries of the Stone and Copper Ages are blurred but we may assume that the change happened about the middle of the period assigned to the Beaker folk (2000-500 B.C.).

There is no need to go into the minutiae of the various metal ages. Suffice it to say that a new era of change was dawning. Although the first metal tools were little more than thin blades of hammered copper, they were more efficient than anything that preceded them, and so enabled man to intensify his influence on his adopted terrain. Whether this technical advance contributed to increase his numbers, increase they must have done, otherwise he could not have constructed the 18,000 tumuli that have been recorded in Britain. To accommodate the increasing population the 'slash and burn' techniques of Neolithic man no doubt continued, producing a countryside that was a mosaic of virgin forest, cut forest perhaps regenerating, dotted with rough pasture and patches of tillage. But neither nature nor man remain static for long. Late in the Bronze Age, Celtic peoples arrived bringing with them a higher technology characterised by the *cire perdue* method of casting, socketed axes, and more sophisticated woodworking tools. The latter made possible an advance to timber-framed structures, which took their place alongside the wattled huts that had till then provided man's most hospitable habitation. Technological changes were not confined to metallurgy, however, though they no doubt derived from it. These Celtic peoples also progressed in agriculture, introducing new crops (oats, rye, and spelt) and for the first time sheep exceeded wild forest animals in number. Cattle, and especially pigs, helped to check the regeneration of such land as had been cleared of forest. Among mechanical inventions, the horse-drawn chariot improved transport although roads remained deplorable, and the Celtic plough gave a new appearance to the cultivated areas. These rectangular strips some 400 ft by 100 ft – remains of which can still be revealed by aerial photography – may be said to be technological in origin in that they resulted from the use of a heavy plough drawn by oxen, in contrast to the little oval patches of earlier times.

For the best part of two millennia (2000-500 B.C.) bronze remained man's supreme achievement in metallurgy but as we approach Roman times increasing knowledge of the properties of minerals must have revealed that iron ores were of wider occurrence than those of tin and copper, so the greater accessibility of iron for tools and weapons furthered still more the impact on the environment. There is no need here to discuss in detail the archeologists' classification of the age of iron dominance. The important thing is that with the improved metallurgy the oak forests fell more easily to the woodman's axe and elaborate heavy timber fortifications became a characteristic of the age. About 600 hill forts, some extending to 160 acres, are known to have existed.

The agricultural potential of the various soils still had a marked influence on the location of settlement, and the Celtic field system remained dominant, the cultivators living in widely spaced 'farm-towns' associated with their fields.

In mechanics, rotary motion was applied in wheel-thrown pottery and in the quern used to grind corn.

With the arrival of the Belgae (a Germano-Celtic people), a few tribal capitals were established (Winchester, Silchester, Colchester and Leicester) as they spread over the whole south-east and into the Midlands.

Coming to Roman times we leave the realm of archeological speculation, but despite the fact that we had entered the era of recorded history there is still much difference of opinion among social technologists as to the real effect of the Roman occupation upon the landscape as a whole. The total population of the islands was probably about the half million mark, no more than a single city like Bristol today. So settlement overall must have been thin. Wreford Watson goes so far as to say categorically that 'Roman culture had little effect on life and landscape'. We have to bear in mind that under the Romans there were three zones of occupation: civil zones, military zones, and the rest, which for simplicity may be subsumed under the category of the remoter parts of Scotland. The excellence of Roman civil engineering techniques and strategy may have led us to exaggerate their overall influence. True, they built in excess of 300 known villas and established upwards of sixty towns, though perhaps half of these were rather in the nature of permanent camps or administrative centres, which nevertheless added a new environmental feature to the British scene. Even regions of the country most accessible to Europe, e.g. the Weald, remained mostly unsettled except where there were clearings for iron-workings.

The mention of iron raises an important point in technology. 'Why did the Romans seek to extend their Empire beyond the barrier of the Channel?'

One answer is the attraction of mineral wealth. If we study a map showing the distribution of mines known in Europe in Roman times, it is immediately obvious that Britain compares favourably with Europe as a whole. The geology of Britain south of the Highland line was particularly favourable to economic development; coal could be obtained from the Forest of Dean or Somerset; iron-stone from the Weald, Forest of Dean and Northumberland; salt from the sea or Triassic measures; and especially tin and silver from Cornwall, the Mendips, Derbyshire, Yorkshire and Flint. If the motivation for the Romans was to acquire British minerals, then we can say that the age of extractive industries with all its consequences was on its way. But extraction is only the first step in the technological chain. It is economic to smelt ore with the nearest source of fuel. We know that the Romans made bricks and other ceramic products with local clay, and this, with their metallurgical operations, helped to disrupt the established ecology. So the clearance of forests continued, and was extended into lower less tractable lands. Coal was probably also mined in Somerset and the Forest of Dean.

The Celtic field system expanded and sheep rearing began to move towards becoming the great source of wealth that it was in subsequent ages; but as Roman influence declined, cleared forest reverted to go out of cultivation for centuries, and the Fenland drainage system collapsed.

Whatever the Roman influence on landscape, it is certain that they left vast areas of still untamed forest. The heavy soils of the Midlands remained a problem; in fact they have been described as an 'archeological vacuum' – which suggests that in these 'sodden and unkind lands' there was still much dense forest. Although the departure of the Romans is followed by a period of obscurity it is certain that some of the techniques they had introduced survived in the knowledge of the native population, and the trends of the past continued. But it was their successors, the Anglo-Saxons, who between 450 and 1066 A.D. extended a far greater influence on the landscape than the Romans ever did. This English settlement exerted its influence not so much by technology as by social change. The Saxon pattern of manor, hamlet of mud and wattle dwellings, and a method of cultivation in open common fields divided into strips – a furlong – exerted a more lasting effect on the English landscape than anything produced by the Roman occupation. Exploiting the soil potential, they sought out good deep loams, and ploughed in such a way that produced 'ridges and furrows', many of which can still be seen. We find them colonising river terraces, the boulder clays of East Anglia, parts of the North and South Downs, and the Chilterns, later spreading on to the heavier Midland soils. The village geography of the sixth century is a basic element in the pattern of rural England today. It lasted for a thousand years practically unaltered, until overtaken by a new technology which necessitated enclosure of the land. Owing to the impermanent material from which the domestic dwellings of the era were made, however, none remain, though there are a few Saxon churches still extant.

Although in retrospect the Anglo-Saxon period may appear technologically static, progress was being made. W. H. Hoskins, for example, has suggested that in addition to the axe, mattock, and bill-hook, fire was now being used to speed up the clearance of the land. This is certainly borne out by place names such as Brentwood, Brindley, and possibly Barnet. Also, in the eighth century, we see the beginnings of the power revolution that has had such a dominant effect on Britain's economy. Water-mills were introduced into eighth-century England and by the Norman Conquest had spread widely over Eastern England and the Midlands. They were all corn-mills of which 6000 are recorded in Domesday Book – ten of them for every church.

The next social and political upheaval in England was more the transfer of an aristocracy than a folk-movement or occasion for technological innovation, except in that in its aftermath some citizens came to realise that the production of wool might lead to more security than war. So we see the advance of an industry that was, as the years passed, to have a lasting influence on the English environment.

Sheep farming and the production of cloth from the wool produced became a primary English occupation and so remained for many generations. Between 1150 and 1250 there were no less than 600 monasteries in the country and many of these helped to push sheep-rearing into the remoter parts of the country. The sheep themselves held back natural regeneration that might have taken place, so hitherto wooded land tended to change to grass or even heather moor.

Existing farms, for example in Devon, can be traced back to the eleventh to thirteenth centuries. Their still irregular fields had been made by the haphazard clearing of the woods, and the meandering lanes or roads of today are the successors of old woodland paths.

Although many generations of warfare were to pass before the last battle was fought on British soil, by the time we came to the Middle Ages towns were no longer sited for strategic reasons. The basis of their development was now in the main economic, and the basis of the economy was not yet the extraction industries but, as has been mentioned, wool.

We must not, however, overlook the search for minerals that continued in the twelfth and thirteenth centuries. Copper, tin, lead and coal all had their place in the economy and this background of technology may well have had the effect of 'opening up' regions of the country which otherwise might have long remained unexplored. We have only to recollect much later maps on parts of which there is the off-putting legend 'Here be stony places'. But it was these stony places that often became sources of mineral wealth.

The end of the twelfth century also saw the development of two significant types of mill: the windmill applied to the grinding of corn, and the first mechanical power-driven invention related to the expansion in sheep husbandry – the fulling-mill. The latter was the first extension of water-power to an industrial process and the two developments taken together have led Professor E. M. Carus-Watson to speak of a thirteenth-century industrial revolution. But technically speaking, Britain was still underdeveloped and a late starter, its foreign trade still confined to the export of wool and leather and unfabricated metals, principally tin and lead. At home, however, malleable iron-making probably satisfied domestic needs, and ceramics in the form of brick and tile-making had advanced sufficiently to enable some towns to decree the compulsory substitution of tiles for thatch. To sum up: apart from agricultural changes, the most spectacular advances in medieval technology, excluding power-mills, were in the fields of mining and metals, which produced bronze and iron for cannon, copper and iron for domestic utensils, and lead and tiles for roofs.

Whether the next part of English history can be considered part of its technological history is a matter of opinion. It certainly had a profound effect, albeit indirectly, on the landscape in consequence of the change in agricultural technology that it brought in train. The event was the epidemic of bubonic plague (1348/9) which it is estimated carried off between a third and a half of the inhabitants, putting the population back to about the Domesday level.

The scarcity of labour was such that land went out of cultivation. Whole villages were deserted and sheep took the place of corn because they needed less attention. Landowners were able to increase the size of their domains because common-rights were no longer safeguarded. Thus, certain sections of the population wrung personal prosperity from general misfortune, and we have the so-called wool-churches they built to bear witness to a possible attempt to square their consciences. As a consequence of the change in husbandry, new sheep-runs called for some sort of enclosure, and although powers of enclosure had existed since the statute of Merton (1235) it was only in the aftermath of the Black Death that they began to be put into operation. Once-cultivated strips were put down to grass; open fields became hedged enclosures. In some parts of the country something akin to present-day rural England began to emerge although much of it remained as described by Thomas Sharp in his *English Panorama:*

> A great part of the country was still in an unredeemed primeval state. In the fifteenth century an unbroken series of woods and fens stretched across England between Lincoln and the Mersey. The great eastern fens covered hundreds of thousands of acres: north and south of them extended a vast area of bog and swamp. Yorkshire was swamp, heath, forest and bare woodland. Lancashire was largely marsh and peat moss. Warwickshire, Northamptonshire and Leicestershire were covered with forest. Sherwood Forest covered nearly the whole of Nottinghamshire; much of Sussex was still the forest of Andredsweald: Cannock Chase was crowded with oaks; the Chiltern district of Buckinghamshire and Oxford was thick with woods – and so on over most of the country. In some counties there were now great clearings; but where the landscape was not waste and wild, it was generally quite open: it was also scrubby and patchy in effect and seen from the air it would probably have had the appearance of a vast area of modern allotment gardens.

With wool in the ascendancy a whole network of clothing villages and towns developed, although their populations remained small by our standards (Leicester 2000, Oxford 2500, Lincoln 3000) and the words rural and urban had little meaning outside London. There were still too few people to civilise the whole landscape, if we can so describe man's impact on nature. For example, between 1450 and 1600 only 2 per cent of the total area of the country was enclosed; common-fields were general, and there were probably three times as many sheep on the land as men.

By the 1700s, however, it became apparent that the thousand-year-old system of agriculture had outlived its usefulness. Profound technical, legal, and social changes were afoot. In 1701 the first modern Enclosure Act was passed. New crops were introduced or their cultivation extended (potatoes and turnips), new techniques were experimented with (Tull's *Horse Hoeing Husbandry*), and stock was improved by men like Bakewell of Leicester and Coke of Holkham.

By the end of the century three and a half million acres had been enclosed, much of it originally common-field. Hedging with thorn was often a condition of enclosure, so we get the establishment of the typical landscape and hedgerows and hedgerow trees, now alas often disappearing to accommodate yet another new technology of monoculture, mechanisation, and chemical insecticides.

With much of the land enclosed, the countryman had made his contribution to the rural pattern, though the landowner continued to exert his influence through the laying out of parks, some of which have preserved for us valuable green open spaces. But the eighteenth-century landowners' activities were far from purely aesthetic. The great landowners were not slow to realise that there was wealth in the minerals under their hills, fields, and woods. Landowners had worked iron in a small way for many years. Blast furnaces in the Weald date from 1490 though they did not expand rapidly, there being only some sixty a century later – an expansion in all probability limited and controlled by the available timber supplies. Similar small-scale developments took place in South Wales, Staffordshire, Yorkshire, and Derbyshire before the end of the sixteenth century. They served needs mostly domestic and agricultural. In Elizabethan times, the Navy expanded and created a further demand for timber – for construction in the first place, but also as fuel needed for smelting iron to furnish the necessary chains, anchors, armaments and so on.

Both agriculture and mineral working, and the utilisation of water-power, created new landscapes and we are in error if we assume that the Industrial Revolution was solely dependent on the development of the coal-iron-steam-transport complex. While obviously the nineteenth-century part of the Industrial Revolution is the great age of steam, profound changes, social and economic, preceded the coal/iron era.

In fact the transition from cottage to factory in textiles took place half a century before James Watt was granted his steam-engine patent (1769). The first real textile-mill, which employed some 300 operatives, was that built on the River Derwent between 1718 and 1722 by J. Lombe (1693-1722) and his brother T. Lombe (1685-1739), and it was not a wool-mill, as we might expect, but a silk-mill, and it was powered by water. Richard Arkwright's first spinning-mill at Nottingham (1768) was powered by horses; his second at Cromford (1771) was, like the Lombes', on the Derwent and it too relied on water.

Even quite massive metal-working machinery was powered by water-wheels. An example from the Abbeydale Works on the River Sheaf (Sheffield, 1780) can still be seen. And practically all the main textile inventions – Kay's flying shuttle (1733), Hargreaves' spinning jenny (1767), and Arkwright's water-frame (1769) – were established in the age of water-power. Water-wheels themselves were the subject of research towards improved power output and were widely used to grind corn, for fulling, to drain the ever-deepening mines, and crush the ore taken from them. In metal production they were used to generate the blast for furnaces, and operate tilt hammers.

The availability of water, which in the production of textiles was also needed for scouring and bleaching, dominated the siting of the early mills. Early cotton-mills, for example, were often built in remote valleys, near water obviously, but with the added advantage of being away from prying eyes. To us today, who can only see them through eyes conditioned to steam, many of the sites look incongruous. But we have to bear in mind that the supply of water was not limitless. Indeed, in some regions, all available supplies were utilised and the same water often used over and over again if there was a sufficient fall to give an adequate head to generate useful energy. There was, however, another source of energy, fossil fuel. Where it was simply heat that was required, in favoured districts coal had been used from early times, e.g. for salt-boiling on the shores of the Firth of Forth, where it was an early cause of atmospheric pollution. Already in

1700 there were 1600 vessels engaged in coastal trade between the Wear and London where it augmented the failing timber supplies, though there too the pollution caused by the substitution was not always welcome.

But considerable changes were to take place in the landscape before it succumbed to the age of coal and iron. The premier position of the Northumberland and Durham mines stemmed from their access to the sea, which provided the only route over which a heavy material could be transported in bulk. But regions other than London wanted coal and had industrial products that they needed to distribute, so while technology facilitated and multiplied the output of industry, even in the absence of a machine to convert energy into rotary motion, a transport system of some magnitude developed – in the main between 1760 and 1825. This was the now largely forgotten and derelict canal system.

Till the canals were developed, the sea and the rivers were virtually the only routes over which any but the lightest and most robust merchandise could be carried. The Exeter Canal of 1664 was something of a preview, but the period 1760-1825 saw water transport brought to many parts of the country. First the rivers were improved, a thousand or more miles of them, and early engravings illustrate the busy scene on many now neglected rivers.

The canal built by James Brindley between 1760 and 1761 for Francis Egerton, third Duke of Bridgewater (1736-1803) who had seen the French canals at Briare and Languedoc, was literally a landmark in transport history. It connected the Duke's mines at Worsley with Manchester. Brindley did not stop at half measures. He carried the canal underground into the mine, and with this new facility linking source and consumer he halved the price of coal to the latter in Manchester.

In our era of motorways and inter-city express trains it is easy to forget that canals, while serenely adding something new to the environment, also embody many of the civil engineering features we are prone to think of as the products of the railway pioneers. It is unnecessary to go into details here, but the cuttings, embankments, tunnels, locks, lifts, bridges, and inclined planes all foreshadowed the changes of the Industrial Revolution. By 1820 there were 3000 miles of valuable inland waterway, the banks of which provided, for obvious reasons, a venue for the siting of many of the new factories of the Industrial Revolution.

Wedgwood was prominent in backing canal development, and, when he moved from his original pothouse, built Etruria on the banks of one of them. Indeed there is a rather closer connection between industry and canal-building than between canals and growth of towns. There was one town, however, Stourport, that developed from an isolated inn into what has been described as 'the emporium of the Midlands'. It even had a Customs House – a direct result of its development as an entrepôt on the expanding canal system.

Fig. 1. The attraction to industry and trade presented by canals in the pre-railway age. A warehouse on the Liverpool to Leeds canal built *c.* 1828

Parallel to the opening up of the country to transport of industrial products by water, there was a long-overdue expansion of road-building, though the technology employed was less a new one than a reversion to the practices of Roman civil engineers that had long been in abeyance. Among the notable figures of the period were Blind Jack of Knaresborough, alias John Metcalf (1717-1810), who built between 1765 and 1792 many miles of excellent road in Yorkshire, Lancashire, Derbyshire, and Cheshire; Thomas Telford (1757-1834), who became surveyor of public works in Shropshire and whose canals and roads are equally remarkable; J. Loudon McAdam (1756-1836), whose system of road construction revived many of the principles of road engineering that had been lost since Roman times.

One signal difference in the second half of the eighteenth century was the availability of a material unknown to the Romans, cast-iron, which enabled Abraham Darby III (1750-91) to build in 1779 the world's first cast-iron bridge at Coalbrookdale, and Rowland Burdon to span the Wear at Sunderland in a way that would hitherto have been impossible.

But this is to anticipate a discussion of the influence of technology on environment through the solution of the problem of smelting iron ore in an age of acutely declining supplies of traditional fuel, viz. charcoal.

Fig. 2. Iron gave the civil engineer a new freedom to cross large gaps hitherto impossible. With its 250 feet span, Rowland Burdon's bridge over the River Wear merits a place alongside its more publicised predecessor at Coalbrookdale whose dimensions it greatly exceeded

Repeated allusion has already been made to man hewing for himself a habitat out of the time-made environment he came to inherit. There are many references to woods in the Domesday Book, but from the time of the Norman Conquest to the end of the Middle Ages attrition was continuous, and ultimately this unending attack began to tell. By the seventeenth century the extent of man's predation had reached alarming proportions. And well it might. In 1629 it was recorded, for example, that a single man with his own axe had brought down no less than 30,000 oaks during the course of his lifetime. While the thesis has not gone undisputed, it is the author's conviction that by Elizabethan times not only England but Europe was in the throes of a timber crisis and that the innovations necessitated to overcome this shortage were vital determinants in the subsequent evolution of European technology. We must bear in mind that for countless generations timber had been an indispensable raw material. Apart from relatively trivial quantities of peat and coal it was the only source of domestic or industrial heat. Bridges, castles, and even churches were built of it. Tin, lead, copper, and iron could not be smelted without it. In selected regions prodigious quantities were used in salt-boiling, and as navigators demanded stouter ships to carry them to the ends of the earth, and the necessity arose to defend the kingdom against the predations of other mercantile nations, timber had to be found to build the 'wooden walls' and smelt the iron to make their anchors and other fittings. To a lesser, but by no means less important, degree, neither glass nor soap could be made without potash, the alkaline residue of calcined timber, and from early times an important commodity in the international trade.

The destruction of trees and woodland is not an obvious activity to attract the contemporary artist, but there is a charming woodcut of the felling of trees to make way for a road in a fifteenth-century woodcut in the Royal Library in Brussels, and it has always seemed to the writer that there is an unconscious representation of the ruthless attack on woods by metal-producers, in particular, in many of the woodcuts in Agricola's *De Re Metallica.* The rapidity with which this essential resource was dwindling is illustrated by Navy estimates of timber reserves over the years 1608-1707. In the former year it was reckoned that there was a reserve of 124,000 trees fit for naval construction, but a century later the figure had been reduced to 12,500. The banks of every navigable river had been denuded and it was only the less accessible forests, such as Sherwood, the Weald, and Epping that remained. As we shall see, solutions to this critical situation came from various directions. Replanting was an obvious possibility although requiring at least a generation to show its effect. Evelyn's *Silva,* published in 1664, was a by-product of the timber famine and a *cri de coeur.* While effective solutions to the problem came from other directions – particularly the application of chemical knowledge to social and economic problems – it is no exaggeration to claim that the pursuit of policies advocated by Evelyn did much to alter the appearance of many parts of the English landscape.

But it is indisputable that had Britain been forced to depend on the availability of timber and its diverse application, the whole history of Britain as a technological society would have been different. There would undoubtedly have been an industrial revolution, but it would not have been the industrial revolution in the terms we recognise. The reason is simple: the geology of the British Isles was to prove to be its salvation.

Fig. 3. Mining as illustrated in Agricola's *De Re Metallica* (1556) but also suggestive of the unconscious portrayal of disafforestation

If we look at a geological map of Europe we see that nature endowed Britain with some of the richest coal deposits in the whole of Europe, and the subsequent story of the influence of technology on environment centres on the utilisation of coal. When the age-old sources of energy, apart from water, became critically inadequate, mineral deposits of fossil fuel redeemed the situation. Deposits of coal were widespread from the Lowlands of Scotland to Somerset, indeed to Kent, and following the dissolution of the monasteries by Henry VIII, rich deposits fell into the hands of those who were only too anxious to exploit them. This was particularly true in Durham, Shropshire, and South Wales, but the same was true in Scotland.

While in some processes the substitution of coal for charcoal raised no insuperable difficulties, as in the salt-pans on the Forth littoral, early patent literature abounds in references to the problem of the utilisation of coal or coke in place of wood in industrial processes. In the main the problem was to get rid of the sulphur which is a natural constituent in many coal deposits. As early as 1650 malt had been successfully dried with coke: in 1686/7 C. and R. Clark had succeeded at Bristol in smelting copper without timber, and the lead smelters achieved success about the same time.

Cornwall, which had, even on an international scale, important copper and tin mines, lacked coal, so the ore had to be shipped across the Bristol Channel to the nearest accessible source of coal, namely Neath and Swansea, thus giving rise to the important industrial complex of that region, where the degradation of environment became at least as catastrophic as anywhere else in the British Isles.

Between the Elizabethan Age and the beginning of the Industrial Revolution in the middle years of the eighteenth century, output in the production of English coal mines had increased tenfold, and in view of what has been said about transport it is not unexpected to discover that the coal mines that figure most prominently in the early industrial scene are those with easy access to transport by water. In 1640, for example, the Tyne shipped half a million tons of 'sea coal' to London; the Durham coalfield had access to the Wear; coal from Broseley could reach the sea *via* the Severn. There was the Irwell in Lancashire. Such were the early activities in these regions that British output was probably three to four times that of the whole of the rest of Europe and it is in these parts of the country that we may be said to encounter the first true industrial revolution landscapes, such as that of Dudley, the nail-making centre.

The iron needed for production of this kind was malleable iron produced in a host of 'bloomeries' spread over many regions of the country, but concentrated naturally where sources of ore and fuel coincided. Whereas these bloomeries were simple primitive devices depending on charcoal to reduce the iron ore, the metallurgy of iron is sophisticated so that, while in some processes the transition from charcoal to coal could be made with few technical innovations, this was not so with iron. Thus we encounter one of the major impediments to industrial progress which bedevilled a timber-starved land. The problem of making iron with coal was solved by Abraham Darby in 1709; Darby succeeded in smelting iron ore with 'charked coal' (coke) made from the 'Clod' coal of Shropshire. He did this at Coalbrookdale in a pleasant valley which had been chosen neither for its iron ore nor coal mines but because of the availability of water for power and transport down the river to the already important port of Bristol. Coalbrookdale became the largest unit of its kind in the kingdom – it was portrayed in various guises by celebrated artists of the day – but Darby's technically successful process took a long time to spread to other areas, possibly because of the almost superstitious conservatism of the traditional ironmasters in a pre-scientific age. In fact there was little reason why they should not have been assured of economic success since, if we are to believe William Wood, a decade after Darby's process became available two-thirds of the British requirements for iron were still having to be met by importation from abroad.

With a major technological problem solved, from approximately 1700 new regions where coal was available began to develop: Carron near Falkirk, 1759; Merthyr, 1760; Workington, 1762; all of which became focal points in subsequent industrial development. During the remaining years of the century, technical innovations were effected in Britain that changed the face not only of this country but of many other parts of the world as well.

Abraham Darby's successful smelting of iron with coke has been referred to. Both he and John Wilkinson improved the quality of cast-iron. Germinal ideas contained in various patents were brought together by Henry Cort (1740-1800) in two master patents in 1784, and in contrast to the slow progress of Darby's invention, so enthusiastically were Cort's processes taken up, especially in Wales, that by 1790 it was being referred to as the 'Welsh Process'. Taken together these developments virtually put an end to the life of the traditional centres of iron production in Britain. The scattered local bloomeries disappeared: The Weald, which for generations had enjoyed the advantages of ore from the Sussex mines and charcoal from the forests of the Duke of Norfolk, had succumbed by 1820.

Nor was there any longer need to send English ore to be smelted with charcoal made from trees on the west coast of Scotland.

The increased availability of malleable and improved cast-iron gave architects and designers a new material to experiment with. The resulting advances may not be so obvious as those that took place over the centuries in agriculture, but they are worth looking for in the shape of cast-iron pillars, girders, vaulting, fanlights, and market buildings. A little later we can think of the balustrades and verandahs of Regency Brighton, Cheltenham, and Bath, and the parts of London, Liverpool, and Bristol built about the same time, as all harking back to the technical successes of the metallurgical pioneers of the late eighteenth century.

But the effects of Cort and his predecessors were not confined to the elegance of Bath and Brighton. Cort changed the location of the British iron industry. In the early eighteenth century the region of maximum population in Britain, excluding Middlesex, was a crescent sweeping from Somerset, through Gloucestershire and Wiltshire to East Anglia, with woollen cloth providing half the exports; by 1800 the whole pattern was in a process of rapid change. Freed from its dependence on wood for fuel, the iron industry gravitated towards the coalfields with which Britain was so richly endowed. As a result the Black Country (with its fantastic 'ten-yard seam'), South Yorkshire and its border with Derbyshire, Glamorgan, and the Scottish industrial belt, took on a new look. The old small furnaces and forges became obsolete and gave place to 'steam-powered iron-works'. By any standards some of these were large organisations – such as those of the Darbys at Coalbrookdale and of Wilkinson at Broseley. By the end of the eighteenth century Britain had become an exporter of iron, and by 1830 over 40 per cent of the production centred on South Wales, and another 30 per cent in Shropshire. Technological innovation was now shaping the environment, and also steam-power had become available to industry, although it should not be forgotten that at the beginning of the century water-wheels were still far more numerous than steam engines. Moreover, Cort's activities coincide with the start of one of the most remarkable expansions in the history of economic man. Industrial growth, which had been jogging along at a rate of increase of about 1 per cent per annum, changed to from 3 to 5 per cent and so remained for a hundred years. As a result, within half a century much of the map of England was completely transformed. Reference was made above to the 'steam-powered iron-works' that supplanted the eotechnic forges and furnaces, and clearly the Industrial Revolution could never have taken the shape it did if advancing industry had been forced to remain dependent on water as its main source of power, especially as it has been recorded that in some regions every scrap of water-power was utilised not just once but repeatedly. It was necessary,

Fig. 4. Scene characteristic of the profligate era of iron smelting. Blast furnaces at Summerlea Iron Works, Coatbridge, both polluting the atmosphere and wasting heat through lack of regenerative heating

therefore, to look for an alternative. This evolved in the context of the difficulties experienced in maintaining one of Britain's few exports in the later part of the seventeenth century. If we bear in mind that mining in Cornwall dated back at least to Roman times, it is not unexpected that by the seventeenth century some of these mines had penetrated deeply underground and in so doing were liable to serious flooding. So there was an urgent need for an efficient pump if output was to be maintained and expanded. It was to this end that Thomas Savary (1650-1718) invented his engine for 'raising water by the help of fire' (1698). This was followed (1705) by an improved device due to Thomas Newcomen (1663-1729), the first of which was installed at Huel Vor in Cornwall, and the second at collieries at Dudley Castle – coal mines sharing with those producing tin and copper the problems of flooding as they were forced to ever greater depth.

While it served its purpose, Newcomen's engine was a thermodynamically inefficient device, and it was while contemplating this poor power output for fuel consumed that James Watt invented his separate condenser engine, patented in 1769. To produce engines on a commercial scale, Watt joined forces with Matthew Boulton, an established manufacturer of Birmingham metal goods. So yet another industrial development, which originated elsewhere – Watt was a surveyor and instrument maker in the University of Glasgow – gravitated to the Midlands. To what was in essence a mechanical pump Watt added rotary motion. By 1800 Boulton and Watt had built 321 engines. The localities in which they operated were either the expanding industrial regions or those regions in which there was an unsatisfied demand for power.

The change from water to steam was neither instantaneous nor complete; water-power remained an important source of energy for many generations. But there was one application of steam that water could not rival, and one that had the profoundest effect on the environment – the application of steam to transport. While at the turn of the century metals and metal products were rapidly growing in importance, as was the production of textiles, it was the application of steam-power to transport both on land and at sea that was the most significant feature of the age that followed.

Railways had originated as local mine facilities, and with the application of steam the association became more and more intimate. Following the successes of William Hedley (1813) and George Stevenson (1814), a voracious new consumer of coal and iron came into existence. The demand for rails to run on increased the demand for iron; and the necessity for iron created a demand for coal to smelt it, and for railways to get it from the regions where it was mined to where it was most wanted. These, of course, were often contiguous. Even before the impact of these railway-age pressures, the output of coal had increased prodigiously – by three times between 1770 and 1826 – and the older shallow mines had been forced to give way to the deeper mines characteristic of the expansion in Northumberland and Durham, which by mid-century were contributing a quarter of the total British output but also unhappily laying up a store of unparalleled dereliction to come. While the railways, in association with the factories into which they brought raw materials, and from which they took manufactured goods, ultimately came to dominate much of the urban scene, it was not railway transport in itself that set off the phenomenal rise in the populations of the industrial towns of Britain. Canals and associated factories, as has already been explained, preceded the railways. The Stockton to Darlington Railway dates from 1825, but already industrial towns were growing like evil fungi, often doubling in population in as little as twenty years. Thomas Sharp speaks of 'a nightmare rate of growth producing nightmare towns'. Figures substantiate his comment:

	1801	*1821*
Liverpool	77,000	118,000
Manchester	95,000	238,000
Leeds	60,000	123,000
Sheffield	45,000	91,000
Birmingham	73,000	146,000

According to one, Langford, quoted by W. H. Hoskins:

The traveller who visits [Birmingham] once in six months supposes himself well acquainted with her, but he may chance to find a street of houses in the autumn, where he saw his horse at grass in the spring.

The population of the town doubled in the last forty years of the eighteenth century, but it was as yet far from being the dark and horrible landscape that it eventually became. Even in the early years of the nineteenth century the middle-class streets had prospects of the country, and the older working-class at least still had gardens. The dirt and overcrowding came with the Steam Age in the nineteenth century.

In Lancashire and the Potteries the worst had still to come. Chorley was, when Aiken wrote (1795) 'a small, neat market town' with its river flowing through a pleasant valley, turning 'several mills, engines, and machines. . . . '

In the south of the county what was to be the most appalling town of all – St Helens – was just beginning to defile its surroundings. The British Plate Glass Manufactory had been erected at Ravenshead near the village, in 1773, and other glassworks followed. And about the year 1780 'a most extensive copper-work' was erected to smelt and refine the ore from Parys Mountain in Anglesey. The atmosphere was being poisoned, every green thing blighted, and every stream fouled with chemical fumes and waste. Here, and in the Potteries and the Black Country especially, the landscape of Hell was foreshadowed.

So far reference has been made to such effects of technology as were either (*a*) virtually universal, as was the effect of agricultural development on the landscape; or (*b*) widespread, but covering limited areas at any one point, as in the development of canals and railways; or (*c*) regional development, where locally the influence might be intense – as in coal and other mining, iron-working, and the like. But it would be a mistake to leave the analysis at that point. In particular there evolved, in parallel with the textile industry, a heavy chemical industry – a hydra-headed organism without which

Fig. 5. Staffordshire industrial complex in the early Industrial Revolution

the Industrial Revolution would have been the victim of numerous bottlenecks due to unphased expansion. To take but one example, the mechanisation of spinning and weaving implies the need to speed up the various finishing processes; bleaching, dyeing, etc. Moreover, to see the influence of technology in perspective, we must bear in mind that where it did operate, the unfettered early chemical industry could cause devastation unequalled by any other industry, with the possible exception of the Potteries.

What to include under the heading 'chemical industry' and to decide when it became effective are subjects for debate. There is much to be said for taking as the starting-point the foundation of two vitriol (H_2SO_4) works by Dr John Roebuck and his partner, the first at Birmingham in 1746 and the second at Prestonpans, on the Firth of Forth, in 1749. The background to the Birmingham development was metal refining; there is no doubt that a large proportion of the output from Prestonpans went to the bleachers of linen, which was widely produced in the East of Scotland, and also to some extent to cotton finishers. Apart from wool, which was bleached with sulphur dioxide, made by burning sulphur – a process that caused a degree of local pollution – the traditional method of 'whiting' cloth was by 'grassing', exposure to the open air on bleachfields accompanied by alternate saturation with weak acid and alkaline solutions. Till vitriol became available, sour or buttermilk was the acid used but the process was a tedious one and many acres of land were given over to bleachfields, particularly in the neighbourhood of Perth in Scotland, and Bolton in England. So great was the reduction in bleaching time that resulted from the use of chemical bleaches that their introduction was regarded as a great blessing in that it returned land to agriculture and the buttermilk to the hungry.

Repeated reference has been made to the impetus to invention resulting from the lack of timber as fuel. The early patent literature abounds in references to improved furnaces that would burn coal without contaminating the products; the covered-in glass pot is a consequent invention. But wood, apart from its importance as an energy source, was also an important raw material, in that the ash left after it had burned away was one of Europe's few sources of alkali (in this instance principally potash) which was required for textile finishing either directly or in the form of soap, and without which glass also could not be made. Fortunately, wood ash is not the only source of alkali and until the application of chemical principles led to a lasting solution of the shortage, various palliatives were tried: Spanish *barilla* was imported, as were Muscovy ashes, and an extensive trade in kelp (calcined seaweed) developed in the Scottish islands and on the shores of the Highland counties. These were, however, no more than stopgaps and one of the dominant activities of chemists in the latter part of the eighteenth century was the search for a means of synthesising alkali from a cheap readily available raw material – the most obvious being common salt. Experiments were made in the Forth and Tyne areas, in Glasgow and at Tipton in Staffordshire. None of these pioneer ventures was of sufficient magnitude to have an environmental effect, but experiments were also going on in France and the importation of the resulting successful process became the cause of desolation that for generations seemed to be the inevitable accompaniment of industrial chemical operations.

The successful process was that of Nicolas Le Blanc and its importer into England, James Muspratt, who established an alkali works in Liverpool in the early 1820s. The process involved the treatment of common salt with sulphuric acid, which liberated large quantities of highly corrosive gaseous hydrogen chloride. Since initially there was no market for the hydrogen chloride – which later became a source of chlorine – it was allowed to run to waste in the atmosphere. Although he operated in Liverpool it is reported that Muspratt's activities blighted the vegetation on the Birkenhead side of the Mersey. What it did locally can be imagined. Even in the pollution-permissive society of the early nineteenth century this could not last and eventually Muspratt was told to leave. As salt and sulphuric acid were his principal raw materials it is not surprising that his next move was to the proximity of the Cheshire saltfield, where in time there developed one of the great chemical complexes of Europe, the derelict aftermath of which remains with us. Perhaps fortunately, the chemical industry tends to form interlocking complexes in which the by-products of one part become the raw materials of another. The debit side was that the hard core of the heavy chemical industry, the alkali producers, also produced large quantities of solid waste which had to be dumped in an environment already rendered vile by acid fumes and soot in the atmosphere. Langford's landscape of hell became a reality.

Similar developments to those initiated by Muspratt in Lancashire were also taking place in the neighbourhood of Glasgow, where Charles Tennant had succeeded in taming chlorine in the form of bleaching powder. To exploit his discovery he founded the St Rollox Chemical Works, which, when many ancillary activities including the production of sulphuric acid and alkali had been added, became in its heyday the greatest complex of its kind in the world. One of Tennant's chimney stacks, over four hundred feet high, was one of the wonders of the early industrial scene: its function, of course, to transfer the pollution to the Highlands as quickly as possible.

In so far as effect on environment is concerned, there was little to choose between the effects of the chemical industry on Merseyside and the Clyde with those on the conurbations of the Tyne, Wear and Tees. Money can be made from waste so the manufacturers themselves sought means to recover their noxious by-products; but protective legislation was necessary and the first of the Alkali Acts was passed in the 1860s.

Excluding coal, so far nothing has been said about the extraction industries except by implication. But at the present day open-cast working has had at least a temporary effect on the environment in selected regions, and, in the past, scenes not lacking in drama have been created as can be seen in the quarry-scape of Penrhyn painted by William Crane in 1842.

Fig. 6. The chemical industry at its most primitive: calcining aluminous shale at Macintosh's Hurlet Chemical Works

Mineral-working is important in its effect on environment especially when, as has happened in Britain, the once widely spread local brick-works have largely died out and there has been a massive concentration of brick-working on the Oxford clay formations in the neighbourhoods of Peterborough, Bedford, and Bletchley – an area which today produces half the country's building bricks.

As with brick-making, the winning of clay for pottery making was once widespread, and there are still many widely spread craft potteries, as there were in Staffordshire long before the rise of 'The Potteries'. In the eighteenth century scientific potting was given the lead by Josiah Wedgwood who, as Matthew Boulton did in relation to the metal trades of Birmingham, applied the scientific knowledge of those with whom he associated in the Lunar Society. He experimented with bodies made from local clay and was quick to realise the advantages of the china clay and china stone discovered by William Cookworthy in Cornwall. The traditional potteries were in a somewhat landlocked area and Wedgwood was one of the chief promoters of the Trent-Mersey canal. In fact he built his new Etruria factory on its banks. Wedgwood was not by any means the only

Fig. 7. Josiah Wedgwood's new pottery at Etruria built on a canal he did much to sponsor, and which improved his access both to raw materials and markets

potter of note and the potteries in general kept pace with the general expansion of industry in the second half of the eighteenth century. Unfortunately, the crude methods of firing used, and in particular the technique of production of one species, salt-glazed ware, led, together with the products of combustion of the firing process, to pollution which possibly outdid that arising from the early chemical industry. All this has changed and the early cones which gave such a characteristic appearance to the pottery townscape are no more than museum pieces – even the few that are left. In Cornwall too, from which all the china clay comes, a curious situation has arisen. Contemporary Cornwall has two industrial landscapes, one largely dead and the legacy of its pre-eminence as the producer of metal ores, and the other much alive and, in the region of St Austell with its moonscape heaps of kaolin-spoil, the cause of considerable concern to conservationists. The dead hand of altered economic conditions has also fallen on nearby Devon, where in the mid nineteenth century, Devon Great Consols, at Blanchdown, west of Tavistock, was the richest copper mine in the world. This position of British eminence is now easily overlooked, but since it has left its scars in various parts of the country we will conclude this essay with a brief look at the developments that took place over the centuries. The attraction of mineral deposits in Britain even in Roman times has been referred to earlier. Cornwall was the main point of attraction possibly because it was nearest the Continent, but deposits in other parts were known and worked.

In the Lake District by 1560 the Mines Royal Company was an organisation of some magnitude engaged in smelting local copper ore, almost certainly with charcoal, though we must not forget the introduction of coke as fuel in copper smelting much earlier than in the iron industry. Copper deposits were also found in Cornwall, but there was no indigenous source of fuel, so the Mines Royal Company established its first smelter at Neath in South Wales in 1584; the next was at Llangavalach in the early 1700s. By 1800 Cornwall was providing a large proportion of the world's copper ore – smeltered in the Swansea region.

Other important deposits were also expanding. For example, a solicitor, Thomas Williams, became the principal partner in 1778 in the Parys Mining Co., in Anglesey. He too set up smelters in Swansea, as well as at Holywell in Flintshire and at St Helens. In less than ten years he had gained control of the Mona Mine Co., and for several years exercised virtual control of the whole output of copper in Britain. With the expansion of industrial trade the Cornish ores ceased to hold their premier position and the copper industry of South Wales came to rely more and more on imports from Chile and Cuba. Copper alloyed with zinc gives brass. The Society of Mineral and Battery Works was founded in 1565 and the next year found deposits of zinc ore in Somerset, and set up works at Tintern to produce brass and wire. (This development, claimed by some to be the introduction of brass, is commemorated by a plaque at Tintern Abbey.) But so far as copper is concerned it is to South Wales that we have to look to appreciate the price we have to pay for the position we once occupied as a producer of copper.

Lead, of which deposits were found in various localities including the Pennines, the Mendip and the region of Leadhills and Wanlockhead on the Lanark/Dumfries borders of Scotland, contributed its share to the desolation often associated with mineral working. British lead had found its way to Rome and when the ore began to be smelted with coal in 1690 several companies emerged. In general, lead-smelting was carried out in small units although there were a number of large enterprises. While the disposal of the sulphurous gases from copper-smelting was itself a problem, lead had the added disadvantage that the lead cation is itself toxic and cumulative. This was early appreciated and elaborate precautions had to be taken to conduct away the fumes associated with the reduction process. Mile-long flues were often built up the hillsides and remnants of these can still be examined in the Northern Pennines as well as, in Allendale, the still persistent effect of the toxicity of lead on the surrounding vegetation. Lead production in Britain suffered the same fate as copper in that more lucrative deposits were found in other parts of the world, notably in Spain in the 1870s.

From 20,000 B.C., when the British Isles began to provide a habitat for man, to the Industrial Revolution of the eighteenth century, is a short time in the lifespan of the human race as a whole, but it is the period of what Frank Fraser Darling has called the technological exponential, the ever-accelerating effect that technology is having on the face of the earth. So rapid are these changes now that it may come as a surprise that it was not till the Census of 1851 that maps were available showing 'the places where certain well-defined works and manufacturers are concentrated' (these maps were the work of Augustus Petermann). If we compare maps showing the distribution of population in 1800, when there were still many more mills than steam-engines, with those for 1851, the year in which Britain exhibited herself as the workshop of the world, we see the effects of the technological changes that have been the subject of this essay. In brief summary, they were:

1. The concentration of heavy industry in the central belt of Scotland, where John Roebuck founded the Carron Iron Co. in 1759, with particularly heavy concentrations in parts of Lanarkshire which responded to the invention of the hot-blast by James Beaumont Neilson in 1829, and the utilisation of the indigenous black-ironstone discovered by David Mushett. While the tobacco trade of Glasgow lost its significance and the cotton industry failed to take root, capital was diverted to heavy engineering and shipbuilding.

2. Access to the sea led to the early exploitation of the Northumberland and Durham coalfields, with the subsequent development of chemicals, and shipbuilding as on the Clyde.

3. The textile complex of Lancashire, and the woollen districts of

Fig. 8. Cottonopolis (Manchester) as seen through contemporary eyes in the heyday of the textile industry there

Yorkshire, which benefited from the steam-power that supplemented the water which had been an early attraction to them.

4. The Potteries, something of an anomaly in that they were disadvantageously situated from the point of view of transport, and early came to use a raw material that had to be transported over long distances. As a fire industry they were well placed in relation to coalfields.

5. The chemical complex situated in the region of St Helens, Runcorn, Widnes, which produced not only chemicals but had inter-

connections with the smelting of metals (by-products from which the chemical industry could absorb) and the manufacture of glass, which in its turn depended on the output of the chemical industry. The economic advantage of this area was again geological – the near congruity of coal and the salt mines of Cheshire.

6. The expansion of regions within the Birmingham area till they coalesced into the great conurbation of the Black Country.

7. The mines of South Wales with their associated industries like copper-smelting developed there because there was no coal near the early sources of ore. Once established, however, iron and steel were added to the copper. Again for reasons of geology – this time the desirable qualities of Welsh steam coal – a truly remarkable export trade developed.

8. The continued expansion of the administrative centre, London, once the only considerable town in the whole island and a region whose metropolitan status has tended to overshadow its very considerable contribution to the industrial output of the country as a whole.

These changes are in a nutshell the summation of 20,000 years of the effect of technology on environment – whether it be a new bow and arrow, or an improved plough, or a sophisticated chemical process. Although there has not been an opportunity to analyse here the changes of the later nineteenth century and the twentieth, obviously they did not stop with the Industrial Revolution. For a complete picture we should have to take cognisance of new iron towns like Middlesbrough and Barrow, which were just as much the outcome of advancing technology as was the release of land for agriculture due to the introduction of chemical bleaching; of railway towns like Crewe and Swindon; even of resorts like Blackpool and Bournemouth, escape to which, from the vile environment of the industrial towns, was made possible by the expanding railway network. But the overall pattern established during the Industrial Revolution, and many of the problems it laid up, are still with us. While new and critical problems arise from an ever more sophisticated technology, it is beginning to be realised that if we fail to do something soon the 'landscape of Hell' will be hell indeed.

NOTES

1. There are, of course, a number of volumes that deal broadly with the subject. Since specific references are not detailed in the text, a number

of these volumes are listed here in acknowledgement of the present author's indebtedness to them.

W. H. CHALONER AND A. E. MUSSON (1963) *Industry and Technology*, London.

S. D. CHAPMAN AND J. D. CHAMBERS (1970) *The Beginnings of Industrial Britain*, London.

GRAHAM CLARK (1952) *Prehistoric Europe: The Economic Basis*, London.

NAN FAIRBROTHER (1969) *New Lives, New Landscapes*, London.

W. H. HOSKINS (1969) *The Making of the English Landscape*, London.

F. D. KLINGENDER (1968) *Art and Industry in the Industrial Revolution*, rev. Arthur Elton, London.

JOHN NEF (1964) *The Conquest of the Material World*, Chicago.

THOMAS SHARP (1950) *The English Panorama*, London.

R. L. SHERLOCK (1922) *Man as a Geological Agent*, London.

L. D. STAMP (1955) *Man and the Land*, London.

LYNN WHITE Jr (1962) *Mediaeval Technology and Social Change*, Oxford.

5

THE CITY AND ITS ENVIRONMENT

PETER SELF

INTRODUCTION

THE purpose of this essay is to explore some theories and beliefs about the nature of cities, and about the relationship between cities and their environment. This subject can be explored from the standpoint of many academic disciplines, such as history, geography, demography, economics, sociology, politics and administration. It would be impossible within one essay to do justice to these various approaches, all of which provide fruitful insights into the nature of cities and of urban problems. On the other hand, no single 'discipline' can provide us with adequate theories about the structure or functioning of cities, or about the characteristics and consequences of massive urbanisation.

It is interesting, therefore, to attempt a more synoptic view of the state of our knowledge about cities, even though the result is bound to be patchy and inadequate. Moreover, the current attention given to broad 'ecological' issues urgently requires a more synoptic study of urbanisation. Ecology deals in principle with the relations between men and their total environment. What more necessary focus for such a study than the massive concentrations of humanity in vast and swelling urbanised areas?

An ecological approach to cities is not new. The Chicago School of Social Geographers attempted an ecological type of approach to the spatial structure of cities which is considered below. But contemporary and popular 'ecological' views of the city are problem-oriented and are usually pessimistic or even traumatic. Great cities are seen very often as the supreme exemplars of population overgrowth and overcrowding, and as causes of the overloading and destruction of natural resources. Associated with such ideas, but in principle quite different, is an altered view of urban-rural relations, whereby the city is no longer admired as a centre of economic growth and of cultural enlightenment, but is deplored as a destroyer of the more humanised values of its surrounding countryside.

These general beliefs or impressions are but rarely tested against such light as the social sciences can throw upon the causes and results of urbanisation. This essay suggests that the grave problems of urbanisation, which have become increasingly apparent, cannot sensibly be understood (much less dealt with) as ecological or biological disasters, but have detailed social causes that can be analysed. Unfortunately, the splintered condition of the social sciences impedes this analysis, but some progress should be possible towards understanding the complex causes and interactions of social behaviour in cities. The general conclusion reached here is that many familiar problems of urbanisation are the unwanted results of processes of economic growth and of social and technical change, and that these problems can only be alleviated through improvements in the political systems of cities, and in the quality of public policies. Urbanisation is indeed more of a political and administrative, than a biological, problem for mankind.

The last section of this essay turns to theories about the desirable form and structure of modern cities. It considers the conflict between the 'urbanistic' school of thought and those who foresee the gradual dissolution and disappearance of cities as we now know them; and discusses how far the idea of the regional city can provide a worthwhile framework for structuring urban growth under modern conditions.

First we should briefly note the scale of urbanisation. While it is true that we live in a rapidly urbanising world the great bulk of population has lived throughout history in small rural places, and a substantial majority of people still does so today. In 1800, only 2·4 per cent of world population, equal to about 21½ million people, lived in towns of over 20,000 people. By 1950 this figure had risen to 21 per cent, and represented about 500 millions.[1]

By modern standards, a town of 20,000 people is still a smallish place. When we think of urbanisation, we think above all of the great 'millionaire' cities or conurbations. There are six such areas in Britain, covering only 4 per cent of the land but having 40 per cent of the population; and the continued outward sprawl of these areas makes even these figures out of date. In the United States the number of 'millionaire' metropolitan areas rose from five in 1900 to twenty-four in 1960, and the proportion of national population living in them from 16 to 34 per cent.[2]

These countries are exceptional. The proportion of world population living in great centres of over a million was only about 4 per cent in 1950. It is of course rising rapidly, because of the rapid growth of urban concentrations not only in Europe and North America but still more strikingly in Latin America and Asia. Mexico City is rapidly approaching Paris in size, and Greater Calcutta may have 50 millions by the turn of the century.[3]

Similarly our notions of what constitutes a city are changing. Once it was a fairly self-contained community, clearly demarcated from the surrounding countryside. Then came the conurbation, a fusing together of towns into one large sprawl of bricks and mortar, separated sometimes by large open spaces or topographical features. Now the tendency is to talk about the urban region, meaning by this an enlarged and diffused phenomenon, containing large wedges of countryside and incorporating a polycentric pattern of business centres with one great centre usually predominant. Thus defined, the urban region of London extends somewhere between twenty-five and sixty miles from Piccadilly, depending upon the measurements used.

My purpose is not to discuss the statistics of urbanisation, or possible definitions of urban regions. My aim is to ask what theories exist, or could exist, about these processes of urban growth; what relationships hold between a great urban centre and its environment; and what distinctive problems for human society are posed by massive urbanisation.

THE CITY AND THE SOCIAL SCIENCES

Looking around at the growth of the city, it is easy to turn to botanical analogies. One looks at London, and sees the great tide of office development gobbling up the residential and even cultural facilities of the West End; or at choice inner areas of potentially attractive housing and environment, where one sees the middle-class salariat taking over and renovating working-class dwellings; or at outer suburbia, where distinctive suburbs grow up that reflect the incomes and life styles of what appear on the surface to be homogeneous groups. It almost seems as if offices are exotic species of plant which under appropriate ecological conditions necessarily oust other types of plant which previously flourished in the same habitat.

These analogies arise easily from a reading of the Chicago School of Human Ecology, which sought to discover the laws which guide the spatial distribution of uses within a city. Burgess believed that all modern cities, at any rate in the United States, grew in a series of concentric zones. At the hub of communications is a central business district, comprising office and commercial uses, surrounded by factories. The next or 'transitional' zone contains less intensive commercial and industrial uses such as warehousing, together with lodgings for transient population, vice zones and deteriorating residential areas for the poorest groups. The third zone is that of independent working men's homes; what in England would once have been called artisans' dwellings and now public housing; here live the working-class population which man the many basic services of the central area. A fourth zone contains the better residences of the middle class and a fifth zone is inhabited by still wealthier longer distance commuters [4]

Clearly this distinction by Burgess has some rough correspondence to the pattern of many western cities. It reflects the concentration of many intensive uses at the centre of the city, and the tendency for some correlation to exist between the wealth of an individual and the distance he lives from his work. One could modify the theory in various ways, of course. For example Hoyt's sector theory draws attention to the tendency for people to move and migrate outwards in a sector pattern, as happens when a London Eastender moves to suburbia in Essex or finally to Southend or Basildon. The same theory allows for the clusters of relatively rich or poor residences along the same sector; for example London's richest sector extends south-westwards from Chelsea and South Kensington to Wimbledon, Richmond, Kingston and the Ascot country beyond London airport. The sector theory allows, which the concentric theory does not, for the existence of pockets of wealthy residences in inner areas; this is clearly the situation in any city worth the name, although not necessarily true of the more debased type of industrial city.[5]

One could play with such theories for a long time. These are empirical generalisations, holding roughly true of certain types of city at certain periods. But spatial patterns shift with technology. Burgess's city describes the situation which had been reached after the Industrial Revolution and the development of mass public transport, but before the full impact of the motor car and aeroplane. Under modern conditions, many central area uses are dispersing themselves to new locations, industries are growing up along major transport routes and in satellite towns or new towns, and residences are being spread more flexibly according to the range of car commuting to nodal transport points. Many elements of the concentric city remain, just as within the framework of the concentric city one can see the impact of an earlier stage when technology was advanced enough to promote heavy concentrations of commerce and industry but not advanced enough to provide adequate local transport for the mass of workers, who had to live crammed at very high density near the centre. Conditions dating from this still earlier period partly continue in Inner London at the same time as the urban region is acquiring a quite different morphology from that sketched by Burgess, even when modified by Hoyt.

There are also cultural influences upon the urban pattern. The tendency to live further from your work as you grow richer, which is prevalent in modern English-speaking countries, was reversed in most cities in the pre-industrial age, and is still reversed to a large extent in cities of Latin culture. In Rio de Janeiro for example, the rich live near the cultural and amusement facilities of the central area and the bathing beaches, while the poorest groups face a long daily commute to distant favellas. Schnore tells us that this pattern antedates the Iberian invasions, and that in Cuzco the distance of one's habitation from the centre depended upon the degree of relationship to the Inca ruler. We have here the model of an urban structure based upon the glamour and the power of the Court, in which to be fashionable was to be near the centre of things – an association which the Industrial Revolution partly, though of course never completely, broke in English-speaking countries. But it also seems that many Latin American cities are moving somewhat towards the concentric patterns sketched by Burgess or more modern variants thereof. In a sense this is hardly surprising. Industrialisation, where it occurs, reduces the charm of central areas, and modern transportation enables the middle class and perhaps the rich to take themselves to the pleasantest suburbs available.[6]

This brief look at the Chicago school has left us with some empirical insights but no workable theories. One sees the influence of technology and culture upon urban patterns in varying degrees, but there are no clues to the human motivations which use technology and modify culture. Quite clearly, the botanical analogy will not do. Land uses are not in fact competing species, but the products of diverse human motivations and interactions working under shifting technological conditions. If we consider the example of office growth in London, this is the result of many subtle causes. One cause presumably is the strong economic advantage of a central location for growing numbers of large firms. Another reason may be the prestige which top managers acquire and the social advantages which they enjoy by operating from such a location. Yet another factor is the resistance of a body like the Greater London Council to office growth, where it threatens for example some well-known theatre. In defending the theatre against the office the GLC is adding a political objective to the economic and sociological aims already noted, but in doing so it may even be reflecting the norms of many managers themselves.

An adequate theory of the city requires an adequate theory of human behaviour; and we have no such theory. The social sciences are of limited help, because they fragment human behaviour into different dimensions and leave the interactions unexplained. Of some use is the distinction which runs through all the social sciences between micro and macro aspects of human behaviour. Micro theories start with individual behaviour, whereas macro theories deal with the functioning of a total system. Thus micro-economics partly explain the growth of a city in terms of the economic calculations made by firms and individuals; whereas macro-economics partly explain the growth of a city once a certain pool of capital and labour has been established in a given place. Similar distinctions exist in the other social sciences.

We may picture the city as a self-regulating system powered by calculations of individual advantage. For example, an individual will choose his place of residence according to a calculus of advantage, in which the costs and nuisance of travel will be weighed against the superiority of residential environment, schools, social conditions, etc. Calculations by individuals or organisations will often be complex, and will shift with technology, but enough information might enable us to predict rational behaviour. The model can also be expanded to political behaviour, which can be seen as bringing in the power of government to support the maximisation of individual advantage; as happens, for instance, when wealthy suburbanites utilise town planning laws to protect their residential densities or golf courses.

The limitation of such a model is that it concentrates upon individual not group behaviour, thus mirroring a typical dilemma of the social sciences. Groups may be added in two ways. One way is to see the group as a coalition of individual interests whether formally organised or not. There is no need to accept Marxism to observe the tendencies of modern cities to segregate along economic class lines with the richest groups getting the best locations.

However, group culture in cities has a more pervasive influence than is covered by these atomistic or class explanations. For many ethnic groups, and for some traditional working-class groups, the city is not seen as a great arena of opportunity and mobility, as the atomistic theory suggests, but is perceived through a narrow but strong set of group institutions and loyalties. For an individual within such a group, the traditional cultural pattern provides both socialisation and satisfactions. Of course, such influences are not absent among any part of the community, but they are strongest among poor and minority elements and perhaps among such special groups as young people drawn together by a quest for emancipation and excitement. These elements of group culture and behaviour mean that neither the pattern of a city nor the behaviour of its inhabitants can be adequately explained by any mechanistic model.

Redfield contrasted urban society with 'folk' society, at opposed ends of a spectrum, and Wirth viewed the city as producing basic changes in personality. On both views the city broke down a more traditional type of rural or peasant traditions and norms. The result was a collapse or undermining of the extended family and of kinship groups; secularisation and the decline of religion; the reduction of primary in favour of secondary contacts; and the growth of sophistication, calculation, impersonality, anonymity.[7]

Oscar Lewis in his studies of Mexico City has shown the erroneousness of these assumptions. He concludes that peasants in Mexico City adapt to city life with much greater ease than these theories assume; that family life remains stable and strong; that religious life becomes more catholic and disciplined and that many village remedies and beliefs persist. He also stresses the point, that others have also made, that the city in a poor country very frequently comprises a number of districts or neighbourhoods, each of which has a largely self-contained social and economic life. The same generalisation would hold true on a much more modest scale of the Bethnal Green once investigated by Young and Willmott.[8]

On the other hand, as urban technology and economy develops and as earlier rural roots are left behind, it may be that some of the transformations of personality stressed by Wirth come about. The city will cease to function as a series of largely separate 'villages' or townships; more specialisation of labour will occur and physical mobility will grow; the more ambitious workers will move to pleasanter environments, and particularly to better housing selected on an income basis. These pressures will tend to disrupt the traditions and norms of the less successful groups, without adequately replacing them with the individualist and public ethic of the middle class. Or so we may hypothesise. But how far the process of conversion to 'middle-class' norms is bound to occur under urban conditions is the question which has not been satisfactorily answered, if it ever can be.

THE CITY AS AN ECONOMIC AND POLITICAL SYSTEM

As a total system the city produces results not foreseen or intended by any individual. In advanced countries, the economic effects of this situation are generally welcomed. A pool of capital, skills and labour is built up, which serves to generate further economic growth. There is pressure on land resources, of course, and this situation influences the dispersal of many economic activities to the edges of the city or to satellite towns. In general, however, economic success begets further growth. Wilbur Thompson has noted the 'ratchet effect' in western cities, whereby once a certain size is reached, the level of population and economic activity is most unlikely to fall, and will probably continue to rise.[9]

The condition of cities in developing countries is usually very different. Here large numbers of people are attracted to the city in advance of adequate economic growth. Considerable unemployment and under-employment results, and economic development fails to provide a satisfactory livelihood for the growing population. The total amount of poverty and unemployment may be no greater than if the population had remained in rural areas. However, the squalor is more visible and more likely to be associated with crime and with political riots or revolution. Indeed, the opportunities for exerting political pressure through force of numbers may be a reason which draws poor and unemployed individuals into the city in the first place.[10]

Whilst in richer countries the economic effects of urban growth may be welcomed, the social effects are much less desirable. There is, of course, a growth of cultural, educational and other opportunities, although many city dwellers may make little use of them. In any event, there is overcrowding and high residential densities; lack of parks or green spaces; shortage of land for basic community services; traffic congestion and delays; long and sometimes expensive journeys to work; unpleasant noise levels; pollution of the atmosphere and sometimes of water supplies. In wealthier societies these ill-effects are capable of being controlled and remedied to a considerable extent; but this requires considerable government intervention and investment, which is hard to achieve. Moreover, the more such actions are delayed, the greater becomes the eventual cost to improve the functioning of the city and provide a better environment.

This typical political dilemma is seen differently by the economist, the political scientist, and the social anthropologist. To the economist, the provision of collective goods will be necessary to the extent that the market cannot conveniently or adequately provide such goods, while the case for administrative regulation will be related to a calculation of the indirect social costs produced by uncontrolled individual action. This economic concept of rational behaviour is at variance with political sociology which observes the pressure of various groups to gain advantages from government (such as subsidised commuter transport, housing subsidies or tax concessions, etc.) and to oppose regulations which are burdensome. The political system of a city does not work according to any concept of rational economic laws. Additionally, however, the political scientist will observe the presence of a public ethic, which conditions the reconciliation of group demands and which accepts some forms of common provision and regulation as being in the general interest, even when disadvantageous to the individual participant. Thus, many people will accept the case for subsidised transport or cultural facilities, even if they do not make much use of these facilities, or for regulations over the use of cars even if this is a nuisance. Finally, the social anthropologist would note considerable variations in cultural values which influence the scope and also the acceptibility of governmental action.

The problems of large cities increasingly demand governmental management and investment on a vast scale. Unfortunately, political management seems increasingly unable to cope with the enormous social problems of cities due to (*a*) the sheer multiplicity of collective needs and problems; (*b*) problems of scale, which tax the capacity for organisation; (*c*) the breakdown in the social cohesion of subgroups and their internal regulation throws added burdens upon general government. Increasing weight is thereby thrown upon a general public ethic for reducing differences and supporting effective public action.

To some writers the city itself becomes the cause of our social discontent. Professor Stafford Beer: 'The city is a settlement grown beyond viable limits, technologically souped-up beyond the threshold of physiological endurance and perhaps 10 per cent efficient in terms of its group purposes. It is a machine for generating problems of noise, carbon monoxide, logistics, ghettos, and so forth.'[11]

As I shall suggest later this apocalyptic view of the city is exaggerated and largely false. The city is not an ecological monstrosity, it is rather the place where both the problems and the opportunities of modern technological civilisation are most potent and visible. But it cannot be denied that the social and management problems of the city are increasingly severe.

Part of the answer to these problems can be found in measures of local government reorganisation. Many people see the creation of a large metropolitan government covering an entire urbanised area as a recipe for tackling these problems. Arguments over local government reform reveal a clash of substantive and procedural values. Those favouring the reform stress the technical efficiency of large organisation in an urban context, and the value of uniform standards of service and a uniform distribution of costs. Those opposing reform cling to the values of more localised and traditional forms of local government and accept the freedom of such authorities to vary services and charges. In the western world the reformers seem slowly to be winning the argument, although sometimes blocked by a combination of traditional values and special interests.[12]

However, the monster city government is only a partial remedy. For one thing there are difficulties about its size; the Greater London Council, the result of a notable reform of this kind, is responsible for $7\frac{1}{2}$ million people, but this is a mainly built-up area of falling population. Many consider that the 'super city' ought to take in the surrounding region of new growth as well, in the interests of balancing new and old development; easing housing pressures in the urban core; planning transportation, water supplies, and other utilities; and controlling the impact of the giant city upon natural resources. Additionally, it seems clear that so vast an urban government cannot provide all of the more localised services now demanded, nor achieve a close enough relation with the local population. Partly for technical efficiency but mainly to sustain the values of participation, it becomes necessary to create or maintain also a second level of local government within the great city, as was done with the creation of the present thirty-two boroughs of Greater London. Even so the borough is large, and popular participation is limited.[13]

Metropolitan reorganisation is essential for technical and financial reasons, but the system of government which it can produce will necessarily remain very complex. Improved technical efficiency will not itself bring about the changes in political attitudes and behaviour, which are urgently required to cope with the multifarious social problems of the modern city. As noted above, the problem is to achieve sufficient public investment and public regulation to avert a deteriorating environment and to secure satisfactory community services. The demands upon 'civic spirit' or the public ethic are increased, under conditions which necessarily make government more remote and highly specialised. Political apathy or indifference, save in relation to obvious examples of individual or group interest, tend to be the result. These political failures are probably the gravest challenge before western cities, and suggest the need for building into the institutional structure new channels for the flow of information and opinion.

CITY AND COUNTRYSIDE

The most obvious functional relationship of the countryside to the city derives from the food requirements of the urban population. In preindustrial societies, the city was the home of the Court, the military, and the social elite, as well as performing commercial and administrative functions. The city could often be seen as exerting military and political power in order to exploit impotent rural populations of peasants for the benefit of its food requirements. This is still, at least partially, the situation in many relatively poor countries, particularly in Latin America.[14]

Industrialisation transformed this relationship. It created a large demand for labour in the towns, which in turn reduced pressures on the land and hastened the modernisation of agriculture with the aid of urban technology. Thus towns and countryside became complementary partners in the process of economic development which produced great industrial strains but eventually benefited both elements. Under this relationship the countryside could sometimes be seen as seeking to exploit the towns, by using its political power to sustain an inefficient agriculture and deny cheaper food to the town dwellers. In Britain the repeal of the Corn Laws in 1846 broke this political power of the countryside and led to a process of integrated economic development which has finally reduced the farm population to a mere 4 per cent of all workers. Aided by this shrinking manpower, agriculture has become technically advanced and efficient, and paradoxically has achieved the subsidised support denied when it was far larger.

This process of agricultural depopulation and modernisation and subsidies has been pushed to extreme limits now in the United States, Britain, Japan and some Western European countries. But over most of the world, agriculture still retains vast numbers of poor and under-employed workers. Even though many move to towns industrialisation is inadequate to support them. Thus the complementary process of economic development, almost ended for Britain, has still not occurred throughout most of the world.[15]

In Britain and in most western countries, the traditional relationship between town and countryside is being drastically altered. Modern technology has set industries free from their once limited choice of locations, and industries have spilt into the countryside, particularly around the big cities. Conversely, agriculture and the countryside can no longer be identified. Modern agriculture is more and more like any other industry; highly capitalised and mechanised, making intensive use of land, and not particularly romantic or attractive. The standards of life and the ways of living of town folk and country folk are increasingly approximated, although regional differences continue to exist. The farm population constitutes only a minority of those living in the countryside, many of whom are retired or ex-urbanites or industrial workers. In Britain, the traditional countryside is now largely valued as a picturesque recreational area, a historical museum, and a choice residential area for those who can get through the net of planning controls. The traditional dichotomy between towns and countryside is broken and one finds a tension between development pressures of all kinds (including 'agribusiness') and the protection of the traditional, humanised rural landscape.

URBANISATION AND ECOLOGY

So far, the problems of cities and the relationship between cities and countryside have been seen in the context of social behaviour and technological development. An entirely different perspective is offered by those who see the cities as tension points of excessive population growth. Some writers have compared the biological tensions which harmfully affect some animal species above a certain population density with the kind of situation which they claim to exist in the large modern city. On this view, high urban densities are a source not only of psychological and social disturbances contributing to crime and delinquency, but also of potential crises and disaster involving probably a sudden population decline.[16]

There is in fact little evidence for such general theories. In the western world, at any rate, population densities in the cities are steadily falling as the urbanised area expands.[17] The total area under bricks and mortar becomes greatly enlarged but it is also interspersed with much more open space. The plight of certain fairly high density 'ghettos' of poor population within inner urban areas constitutes an exception, though an important one, to this general trend. Moreover, there is little real evidence that psychological instability is correlated with high density, at any rate within any normally experienced range; indeed, the correlation with low density could be as plausibly argued. The high crime and delinquency rates of some cities can be more plausibly seen as resulting from the greater opportunities for crime and bad behaviour which the city offers. Additionally, there is social disorganisation due to the tensions of migration.

At the biological level if there were indeed intolerable stress occurring in the big cities, it seems strange that there is little movement from them to the great open spaces which still exist. It is often forgotten that even within the United Kingdom over half of the land area is sparsely populated and in these areas the population as a rule is either static or declining.

Once again we are forced back into seeing the problems of the city as those of social adjustment and political management; rather than viewing these problems in terms of some biological or ecological unbalance. This is not to deny that there would be very considerable advantages in dispersing some of the population of the largest cities to smaller places, or at the least in deterring further growth until existing problems have been tackled more effectively. It is not to deny either that total population growth may constitute a substantial ecological danger; but this danger, if it exists, is a function of total society, and not of cities as such.

CITIES IN THE FUTURE

Modern technology steadily reduces the frictions of space; it thereby allows increasing personal mobility in terms of work and leisure choices, and gives to both economic enterprises and households an increasing freedom over choice of location. Further developments in technology are likely to strengthen these trends; both through faster transportation (e.g. super express trains) and more especially through the growth of instant communications, such as closed-circuit television, which permit decision-makers to confer together quite easily from a distance.

Without doubt the values of local communities, that is of associations based primarily upon geographic contiguity, have been eroded both through increased physical mobility and through specialised public services. The former factor removes functional, professional and cultural organisations from close dependence upon geographical factors, while the latter factor reduces the need for localised forms of government or community self-help.

The questions are: how desirable is this process? how far will it go? could it conceivably be reversed? are we seeing the complete disappearance of the city as conventionally understood or will it take fresh shape in some new form? Three views on these issues will be briefly considered.

1. *The urbanist school*, typified by Jane Jacobs,[18] stresses the continued values of localised interests and contacts. In their view, these values require a diversity of functions and occupations which is found in the traditional type of city, but which is eroded by the segmented geographic specialisation of activities typical of modern urban growth. Their preferred image is Chelsea (London) or Greenwich Village (New York), which have a richness and variety of land use, social activities, and social groups, in contrast with the homogeneity of the one-class suburb or the large public housing estate.

Undoubtedly, there is much that appeals to many people in this summons to return to the traditional notion of what makes a city. Unfortunately, the 'urbanists' tend to be both falsely romantic and socially blind. Chelsea and Greenwich Village are not in fact strong or durable social communities. Those who most enjoy these places are typical transients within an urban life cycle and relatively rich. They are the youthful or sometimes middle-aged 'upper bohemians' who flourish in these habitats, and usually move on as they grow older to the type of suburban or ex-urban area which they had previously despised. Often, too, such people have a second dwelling in the countryside or at any rate outside the congested central area.

Moreover, the traditional type of inner urban zone typically offers a poor and congested environment occupied by relatively low income groups. These zones are frequently not very diversified or picturesque, and where the environment has good elements it is often pre-empted by the middle class or 'upper bohemian' overspill from places like Chelsea. The maintenance of these drab high-density working-class zones is hardly consistent with any cultural ideal of urbanisation, save in the sense that the working population man the specialised facilities of the city centre; but these facilities appeal mainly to a large and dispersed population, not to the nearby lower income groups. At present, many public policies tend to maintain these high-density inner zones; for example, subsidised commuter fares which enable economic activities to stay clustered in central areas, and high housing subsidies for accommodating workers in densely built blocks of flats. Instead, town planning ought to be offering a choice of more and better locations to the residents of such zones. Greater mobility for these groups requires a planning policy which overcomes suburban or ethnic hostilities to the relocation of low income groups, as well as financial assistance to enable more members of these groups to achieve improved housing in a better environment.

Thus it could be urged that an ideological view of the traditional city inhibits measures of dispersal which are socially desirable, and pens up the poorest groups in the name of urbanity. Given an acceptance of the middle-class values of personal mobility and opportunity, this comment is certainly justified. This situation is particularly true of the United States, which explains an increasing tendency there to view town planning in terms not of ideal urban forms but of ladders of social opportunity. The same critique is partially true of Britain, although much modified by the scale of public housing and overspill schemes.

Still, there is some point in the Jane Jacobs thesis. At its best the traditional diversity of urban uses and occupations can be personally enjoyable, as well as a source of social understanding and (as she says) a defence against crime. It is also true that town planning principles and practice have tended to separate and fragment land uses to an excessive degree. This is a pity; and there is a strong case for leaning in the opposite direction, since a considerable segmentation of land uses anyhow results from the organisation of the housing market, as well as from the apparent play of social tastes. How far these trends can be modified in the interests of greater social diversity and communication remains an open question.

2. The opposite position from the urbanists is held by those who foresee the *complete dissolution of the traditional city*. This theory is expressed in Melvin Webber's concepts of the 'non-place urban realm' and 'community without propinquity'.[19] These concepts express the dissolution of any kind of localised community made possible by the increasing range and speed of communications. Of course, these concepts could never be fully realised even in technological terms. Since communication costs will never be zero, there will always be some bias towards geographical contiguity as a factor in economic and social life.

The extent of this bias depends partly upon time-costs. It is commonplace that speed of travel increases with distance covered, and that long journeys are now relatively quick and sometimes comfortable when compared with short ones. This factor might be thought to encourage still greater dispersion of activities were it not that the long distance journeys have to operate from nodal points, from which the more awkward localised journeys have still to be covered. In any event the long journeys are and will remain relatively expensive and this fact alone puts a premium upon proximity for most of the activities of most people. Webber's illustration of the way that western scholars form communities based upon common intellectual interests that are singularly free from frictions of space owes a great deal to the existence of lavish travel grants from American foundations. It will never be typical of the workaday world.

The extent to which physical mobility is worth the time and money involved, and the associated restlessness, is also a question differently answered by individuals, classes and cultures. It seems probable that many traditions will continue to be resistant to the values of mobility, and in the more mobile western world there are some indications of a revulsion from mobility in favour of greater attachment to some expression of local community. It seems that the modern unit of direct local interest typically extends no further than a small neighbourhood of streets and houses, and the associations sought are social rather than functional. But it does seem possible that the functional advantages of neighbourhood association will also grow, because of the difficulties or failures of public authorities over controlling crime and maintaining or guaranteeing basic services. Equally, the increasing interest in the maintenance of local 'amenities' and cultural facilities will lead more and more people to take part in limited forms of political action at the neighbourhood level. This possibility is deliberately cultivated in the proposal by the British Royal Commission on Local Government to create small urban councils based on the idea of the rural parish. Such councils would have few executive powers but would act as pressure groups and communication channels in relation to larger scale government.[20]

3. Finally, *the city region* (*or regional city*) is an attempt to develop a new morphology of urban form attuned to modern cultural demands and opportunities.[21] This concept is based upon creating a satisfactory hierarchy of life styles and opportunity levels, available to all citizens. These advantages would be realised through a polycentric pattern of urban centres, each of which would be related in differing ways to a nucleated and partly self-contained block of development. Thus, a new town created within the framework of an urban region would offer to its citizens a good local choice of work and social opportunities; but by being located within a mobile urbanised area, the residents would also have the choice (if they wished) of seeking their satisfactions within the central area of the whole urban complex, or elsewhere within it. As one moves towards the centre of such an urban region each block of development would become relatively more diversified and urbanised in a traditional sense and somewhat less self-contained. Thus a choice would be offered between different styles of living. No citizens therefore need be condemned to areas of poor environment or to areas of high density unless deliberately chosen. The theory of the city region is that it should exploit to the full the modern opportunities of physical mobility in such a way as to break the grip of the 'ghetto' while simultaneously reducing the need for an excessive degree of mobility through the creation of a wide range of localised facilities and opportunities. Similarly, the specialised central area facilities would be opened up to all without the need of continuing to be associated with the labour of a deprived urban proletariat.

This concept or vision resists both the highly fluid pattern of development associated with Los Angeles, whilst also opposing the maintenance of more static and traditional types of urbanism. It is a vision well worth pursuing although it leaves open several questions.

Can the dissolution of the city be stopped at any particular point or will it continue to spread further? Like the traditional urbanists, and unlike the Webber school of thought, the theorists of the city region are morphologists. They believe in the value of a particular urban form as a goal to be achieved. But the pursuit of ideal physical forms has become unpopular with many social scientists, who argue that urban planning should be based upon *social policies* whose physical effects cannot be closely foreseen, and will in any event be constantly shifting so that no ideal concept can ever be realised.

This criticism is partly true, but is also in many ways irrelevant or circular. The regional city concept need not be recommended as a Platonic essence, but as the physical framework which seems most likely to satisfy desirable and widely shared social aims under modern technological conditions. Urban planning has to work largely through the manipulation of land uses and channels of communications, so that meaningful policies have ultimately to be expressed in physical terms. A regulative ideal form to guide urban change should therefore be welcomed unless the ideal is too fixed and precise, which is hardly the case with the regional city concept.

The structuring of the regional city could take a variety of forms. It is also true that the total complex can be only very partially self-contained in terms of social interactions. Not only will some functional communities (such as scholars) operate to some extent within much wider orbits, as in fact they always have done, but, more to the point, the edges of the urban region are bound to be vague and blurred, and much interaction will occur with other complexes. The nature of these interactions will depend not a little upon the time-costs of travel, which at present are tending to expedite both centre-to-centre and periphery-to-periphery forms of movement, but to retard localised journeys within densely developed areas. Even so the volume of interactions *within* an urban region currently seems, on any reasonable definitions, to be enormously greater than that occurring *between* urban regions. More skilful and deliberate structuring of this new kind of urban complex would strengthen this situation, as of course would breakthroughs in the technology of transport in congested areas.

Geographic prognoses aside, the structuring of urban regions is also a reflection of political culture. In the United States the liberty accorded to market and organisational competition (including competition between public authorities and adjacent local governments) creates a bias against any attempts to plan urban form, and is linked with a rather phrenetic stress upon the values of flexibility and mobility. The Webber thesis is more of a cultural document than a predictive or normative type of theory. But although little represented in the academic debate between social scientists, many Americans are in fact rediscovering some of the values of local community and of more stabilised physical forms.[22]

British political culture is more favourably disposed towards a systematic ordering of the physical environment, the main examples to date being the conservation of the countryside and the planning of new towns. However, the planning of great cities and urban regions has been much less systematic, and has been vitiated by a rather fruitless conflict between the traditional urbanists and the advocates of urban dispersal. Better intellectual foundations for more effective planning policies have now been laid, but urban restructuring remains inhibited by unsolved dilemmas. These include, particularly, doubts about the acceptability of 'motorisation' for inner urban areas, and problems over how to diversify the social composition of these areas without adding to problems of overcrowding and poverty.

The regional city concept is partly predictive, for western cities appear to be evolving in this direction, but also normative in that massive governmental action seems necessary both to maximise and (particularly) to share equitably the potential social gains. A precise programme cannot be written here. I can only conclude by repeating that the crisis of modern cities is essentially social and political in character, and that the challenge to political innovation has rarely been so awesome.

1. CHARLES ABRAMS (1964) *Housing in the Modern World*, London, p. 1, n. 2.
2. PHILIP HAUSER (1965) 'Urbanization: An Overview' in Philip M. Hauser and Leo F. Schnore ed., *The Study of Urbanization*, New York, p. 8.
3. HAUSER, *op. cit.*, p. 7. For problems of urbanisation in developing countries see Abrams, *op. cit.*
4. ROBERT E. PARK, ERNEST W. BURGESS, AND RODERICK D. MCKENZIE (1925) *The City*, Chicago, pp. 47-62.
5. HOMER HOYT (1939) *The Structure and Growth of Residential Neighborhoods in American Cities*, Washington, Federal Housing Administration.

6. LEO SCHNORE, 'On the Spatial Structure of Cities' in Hauser and Schnore, *op. cit.*, pp. 356-89.
7. For a summary of these theories see 'The Folk-Urban Ideal Types' in Hauser and Schnore, *op. cit.*, pp. 491-514.
8. *Ibid.*, pp. 491-503. Michael Young and Peter Willmott (1957) *Family and Kinship in East London*, London.
9. WILBUR R. THOMPSON in Hauser and Schnore, *op. cit.*, pp. 442-4.
10. For analysis of the causes of migration into cities in poor countries see Abrams, *op. cit.*
11. STAFFORD BEER, *The Liberty Machine*, address to Conference on the Environment, American Society for Cybernetics, Oct. 1970, p. 5.
12. For conflicts over metropolitan reorganization see Gerald Rhodes (1970) *The Government of London, The Struggle for Reform*, London; L. D. Feldman and M. D. Goldrick ed. (1969) *Politics and Government of Urban Canada*, Toronto, Parts 6 and 7; Edward C. Banfield ed. (1969) *Urban Government: A Reader in Administration and Politics*, New York, pp. 68-116.
13. P. SELF (1971) *Metropolitan Planning*, London.
14. NATHAN KEYFITZ in Hauser and Schnore, *op. cit.*, pp. 265-311.
15. COLIN CLARK (1967) *Population Growth and Land Use*, London, Chs. 4, 7 and 8.
16. For example see Gordon Rattray Taylor (1963) *The Biological Time Bomb*, London.
17. The fall of urban densities is fully analysed in Colin Clark, *op. cit.*, Ch. 9.
18. JANE JACOBS (1965) *The Life and Death of Great American Cities*, London.
19. MELVIN M. WEBBER (1963) 'Community without Propinquity' in Lowdon Wingo Jr ed., *Cities and Space*, Baltimore. See also Scott Greer (1962) *The Emerging City*, New York.
20. Royal Commission on Local Government in England 1966-69, Report, i, pp. 95-109; ii, pp. 126-34. Research Study No. 9 (Community Attitudes Survey).
21. Theories of the city region are developed in Derek Senior, ed. (1966) *The Regional City*, London; Maurice Ash (1969) *Regions of Tomorrow*, London; Peter Self (1969) in Henry J. Schmandt and Warner Bloomberg Jr ed. *The Quality of Urban Life*, California.
22. An excellent example is the movement to plan the San Francisco Bay Area of California as a regional complex, by knitting the parts together through public transport, protecting green areas and open space, and conserving local communities while facilitating mobility among the poorest groups.

Model Ecosystems

6

A MODEL MARINE ECOSYSTEM: 24 HOURS IN THE LIFE OF A ROCK-POOL

RAYMOND VAISSIÈRE

THIS paper deals with marine ecology and, in a more general way, with aquatic ecology. Whenever marine or aquatic ecology is defined, there is an underlying feeling of restriction, of the arbitrary categorisation of a young and dynamic science which is evolving with contemporary thought towards a better understanding of sets and systems.

Today, ecology is a much publicised word, forced on the public because of the ever-increasing injuries to our surrounding biosphere by events which continually modify a balance originally thought to be well established. According to the definition given by Haeckel, hardly a century ago, ecology is the science of relationships between organisms and their environment, it being understood that these organisms are themselves a part of their own environment. In my opinion this is the most acceptable definition. Although it does not specify the meanings of interaction and environment, it does suggest the principle of an organisation, with stable or evolving states, which depends on the relationships between its various constituents.

The definition of biology must also be considered. According to Littré's dictionary, biology is the science which concerns living organisms and whose eventual object is the understanding of the laws governing the behaviour of these beings, by a study of the laws of their organisation.

An ecological system or ecosystem possesses its own organisation which is represented by plant-animal groups in continual interaction and existing in a physico-chemical environment where exchange occurs. In the same way a living being is composed of organs having functional relationships and maintained in a fluid internal environment, with which exchange also occurs. Ecology is thus a study of the biology of ecosystems.

It can be established that an organisation is logically followed by a manifestation, which in the case of the living being could be an act, and which can be defined as a signal in ecology. What parallel can be drawn between act and signal? The term 'act' can have several meanings depending on the level and context of the discussion. However, by successive analyses towards simplification, and thus by progressive elimination of the complex meanings given to the word act according to its various uses, it is possible to consider an act as a response signal to one or many external signals. The system has received a signal and emitted a response which in turn becomes a signal, indicating the state reached by this receiver. In other words, one system transmits its state to another by a signal which can take on various forms equal in number to the forms of the states.

This line of argument originated with the Information Theory proposed by Shannon and Weaver in 1949. No attempt will be made here to expound this theory, which is the province of highly qualified mathematicians. But it is evident that all forms of signal exist and take place in time. Consequently, the signals order themselves chronologically and make up one message or a series of messages; the succession of messages permits a reconstitution of the past from a knowledge of the present state of the system. It is obvious that the state of the system projects information into the future.

Proceeding from the simple to the complex, let us consider organisation on our own planetary level, avoiding pure energy and elementary particles. We have a sequence: (atom-molecules)→(protoplasm)→(cells)→(tissues)→(organs)→(organisms)→(groups of organisms)→(biosphere).

At the level of the atom, and maybe even before, there exists one system which transmits its state to another system. The information carried by this system indicates its history but also projects into the future, since in conventional classical language an atom is said to possess physical or chemical properties, which is one way of expressing information; and this will be the same at all levels. There will be signalling between heterogeneous elements, and signalling is impossible without differentiation; consequently, the more differentiated the system, the more information it will bear. This means that within the limits voluntarily imposed by the ecologist, the biosphere is the most highly differentiated system.

This information projecting into the future should allow us to envisage the next states of a system, knowing that the number of these states is limited by the interaction of elements constituting the system.

Let us consider a simple system consisting of the three elements A, B and C: A being an effector, B a detector of the state of A and C a reactor to the condition of B and acting on A. What will happen?

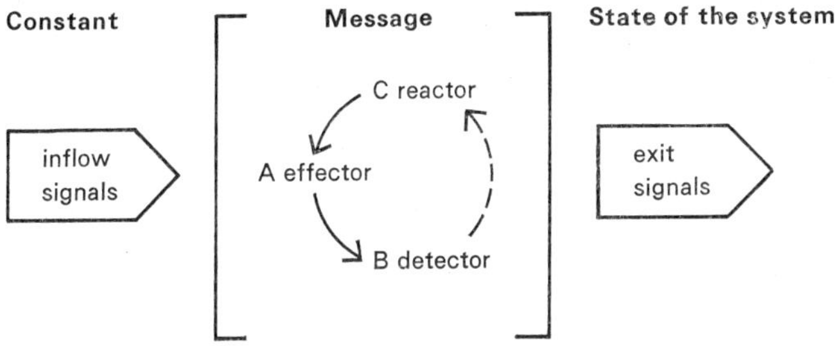

It is clear the A state will be indicated by a special state of B which will make itself felt on C. The latter will react on A, the effector, and will regulate its state, in other words, its action. Consequently, for one or many constant inflow signals received, the system, with its constituent elements, is in a predictable state, limited by interactions of C on A and A on C by means of B and giving off a constant exit signal.

Here again we find the cybernetics of Wiener, in other words, the science of autocontrol and communication within systems. The best example is presented by the prey/predator interactions where C would be the predator-reactor, A the prey, thus the effector, and B the detector, represented by the number or proportion of prey. I would now like to take up the actual text of Margalef (1968):

> Organisms are the bearer of [a] huge amount of information. Since they can be destroyed but cannot be produced from nothing, any regulatory mechanism implies an initial overshoot. An excessive number of offspring is produced by the prey. This number is reduced to a lower level through destruction by the predator. Such destruction is density-dependent, because the numbers of the predators themselves are dependent on the numbers of the prey at a previous time. The interactions between species can be considered as cybernetic mechanisms. Their goal can be stated, for our own special and descriptive purpose, as the maintenance of a reasonable constancy in numbers. Such constancy in numbers means the preservation of information, inasmuch as future states of the system become more predictable from the present situation.

We have already stated that, from the atom to the biosphere, the sequence atom→molecule→protoplasm, etc., makes up successive levels corresponding to increasingly complex mechanisms. They correspond to an augmentation of the quantity of information, which has become enormous at the biosphere level. The mere fact that the ecologist limits himself to the biosphere indicates the necessity for arbitrary limits which will circumscribe the sub-systems. The interactions of the constituents of these sub-systems will be studied in order to disengage the significant factors or parameters and the essential laws. We must bear in mind that these heterogeneous sub-systems will interact with each other.

Consequently, we can already consider the biosphere as being formed by at least two systems, the aerial and the aquatic. The latter is the object of our study and is composed of an indefinite number of sets such as the oceans and seas, which are in contact with other systems by their limiting surfaces, such as the ocean-atmosphere interface, the ocean-floor interface and other specific regions – on the continental shelf for instance – where three systems are simultaneously in contact.

We can now proceed to consider a rock-pool as a hypothetical model ecosystem. Let it be of an average size, neither too large nor too small but of a certain complexity without which it would not provide a satisfactory model for investigation. Thus on a reduced scale we have the three limits defined above: the two interfaces water-air and water-sediment and also the fringe area where the water, the air and the land are in contact. The system is thus not isolated, since its existence depends on the presence of water, which is supplied by wave action and tidal movements. This latter point stresses the fact that although we are limited to the scale of the biosphere, this biosphere exists as such because our globe is part of a solar system and its position with its satellite is evident from tidal action. Thus there is a cycle imposed on the whole system. In fact if the cycle did not exist, the system we are studying would not exist as such. Without going into unnecessary detail, it can be said that the cycle is a 24-hour constant in two phases, symbol of the numerous *circadian* rhythms to which the components of the system are subjected. (*Circadian* rhythms are those with a cycle of 'approximately 24 hours', from the Latin *circa diem*.)

The rock-pool is first observed at a given time, in a state which obviously tells us of the present but also of the past and to a certain extent allows prediction of the near future. The tide goes down, leaving behind, in a hollow, a kind of vast basin, containing salt water which cannot escape since it is held back by a rocky barrier. It is immediately evident that the populations of animals and of algae differ in composition according to whether they are situated on the edge of the pool or in the water. The first obvious conclusion to be made is that fixed organisms out of the water can support a temporary lack of water and can even make do with the spray action. Here we approach, in an approximate way, the notion put forward by Shelford of the limiting factor and the law of tolerance. The absence of an organism or of a group of organisms depends on the limits of tolerance of the organism. We shall see later that these limits of tolerance are extremely complex and could be in some cases expressed by interactions of numerous environmental parameters.

Thus, from the land as far as the aquatic limit, that is to say, in the transition zone where the aerial-geological-aquatic ecosystems exist simultaneously in contact, only those organisms will develop and multiply which can tolerate simultaneously or successively the organisation of the three systems. In this region we find not only barnacles, which require humidity to be able to respire but can exist several hours in the air, but also terrestrial crustaceans which can withstand several hours of immersion. It should be noted that the life cycle of barnacles involves an aquatic larval stage and thus their survival depends on an accessible substrate and the survival of the larvae. Finally, the rock is covered with flora: yellow or black lichens or microscopic algae which are grazed on by molluscs such as periwinkles and limpets. In addition to these herbivores, certain molluscs such as whelks are carnivores and feed on barnacles, periwinkles and many other molluscs.

In this border zone we can already consider an ecosystem or more correctly a zone of exchange and thus of transition. However, it is very complicated to analyse since its existence depends on the simultaneous existence of terrestrial, aerial and marine systems, the latter being represented by the pool. Thus the respective exchanges are difficult to define, as long as the organisation and function of the three systems are not specified.

In the pool of sea water, a juxtaposition of populations takes place, each of them being a structural element of the rock-pool ecosystem. All indicate particular ecological conditions, since here again the limiting factors impose certain distributions. In addition, the plant environment creates its own physical, chemical and biological conditions, thus creating a secondary fauna and flora, fixed or not, which will be additional elements in the system. It is evident that the structure of the system is bound up with the diversity of the species, and we shall see that this diversity can be equally well expressed by a flow of energy or by a quantity of energy bound within the system.

This rock-pool is studied over a 24-hour period according to a semi-diurnal cycle in which time 0 corresponds to the beginning of the tidal reflux or backward flow and time 12 corresponds to the second reflux. The end of the semi-diurnal cycle is just before high tide. In fact every twelve hours the system is exposed to the tide. Time 0 is chosen arbitrarily to coincide with sunrise, for the purpose of this illustrative exercise. Time 12 will thus coincide with sunset.

As we have aready stated, two types of parameter need to be known, corresponding to the abiotic and the biotic factors. Among the abiotic factors, measurements should be made of the amount of light energy, the salinity of the environment, its temperature, pH (which I shall define in a moment), the amount of dissolved oxygen, nitrogen salts and phosphates, and if need be the carbon dioxide content. Obviously these measurements are to be made simultaneously at several points and at different levels of the pool to obtain a physico-chemical spectrum of the system over twenty-four hours.

The light energy is measured using quanta-meters and thermopiles at depth in order to establish a correlation between the energy arriving at the surface and that which reaches the deepest parts. The progressive disappearance of the spectrum constituents will also be optically measured. In the present example, the rock-pool being shallow, only infra-red is eliminated in the first millimetres of water; red is slightly diminished.

An accurate salinometer for measuring the conductivity of the environment indicates that the salinity seems to be the same everywhere and that the water contains 36 g of salts per litre. There is a uniform temperature of 20°C. No wind is disturbing the surface.

The hydrogen-potential or pH meter, which indicates the acid or alkaline character of the environment, registers 8·2. Fresh water has a pH of 7, being neutral, with an equal number of H^+ and OH^- ions. A pH value less than 7 would indicate an acid environment with an excess of H^+ ions. The inverse with a value more than 8 would indicate an alkaline environment in which the OH^- ions are predominant. Thus in our case, the sea water is alkaline, which is normal. It is known that the sea water constituents are able to maintain this value of 8·2 by the action of the 'buffer system'. Even if small quantities of acids or alkalis are added, an auto-regulation takes place.

The dissolved oxygen is measured by means of an electrode giving a measurement of 5·38 ml/L. The environment is completely oxygenated by the air, even at the bottom of the pool.

Finally, samples taken for laboratory analysis reveal the presence of inorganic nitrogen salts (nitrate and nitrites) and phosphates at concentrations of approximately 35 μg-atoms of nitrogen per litre for the first and 1·9 μg-atoms/litre for the second. Nitrate-nitrites and phosphates indispensable for plant nutrition are known as nutrients.

As the sun rises and the light intensity increases, the quantity of oxygen and the pH are found to increase. (This increase is due to the algal chlorophyll giving off oxygen and metabolising carbon dioxide [CO_2]. This metabolism reduces the buffer effect of the environment; simultaneously the quantity of nitrate-nitrite and phosphates will decrease.)

What takes place during these light hours? Quite simply a continuation of the action of chlorophyll. The algae take up CO_2 and release oxygen so that finally the sea water is supersaturated. The uptake of CO_2 results in a decrease of the carbonate and bicarbonate content of the water and consequently diminishes what we call the buffer effect, this being a property of weak acids. The OH^- ion concentration increases and the environment tends to become alkaline. As for variation in the nitrogen salts and phosphate concentrations in relation to time 0, this depends on the use of these salts by the plants and by certain unicellular organisms.

These phenomena have many other results: for instance larval or delicate mature organisms with low tolerance will disappear as living communities. Here, Shelford's law is illustrated. But a more important result is the conversion of energy which takes place. In fact a part of the light energy, by way of the chlorophyll which acts as a conversion agent or energy-transducer, has become chemical energy in the form of organic molecules which constitute and are stored in algae. These molecules are then available for organisms unable to effect this conversion. Thus we find the beginning of the food chain at a level which is generally defined as primary production.

Thus two simultaneous and associated processes are evident; a production and a consumption. The production is organic matter, and there is a consumption of CO_2, nitrates, nitrites and phosphates. It is obvious that production would end rapidly if there were no sources of nutrients.

So we have to consider the origin of these nutrients. At the bottom of the rock-pool, sediments have accumulated in certain places. In the same way organic matter, originating from the remnants of the dead bodies of organisms, collects at the base of or underneath the algae. It is in these areas that the microorganisms carry out an important transformation role. At time 0, the environment acts as a slight oxidiser and is thus favourable for the aerobic bacteria. These bacteria will oxidise the detritus, breaking up their molecules into smaller and smaller groups of atoms and recirculating the nitrogen, the phosphorus and other elements in a mineral solution form, making them available for the plants, so that the nutrients are re-formed.

Since during the following twelve hours the water will remain stagnant, the return and recirculation (diffusion) of these nutrients in the environment can only take place by the action of several burrowing animals, which by stirring up the sediment will not only find their food but also mix the water by their movements.

It is possible that another source of mineral salts exists, in the form of freshwater streams from the land. It can be seen that where this water mixes, there follows a decrease in salinity and pH. Here only certain organisms, such as sea lettuces and certain bivalve molluscs, the common oyster for example, can exist and develop: such species are described as *euryhaline* since they undergo a salinity change during the cycle.

During the course of the day, the water temperature will increase considerably, especially at the surface. This means that the organisms present have to support temperature variations, and such organisms are described as *eurythermic*. One has to suppose that all organisms living permanently in the pool have these characteristics even in their larval or juvenile stages, otherwise they would not exist.

The ecologist has now defined the abiotic factors – which are only a part of the environment – and has measured the variations. The upper and lower limits of all possible combinations can be made evident by correlations, and these will constitute some of the limits of the ecosystem. Beyond these limits such a system could not exist.

We have already outlined the importance of energy in the system, energy in the form of organic molecules synthesised by plants and transferred in the food chain by various channels. This food chain is made up of links which join the primary producers to the first-stage feeders. These are in turn linked to the second-stage feeders, and so on. Thus links of food energy are made between each trophic level.

The flow of energy through the system starts with the fixation of sunlight by plants, and the total result from photosynthesis is the gross primary production. From this production energy is expended for maintenance, reproduction and growth; and only part of it is disposable for other levels to preserve the equilibrium of the system. This part is called net primary production. It is obvious that this disposable fraction decreases between each of the higher levels. Let us suppose ideal conditions so that the production is not dispersed to another food chain by migration from one system to another.

Quantification of energy flow is difficult to track, especially in marine ecosystems. Methods involving the analysis of stomach contents furnish important information. For example, bottom-dwelling fish like the Gobius have, on the average, a stomach capacity of about 3 per cent of their own weight and feed twice a day; thus they absorb about 6 per cent of their own weight per day. But on the other hand, certain molluscs like the Conus feeding on polychaete worms eat 15 to 50 per cent of their own volume in a single meal. Such investigations have to be numerous and many computations are required to determine the real state of the system at each level and as a whole.

Another method is to analyse the composition of the communities, their diversity and, subsequently, in the system considered, the number of different communities. This estimate can be made by studying a surface unit, a single square metre for example, or a volume unit. Species identification and their reported numbers, in each of the samples analysed, will be an indication of the structure of the biological components of the system. By following the changes that can happen in a succession of samples we can elucidate the evolution of the system.

These considerations lead us to examine the prey-predator relationships, and for this we should conside.. once again the simple feed-back scheme indicated on p. 103, where A is the prey and C the predator, the detector B being the proportion of preys. This proportion will represent the signal which affects directly the number of predators. Thus, as the number of preys increases, so will the number of predators, which will thus keep down the preys to a value. The proportion

– and thus the detector – having decreased, the number of predators will also decrease.

However, the regulatory systems of predator and preys is usually much more complex, especially in the aquatic environment. For example in the case of the starfish and the molluscs on which they feed, the larvae from which they have developed must also be considered. These larvae feed on microscopic algae which are not necessarily the same. According to which of these larvae find the conditions the most favourable, the prey-predator balance will be upset.

From these statements we understand that the amount of energy bound to each level is symbolised by a biomass, or biological mass, measured in weight or in calories, which is in equilibrium, or in other words constant, as long as the amount of energy received is equivalent to that expended. Consequently, an important parameter is represented by the ratio of primary production to the whole biomass. In fact, the smaller the quotient, the greater is the diversity of the system. Inversely, the larger the quotient, the less is this diversity. It can be concluded that the more biomass units there are, the smaller will be the quotient and *vice versa*. In the first case, the system will be highly diverse with a complex organisation; and in the second case not very diverse and of low organisation.

But this conclusion has another aspect. The diversity involves a multiplication of the transport routes from one *trophic level* (i.e. level of nutrition in the food chain) to another, and the same action on one of the components of the same level will not have the same effect in different systems. Let us consider a system having a single trophic level following primary production; that is to say, a plant-herbivore system. It is evident that any action on the primary producers will involve a variation in the mass of the consumers. But this variation will be less if the consumers are themselves diverse. If we can now imagine a system with three trophic levels, for the same variation, the consequences will be considerably less at the third level. Thus, supposing a constant flow of energy, the system will tend to evolve towards a diverse condition necessary for its stability. At this stage the biomass will not be increased and the flow of energy per unit of biomass will be the lowest possible.

Let us now consider an ecosystem in which the incoming amount of energy is suddenly increased greatly at the primary production level. The species of the second trophic level can only produce a reaction after a certain lapse of time. The increase of the biomass will be appreciable at the beginning of the chain, but will decrease regularly and sharply at higher levels if the time factor is insufficient. In other words, the diversity may decrease and this is what happens when ecosystems are subject to frequent changes.

This diversion towards theoretical considerations does not, as might be imagined, distract us from our rock-pool. In fact, the water exchange following tidal action is a fluctuation, an important periodic change which conditions the system. A constant flow of solar energy, a regular income of nutritive elements, and of phytoplankton in the form of microscopic unicellular algae, will favour (*a*) the maintenance and eventually the increase of the primary producers represented by the fixed algae; (*b*) the filtering animals, mainly represented by the bivalve molluscs, which retain unicellular organisms in their gills. In each case, the augmentation of the biomass will be limited by the abiotic conditions already listed, but also by a maximum degree of occupation, which cannot be exceeded.

Owing to the turbulence caused by the incoming or outgoing tide, very many species will be unable to be part of the system and must be considered as incidental elements, although the statistical parameter they represent can be included. Beyond this, at the highest level of the chain, man can intervene to make his collection between the two tides.

Thus, the disturbance caused by periodic changes will have an effect and is classed with the limiting factors. Only fixed organisms, or those sturdy enough to resist being washed away, will survive, provided that they find their food on the spot and also favourable conditions for reproduction and larval fixation. Obviously, these conditions will never be simultaneously favourable for all species and only certain ones will be able to install themselves along the different levels of the chain. The system will have a poor diversity, but will be interesting to the ecologist because of its relative simplicity, the restricted number of species being an indication of certain specific factors. In addition, an action on one or other of these populations will affect the structure of the ecosystem much more rapidly and make evident more quickly any eventual compensation process.

But we must keep within the symbolic 24-hour cycle.

The water is thus reheated and certain planktonic populations will develop accordingly; and among them, the larval stages will metamorphose and become attached to the rock. Others will not be able to withstand the new conditions and will die. Falling to the bottom, they will enrich the organic deposits and favour the development of the decomposer species in the system, that is species which require much energy. Nightfall brings with it a temperature drop, and this, together with an increase of CO_2 content from plant respiration and the modified pH, will exert a complex selective pressure which will cause the disappearance of a certain number of other young species. Finally, at high tide (time 12, according to our clock), all this evolution of the system towards a diverse and stable state will once again be put to the test. This new overthrow will be resisted only by the populations adapted to the rhythm – a rhythm which is part of the structure of the ecosystem.

It might be considered wrong to try to describe an ecosystem and its evolution over a period of twenty-four hours, during which such considerable changes take place. In fact, the analysis has allowed us to be aware of and correlate certain response mechanisms to distinct parameters, isolated or in groups; the analysis has also demonstrated that in ecology a study of organisation can be made at a micro- or macroscopic level.

The microscopic aspect leads us to a study of the microphenomena which certainly take part in the organisation and are extremely important, but which do not reflect the integration of all conditions. This is evident only from a macroscopic viewpoint.

The rock-pool ecosystem is made up by the tidal rhythm, by an average value for the other abiotic conditions and by an average equilibrium of the populations. The whole may be described as a poor organisation and we now know that the double exchange of energy provoked by the solar cycle and the tidal rhythm limits the evolution potential towards the formation of a mature system – in other words, limits the diversity and the trend towards equilibrium.

These conclusions have important consequences since they should lead man in the second half of the twentieth century to a better understanding of the effect he has on the biosphere surrounding him when he modifies it in any way; and also to plan his interventions more suitably, and to realise that any important change forced upon natural systems will result in a disturbed equilibrium, involving an energy loss by the system and eventually for himself also.

But this little pool of water has taught us certain other lessons. The ecologist is always a naturalist, a biologist, even if he touches on certain mathematical aspects; his observations of all the beings that surround him enable him to discover a new secret of nature each day, whether it be a reproduction cycle and the conditions necessary for this reproduction, or whether it be a behaviour pattern. All new discovery is an additional contribution to science and also to a better understanding of our planet. Following the study of hundreds and thousands of rock-pools throughout the world, many practical problems concerning the culture of marine organisms, as well as the exploitation of natural resources, have been solved.

R. MARGALEF (1968) *Perspectives in Ecological Theory*, Univ. of Chicago.

7

THE HUMAN SKIN AS AN ECOSYSTEM

MARY MARPLES

THE word ecology brings to mind countryside and sea and pollution, and it is not always realised that each of us can be regarded as a complex of ecosystems to the study of which ecological principles can be applied. It can most truly be said that no man lives alone, for all mammals and probably all animals support microbial populations of what are frequently called 'germs', on those tissues available for colonisation. In man and the other mammals a complex flora and fauna lives on those surfaces which are in contact with the outside world, that is the skin and the alimentary tract. In fact man is swarming with germs of all kinds. These are not harmful but beneficial to him. It is wrong to think that all germs associated with us cause disease. Only a very few are capable of doing so and these have to break through the body defences before they can establish themselves. It is also incorrect to imagine that we can by any means rid ourselves of our resident flora. We can reduce the numbers of individuals by various means, but some will always survive to recolonise our surfaces. We are fortunate enough to support our inhabitants for life, no matter how unattractive to some people is the idea of their presence. These microbial communities live in a delicate balance with each other and with their host, and their presence is beneficial rather than harmful. Disturbance of this balance may in some circumstances be followed by the appearance of disease in the host.

These microbial communities are called the normal flora, whose presence has long been recognised, but whose ecology has only recently received much attention. The flora of man and some of his domestic animals have to some extent been studied, but very little is known about the inhabitants of vertebrates other than mammals, and almost nothing about the flora of invertebrates. Ecological studies concerned with population changes or community structure have been almost confined to man and the intestines of domestic ruminants, and even these are only at their beginning.

In man the densest and most varied microbial populations are found in the mouth and in the large intestine. These are not easy of access, and the communities are so complex that very little indeed is known about their ecology. The human skin, however, provides a much more favourable region for investigation, for several reasons: a very great deal is known about its structure and physiology, it is readily accessible for sampling, it provides a specialised habitat which only a limited number of species can exploit, and most of these can be cultivated in the laboratory. Finally, both the substrate and the inhabitants are rapidly replaced, so that repeated sampling does not alter the ecosystem. Consider the number of years required for the regeneration of a forest after it has been destroyed. All of us have at some time suffered from a minor wound or burn and know that the skin is replaced and the area healed in a few days. The normal flora regenerates even more quickly for it returns within a few hours after skin sterilisation.

In view of these manifest advantages it may seem strange that the ecosystem of the human skin has not been more extensively studied, but the reason for this is not far to seek. Our cutaneous inhabitants are so very small – none of them is visible to the naked eye and most can be seen only under the higher powers of the microscope. It is difficult to appreciate how very small bacteria, the most prominent members of the flora, really are. The rod-shaped bacteria which inhabit the skin are 2 to 4 μ in length, while the cocci, or spherical forms, are about 1 μ in diameter. 1 μ is 1/1000 of a millimetre. A millimetre is clearly visible on a ruler, so if the coccus was enlarged 1000 times it could readily be seen and would look like the head of a pin. But if its human host were enlarged to match he would be more than a mile in height. Another way of picturing the relative sizes of man and a member of his normal flora is to imagine the man enlarged until his feet were at Land's End and the top of his head at John O'Groats. A coccus enlarged to the same scale would be about the size of a half-grown lamb in one of the fields which he would cover. This very small size of microorganisms makes it impossible to investigate and measure the activities of individual cells. Many can, however, be cultivated on artificial nutrient media, so that large populations can be obtained and their physiology studied. But although these populations are regarded as uniform, they are composed of individuals as subject to mutation and variation as are larger living things.

Another great difficulty which delays the study of the normal flora is that so far no satisfactory classification of bacteria and other microorganisms has been devised. Microorganisms from the skin, as from other habitats, are by no means easy to identify for they are exceedingly variable. In recent years valiant attempts have been made to provide a reasonable classification of skin bacteria, and the work of Baird-Parker (1963) and Richard Marples (1969) is noteworthy in this context.

In spite of these difficulties, extensive studies of the ecosystem of the human skin have been undertaken. The results, fascinating in themselves, also serve to show that the principles of ecology are as applicable to the curious world we ourselves provide as to the world which we inhabit. In the following paragraphs an attempt is made to describe that world, and to give an account of some of its inhabitants.

THE STRUCTURE OF THE SKIN

Any account of a classical ecosystem includes a description of its non-living environmental component, and of the different habitats provided. Although no part of the cutaneous ecosystem can be regarded as truly non-living, for the purposes of comparison the skin itself can be equated with the soil, or with the rock-pool or the pond. The analogy is not too extravagant, since the cells forming the inhabited part of the skin are in fact fully differentiated and dead. Fig. 1 is a diagrammatic representation of a section through human skin, which consists essentially of two layers, the superficial *epidermis* and the deeper *dermis*. The dermis can be ignored in the present discussion, since in health it does not support a resident population. It is, however, of immense importance to the cutaneous inhabitants, since it contains among other structures the blood and lymph vessels which transport nutrient to the superficial layers, and indirectly to the cutaneous community.

The epidermis is mainly composed of cells undergoing differentiation or keratinisation. In this process the individual cells die and are converted into tough, flat, interlocking plates. The most superficial of these are shed to the exterior, but are constantly replaced from below. Two main layers are recognised in the epidermis. The deeper granular layers are made of cells not yet dead and fully differentiated. The more superficial *stratum corneum* is composed of tough, flat, dying or dead cells. This cornified layer acts as a barrier which prevents loss of water from the deeper tissues, and penetration of

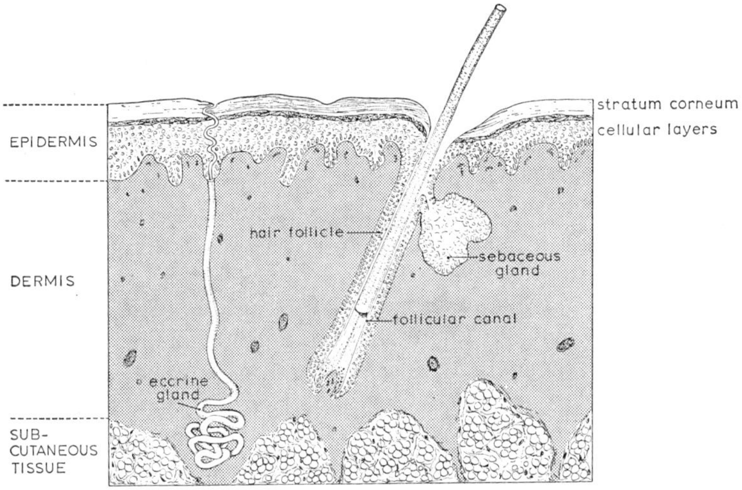

Fig. 1. Diagrammatic representation of a section through human skin

liquid water and other substances into the body. This barrier is of considerable importance to the microorganisms, since because of this property the skin is too dry for its colonisation by many species.

CUTANEOUS APPENDAGES

At intervals over the surface, the skin is invaginated into the deeper layers to form two groups of structures. The first consists of the sweat glands. These secrete a slightly salty, slightly acid secretion, which is constantly poured over the skin surface. The glands are primarily concerned with the regulation of body temperature, but their secretions are of major importance in the ecosystem, since they provide most of the available water. In areas such as the armpit there are additional sweat glands with a more complex secretion. The substances which they produce can be metabolised by a variety of microorganisms and probably contribute to the development of the dense populations found in these areas.

The other appendage, the hair follicle, is a complex structure. It consists of a tube or canal containing a hair whose root dips into the dermis from which it draws its nutrients. Some distance up the canal is the opening of the sebaceous gland, which secretes an oily substance known as sebum. The sebum mixes well with sweat, so that the skin is covered with a fine oily film. The hair follicle is of particular importance to the cutaneous inhabitants, since its opening forms the headquarters of most members of the community.

These appendages are not evenly distributed over the skin. Hair follicles, for example, are absent from the palms and soles. In such areas as the scalp and eyebrows they are closely packed and support long tough hairs, while elsewhere they may be scanty and carry fine, fragile hairs. The size of the sebaceous gland is unrelated to the diameter of the hair, and in areas on the face very large glands are associated with inconspicuous hairs.

The unequal distribution of appendages, together with variations in temperature, humidity and other characters. divides the skin into several different habitats. In general, warm moist regions, such as the nostrils and armpit, are the ones most densely colonised, while exposed, arid areas, for example the skin of the forearm, are only sparsely inhabited. But it must be stressed that the human skin provides an unfavourable substrate for almost all microorganisms. Soil and water species in general cannot colonise the skin, and even those causing human disease have great difficulty in establishing themselves on undamaged skin.

THE RESIDENTS OF THE HUMAN SKIN

Only one animal can be regarded as representing a resident fauna. This is *Demodex folliculorum*, a microscopic mite which has its headquarters in the hair follicles of the face. This tiny animal has an elongated worm-like body and four pairs of stubby legs. Closely related species are found in the follicles of other mammals.

Demodex is rare in children but is found in the follicles round the nose and chin of most adults (Riechers and Kopf 1969). Its life history has been worked out by Spickett (1961). The larval stages are passed within the sebaceous glands. The adult females migrate to the openings of the hair follicles, while the males roam over the skin surface. (See Fig. 2.)

It would be satisfactory to regard *Demodex* as representing the consumer level of the ecosystem, but it is not yet clear whether the mite derives its nutrients from the sebaceous secretions or from the bacteria inhabiting the follicles. It appears to be a truly harmless resident of the skin, for although there have been attempts to associate it with various skin diseases, its universal presence in

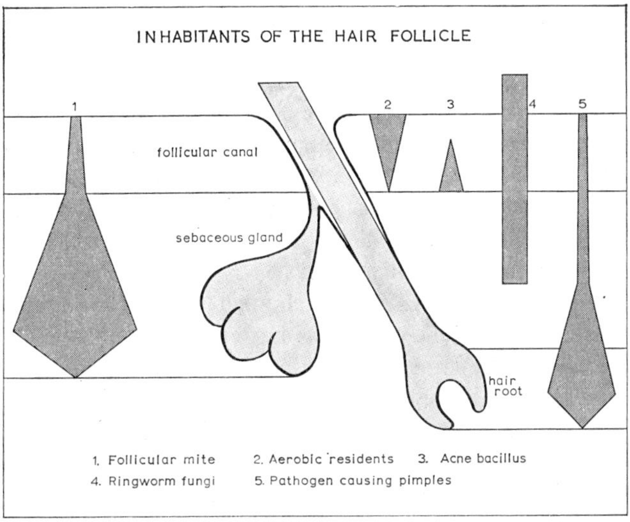

Fig. 2. Diagram of a hair follicle to show the parts colonised by different microorganisms

adults, sometimes in very large numbers, precludes any such relationship.

Although several other animals spend some or all of their time on the skin, they cannot be regarded as members of the normal fauna, since they all damage the substrate. Mosquitoes and other blood-sucking arthropods visit the skin and pierce it, but their headquarters are elsewhere. Human lice complete their life histories on the skin surface, and *Sarcoptes scabei*, the itch mite, lives in burrows in the epidermis, but the presence of these organisms is recognised and resented by the host. The same is true of the various larval worms and protozoa which may spend considerable periods of time in the skin. The substrate is damaged and the host is aware of their presence.

Among the plants, no algae have colonised the skin of man, though they could be regarded as members of the normal flora of some other animals. Fungi, however, are represented by two important groups.

Certain of the filamentous fungi, which cause ringworm of the hair and skin, can live for long periods as harmless residents. The condition known as 'athlete's foot' is a recurrent one, and it seems clear that the fungus remains as a cutaneous inhabitant of the sole and web-spaces of the foot in between attacks. Moreover, the organisms can be isolated from the feet of a few individuals who have never suffered from an overt infection. It is of interest that some of the soil fungi can become residents of the toe-nails, especially if these are damaged (English 1968).

The other group, the yeast-like fungi, have several cutaneous representatives, and one genus named *Pityrosporum* includes two species which may occur in abundance, especially on the scalp when dandruff is present. These yeasts are lipophilic and lipid-dependent, but many individuals carry a few additional yeasts which do not require fat for their multiplication.

It is difficult to list the viruses which might be regarded as residents of the skin. Many of the cutaneous bacteria are themselves known to be parasitised by viruses, and in addition one organism, *Herpes virus hominis*, can be regarded as spending much of its time as a harmless member of the flora. This virus is the cause of 'cold sores', which tend to recur in the same small area of skin in response to such stimuli as fever, anxiety or sunburn. It seems clear that in between attacks the virus is retained within the living cells of the granular layers of the epidermis.

THE CUTANEOUS BACTERIA

The bacteria living on normal skin have received much more attention than have the other groups. They are the dominant members of the community, and such population studies as have been undertaken have dealt largely with bacterial species.

BACTERIAL POPULATIONS

The skin can be sampled in a variety of ways: a measured area can be swabbed or scrubbed, a pad of sterile velvet or of some appropriate nutrient medium can be applied to the surface, or layers of epidermis can be successively removed with scotch tape. Regardless of the method of collection the next step is basically the same. The sample, with or without dilution, is inoculated on to appropriate nutrient media. It is then incubated at a favourable temperature so that the individual bacteria multiply until each has formed a visible colony. This takes twenty-four to forty-eight hours, by which time the original cell has produced many million offspring. These visible colonies are counted, and, since each is regarded as having arisen from a single bacterium, the number of organisms in the original sample and hence living on a unit area of skin can be calculated. Although there are many errors in this technique, the results can be made sufficiently repeatable to permit comparison of bacterial populations living on the same site in different individuals, and of different sites in the same host.

On the basis of numerous investigations of this kind the following facts have been assembled:

1. *The individual host.* Some individuals regularly support more bacteria per unit area than do others living in a comparable situation. For example, Williamson (1965) could distinguish two groups of men living in the same enclosed social conditions, on the basis of the population densities living on the forearm. Among thirty-two subjects seventeen were described as forming a 'high count' group with an average population of 4500 bacteria per sq cm of skin. The remaining fifteen formed a 'low count' group, with an average population of only 105 per sq cm. Similar differences have been found by investigators in very different countries, so that there seems to be no doubt that the skin of some human hosts provides a much more favourable habitat than that of others.

2. *The skin site.* Warm, moist areas of skin, such as are found in the armpit or groin, are the most densely populated, while among exposed parts of the skin the scalp and face carry more micro-organisms than are found on the arms or legs (see Fig. 3). R. Marples and Williamson (1969) recorded a mean count of $3{\cdot}2 \times 10^6$ per sq cm (that is, over 3 million bacteria residing on a square centimetre of skin) in the armpit, while the average count for the foreheads of the same fourteen individuals was 7880 per sq cm. In another investigation R. Marples and his colleagues (1970) found population densities of almost 900,000 bacteria per sq cm, in male scalps. In contrast, the forearm may carry as few as twenty-five bacteria on the same unit area (Williamson 1965). The web-spaces of the feet also carry very dense populations, but their anatomical structure makes it more difficult to take quantitative samples. It seems clear that moisture is the most important environmental factor affecting population

densities. R. Marples (1965) has shown that if the skin of the arm is covered with an impermeable dressing, the bacterial population rises from its original level of a few thousands per sq cm to more than 11 million in twenty-four hours, and to a peak of 38 million by the fourth day of occlusion.

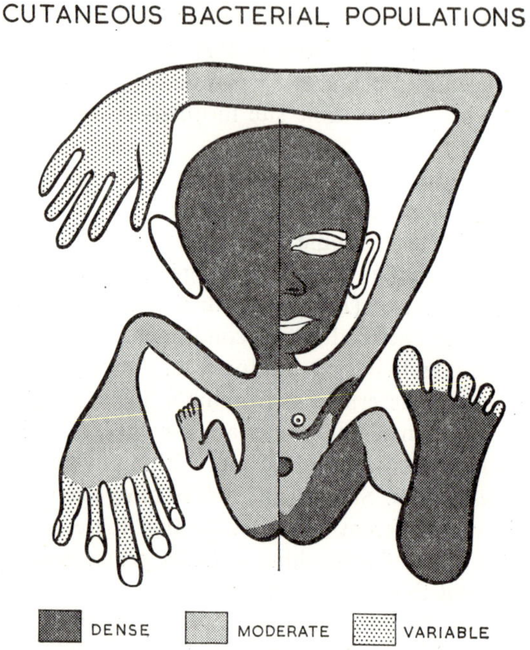

Fig. 3. Diagram illustrating the density of bacterial populations at different skin sites

In no anatomical area are bacteria evenly distributed over the surface. Most are located at the openings of the hair follicles, a few are scattered among the most superficial layers of the epidermis, but in health none is found below the fully cornified layers of the skin (see Fig. 4).

3. *Age*. The age of the host influences both the density and the composition of cutaneous populations. Sarkany and Gaylarde (1968) have shown that during birth the infant's skin is colonised by a sparse population derived from its mother. Somerville (1969) made an extensive study of the cutaneous flora in different age-groups. She found the most varied communities on the skin of children. In

young adults there are dense populations in various sites, but they are composed of only a limited number of species. In old age, the number of resident species increases, so that to some extent the flora of old age resembles that of childhood.

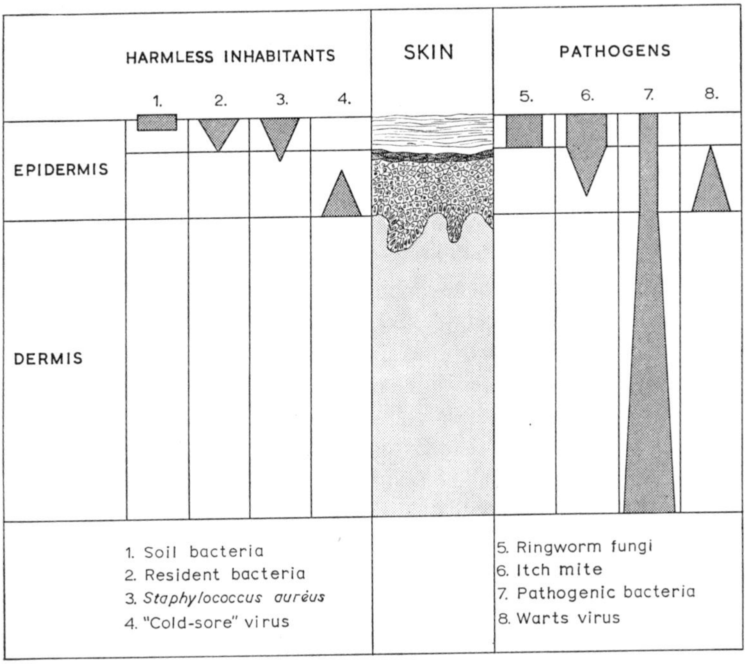

Fig. 4. Diagram illustrating the depths of penetration of the skin by various microorganisms

4. *Environmental factors.* It is generally accepted that the carriage of surface bacteria is greater in tropical than in temperate countries. Some experimental evidence is available to support this opinion. Duncan, McBride and Knox (1969) sampled the skin of subjects exposed to three controlled environments. They found that in hot, humid conditions the bacterial populations on the back and hands increased significantly, but that no such increase occurred on exposure to hot and dry, or cold and wet, conditions. It is interesting that the populations of the feet of their subjects were unaffected by external conditions. This finding probably reflects the special response to temperature changes of the superficial blood vessels of the legs and feet.

It is probable that changes in the internal environment of the host also influence skin populations, but this aspect of cutaneous ecology has not been extensively studied. M. Marples (1965) found significant differences in the types of organisms living on the skin and in the mouths of diabetic as compared with normal subjects. Stratford and his colleagues (1968) reported profound changes in the superficial flora during severe, prolonged illness of the host.

THE TYPES OF BACTERIA LIVING ON HUMAN SKIN

The bacterial communities found on human skin include only a few bacterial groups. Bacteria can be separated into two great divisions on the basis of their response to the Gram Stain. In a stained preparation some cells are coloured dark purple, and are known as Gram-positive, while others which are stained red are called Gram-negative. Although this simple technique was introduced to demonstrate structural differences, it has since been found that Gram-positive and Gram-negative species differ not only in their structure but also in their physiology and disease-causing properties.

Gram-positive bacteria predominate on the skin and can be divided into two groups. The first includes the cocci, small spherical cells about 1 to 2 μ in diameter. Two genera and several species are represented. The majority of these are harmless or even beneficial to the host, but one species, *Staphylococcus aureus*, can cause pimples, boils and sometimes more serious infections. The other Gram-positive bacteria appear under the microscope as fragile rods, showing considerable variation in size. These are known as diphtheroids, of which three ecological groups can be recognised. One is known as the 'acne bacillus'. It lives in the depths of the hair follicle and is anaerobic, that is, it does not require oxygen for its respiration. Both the other groups of diphtheroids are aerobic, but they are separated by their fat requirements. The large-colony diptheroids grow well in ordinary nutrient media, but the third group, the lipophilic diphtheroids, are stimulated by various forms of fat, and grow poorly without fat supplements.

It is doubtful if any diphtheroid should be regarded as causing disease. The acne bacillus is found in large numbers in the blackheads of acne, but its role in the causation of acne is controversial. Another species is associated with the development of superficial scaling of the skin. The rest of the diphtheroids appear to be beneficial, rather than harmful, to their hosts.

In addition to these Gram-positive bacteria, most individuals support a scanty population of Gram-negative organisms. The majority of these are rod-shaped, a few are motile, swimming by means of flagella. Several species are represented, and some of them can cause clinical disease in appropriate circumstances.

The organisms described above comprise the true, resident bacteria of the skin. Most disease-causing species find the undamaged skin so unfavourable a habitat that they cannot establish themselves, so that even when large numbers are transferred to the skin they very soon die. Organisms from soil or water are even less capable of becoming residents, although they constantly reach the skin during normal human activity. Similarly, the cocci and diphtheroids of the skin do not multiply in soil or water. Some strains can survive in dust, and a few can grow in complex organic substrates such as milk, but their true headquarters is provided by the mammalian skin.

TRANSMISSION OF THE FLORA

Although the cutaneous bacteria may not survive long away from the host, they can be readily transmitted through the air to new hosts. Noble and Davies (1965), and other workers, have shown that all movements of man are accompanied by the shedding of fragments of skin. The fragments provide minute 'rafts' on which a bacterium may be carried by air currents long distances from its origin. Sciple and his colleagues (1967) found that an individual spending forty minutes in a sterile chamber released more than a million rafts carrying a living organism. It has been found that the optimal size of a raft is one of equivalent diameter of 14 μ, that is, rather larger than 1/100 of a millimetre. It is generally believed that transfer of disease-causing bacteria on these cutaneous rafts is responsible for much of the cross-infection which occurs in hospitals.

ACTIVITIES OF THE CUTANEOUS COMMUNITY

It seems clear that the cutaneous inhabitants are living on the by-products of keratinisation and on the glandular secretions of the skin. Very few species can decompose keratin itself, even after it has been shed. It is for this reason that hair or feathers of dead or even fossil animals may remain, long after the soft tissues have completely disappeared.

The nutrients available to the microorganisms are reasonably adequate. Free amino acids are liberated during keratinisation, and these contain both nitrogenous and carbohydrate components. Sweat provides water, salt and some nitrogen-containing residues. Sebum is rich in fats of various kinds. All these substances have been shown to be capable of supporting bacterial life in a test-tube. Additional nutrients in varying amounts come from food, drink, cosmetics and the excretory products of the host. Many of the cutaneous bacteria have been shown to possess enzymes capable of utilising these various substrates. In particular, both diphtheroids and cocci are provided with lipases which break down the components of sebum. The acne bacillus has recently been shown to be very active in this process (R. Marples *et al.* 1970).

COACTIONS OF THE CUTANEOUS INHABITANTS

1. *With the host.* There is good evidence that the presence of a cutaneous community is advantageous to the host. For many years the 'self-sterilising' power of the skin has been a clinical dogma. It now seems that the resistance of the intact skin to infection exemplifies the well-recognised character of an established ecosystem, namely that all influences tend to maintain the *status quo*. This 'homeostasis' is characteristic of fully developed ecosystems, and can be clearly demonstrated in that of the human skin. For example, infant skin rather easily succumbs to invasion by disease-causing bacteria, for should these be the first to arrive, they can establish themselves before the better adapted, harmless residents have become competitors. If the harmless organisms are already there the pathogens are much less likely to colonise the area. This fact has been utilised by Shinefield and his colleagues (1965) who were able to prevent skin infections in infants by prior inoculation of harmless cutaneous strains.

Similarly, if the resident flora is reduced or destroyed by the application of disinfectants or antibacterial preparations, the ecological vacuum is filled by organisms which are not susceptible to the drug. R. Marples and Kligman (1969) have reported the appearance of clinical infection in six out of ten normal males, an area of whose skin was treated for one week with neomycin, a widely used topical antibiotic. In each case the organism causing the infection was a strain of *Staphylococcus aureus* resistant to neomycin. Yeast populations also increased in the treated areas.

When the skin is damaged by any means, it becomes a much more favourable habitat for invasive bacteria. Disease-causing organisms which cannot multiply on intact skin can invade a wound and grow luxuriantly, so that a local or general infection may develop. The human body has other defences than those provided by the skin, but the presence of this watertight covering and its inhabitants provides a formidable barrier to the agents of disease.

2. *With each other.* Several studies have shown that the Gram-positive cutaneous bacteria in some way limit the growth of Gram-negative populations. Selective removal of the Gram-positive residents is followed by an overgrowth of Gram-negatives until the original population density is reached (Shehadeh and Kligman 1963). These Gram-negative communities may be harmless but can be dangerous to the host.

There also appears to be competition among the Gram-positive species. R. Marples and Williamson (1969) divided their subjects into 'diphtheroid' men, in whom lipophilic diphtheroids were dominant in the armpit, and 'coccal' men in whose armpits cocci were the major bacteria. Diphtheroid men carried significantly larger populations in the armpit than did the coccal men. Inhibition of the diphtheroids in the diphtheroid men was followed by a rapid increase in the growth of their cocci. Removal of the inhibition was followed by renewed dominance of diphtheroids and a reduction in the number of cocci. It appears that in the diphtheroid men, the diphtheroids were limiting the number of cocci in the cutaneous community.

The mechanism of these interspecific inhibitions is not yet known. Some of the products of fat decomposition can be shown to depress the growth of some disease-causing species, but these do not appear to be specifically active against cutaneous residents, and other factors must be involved.

Enough has been said to show how fascinating a community lives on the dry, acid surface of the human body. Study of the interactions of this highly accessible community might lead to a better understanding of the problems arising in a classical ecosystem. Above all, study of the cutaneous ecosystem reminds us that we do not live alone, and that every action we make affects not only our human and animal contacts but the microorganisms who depend on us for their every requirement. When you wash your hands, or scratch your nose, please give a thought to the small ones you are launching off into outer space.

A. C. BAIRD-PARKER (1963) 'A classification of Micrococci and Staphylococci based on physiological and biochemical tests', *J. gen. Microbiol.*, **30**, 409.

W. C. DUNCAN *et al.* (1969) 'Bacterial flora, the role of environmental factors', *J. Invest. Derm.*, **52**, 479.

M. P. ENGLISH (1968) 'Invasion of the skin by filamentous non-dermatophyte fungi', *Br. J. Derm.*, **80**, 282.

M. J. MARPLES (1965) *The Ecology of the Human Skin*, Springfield.

R. R. MARPLES (1965) 'The effect of hydration on the bacterial flora of the skin' in *Skin Bacteria and Their Role in Infection*, New York.

—— (1969) 'Diphtheroids of normal skin', *Br. J. Derm., Suppl. I*, **81**, 47.

R. R. MARPLES *et al.* (1970) 'The role of the aerobic microflora in the genesis of fatty acids in human surface lipids', *J. Invest. Derm.*, **55**, 173.

R. R. MARPLES AND P. WILLIAMSON (1969) 'Effects of systemic demethylchlortetracycline on human cutaneous flora', *Appl. Microbiol.*, **18**, 228.

W. C. NOBLE AND R. R. DAVIES (1965) 'Studies on the dispersal of staphylococci', *J. Clin. Path.*, **18**, 16.

R. RIECHERS AND A. W. KOPF (1969) 'Cutaneous infestation with *Demodex folliculorum* in man', *J. Invest. Derm.*, **52**, 103.

I. SARKANY AND C. C. GAYLARDE (1968) 'Bacterial colonisation of the skin of the newborn', *J. Path. Bact.*, **95**, 115.

G. W. SCIPLE *et al.* (1967) 'Recovery of microorganisms shed by humans into a sterilised environment', *Appl. Microbiol.*, **15**, 1388.

N. H. SHEHADEH AND A. M. KLIGMAN (1963) 'The effect of topical antibacterial agents on the bacterial flora of the axilla', *J. Invest. Derm.*, **40**, 61.

H. R. SHINEFIELD *et al.* (1965) 'Bacterial interference' in *Skin Bacteria and Their Role in Infection*, New York.

S. G. SPICKETT (1961) 'Studies on *Demodex folliculorum* Simon 1842. 1. Life History', *Parasitology*, **51**, 181.

D. A. SOMERVILLE (1969) 'The effect of age on the normal bacterial flora of the skin', *Br. J. Derm., Suppl. I*, **81**, 14.

B. STRATFORD *et al.* (1968) 'Alterations of superficial bacterial flora in severely ill patients', *Lancet*, **1**, 68.

P. WILLIAMSON (1965) 'Quantitative estimation of cutaneous bacteria' in *Skin Bacteria and Their Role in Infection*, New York.

Culture and Nature

8

ENVIRONMENTS AT RISK

MARY DOUGLAS

WHEN the scientist has a very serious message to convey he faces a problem of disbelief. How to be credible? This perennial problem of religious creed is now a worry for ecology. Roughly the same conditions that effect belief in a denominational god affect belief in any particular environment. Therefore, in a series of lectures on ecology, it is right for the social anthropologist to address this particular question. We should be concerned to know how beliefs arise and how they gain support. Tribal views of the environment hold up a mirror to ourselves. Putting ourselves in line with tribal societies, we can try to imagine the figure we would cut in the eyes of an anthropologist from Mars. From our own point of view he would take an agnostic stand. But today, to do justice to this lecture's subject, we should ourselves attempt the difficult trick of letting go of what we know about our environment – not forgetting it, but treating it as so much science fiction. Like the alien anthropologist, let us suspend belief for a little while, so as to confront a fundamental question about credibility.

We are far from being the first civilisation to realise that our environment is at risk. Most tribal environments are held to be in danger in much the same way as ours. The dangers are naturally not identical. Here and now we are concerned with overpopulation. Often they are worried by underpopulation. But we pin the responsibility in quite the same way as they do. Always and everywhere it is human folly, hate and greed which puts the human environment at risk. Unlike tribal society, we have the chance of self-awareness. Because we can set our own view in a general phenomenological perspective, just because we can compare our beliefs with theirs, we have an extra dimension of responsibility. Self-knowledge is a great burden. I shall be arguing that part of our current anxiety flows from loss of those very blinkering or filtering mechanisms which restrict perception of the sources of knowledge.

First, let us compare the ecology movement with others of historical times. An example that springs to mind is the movement for the abolition of slavery of a century ago. The abolitionists succeeded in revolutionising the image of man. In the same way, the ecology movement will succeed in changing the idea of nature. It will succeed in raising a tide of opinion that will put abuses of the environment under close surveillance. Strong sanctions against particular pollutions will come into force. It will succeed in these necessary changes for the same reason as the slavery abolition movement, partly because of its dedication and mostly because the time is ripe. In many countries in the nineteenth century slavery was becoming more costly than wage labour.[1] If this had not been the case, I doubt if that campaign would ever have got off the ground. Where locally it was not the case, all the arguments about brotherly love, Christianity and common humanity were of no avail. The Clapham Sect, I believe, abstained from sugar as a protest against plantation slavery. In the same spirit some of my friends have abstained from South African sherry. This is a less impressive sacrifice since there are other better sherries. But those of us who do not own a car will not end exhaust fume pollution any more than the Clapham Sect diminished by one whit the place of sugar in the native diet. The tide of opinion against slavery was not against industrial development. And the tide of opinion which will reduce the worst pollution effects will not stem industrialisation. Here is the crunch of the environmental problem that leads it far beyond the nuisance of water and air pollution and increasing noise. The ecologists have had to raise their sights to the global level. Their gloomy forecasts for the imminent end of our planet put us, the laymen, in the role of the helpless hero of a thriller. Several nasty deaths are in store for us. Time will reveal whether the earth will be burnt up by the unbalancing of its radiation budget, or whether a film of dust will blank out the sun's rays, or whether it will explode in an atomic war. Over-population and over-industrialisation are the twin causes. But herein lies the dilemma. The obviously overpopulated and starving masses are in the non-industrial regions. Their hope of food lies in new technological developments. But these come from the already industrial countries. Must we stop the growth of science which may one day feed the existing hungry? How do we control population anyway? And which ones should we start with? On a giant hoarding over the Chicago Expressway is a notice which says: 'Think before you litter.' A rather coarse expression, I thought, when I first assumed it to be family planning advice. But if I understand Dr Paul Ehrlich aright the anti-litter campaign could do well to take on the double objective, especially in Chicago. The starving millions of Asia are not the ones who own two cars, whose factories discharge effluents into lakes, or whose aeroplanes give off loud bangs. Ehrlich says: 'The birth of every American child is fifty times more of a disaster for the world than the birth of each Indian child. If you take consumption of steel as a measure of overall consumption, you find that the birth of each American child is 300 times more of a disaster for the world than the birth of each Indonesian child.'[2]

At the top global level the scientists speak with different voices, and none has a clear solution. This is the level at which we are free to believe or disbelieve. The scientists would not wish to be treated as so many old sandwich-men bearing placards which say: 'The end is near.' Our disbelief is just as much a problem for them as our gullibility. Therefore, whether their message is true or false, we are forced to study the basis of plausibility.

Another movement of ideas which this current ecology question recalls is the growth of classical economics. A realisation which transfixed thoughtful minds in the eighteenth century and onwards was that the market is a system with its own immutable laws. How can we appreciate the boldness of the illumination with which Ricardo discerned that system and its homeostatic tendencies? In our day and for this audience I can only hope to give an idea of the thrill of analysing its complexity, and the power and even sheer beauty of the system as it revealed itself, by reminding you of the excitement engendered in linguistics by Chomsky's revelation of the structural properties of language. But that is a very pale analogy. Consider how few political decisions are affected by linguistics compared with the implications of economic science. For the sake of that system and its unalterable laws, many good men have had to harden their hearts to the plight of paupers and unemployed. They were deeply convinced that much greater misery would befall if the system was not allowed to work out its due processes. In the same way, the ecologists have perceived system. In fact, their whole science consists in assuming system, reckoning inputs and outputs and assessing the factors making for equilibrium. The pitch of excitement in the ecological movement rises when the analysis is lifted to the level of whole continents and even to the level of this planet as a whole. In exactly the same way as the old economists, the ecologists find themselves demanding a certain toll of human suffering in the name of the system which, if disturbed, will loose unimaginable misery on the human race. Sometimes there is a question of bringing water a thousand miles to irrigate a desert. The ecologists know how to do it. They can easily make a desert blossom and so bring food and life to starving people. They hesitate to answer for the consequences in the area from which the water has been diverted. Their professional conscience bids them consider the system as a whole. In the same spirit as Ricardo deploring the effects of the Poor Laws, ecologists find themselves unwillingly drawn into negative, even reactionary positions.

These digressions into economics and slavery suggest a way of restricting somewhat the problem of credibility which is altogether too wide. It will be rewarding to watch how belief is committed along the bias towards or away from restriction. For ultimately this is it – restriction or controlled expansion? Which of us tend to believe the experts who warn that our system of resources is limited? And which of us optimistically follow those who teach that they cannot possibly tell yet what resources may lie unknown beneath the soil or in the sea or even in the air? And the same question about our own bias may be raised for the bias of the experts themselves.

Phenomenology, as I understand it, is concerned with what it is we believe we know about reality and with how we come to believe it. An anthropologist's survey of tribal environments is different from the ecologist's survey. Ecology imports objective measures from a scientific standpoint and describes in those terms the effects of the system of cultivation on the soil and of the soil on the crop yield, etc. It is concerned with interacting systems of physical realities. The anthropologist, if he is not lucky enough to have access to an ecological survey in his research area, has to make a rough dab at this kind of assessment and then use it to check with the tribe's own view of their environment. In this sense an anthropologist's survey of tribal environments is an exercise in phenomenology. Each tribe is found to inhabit a universe of its own, with its own laws and its own distinctive set of dangers which can be triggered off by incautious humans. It is almost as if there were no limit on the amount of variation two tribes can incorporate into their view of the same environment. Some objective limits must apply. Nevertheless, if we were to rely entirely on tribal assessments, we would get wildly incongruous views of what physical possibilities and constraints are in force.

For example, I worked in the Congo on the left bank of the Kasai river, among the Lele. On the other bank of the same river lived the Bushong, where my friend Ian Vansina worked a little later on. Here were two tribes, next-door neighbours, who celebrated their cold and hot seasons at opposite points in the calendar. When I first arrived, green to Africa, the Belgians said how wise I had been to arrive in the cold season: a newcomer, they said, would find the hot rainy season unbearable. In fact it was not a good time to arrive, because all the Lele were working flat out to clear the forest and fire the dead wood, and then to plant maize in the ash. No one but the very aged and the sick had time to talk to me and teach me the language, until the rains arrived and ended their period of heavy work. When I knew the language better, I learnt of a total discrepancy between the European and native assessment of the weather. The Lele regarded the short dry season as unbearably hot. They had their sayings and rules about how to endure its heat. 'Never strike a woman in the dry season', for example, 'or she will crumple up and die, because of the heat.' They longed for the first rains as relief from the heat. On the other bank of the Kasai, the Bushong agreed with the Belgians that the dry season was pleasantly cool and they dreaded the onset of the first rains. Fortunately the Belgians had made excellent meteorological records, and I found that in terms of solar radiation, diurnal and nocturnal temperatures, cloud cover, etc., there was very little objective difference that could entitle one season to be called strictly hotter than the other.[3] What the Europeans objected to, apparently, was the humidity of the wet season and the absence of cloud which exposed them directly to the rays of the sun. What the Lele suffered from in the dry season was the increased radiant heat which resulted from the heavy screen of clouds. They recognised and hated the famous glass-house effect that we are told will result from an excessive carbon dioxide screen for ourselves. But above all, the Lele time-table required them to do all their agricultural work in one short, sharp burst, in the dry season. The Bushong, across the river, with a more complex agricultural system, worked away steadily the whole year round. They also distinguished wet and dry seasons, but they concurred with the Europeans about the relative coolness of the dry period. How did the Europeans arrive at their assessment, since objectively there was so little to choose? No doubt because the seasons were named and their attributes set at Leopoldville, the capital, where temperature readings showed a difference between the seasons that did not obtain in the interior. In this example, credibility derives from social usage. If the Lele could have changed their time-table, their perception of their climate could have been altered. But so would a great deal else in their life. They were relatively backward technologically, compared with the Bushong. A different time-table, spreading their work through the calender and through the whole population, would have greatly bettered their exploitation of their environment. But for such a fundamental revolution they would have had to create a different society.

Time-tables are near the heart of our problem in the phenomenology of environments. Andrew Baring, in studying a Sudanese people, tells one that their mythology is full of dynastic crises, plots, unrest and revolution. Whenever discontent reaches boiling-point in the myth cycle, a new king takes over the palace. The upstart always shows his administrative flair by changing the times of meals. Then the discontent simmers down and all is well until something goes wrong again with the order of day in the royal household. Then the stage is set for a new dynastic upheaval and a new king to settle the time-table problem afresh. Largely, the doom ecologists are trying to convince us about a kind of time-bomb. Time is running out, they say. Whenever I suggested to the Lele small capital-intensive projects that would improve their hunting or the comfort of their houses, they would answer 'No time'. The allocation of time is a vital determinant of how a given environment is managed. It is also true that time perspective held by an expert determines what answer he will give to a technical problem. Therefore, we should start our discussion of how credibility is engendered by considering the time-dimension.

Among verbal weapons of control, time is one of the four final arbiters. Time, money, God, and nature, usually in that order, are universal trump cards plunked down to win an argument. I have no doubt that our earliest cave ancestress heard the same, when she wanted a new skirt or breakfast in bed. First 'There wouldn't be time', and then, 'We couldn't afford it anyway'. If she still seemed to hanker: 'God doesn't like that sort of thing'. Finally, if she were even prepared to snap her fingers at God, the ace card: 'It's against nature, and what is more, your children will suffer'. It is a strong hand when the same player, by holding all these cards, can represent God and nature, as well as control the time-table and the bank account. Then the time-scale, as presented by that player in control, is entirely credible.

It is only just beginning to be appreciated how much the perception of time-scale is the result of bargaining about goals and procedures. For a touching insight, read Julius A. Roth's little book *Timetables, Structuring the Passage of Time in Hospital Treatment and Other Careers*.[4] Here he describes the attempts of long-term patients in a T.B. hospital to get some satisfactory response out of their doctors. Spontaneously and inevitably the clash of interests expressed itself in a battle about the time-tabling of diagnosis and treatment. For the patient, his whole life is held in suspense, no plans can be made, no sense of progress enjoyed until he knows when he can go home. His anxiety concentrates in a passionate study of the time-scaling of the disease and its treatment. With no means of extracting from them any clue to his central preoccupations, and no sanctions to employ to enforce their collaboration, the patient would try to impose on the medical staff a kind of natural time-table. 'I've been here six months now, doctor, by this time you ought to have decided whether I need surgery.' 'Massey got a pass after only three months here – why can't I?' 'Hayton got discharged three months after surgery – why should I have to wait four months?' The doctors' strategy is evasive. They consistently reject the very idea of a rigid time-table, and struggle to refute the culture of the ward where patients go on working out a clear set of phases by which they judge the competence of the doctors and the course of their illness. Sometimes if the doctor does not seem to accept these spontaneously emerging laws of disease and treatment, the patient discharges himself, feeling that the basis of mutual understanding has failed.

The Lele afford another example of how time-tabling is used as a weapon of control. They think that they can do something to bring on the rains. This technique of weather control was not a rain-dance, or a magic spell. It was something which any individual might do, with the effect of hastening the onset of the rainy season. The belief in its effectiveness became an instrument for mutual coercion. Laggard farmers would beg others to wait until they had had time to clear their fields and burn the wood. The punctual ones would warn them to hurry up, lest the rain be provoked by action in the north. It seemed to me, sceptical as I was of the value of their technique, exactly like the departmental head who creates artificial deadlines to hasten decisions or otherwise keep his staff on their toes. 'I can only vouch for the students' reaction if we get our policy settled by the next meeting.' Much later I learnt that the Lele techniques of seeding the clouds by the smoke of their burning forests might indeed be effective. Air pollution can increase condensation and precipitation of moisture. It seems that a district in Indiana, thirty miles downwind of South Chicago's smoky steelworks, tends to have 31 per cent more rain than other communities where the air is clearer.[5] The joke was on me that the Lele weather control turned out to be scientifically respectable. For the purpose of my present argument, its efficacy is irrelevant. All that matters is that time is a set of manipulable boundaries. Time is like all the other doom points in the universe. One and all are social weapons of control. Reference to their power sustains a view of the social system. Their influence is thoroughly conservative. For no one can wield the doom points credibly in an argument who is not backed by the majority view of how the society should be run. Credibility depends so much on the consensus of a moral community that it is hardly an exaggeration to say that a given community lays on for itself the sum of the physical conditions which it experiences. I give two well-known examples.

In many tribal societies it is widely agreed that wives should be faithful to their husbands. Women probably concur in that ideal, and they would perhaps like to add to it that husbands should be equally faithful to their wives. However, the latter view does not obtain whole-hearted male support. Therefore, since the men are the dominant sex, to sustain their view of sexual morality they need to find in nature a sanction which will enforce the chastity of wives without involving male infidelity. The solution has been to fasten on a natural danger to which only female physiology is exposed. Hence we find very commonly the idea that miscarriage is due to adultery. What a weapon that provides: the woman tempted to adultery knows that her unborn baby is at risk, and her own life too. Sometimes she is taught that the health of her older children will also suffer.[6] What a paraphernalia of confession and cleansing and compensation attends the guilty mother in her labour. What she has done is against nature and nature will retaliate.

For a different example – a warlike tribe of Plains Indians, the Cheyenne, believes that murder of a fellow tribesman is the ultimate wickedness. The tribe used to depend on wandering herds of bison for its food. The bison, it was thought, did not react to the murder of men of other tribes. The bison were not affected by ordinary homicide as such. But a fratricide emitted a putrid stink which frightened off the herd and so put the vital resources of the tribe at risk. This danger from the environment justified special sanctions to outlaw the murderer.[7]

When homicide and adultery are seen to be triggering agents for danger points in a physical environment, the tribal view of nature begins to emerge as a coherent principle of social control. Red in tooth and claw, perhaps, but nature responds in a highly moral and avenging form of aggression. It is on the side of the constitution, motherhood, brotherly love, and it is against human wickedness.

When I first wrote *Purity and Danger* about this moral power in the tribal environment, I thought our own knowledge of the physical environment was different.[8] I now believe this to have been mistaken. If only because they disagree, we are free to select which of our scientists we will harken to, and our selection is subject to the same sociological analysis as that of any tribe.

We find that in tribal society certain classes of people are liable to be classed as polluters. These classes are not the same for all tribes. In some social structures the polluters will be one type, in others another. Imagine a tribal insurance company which set out to cover people against the risk of being accused of causing pollution. Their market researchers and surveyors should be able to work out where they should charge the highest premiums in any particular social system. In some societies the elite possessors of esoteric knowledge are certain to be charged with owning too much science and misapplying it to selfish ends. Sorcery charges against big operators in New Guinea or against cunning old polygamists among the Lele can be paralleled by our own charges against big business polluting lakes and rivers and poisoning the children's food and air for their commercial profit. The Lele shared with other Congolese tribes an acute anxiety about their population. They believed themselves to be dying out because of malicious attacks by sorcerers against the fertility of women and on their lack of babies. They continually said that their numbers had declined because of jealousy. 'Look around you,' a man said to me on this theme, 'do you see any people?

Do you see children?' I looked about. A handful of children played at our feet and a few people sat around. 'Yes,' I said, 'I see people and children.' 'Look again,' he said, disgusted with my missing the cue. 'There are no people here, no children.' His question had been couched in the rhetorical style expecting the answer 'No'. It took me a long time to learn the tonal pattern which should have led our dialogue to run in this way[9]:

'Look around you! Do you see any people? Tell me – do you?'

Emphatic answer: 'No!'

'Do you see any children? Tell me, do you?'

Emphatic answer: 'No!' Then his answer would come: 'See how we have been finished off. No one is left now, we are destroyed utterly. It's jealousy that destroys us.' For him, the sorcerer's sinful lore was as destructive as for us the science that serves military and business interests with chemical weapons and pesticides.

In another type of society the probability of being accused of pollution will fall on paupers and second-class citizens of various types. Paupers I define as those who, by falling below a required level of achievement, are not able to enter into exchanges of gifts, services and hospitality. They find themselves not only excluded from the main responsibilities and pleasures of citizenship but a charge upon the community. They are a source of embarrassment to their more prosperous fellows and a living contradiction to any current theories about the equality of man. In tribal societies, wherever such a possibility exists, these unfortunates are likely to be credited with warped emotions. By and large they may be called witches, and risk being accused of causing the natural disasters which other people suffer. Somehow they must be eliminated, controlled and stopped from multiplying. If you want to intuit from our own culture how such accusations of witchcraft gain plausibility I recommend you to attend a conference of professional social workers. Over and over again you will hear the objects of the social workers' concern being described as 'non-coping'. The explanation given for their non-coping is widely attributed to their having 'inadequate personalities'. In something of this way, landless clients in the Mandari tribe are said by their patrons to have a hereditary witchcraft streak which makes them vicious and jealous.[10] The fact that they are emotionally warped justifies their fellow-men in withholding the liberties and protections of citizenship.

As for females, in all these societies and anywhere that male dominance is an important value, women are likely to be accused of causing dangerous pollution by their very presence when they invade the men's sphere. I have written enough about female pollution in *Purity and Danger*.

It should be clear now that credibility for any view of how the environment will react is secured by the moral commitment of a community to a particular set of institutions. Nothing will overthrow their beliefs if the institutions which the beliefs support command their loyalty. Nothing is easier than to change the beliefs (overnight!) if the institutions have lost support. If we could finish classifying the kinds of people and kinds of behaviour which pollute the tribal universes we would have performed an ecological exercise. For it would become clear that the view of the universe and a particular kind of society holding this view are closely interdependent. They are a single system. Neither can exist without the other. Tribal peoples who worship their dead ancestors often explicitly recognise that each ancestor only exists in so far as cult is paid to him. When the cult stops, the ancestor has no more credibility. He fades away, unable to intervene, either to punish angrily, or to reward kindly. We should entertain the same insight about any given environment we know. It exists as a structure of meaningful distinctions. In so far as it is only knowable by the powers attributed to it and the practical action taken in its regard, and in so far as its powers are evoked as techniques of mutual control, a known environment is as fragile as any ancestor. While a limited social reality and a local physical environment are meshed together in a single experience, there is perfect credibility for both. But if the society falls apart, and separate voices claim to know about different environmental constraints, then do credibility problems arise.

At this point I should correct some possible false impressions. I have tried to avoid examples which lend themselves to a skull-duggery, conspiracy theory of how the environment is constructed in people's minds. There is no possibility of one group conning another about what nature will stand for, and what is against nature. I certainly would not imply that fears of world overpopulation are spread by frustrated car-owners in the commuter belt who would like a clear run from Surrey to the City. I would not imply that residents on the south coast press for legislation to control population because they know there is no hope of legislating specifically to summer crowds from the seaside. But their personal experience could make them lend a friendlier ear to those demographers who are most gloomy about population increase, and ignore the optimistic ones. It obviously suits Lele men and Cheyenne men to teach that the physiology of childbirth and the physiology of the wild bison respond to moral situations. But no one can impose a moral view of physical nature on another person who does not share the same moral assumptions. If Lele wives did not believe in married fidelity as a part of the social order they might be more sceptical about an idea which suits husbands extremely well. Because all Cheyenne endorse the idea that murder in the tribe is disastrous they can believe that bison are sensitive to its smell. The common commitment to a set of social meanings makes inferences about the response of nature plausible.

Another misunderstanding concerns the distinction between true and false ideas about the environment. I repeat the invitation to approach this subject in a spirit of science fiction. The scientists find out true, objective things about physical nature. The human society invests these findings with social meaning and constructs a systematic time-tabled view of the way that human behaviour and physical nature interact. But I fear that it is an illusion if scientists hope one day to set out a true, systematic, objective view of that interaction. And so it is also illusory to hope for a society whose fears of pollution rest entirely on the scientists' teaching and carry no load of social and moral persuasion. We cannot hope to develop an idea of our environment which has pollution ideas only in the scientists' sense, and none which, in that strict sense, are false. Pollution ideas, however they arise, are the necessary support for a social system. How else can people induce each other to cooperate and behave if they cannot threaten with time, money, God and nature? These moral imperatives arise from social intercourse. They draw on a view of the environment to support a social order. As normative principles they have an adaptive function. Each society adapts itself to its habitat by precisely these means. Telling each other that there is no time, that we can't afford it, that God wouldn't like it and that it is against nature and our children will suffer, these are the means by which we adapt our society to our environment, and it to ourselves. In the process our physical possibilities are limited and extended in this way and that, so that there is a real ecological interaction. The concepts of time, money, God and nature do for human society the adaptive work which is done non-verbally (but otherwise probably by very similar means) in animal society.

I have spoken of pollution ideas which are used by people as controls on themselves and on each other. In this light they seem to be weapons or instruments. However, there is another fundamental aspect of the subject. Pollution ideas draw their power from our own intellectual constitution. Impossible here to describe the learning process by which each individual works out a set of expectations, and derives rules which guide him in his behaviour. The beliefs that there are rules and that future experience is expected to confirm to them underlies social intercourse. There is some fascinating experimental work on this aspect of behaviour by American sociologists. However faulty our probings and conclusions may be, we assume a rule-obeying, stable environment. We expect, as we learn a fairly satisfactory set of rules, that the *et cetera* principle can be left to look after the known. The *et cetera* principle is like the automatic pilot which, once the controls are fixed, will keep the plane on course. *Etcetera, etcetera.* Finding rules that work is satisfying as it allows us to suppose that more of the machine can be turned over to the automatic pilot to look after. Discovering a whole system that works is exciting because it suggests an even greater saving of *ad hoc* painful blundering. Hence the emotional response to discovering that market prices work as a system, or that language or mythology has a systematic element.

The deepest emotional investment of all is in the assumption that there is a rule-obeying universe, and that its rules are objective, independent of social validation. Hence the most odious pollutions are those which threaten to attack a system at its intellectual base. The system itself rests on a number of unchallengeable classifications. One of the well-known examples in anthropology is that of the Eskimo girl in Labrador who would persistently eat caribou meat after winter had begun.[11] A trivial breach of an abstinence rule, it seems to us. But by a unanimous verdict, she was banished in midwinter for committing what was judged to be a capital offence. These Eskimo have constructed a society whose fundamental category is the distinction of the two seasons. People born in winter are distinguished from those born in summer. Each of the two seasons has a special kind of domestic arrangement, a special seasonal economy, a separate legal practice, almost a distinct religion. The regularity of Eskimo life depends upon the observances connected with each season. Winter hunting equipment is kept apart from summer equipment, summer tents are hidden in winter. No one should touch the skins of animals classed as summer game in winter. As Marcel Mauss put it, 'even in the stomachs of the faithful' salmon, a summer fish, should have no contact with the sea animals of the winter.[12] By disregarding these distinctive categories the girl was committing a wrong against the social system in its fundamental form. A lack of seriousness about the categories of thought was not the reason given for why she was condemned to die by freezing. She had to die because she had committed a dangerous pollution which set everyone's livelihood at risk. Contrast this sharp categorisation and this cruel punishment for contempt with the Eskimo experience of the last millennium. Here is a civilisation which has seen precisely what may well be in store for us, a slow but steady worsening of the environment. Are we going to react, as doom draws near, with rigid applications of the principles out of which our intellectual system has been spun? It is horribly likely that, along with the Eskimo, we will concentrate on eliminating and controlling the polluters. It might be a more worthwhile recourse to think afresh about our environment in a way which was not possible for the Eskimo level of scientific advance. Nor is it only scientific advance which lies in our grasp. We have the chance of understanding our own behaviour.

If the study of pollution ideas teaches us anything it is that, taken too much at face value, such fears tend to mask other wrongs and dangers. For example, take the population problem. A straight response to pollution fears suggests we should urgently try to control population. The question is treated in an unimaginative and mechanical way. It is made a matter of spreading information and making available contraceptive devices. At first, people's eagerness to use them is taken for granted, but soon the clinics report apathy, carelessness, lack of determination, lack of agreement between husbands and wives. Then the question moves from voluntary to automatic methods such as sterilisation or compulsion by law. We are almost back to 'Think before you litter' and forcible control of animal populations. But if we were to learn from biologists, Wynne-Edwards' work on animal populations has many a moral for the demographer.[13] In some human societies social factors encourage the voluntary control of family size. Not all tribes tolerate unlimited expansion of their numbers. It cannot be ignored that the world demographic problem is an Us/Them situation. Even in Ricardo's day it was They, the labourers, whose improvident fecundity created the pressure on resources, while We, the rich, could be relied on to procreate more cautiously. And today it is We, the rich nations, who wag our fingers at Them, the poor ones, with their astronomical annual increase. Somewhere a social problem about the distribution of prestige and power underlies the stark demographic facts. Let us not miss the lessons of this confrontation with biology and anthropology.

In essence, pollution ideas are adaptive and protective. They protect a social system from unpalatable knowledge. They protect a system of ideas from challenge. The ideas rest on classification. Ultimately any forms of knowledge depend on principles of classification. But these principles arise out of social experience, sustain a given social pattern and themselves are sustained by it. If this guideline and base is grossly disturbed, knowledge itself is at risk.

In a sense the obvious risk to the environment is a distraction. The ecologists are indeed looking into an abyss. But on the other side another abyss yawns as frighteningly. This is the terror of intellectual chaos and blind panic. Pollution is the black side of Plato's good lie[14] on which society must rest: it is the other half of the necessary confidence trick. We should be able to see that we can never ask for a future society in which we can only believe in real, scientifically proved pollution dangers. We *must* talk threateningly about time, money, God and nature if we hope to get anything done. We must believe in the limitations and boundaries of nature which our community projects.

Here we return to the comparison with the classical economists and the slavery abolitionists. It would be good to know which of our experts is likely to take a restrictive view of the environment, certain that time, money, God and nature are against change, and which of them is likely to favour expansionary policies. It is easy to see why the laymen can't lift their noses above the immediate horizon. The layman tends to assimilate the total planetary environmental problems to his own immediate ones. His horizon is his back yard. For the scientists, as well as this same tendency, there is another source of bias. To understand a system – any system – is a joy in itself. The more that is known about it the more the specialist is aware of its intricacies, and the more wary he is of the complex disturbances which can result from ignorance. The specialist thus has an emotional investment in his own system. As Professor Kuhn has said, in his *The Structure of Scientific Revolutions*,[15] scientists rarely change their views, they merely retire or die away. If there are to be solutions to a grave problem, they will come from the fringes of the profession, from the amateur even, or from those areas of knowledge in which two or three specialisms meet. This is comforting. In the long run, if there is a long run, unless the man in the street specially wants to choose the pessimistic restrictionist view on any ecological problem, he can wait and see. The scientific establishment has its own structure of stability and challenge. Our responsibility as laymen and as social scientists is to probe deeper into the sources of our own bias. Suppose we are really set for the worst terrors that the ecologists can predict. How shall we comport ourselves?

Our worst problem is the lack of moral consensus which gives credibility to warnings of danger. This partly explains why we fail so often to give proper heed to the ecologists. At the same time, for lack of a discriminating principle, we easily become overwhelmed by our pollution fears. Community endows its environment with credibility. Without community, unclassified rubbish mounts up, poisons fill the air and water, food is contaminated, eyesores block the skyline. Flooding in through all our senses, pollution destroys our well-being. Witches and devils ensnare us. Any tribal culture selects this and that danger to fear and sets up demarcation lines to control it. It allows people to live contentedly with a hundred other dangers which ought to terrify them out of their wits. The discriminating principles come from social structure. An unstructured society leaves us prey to every dread. As all the veils are successively ripped away, there is no right or wrong. Relativism is the order of the day. I myself have tried to join the work of taking down some of the veils. We have adopted first this standpoint, then that, seen tribal society from within and from without, seen ourselves as the scientists see us or from the stance of the anthropologist from Mars. This is the invitation to full self-consciousness that is offered in our time. We must accept it. But we should do so knowing that the price is William Burroughs' *Naked Lunch*.[16] The day when everyone can see exactly what it is on the end of everyone's fork, on that day there is no pollution and no purity and nothing edible or inedible, credible or incredible, because the classifications of social life are gone. There is no more meaning. Neither melancholic madness nor mystic ecstasy, the two modes in which boundaries are dispensed, can accept the other invitation of our time. The other task is to recognise each environment as a mask and support for a certain kind of society.

It is the value of this social form which demands our scrutiny just as clearly as the purity of milk and air and water.

1. JOHN HICKS (1969) *A Theory of Economic History*, London, pp. 122-40.
2. PAUL EHRLICH (1970) *The Listener*, 30 Aug., 215.
3. MARY DOUGLAS (1962) 'The Lele, Resistance to Change' in *Markets in Africa*, ed. Bohannan and Dalton, Evanston, Ill.
4. JULIUS A. ROTH (1963) *Timetables, Structuring the Passage of Time in Hospital Treatment and other Careers*, New York.
5. ERIC AYNSLEY (1969) 'How air pollution alters weather', *New Scientist*, 9 Oct., pp. 66-7.
6. MARY DOUGLAS (1963) *The Lele of the Kasai*, International African Institute, Oxford, p. 51.
7. E. A. HOEBEL (1960) *The Cheyennes, Indians of the Great Plains*, New York, p. 51.
8. MARY DOUGLAS (1966) *Purity and Danger, An Analysis of Concepts of Pollution and Tabu*, London.
9. —— (1950) 'Elicited responses in Lele language', *Kongo-Overzee*, **xvi**, 4, 224-7.
10. JEAN BUXTON (1963) 'Mandari Witchcraft', in *Witchcraft and Sorcery in East Africa*, ed. Middleton and Edward Winter, London.
11. E. A. HOEBEL (1954) *The Law of Primitive Man: A Study in Comparative Legal Dynamics*, Harvard.
12. MARCEL MAUSS AND M. H. BEUCHAT, 'Essai sur les variations saisonnières des sociétés Eskimos', *L'Année Sociologique*, **9** (1904-5), 39-132.
13. V. C. WYNNE-EDWARDS (1962) *Animal Dispersion in Relation to Social Behaviour*, Edinburgh and New York.
14. PLATO, *The Republic*, 376-92.
15. T. S. KUHN (1962) *The Structure of Scientific Revolutions*, Chicago.
16. WILLIAM BURROUGHS (1962) *The Naked Lunch*, New York; London (1965).

9

IDEAS OF NATURE

RAYMOND WILLIAMS

ONE touch of nature may make the whole world kin, but usually, when we say nature, do we mean to include men? I know some people would say that the other kind of nature – trees, hills, brooks, animals – has a kindly effect. But I've noticed that they then often contrast it with the world of men and relationships.

I begin from this ordinary problem of meaning and reference because I want this enquiry to be active, and because I intend an emphasis when I say that the idea of nature contains, though often unnoticed, an extraordinary amount of human history. Like some other fundamental ideas which express man's vision of himself and his place in the world, nature has a nominal continuity, over many centuries, but can be seen, in analysis, to be both complicated and changing, as other ideas and experiences change. I've previously attempted to analyse some comparable ideas, critically and historically. Among them were culture, society, individual, class, art, tragedy. But I'd better say at the outset that, difficult as all those ideas are, the idea of nature makes them seem comparatively simple. It has been central, over a very long period, to many different kinds of thought. Moreover it has some quite radical difficulties at the very first stages of its expression: difficulties which seem to me to persist.

Some people, when they see a word, think the first thing to do is to define it. Dictionaries are produced, and, with a show of authority no less confident because it is usually so limited in place and time, what is called a proper meaning is attached. But while it may be possible to do this, more or less satisfactorily, with certain simple names of things and effects, it is not only impossible but irrelevant in the case of more complicated ideas. What matters in them is not the proper meaning but the history and complexity of meanings: the conscious changes, or consciously different uses: and just as often those changes and differences which, masked by a nominal continuity, come to express radically different and often at first unnoticed changes in experience and in history. I'd then better say at once that any reasonably complete analysis of these changes in the idea of nature would be very far beyond the scope of a lecture, but I want to try to indicate some of the main points, the general outlines, of such an analysis, and to see what effects these may have on some of our contemporary arguments and concerns.

The central point of the analysis, as it seems to me, can be expressed at once, in the singular formation of the term. As I understand it, we have here a case of a definition of quality which becomes, through real usage, based on certain assumptions, a description of the world. Some of the early linguistic history is difficult to interpret, but we still have, as in the very early uses, these two very different bearings. I can perhaps illustrate them from a well-known passage in Burke:

> In a state of *rude* nature there is no such thing as a people. . . . The idea of a people is the idea of a corporation. It is wholly artificial; and made, like all other legal fictions, by common agreement. What the particular nature of that agreement was, is collected from the form into which the particular society has been cast.

Perhaps *rude*, there, makes some slight difference, but what is most striking is the coexistence of that common idea, *a state of nature*, with the almost unnoticed, because so habitual, use of *nature* to indicate the inherent quality of the agreement. That sense of nature as the inherent and essential quality of any particular thing is, of course, much more than accidental. Indeed there is evidence that it is historically the earliest use. In Latin one would have said *natura rerum*, keeping nature to the essential quality and adding the definition of things. But then also in Latin *natura* came to be used on its own, to express the same general meaning: the essential constitution of the world. Many of the earliest speculations about nature seem to have been in this sense physical, but with the underlying assumption that in the course of the physical enquiries one was discovering the essential inherent and indeed immutable laws of the world. The association and then the fusion of a name for the quality with a name for the things observed has a precise history. It is a central formation of idealist thought. What was being looked for in nature was an essential principle. The multiplicity of things, and of living processes, might then be mentally organised around a single essence or principle: a nature.

Now I would not want to deny, I would prefer to emphasise that this singular abstraction was a major advance in consciousness. But I think we have got so used to it, in a nominal continuity over more than two millennia, that we may not always realise quite all that it commits us to. A singular name for the real multiplicity of things and living processes may be held, with an effort, to be neutral, but I am sure it is very often the case that it offers, from the beginning, a dominant kind of interpretation: idealist, metaphysical, or religious. And I think this is especially apparent if we look at its subsequent history. From many early cultures we have records of what we would now call nature spirits or nature gods: beings believed to embody or direct the wind or the sea or the forest or the moon. Under the weight of Christian interpretation we are accustomed to calling these gods or spirits pagan: diverse and variable manifestations before the revelation of the one true God. But just as in religion the moment of monotheism is a critical development, so, in human responses to the physical world, is the moment of a singular Nature.

SINGULAR, ABSTRACTED AND PERSONIFIED

When Nature herself, as people learnt to say, became a goddess, a divine Mother, we had something very different from the spirits of wind and sea and forest and moon. And it is all the more striking that this singular abstracted and often personified principle, based on responses to the physical world, had of course (if the expression may be allowed) a competitor, in the singular abstracted and personified religious being: the monotheistic God. The history of that interaction is immense. In the orthodox western medieval world a general formula was arrived at, which preserved the singularity of both: God is the first absolute, but Nature is his minister and deputy. As in many other treaties, this relationship went on being controversial. There was a long argument, preceding the revival of systematic physical enquiry – what we should now call science – as to the propriety and then the mode of this enquiry into a minister, with the obvious question of whether the ultimate sovereignty was being infringed or shown insufficient respect. It is an old argument now, but it is interesting that when it was revived in the nineteenth century, in the arguments about evolution, even men who were prepared to dispense with the first singular principle – to dispense with the idea of God – usually retained and even emphasised that other and very comparable principle: the singular and abstracted, indeed still often and in some new ways personified, Nature.

Perhaps this does not puzzle others as much as it puzzles me. But I might mention at this stage one of its evident practical effects. In some serious argument, but even more in popular controversy and in various kinds of contemporary rhetoric, we continually come across propositions of the form 'Nature is . . .', or 'Nature shows . . .', or 'Nature teaches . . .'. And what is usually apparent about what is then said is that it is selective, according to the speaker's general purpose. 'Nature is . . .' – what? Red in tooth and claw; a ruthlessly competitive struggle for existence; an extraordinary interlocking system of mutual advantage; a paradigm of interdependence and cooperation.

And 'Nature is' any one of these things according to the processes we select: the food-chain, dramatised as the shark or the tiger; the jungle of plants competing for space and light and air; or the pollinator – the bee and the butterfly – or the symbiote and the parasite; even the scavenger, the population controller, the regulator of food supplies. In what is now seen so often as the physical crisis of our world many of us follow, with close attention, the latest reports from those who are observing and qualified to observe these particular processes and effects, these creatures and things and acts and consequences. And I am prepared to believe that one or other of the consequent generalisations may be more true than the rest, may be a better way of looking at the processes in which we also are involved and on which we can be said to depend. But I am bound to say I would feel in closer touch with the real situation if the observations, made with great skill and precision, were not so speedily gathered – I mean, of course, at the level of necessary generalisation – into singular statements of essential, inherent and immutable characteristics; into principles of a singular nature. I have no competence to speak directly of any of these processes, but to put it as common experience: when I hear that nature is a ruthless competitive struggle I remember the butterfly, and when I hear that it is a system of ultimate mutual advantage I remember the cyclone. Intellectual armies may charge each other repeatedly with this or that selected example; but my own inclination is to ponder the effects of the idea they share: that of a singular and essential nature, with consistent and reconcilable laws. Indeed I find myself reflecting at this point on the full meaning of what I began by saying: that the idea of nature contains an extraordinary amount of human history. What is often being argued, it seems to me, in the idea of nature is the idea of man; and this not only generally, or in ultimate ways, but the idea of man in society, indeed the ideas of kinds of societies.

For that nature was made singular and abstract, and was personified, has at least this convenience: that it allows us to look, with unusual clarity, at some quite fundamental interpretations of all our experience. Nature may indeed be a single thing or a force or a principle, but then what these are has a real history. I have already mentioned Nature the minister of God. To know Nature was to know God, although there was radical controversy about the means of knowing: whether by faith, by speculation, by right reason, or by physical enquiry and experiment. But Nature the minister or deputy was preceded and has been widely succeeded by Nature the absolute monarch. This is characteristic of certain phases of fatalism, in many cultures and periods. It is not that Nature is unknowable: as subjects we know our monarch. But his powers are so great, and their exercise at times so apparently capricious, that we make no pretensions to control. On the contrary we confine ourselves to various forms of petition or appeasement: the prayer against storm or for rain; the superstitious handling or abstention from handling of this or that object; the sacrifice for fertility or the planting of parsley on Good Friday. As so often, there is an indeterminate area between this absolute monarch and the more manageable notion of God's minister. An uncertainty of purpose is as evident in the personified Nature as in the personified God: is he provident or absolute, settled or capricious? Everyone says that in the medieval world there was a conception or order which reached through every part of the universe, from the highest to the lowest: a divine order, of which the laws of nature were the practical expression. Certainly this was often believed and perhaps even more often taught. In Henry Medwall's play *Nature* or in Rastell's *The Four Elements*, nature instructs man in his duties, under the eye of God; he can find his own nature and place from the instructions of nature. But in plague or famine, in what can be conveniently called not natural laws but natural catastrophes, the very different figure of the absolute and capricious monarch can be seen appearing, and the form of the struggle between a jealous God and a just God is very reminiscent of the struggle in men's minds between the real experiences of a provident and a destructive 'nature'. Many scholars believe that this conception of a natural order lasted into and dominated the Elizabethan and early Jacobean world, but what is striking in Shakespeare's *Lear*, for example, is the uncertainty of the meaning of 'nature':

> Allow not nature more than nature needs,
> Man's life's as cheap as beast's . . .
> . . . one daughter
> Who redeems nature from the general curse
> Which twain have brought her to.
>
> That nature, which contemns its origin,
> Cannot be border'd certain in itself . . .
>
> . . . All shaking thunder . . .
> Crack nature's moulds, all germens spill at once,
> That make ungrateful man . . .
>
> . . . Hear, nature hear; dear goddess, hear . . .

In just these few examples, we have a whole range of meanings: from nature as the primitive condition before human society; through the sense of an original innocence from which there has been a fall and a curse, requiring redemption; through the special sense of a quality of birth, as in the Latin root; through again the sense of the forms and moulds of nature which can yet, paradoxically, be destroyed by the natural force of thunder; to that simple and persistent form of the personified goddess, Nature herself. John Danby's analysis of the meanings of 'nature' in *Lear* shows an even wider range.

And what in the history of thought may be seen as a confusion or an overlapping is often the precise moment of the dramatic impulse, when it is because the meanings and the experiences are uncertain and complex that the dramatic mode is more powerful, includes more, than could any narrative or exposition: not the abstracted order, though its forms are still present, but at once the order, the known meanings, and that experience of order and meanings which is at the very edge of the intelligence and the senses, a complex interaction which is the new and dramatic form. All at once nature is innocent, is unprovided, is sure, is unsure, is fruitful, is destructive, is a pure force and is tainted and cursed. I can think of no better contrast to the mode of the singular meaning, which is the more accessible history of the idea.

Yet the simplifying ideas continued to emerge. God's deputy, or the absolute monarch (and real absolute monarchs were also, at least in the image, the deputies of God) were succeeded by that Nature which, at least in the educated world, dominates seventeenth- to nineteenth-century European thought. It is a less grand, less imposing figure: in fact, a constitutional lawyer. Though lip-service is still often paid to the original giver of the laws (and in some cases, we need not doubt, it was more than lip-service), all practical attention is given to the details of the laws: to interpreting and classifying them, making predictions from precedents, discovering or reviving forgotten statutes, and then and most critically shaping new laws from new cases: the laws of nature in this quite new constitutional sense, not so much shaping and essential ideas but an accumulation and classification of cases.

THE NEW IDEA OF EVOLUTION

The power of this new emphasis hardly needs to be stressed. Its practicality and its detail had quite transforming results in the world. In its increasing secularism, indeed naturalism, it sometimes managed to escape the habit of singular personification, and nature, though often still singular, became an object, even at times a machine. In its earlier phases the sciences of this emphasis were predominantly physical: that complex of mathematics, physics, astronomy which was called natural philosophy. What was classically observed was a fixed state, or fixed laws of motion. The laws of nature were indeed constitutional, but unlike most real constitutions they had no effective history. In the life sciences the emphasis was on constitutive properties, and significantly, on classifications of orders. What changed this emphasis was of course the evidence and the idea of evolution: natural forms had not only a constitution but a history. From the late eighteenth century, and very markedly in the nineteenth century, the consequent personification of nature changed. From the underlying image of the constitutional lawyer, men moved to a different figure: the selective breeder; Nature the selective breeder. Indeed the habit of personification, which except in rather formal uses had been visibly weakening, was very strongly revived by this new concept of an actively shaping, indeed intervening, force. Natural Selection could be interpreted either way, with natural as a simple unemphatic description of a process, or with the implication of a nature, a specific force, which could do something as conscious as select. There are other reasons, as we shall see, for the vigour of the late eighteenth-century and nineteenth-century personifications, but this new emphasis, that nature itself had a history, and so might be seen as an historical, perhaps the historical force, was another major moment in the development of ideas.

It is already evident, if we look only at some of the great personifications or quasi-personifications, that the question of what is covered by nature, what it is held to include, is critical. There can be shifts of interest between the physical and the organic world, and indeed the distinction between these is one of the forms of the shaping enquiry. But the most critical question, in this matter of scope, was whether nature included man. It was, after all, a main factor in the evolution controversy: whether man could be properly seen in terms of strictly natural processes; whether he could be described, for example, in the same terms as animals. Though it now takes different forms, I think this question remains critical, and this is so for discoverable reasons in the history of the idea.

In the orthodox medieval concept of nature, man was, of course, included. The order of nature, which expressed God's creation, included, as a central element, the notion of hierarchy: man had a precise place in the order of creation, even though he was constituted from the universal elements which constituted nature as a whole. Moreover, this inclusion was not merely passive. The idea of a place in the order implied a destiny. The constitution of nature declared its purpose. By knowing the whole world, beginning with the four elements, man would come to know his own important place in it, and the definition of this importance was in discovering his relation to God.

Yet there is all the difference in the world between an idealist notion of a fixed nature, embodying permanent laws, and the same apparent notion with the idea of a future, a destiny, as the most fundamental law of them all. The latter, to put it mildly, is less likely to encourage physical enquiry as a priority; the purpose of the laws, and hence their nature, is already known: that is to say, assumed. And it is then not surprising that it is the bad angel who says, in Marlowe:

> Go forward, Faustus, in that famous art
> Wherein all Nature's treasure is contained.

What was worrying, obviously, was that in his dealings with nature man might see himself as

> Lord and Commander of these elements.

It was a real and prolonged difficulty:

> Nature that framed us of four elements
> Warring within our breasts for regiment
> Doth teach us all to have aspiring minds.

But though this might be so, aspiration was ambiguous: either to aspire to know the order of nature, or to know how to intervene in it, become its commander; or, putting it another way, whether to learn one's important place in the order of nature, or learn how to surpass it. It can seem an unreal argument. For many millennia men had been intervening, had been learning to control. From the beginning of farming and the domestication of animals this had been consciously done, quite apart from the many secondary consequences as men pursued what they thought of as their normal activities.

THE ABSTRACTION OF MAN

It is now well enough known that as a species we grew in confidence in our desire and in our capacity to intervene. But we cannot understand this process, indeed cannot even describe it, until we are clear as to what the idea of nature includes, and in particular whether it includes man. For, of course, to speak of man 'intervening' in natural processes is to suppose that he might find it possible not to do so, or to decide not to do so. Nature has to be thought of, that is to say, as separate from man, before any question of intervention or command, and the method and ethics of either, can arise. And then, of course, this is what we can see happening, in the development of the idea. It may at first seem paradoxical, but what we can now call the more secular and more rational ideas of nature depended on a new and very singular abstraction: the abstraction of Man. It is not so much a change from a metaphysical to a naturalist view, though that distinction has importance, as a change from one abstract notion to another, and one very similar in form.

Of course there had been a long argument about the relations between nature and social man. In early Greek thought this is the argument about nature and convention; in a sense an historical contrast between a state of nature and a formed human state with conventions and laws. A very great part of all subsequent political and legal theory has been based on some sense of this relation. But then of course it is obvious that the state of nature, the condition of natural man, has been very differently interpreted. Seneca saw the state of nature as a golden age, in which men were happy, innocent and simple. This powerful myth often coincided with the myth of Eden: of man before the fall. But sometimes it did not: the fall from innocence could be seen as a fall into nature; the animal without grace, or the animal needing grace. Natural, that is to say, could mean wholly opposite conditions: the innocent man or the mere beast.

In political theory both images were used. Hobbes saw the state of men in nature as low, and the life of pre-social man as 'solitary, poor, nasty, brutish and short'. At the same time, right reason was itself a law of nature, in the rather different, constitutive sense. Locke, opposing Hobbes, saw the state of nature as one of 'peace, goodwill, mutual assistance and cooperation'. A just society organised these natural qualities, whereas in Hobbes an effective society had overcome those natural disadvantages. Rousseau saw natural man as instinctive, inarticulate, without property, and contrasted this with the competitive and selfish society of his own day. The point about property has a long history. It was a widespread medieval idea that common ownership was more natural than private property, which was a kind of fall from grace, and there have always been radicals, from the Diggers to Marx, who have relied on some form of this idea as a programme or as a critique. And indeed, it is in this problem of property that many of the crucial questions about man and nature were put, often almost unconsciously. Locke produced a defence of private property based on the natural right of a man to that with which he has mixed his own labour, and many thousands of people believed and repeated this, in periods when it must have been obvious to everybody that those who most often and most fully mixed their labour with the earth were those who had no property, and when the very marks and stains of the mixing were in effect a definition of being propertyless. The argument can go either way; can be conservative or radical. But once we begin to speak of men mixing their labour with the earth, we are in a whole world of new relations between man and nature, and to separate natural history from social history becomes extremely problematic.

I think nature had to be seen as separate from man, for several purposes. Perhaps the first form of the separation was the practical distinction between nature and God: that distinction which eventually made it possible to describe natural processes in their own terms; to examine them without any prior assumption of purpose or design, but simply as processes, or to use the historically earlier term, as machines. We could find out how nature 'worked'; what made it, as we will say, 'tick' (as if Paley's clock were still with us). We could see better how it worked by altering or isolating certain conditions, in experiment or in improvement. Some of this discovery was passively conceived: a separated mind observing separated matter; man looking at nature. But much more of it was active: not only observation but experiment; and of course not only science, the pure knowledge of nature, but applied science, the conscious intervention for human purposes. Agricultural improvement, the industrial revolution, follow clearly from this emphasis, and many of the practical effects depended on seeing nature quite clearly and even coldly as a set of objects, on which men could operate. Of course we still have to remind ourselves of some of the consequences of that way of seeing things. Isolation of the object being treated led and still leads to unforeseen or uncared for consequences. It led also, quite clearly, to major developments in human capacity, including the capacity to sustain and care for life in quite new ways.

But in the idea of nature itself there is then a very curious result. The physical scientists and the improvers, though in different ways, had no doubt that they were working on nature, and it would indeed be difficult to deny that this was so, taking any of the general meanings. Yet at just the first peak of this kind of activity another and now very popular meaning of nature emerged. Nature, in this new sense, was in another and different way all that was not man: all that was not touched by man, spoilt by man: nature as the lonely places, the wilderness.

THE NATURAL AND THE CONVENTIONAL

I want to describe this development in some detail, but because we are still so influenced by it I must first draw attention to the conventional character of this unspoilt nature; indeed the conventional terms in which it is separated out. There are some true wildernesses, some essentially untouched places. As a matter of fact (and of course almost by definition) few people going to 'nature' go to them. But here some of the earlier meanings of 'Nature' and 'natural' come in as a rather doubtful aid. This wild nature is essentially peaceful and quiet, you can hear people say. Moreover it is innocent; it contrasts with man, except presumably with the man looking at it. It is unspoilt but also it is settled: a kind of primal settlement. And indeed there are places where in effect this is so.

But it is also very striking that the same thing is said about places which are in every sense man-made. I remember someone saying that it was unnatural, a kind of modern scientific madness, to cut down hedges; and as a matter of fact I agreed that they ought not to be cut down. But what was interesting was that the hedges were seen as natural, as parts of nature, though I should imagine everyone knows that they were planted and tended, and would indeed not be hedges if men had not made them so. A considerable part of what we call natural landscape has the same kind of history. It is the product of human design and human labour, and in admiring it as natural it seems to me to matter very much whether we suppress that fact of labour or acknowledge it. Some forms of this very popular modern idea of nature seem to me to depend on the suppression of the history of human labour, and the fact that they are often in conflict with what is seen as the exploitation or destruction of nature, may in the end be less important than the no less certain fact that they often confuse us about what nature and the natural are and might be.

It is very easy to contrast what can be called the improvers of nature and the lovers or admirers of nature. In the late eighteenth century, when this contrast began to be widely made, there was ample evidence of both kinds of response and activity. But though in the end they can be distinguished, and need to be distinguished, I think there are other and rather interesting relations between them.

We have first to remember that by the eighteenth century the idea of nature had become, in the main, a philosophical principle, a principle of order and right reason. Basil Willey's account of the main bearings of the idea, and of the effects and changes in Wordsworth, cannot, I think, be improved upon. Yet it is not primarily ideas that have a history; it is societies. And then what often seem opposed ideas can in the end be seen as parts of a single social process. There is this familiar problem about the eighteenth century: that it is seen as a period of order, because order was talked about so often, and in close relation to the order of nature. Yet it is not only that at any real level it was a notably disorderly and corrupt period; it is also that it generated, from within this disorder, some of the most profound of all human changes. The use of nature, in the physical sense, was quite remarkably extended, and we have to re-member – which we usually don't, because a successful image was imposed on us – that our first really ruthless capitalist class, taking up things and men in much the same spirit and imposing an at once profitable and pauperising order on them, were those eighteenth-century agrarians who got themselves called an aristocracy, and who laid the real foundations, in spirit and practice (and of course themselves joining in), for the industrial capitalists who were to follow them. A state of nature could be a reactionary idea, against change, or a reforming idea, against what was seen as decadence.

But where the new ideas and images were being bred there was a quite different perspective. It seems to me significant that the successful attack on the old idea of natural law should have been mounted just then. Not that it didn't need to be attacked; it was often in practice mystifying. But the utilitarians who attacked it were making a new and very much sharper tool, and in the end what had disappeared was any positive conception of a just society, and this was replaced by new and ratifying concepts of a mechanism and a market. That these, in turn, were deduced from the laws of nature is one of the ironies we are constantly meeting in the history of ideas. The new natural economic laws, the natural liberty of the entrepreneur to go ahead without interference, had in its projection of the market as the natural regulator a remnant – it is not necessarily a distortion – of the more abstract ideas of social harmony, within which self-interest and the common interest might ideally coincide. What is gradually left behind, in the utilitarians, is any shadow of a principle by which a higher justice – to be appealed to against any particular activity or consequence – could be effectively imagined. And so we have the situation of the great interferers, some of the most effective interferers of all time, proclaiming the necessity of non-interference: a contradiction which as it worked itself through had chilling effects on later thinkers in the same tradition, through John Stuart Mill to the Fabians.

THE WAYS OF THE IMPROVERS

And then it is at just this time, and first of all in the philosophy of the improvers, that nature is decisively seen as separate from men. Most earlier ideas of nature had included, in an integral way, ideas of human nature. But now nature, increasingly, was 'out there', and it was natural to reshape it to a dominant need, without having to consider very deeply what this reshaping might do to men. People talk of order in those cleared estates and in those landscaped parks, but what was being moved about and rearranged was not only earth and water but men. Of course we must then say at once that this doesn't imply any previous state of social innocence. Men were more cruelly exploited and imposed on in the great ages of natural law and universal order; but not more thoroughly, for the thoroughness depended on new physical forces and means. Now of course it soon happened that this process was denounced as unnatural: from Goldsmith to Blake, and from Cobbett to Ruskin and Dickens, this kind of attack on a new unnatural civilisation was powerfully deployed. The negative was clear enough, but the positive was always more doubtful. Concepts of natural order and harmony went on being repeated, against the increasingly evident disorder of society. Other appeals were attempted: to Christian brotherhood and to culture – that new idea of human growth, based on a natural analogy. Yet set against the practical ideas of the improvers, these were always insufficient. The operation on nature was producing wealth, and objections to its other consequences could be dismissed as sentimental. Indeed the objections often were, often still are, sentimental. For it is a mark of the success of the new idea of nature – of nature as separated from man – that the real errors, the real consequences, could be described at first only in marginal terms. Nature in any other sense than that of the improvers indeed fled to the margins: to the remote, the inaccessible, the relatively barren areas. Nature was where industry was not, and then in that real but limited sense had very little to say about the operations on nature that were proceeding elsewhere.

Very little to say. You may think it had a great deal to say. New feelings for landscape: a new and more particular nature poetry; the green vision of Constable; the green language of Wordsworth and Clare. Thomson in *The Seasons*, like Cobbett on his rural rides, saw beauty in cultivated land. But as early as Thomson, and then with increasing power in Wordsworth and beyond him, there is the sense of nature as a refuge, a refuge from man; a place of healing, a solace, a retreat. Clare broke under the strain, for he had one significant disadvantage; he couldn't both live on the process and escape its products, as some of the others were doing and indeed as became a way of life – this is a very bitter irony – for some of the most successful exploiters. As the exploitation of nature continued, on a vast scale, and especially in the new extractive and industrial processes, the people who drew most profit from it went back, where they could find it (and they were very ingenious) to an unspoilt nature, to the purchased estates and the country retreats. And since that time there has always been this ambiguity in the defence of what is called nature, and in its associated ideas of conservation, in the weak sense, and the nature reserve. Some people in this defence are those who understand nature best, and who insist on making very full connections and relationships. But a significant number of others are in the plainest sense hypocrites. Established at powerful points in the very process which is creating the disorder, they change their clothes at week-ends, or when they can get down to the country; join appeals and campaigns to keep one last bit of England green and unspoilt; and then go back, spiritually refreshed, to invest in the smoke and the spoil.

But they would not be able to go undetected so long if the idea they both use and abuse were not, in itself, so inadequate. When nature is separated out from the activities of men, it even ceases to be nature, in any full and effective sense. Men come to project on to nature their own unacknowledged activities and consequences. Or nature is split into unrelated parts: coal-bearing from heather-bearing; downwind from upwind. The real split, perhaps, is in men themselves: men seen, seeing themselves, as producers and consumers. The consumer wants only the intended product; all other products and by-products he must get away from, if he can. But get away – it really can't be overlooked – to treat leftover nature in much the same spirit: to consume it as scenery, landscape, image, fresh air. There is more similarity than we usually recognise between the industrial entrepreneur and the landscape gardener, each altering nature to a consumable form: and the client or beneficiary of the landscaper, who in turn has a view of a prospect to use, is often only at the lucky end of a common process, able to consume because others have produced, in a leisure that follows from quite precise work.

Men project, I said, their own unacknowledged activities and consequences. Into a green and quiet nature we project, I do not doubt, much of our own deepest feeling, senses of growth and perspective and beauty. But is it then an accident that an opposite version of nature comes to force its way through? Nothing is more remarkable, in the second half of the nineteenth century, than the wholly opposite version of nature as cruel and savage. As Tennyson put it:

A monster then, a dream,
A discord. Dragons of the prime
Which tear each other in the slime.

Those images of tearing and eating, of natural savagery, came to dominate much modern feeling. Disney, in some of his nature films, selects them with what seems an obsessive accuracy. Green nature goes on, in the fortunate places, but within it and all about it is this struggle and tearing, this ruthless competition for the right to live, this survival of the fittest. It is very interesting to see how Darwin's notion of natural selection passed into popular imagery – and by popular I mean the ordinary thoughts and feelings of educated men. 'Fittest', meaning those best adapted to a given and variable environment, became 'strongest', 'most ruthless'. The social jungle, the rat race, the territory-guarders, the naked apes: this, bitterly, was how an idea of man re-entered the idea of nature. A real experience of society was projected, by selective examples, on to a newly alienated nature. Under the veneer of civilisation was this natural savagery: from Wells to Golding this could be believed, in increasingly commonplace ways. What had once been a ratification, a kind of natural condonation, of ruthless economic selfishness – the real ideology of early capitalism and of imperialism – became, towards our own day, not only this but a hopelessness, a despair, an end of significant social effort; because if that is what life is like, is naturally like, any idea of brotherhood is futile. Then build another refuge perhaps, clear another beach. Keep out not so much the shark and the tiger (though them when necessary) as other men, the grasping, the predatory, the selfish, the herd. Let mid-Wales depopulate and then call it a wilderness area: a wilderness to go to from the jungle of the cities.

Ideas of nature, but these are the projected ideas of men. And I think nothing much can be done, nothing much can even be said, until we are able to see the causes of this alienation of nature, this separation of nature from human activity, which I have been trying to describe. But these causes cannot be seen, in a practical way, by returning to any earlier stage of the idea. In reaction against our existing situation, many writers have created an idea of a rural past: perhaps innocent, as in the first mythology of the Golden Age; but even more organic, with man not separated from nature. The impulse is understandable, but quite apart from its element of fantasy – its placing of such a period can be shown to be continually recessive – it is a serious underestimate of the complexity of the problem. A separation between man and nature is not simply the product of modern industry or urbanism; it is a characteristic of many earlier kinds of organised labour, including rural labour. Nor can we look with advantage to that other kind of reaction, which, correctly identifying one part of the problem in the idea of nature as a mechanism, would have us return to a traditional teleology, in which men's unity with nature is established through their common relation to a creator. That sense of an end and a purpose is in important ways even more alienated than the cold world of mechanism. Indeed the singular abstraction which it implies has much in common with that kind of abstract materialism. It directs our attention away from real and variable relations, and can be said to ratify the separation by making one of its forms permanent and its purpose fixed.

The point that has really to be made about the separation between man and nature which is characteristic of so many modern ideas is that – however hard this may be to express – the separation is a function of an increasing real interaction. It is easy to feel a limited unity on the basis of limited relationships, whether in animism, in monotheism, or in modern forms of pantheism. It is only when the real relations are extremely active, diverse, self-conscious, and in effect continuous – as our relations with the physical world can be seen to be in our own day – that the separation of human nature from nature becomes really problematic. I would illustrate this in two ways.

In our complex dealings with the physical world, we find it very difficult to recognise all the products of our own activities. We recognise some of the products, and call others by-products; but the slagheap is as real a product as the coal, just as the river stinking with sewage and detergent is as much our product as the reservoir. The enclosed and fertile land is our product, but so are the waste moors from which the poor cultivators were cleared, to leave what can be seen as an empty nature. Furthermore, we ourselves are in a sense products: the pollution of industrial society is to be found not only in the water and in the air but in the slums, the traffic jams, and not these only as physical objects but as ourselves in them and in relation to them. In this actual world there is not much point in counterposing or restating the great abstractions of Man and Nature; we have mixed our labour with the earth, our forces with its forces, too deeply to be able to draw back and separate either out. Except that if we draw back, if we go on with the singular abstractions, we are spared the effort of looking, in any active way, at the whole complex of social and natural relationships which is at once our product and our activity.

The process has to be seen as a whole, but not in abstract or singular ways. We have to look at all our products and activities, good and bad, and to see the relationships between them which are our own real relationships. More clearly than anyone, Marx indicated this, though still in terms of quite singular forces. I think we have to develop that kind of indication. In industry, for example, we cannot afford to go on saying that a car is a product but a scrapyard a by-product, any more than we can take the paint-fumes and petrol-fumes, the jams, the mobility, the motorway, the torn city centre, the assembly line, the time-and-motion study, the unions, the strikes, as by-products rather than the real products they are. But then of course to express this we should need not only a more sophisticated but a more radically honest accounting than any we now have. It will be ironic if one of the last forms of the separation between abstracted Man and abstracted Nature is an intellectual separation between economics and ecology. It will be a sign that we are beginning to think in some necessary ways when we can conceive these becoming, as they ought to become, a single discipline.

But it is even harder than that. If we say only that we have mixed our labour with the earth, our forces with its forces, we are stopping short of the truth, that we have done this unequally: that for the miner and the writer the mixing is different, though in both cases real; and that for the labourer and the man who manages his labour, the producer and the dealer in his products, the difference is wider again. Out of the ways we have interacted with the physical world, we have made not only human nature and an altered natural order; we have also made societies. I think it is very significant that most of the terms we have used in this relationship – the conquest of nature, the domination of nature, the exploitation of nature – are derived from real human practices: relations between men and men. Even the idea of the balance of nature has its social implications. If we talk only of singular Man and singular Nature we can compose a general history, but at the cost of excluding the real and altering social relations. Capitalism, of course, has used the terms of domination and exploitation; imperialism, in conquest, has similarly seen both men and physical products as raw material. But it is a measure of how far we have to go that socialists also still talk of the conquest of nature, which in any real terms will always include the conquest, the domination or the exploitation of some men by others. If we alienate the living processes of which we are a part, we end, though unequally, by alienating ourselves.

We need different ideas because we need different relationships.

> Nature and Nature's laws lay hid in night.
> God said, let Newton be, and all was light.

> Now o'er the one half world
> Nature seems dead.

Between the brisk confidence and the brooding reflection of those remembered lines we feel our own lives swing. We need and are perhaps beginning to find different ideas, different feelings, if we are to know nature as varied and variable nature, as the changing conditions of a human world.

PART II

CONTEMPORARY ISSUES

10

SEWAGE

KENNETH TYLER

INTRODUCTION

MOST countries have a water pollution problem, but the difficulties are more pronounced in those areas which have become urbanised and industrially developed. Although considerable advances have been made in methods of sewage treatment and disposal the demands for cleaner water increase. In the next thirty years the total volume of effluent is likely to double and our dirty water must be disposed of satisfactorily. We see remarkable scientific achievements, but the problems of environmental health and the relationship between man and his external environment must not be overlooked.

This paper looks at some of the inherited problems, current difficulties and techniques in 'sewage' as seen in England. The problems and solutions may differ in other countries.

EARLY SANITARY SYSTEMS

Problems in environmental health probably arose when man first appeared on this planet but the instinct for self-preservation led to the development of certain rules and practices to protect public health.

Over 5000 years ago a civilisation existed in the Indus valley of Sind in North-West India which was remarkable for its standard of living. In this area archaeologists discovered a city with brick sewers and drains which carried water away from one or more bathrooms in practically every house. There were well-built privies and in most houses sloping chimney-like passages which were evidently refuse chutes leading to external bins.

The Minoan civilisation was also astounding with its standard of culture and knowledge of hydraulics and sanitation. In Knossos, the home of King Minos in the island of Crete, clean water was carried in pressure pipes; the royal palace had baths made from pottery; stone drains carried away waste water and there were water-closets which always had clean water in them.

The Greeks, under the watchful eye of their goddess Hygeia, had water-flushed privies, marble wash-basins, hot and cold showers, and drains of burnt clay provided with ventilating pipes. Public conveniences and baths were quite common.

Elements of environmental sanitation took shape in many other countries of the ancient world, in China, Central Asia, Egypt and Russia for example. The Romans, with their policy of attaching a god or goddess to every phase of human activity, did not neglect sewers. Cloacina, Goddess of Sewers, was a vital part of the system, but being alive to the inadequacies of celestial supervision they also appointed the 'aedile'. Slaves and convicts swept the waste and horse-dung into the sewers. The aedile drove through the sewers in a cart, or when there was sufficient sewage, punted down in a boat to see that they discharged freely into the Tiber.[1]

But with the dissolution of the Roman Empire there settled upon the world more than 1500 years of an age which historians describe as 'dark' but which with equal truth might be called 'stinking'. The fact is that Christianity marked the departure of sanitary sciences and their rediscovery has only taken place within the last 140 years. It seems to have been a characteristic of every European nation to show complete indifference to hygiene from the passing of Latin supremacy until the mid-nineteenth century.

A milestone in sanitary history in this country was the Great Fire of London of 1666, as it marks the last great outbreak of plague the country has seen. In 1665 London had been savaged by plague and Samuel Pepys and John Evelyn wrote of 10,000 dying in a week. It was a recurrence of outbreaks which had occurred in England quite regularly and it created a realisation of the dangers that could arise from an insanitary environment. Sir John Simon in *English Sanitary Institutions* describes London thus: 'In general it had only alleys rather than streets, narrow irregular passages wherein houses of opposite sides often nearly met above the darkened and fetid gangway. The houses themselves, mostly constructed of wood and plaster, had hereditary accumulations of ordure in vaults beneath or beside them.' Various historians and other writers have described the appalling conditions which existed at that time and which, through the uncontrolled multiplication of rats, led to the Great Plague.

The Great Fire which burned most of London in 1666 is said to have ended the Great Plague, and to a certain extent this is true because so many plague-bearing rats were incinerated. Some attribute the lull in the outbreaks to the black rat being driven off by the brown rat which is not a plague carrier, others attribute it to higher standards of cleanliness, housing and sanitation. Today experts consider it declined naturally.

What is of importance is that the national economy, based on agriculture, did not at that time require the large number of employees which industrialisation was soon to demand and the government did not have the same incentive to deal with these plague outbreaks as was the case in subsequent epidemics of fever.

AN AGE OF DARKNESS

The period of industrial revolution brought increasing wealth for many, yet misery for rather more. A few men, led by Edwin Chadwick, applied themselves to the task of fighting suffering, disease and the insanitary conditions which existed. It is probable that at this time there was hardly a single town in Great Britain which could compare in hygiene with a second-rate city of the Roman occupation.

At that time industry's demand for labour could hardly be satisfied. Even the poorest of dwellings could not be built quickly enough for the families and many lodgers crowding into the dwellings, which had little or no drainage or sanitary facilities. Fluid contents from cesspits often seeped through the walls and in many instances oozed through into the neighbouring cellars, filling them with the stench and making it necessary for wells to be dug to prevent the occupants from being inundated with the filth. One such well, with four feet of stinking fluid, was found in a cellar under the bed where the family slept. Poverty and misery appeared to be generally accepted and Manchester for example decided that to provide the poor with water-closets would only waste water.

Chadwick believed that disease and smells were synonymous, and although this was later proved incorrect, he continued to want water to wash the smelling wastes into streams which could be cleaned up later on. He also believed that crude sewage, if spread on farmland, would have its impurities removed. He claimed that the land would be richer and the streams protected.

Water can be the source of a number of diseases but in the context of this study cholera is of the greatest importance. In 1854, within a radius of 250 yards, 500 people suddenly died of cholera within ten days. No medieval plague took so many in such a limited area as existed around Broad Street, London. Neighbourhoods served by other pumps did not suffer to the same extent. To Dr John Snow these deaths meant that cholera was spread by water and transmitted by sewage. Dr Snow demonstrated that all of the victims had drunk water from the well on the corner of Broad Street and Cambridge Street. It was proved that the well was almost constantly being contaminated by sewage oozing through its walls. When he dramatically took away the pump handle he did much to take away the scourge of cholera. In the preceding six years a quarter of a million people had died from the disease, but by 1868 it had been eradicated.

Roughly built stone conduits such as the Fleet and the Ditch were the only drains of the time. These, however, were only meant to take surface water. To avoid sewage lying on the streets the connection of house drains to these outlets was allowed, and in 1847 connections were made compulsory. Unfortunately, the sewage did not flow to any great degree in the conduits, and incoming sewage was forced back into the yards and streets again.

In 1877, at a conference on the Health and Sewage of Towns, delegates from Halifax urged the virtues of their dry privy systems. Trenches were dug in covered latrines, and leather shoddy and other industrial wastes added to absorb faecal matter. The pits were periodically cleared out, the contents dried in the sun, ground in mills and sold as manure.[1] Then Sir Henry Doulton, the distinguished potter, and an engineer, John Loe, developed the vitrified clay pipe and the egg-shaped sewer which would carry sewage away even in dry weather. Other important design features were developed.

The 'sanitary idea' was being accepted and by 1891 suspicions and hostilities had been left behind. The period of mains and drains had begun, but all sorts of domestic and industrial wastes started to gush into the streams and watercourses. Dr J. N. Thudickham described the problem when he said that man had removed pollution a little further from his habitation by sending it through sewers, but by a retribution of Providence it turned back upon him in the water which he required for washing and drinking.[1]

A LEGACY FROM THE PAST?

Today's pollution of the environment by solid and liquid waste matter is a staggering burden born of growing affluence, nurtured by rising populations, matured by technology and all but neglected by society.

Through urbanisation and industrial demands, population densities have rapidly increased and made the collection, treatment and disposal of wastes a complicated problem with serious health implications. If present trends continue, by the end of this century there will be some 20 million more people in England and Wales and when this is related to our present population of approximately 49 million and the present total daily flow of all sewage of about 60 gallons per person, the magnitude of the situation can be appreciated. It has been estimated by the Confederation of British Industry that the total volume of water used by industry and consequently the volume of effluent discharged is likely to double by the end of the century.

Then the replacement of obsolete houses, the improvement of substandard homes with modern amenities, the greater use of domestic labour-saving appliances and an increase in disposable goods flushed into the drainage system, together with industrial and agricultural demands – all these result in the volume of sewage effluent increasing by about 3 per cent each year. This has important consequences.

With known increases to be expected in effluent volumes, the expenditure on treatment plants will increase proportionately. Even if the watercourses which receive the effluents remain the same size, the amount of dilution available will drop, so that the efficiency and extent of treatment must increase, with correspondingly higher costs. Also, because increasing quantities of water will be abstracted from the rivers to provide for the higher demand, the natural river flow will not be as large as now, so more efficient treatment will be required to compensate. The World Health Organisation has said that when all these factors are taken together it is clear that even a well-developed country, with adequate authorities, good intentions and no lack of money, must view the future with a certain misgiving.[2]

Sewage effluent forms a considerable proportion of the volume of a number of rivers from which public water supplies are abstracted; and without a returned sewage effluent many rivers would not flow at all in dry weather. It is normal that the liquid waste from a community should be returned to a watercourse after treatment; and to avoid damage to health, amenity or economy the degree of treatment is completely dependent on the circumstances of each case.

One imagines that probably the first water pollutant was dying vegetation and then the natural excrement from animals and man. More recently industrial wastes have been added and, more recently still, the deliberate additives from our twentieth-century civilisation are being washed out of the sky and off the surface of the soil.

A river-pollution survey is now nearing completion, having been undertaken by the Department of the Environment in collaboration with other authorities. Until the findings of this survey are known, a survey made in 1958 gives the most comprehensive picture. It was then estimated that of about 20,000 miles of non-tidal rivers in England and Wales in which the dry-weather flow was not less than about one million gallons a day, 73 per cent of the total length was wholly or substantially unpolluted, 15 per cent was of doubtful quality needing improvement, 6 per cent was of poor quality and 6 per cent was grossly polluted. In general the rivers in the worst condition were in the highly industrialised areas, the Midlands and the North of England, many of which have been grossly polluted for many years. In 1844 Frederick Engels wrote of the River Irk in Manchester: 'In dry weather, a long string of the most disgusting, blackish green slime pools are left standing on this bank, from the depths of which bubbles of miasmatic gas constantly arise and give forth a stench unendurable even on the bridge forty or fifty feet above the surface of the stream.'

Much of the present pollution problem is a legacy from the past and in numerous instances it originated from the Industrial Revolution. Many writers have described vividly the conditions today in some of our rivers. As a brief reminder:

> 40 million gallons of untreated sewage are poured into the Tyne every day. By the time the river reaches Tynemouth it is utterly repellent and virtually de-oxygenated. [H. F. Wallis, 1970.]

> Virtually the whole of the Tame, which drains Birmingham and the Black Country is grossly polluted. Of the 600 local authority sewage works no fewer than 350 consistently fail to meet the far from punitive standards laid down by the river authority. [*The Times*, 24 March 1970.]

> The Irwell is one of the most blighted stretches of moving water in Britain.

No fish can swim in it nor livestock drink its water. [*Observer*, 1 Feb. 1970.]

Two Cornish rivers, the St Austell and the Luxulyan have been written off (at least in the short term) as industrial drains. [*Sunday Times*, 7 Sept. 1969.]

For much of its length the Trent stinks with sewage, foams with detergent and is poisoned with lead, zinc and cyanide. It is death to any fish put in it. [*Daily Telegraph Magazine*, 25 Sept. 1970.]

The eight-mile stretch of the Tawe from Pontardawe to the coast is often black with coal dust and polluted by effluents from a wide range of industries. [*ibid.*]

It is not, however, all a legacy from the previous centuries.

SEWAGE: SOME SOURCES OF POLLUTION

The working definition of 'sewage' which was used by the Government's Working Party on Sewage Disposal, which presented its report 'Taken for Granted' in 1970, was 'the liquid waste of the community'. This is a wide definition embracing the liquid or water-borne wastes from industry, agriculture and the domestic source. The report did, however, provide a more detailed definition.

Sewage is a highly turbid liquid, consisting of a dilute complex mixture of mineral and organic matter in many forms, including: (*a*) large and small particles of solid matter floating and in suspension; (*b*) substances in true solution; and (*c*) extremely finely divided 'colloidal' substances midway between these two categories. It contains living organisms such as bacteria, viruses and protozoa; it is an excellent medium for the development of bacteria, containing several million per millilitre. The solid portion contains paper fibres, corks, soaps, fats, oils, greases, food materials and faeces as well as insoluble mineral matters such as sand and clay. The organic substances present in sewage include carbohydrates, complex compounds of carbon, hydrogen and oxygen, fats, soaps and synthetic detergents and proteins. Ammonia and ammonium salts are always present, some derived from the decomposition of urine. The objectionable character of sewage is due mainly to the presence of organic matter which, in the absence of dissolved oxygen, soon putrifies, with the formation of foul-smelling compounds.[3]

It is appropriate at this stage to look at two of the three principal sources and the pollution factors which can arise. Industrial effluents are to be discussed in another chapter.

Agriculture

The main concern is animal excreta and it has been estimated that 120 million tons of animal excreta are produced each year. This represents a greater amount than man produces (one cow produces as much as six people and a pig as much as two) but 80 million tons is fortunately from ranging animals.

Population and economic problems have compelled the farmer to develop systems on factory lines. New developments so often create new environmental health problems and in Britain the latest sewage problem comes from intensive farming developments. Instead of manure being put on fields as fertiliser, animals reared by intensive farming methods produce, or cause to be produced, a sewage slurry. Individual installations have become larger as smaller establishments are relinquished or consolidated. Waste-disposal problems are compounded as more wastes are created per establishment; and because premises these days are no longer isolated from dwellings the nuisance and health factors are accentuated.

Municipal Wastes

Evidence has been published by the Institute of Municipal Treasurers and Accountants which suggests that of the 5000 local authority sewage treatment plants in England and Wales about 3000 of them discharge an effluent below the recommended standards.

There are various reasons for this situation.

1. An area may be served with works of proper design and effectiveness, but because of the load the plant has to deal with it is often the case that not all the effluent is completely treated and some may not be treated at all. Development in the area has exceeded the planning of sewage treatment. In one town in Sussex the works were built in 1891 and extended in 1939, but there are now nearly twice as many people in the area as in 1939.

2. It is possible that in some districts the particular staff and operatives necessary to maintain efficient treatment are not employed. This situation becomes more serious as wastes become more complex.

3. Many of our older towns were provided with a combined system of drainage. This involves the discharge of surface water from roofs, etc., to the foul sewers. In times of storm, in order to relieve the works, overflows discharge untreated effluent into the water-

course. This discharge in some districts may be operating continuously, owing to the inadequacy of the system to cope with the normal flow from the sewers.

4. The 'dirty jobs' dispute which involved 70,000 dustmen, sewage workers and other council manual employees ended generally on 6 November 1970, when the men returned after a strike of six weeks. The closure, or partial closure, of many sewage treatment works was unprecedented in this country, and there were fears that gross pollution would take place and public water supplies be put in jeopardy. The strike had a less serious effect on the major rivers than was earlier feared and on 25 November Peter Walker, Secretary for the Environment, said that fish were killed in about sixty miles of rivers because of pollution. There were no reported outbreaks of disease.

METHODS OF DISPOSAL

Early Ideas

The system strongly advocated by Chadwick was the removal of sewage by pipes to a distance from all centres of population. The oldest example was the Craigentinny Meadows near Edinburgh, which appear to have been used for sewage irrigation towards the end of the eighteenth century. In spite of the difficulties it did at least offer a more sanitary system for the removal of filth than its collection in cesspits for carting away to a distance limited by the cost of conveyance.

The Towns Improvement Clauses Act of 1847 recognised two methods of sewage disposal: first, getting rid of it without any attempt at making it a source of profit, and second, methods of profitable disposal. Under the first group would be discharges to the sea or watercourses and under the second, collection and sale for agricultural use, provided no nuisance resulted.

The report of the General Board of Health in 1854 expressed the view 'that it was far less injurious to the public health to have the refuse of towns in water in the nearest river than underneath or amidst dwellings'. During this period the dominant opinion was that sewage should be discharged to a river rather than be retained near dwellings. There were doubts as to the public health effects of irrigation of large areas with sewage. Between 1857 and 1870 there was still a pressing need for improving sewerage systems, but this was accompanied by the abandonment of the fear of health risks from irrigation and a growing belief that profitable land utilisation would solve the problem, a recognised problem, of river pollution.

A question put at this time was, is it better to kill fish or men? It was also becoming recognised that if disposal would not pay commercially then it should be made a compulsory local service financed by rates. Many experiments were carried out and money was invested in schemes to try to prove that raw sewage could be dealt with profitably by land enrichment. The sewage farm was looked upon as a solution to purification problems.

Up to 1892 there had been some reference to natural processes, but these had not materialised. But Warrington in 1882, in a paper to the Royal Society of Arts, suggested a form of bacterial filter. For some time work went on without any attention being paid to this possibility. Pasteur had, however, already shown that the conversion of organic wastes by nature was by organisms of different kinds, and when the importance of the anaerobic organisms was appreciated a new light dawned.

In 1898 a Royal Commission was appointed to enquire and report on the treatment and disposal of sewage. The Commission had to deal with the difficulties of trade wastes, storm water disposal and the scarcity of land.[4] Some recommendations still operate today.

Current Policies

The aim is to produce a liquid and solid sludge which can be disposed of without risk to health or nuisance. Because the quantities and strength of sewage are never constant it is necessary for treatment works to be designed for the particular sewage flow they will be required to receive.

Urban communities

The broad principles of treatment carried out at the works designed for urban communities include the following stages:

1. Screening or maceration of the solid extraneous matter.

2. Primary treatment in sedimentation tanks where up to 80 per cent of solid matter is settled out.

3. Secondary treatment where bacterial and biological oxidation of the effluent is carried out by percolating filters.

An alternative system is that known as activated sludge. This relies upon continuous movement of turbulent sewage in contact with air through air being pumped in by jets or by mechanical agitation.

A tertiary stage is often introduced if a high quality effluent is required. By sand filtration, lagoons or surface irrigation up to 99·5 per cent of the effluent's original bacterial population may be removed.

Isolated communities

By the beginning of this century most urban authorities had sewage disposal systems, but in rural areas there were few piped supplies of water or water-carriage drainage systems. The earth closet at the end of the garden was only too familiar. Now only 6 per cent of the population of England and Wales is not serviced by main drainage. Less than 1 per cent of rural dwellings are now without piped water supplies.

Where main drainage does not exist the following systems may be used:

1. Cesspools are, or should be, watertight storage tanks in which the sewage is kept until emptied by a tanker.

2. A septic tank provides a primary stage of purification and the effluent will overflow to some form of oxidation treatment.

3. Extended aeration is a development of the activated sludge process and many manufacturers provide prefabricated units which required only a simple connection to drains and electricity.

Whatever system is used it must be quite clear that the installation cannot be completed and then ignored or forgotten.

Sludge

Methods of liquid waste treatment are designed to separate and concentrate the constituents. The semi-liquid sludges create a problem in that their ultimate disposal is frequently difficult.

The liquid sludges taken from primary or final sedimentation tanks contain between 90 and 99 per cent water; most of them are highly organic, unstable and offensive. There are a number of methods by which the water content can be reduced and the solids converted to a condition in which they may be disposed of satisfactorily. Traditionally the method of treatment has been the drying of the sludge in open beds, but this requires a good deal of land and is largely dependent on weather conditions.

The most widely used process is anaerobic digestion in which the sludge is pumped into enclosed digester tanks. These tanks are heated to about 90°F and anaerobic fermentation takes place with the liberation of methane and carbon dioxide gases. The gas, which often has a calorific value higher than town gas, may be utilised for providing the power source and other needs at the treatment works. Digested sludge can be handled as a relatively compact moist solid and may be further dewatered.

Air-drying, filter pressing, vacuum filtration and centrifuging are some ways of dewatering to produce a material having a potential as a fertiliser. Where its use as a fertiliser is not possible it is either tipped, dumped at sea or incinerated. The development of sludge as a fertiliser will be considered in greater detail in a subsequent section.

Detergents

Foaming at treatment works and on rivers occurred because the materials originally used in the production of synthetic detergents were not completely destroyed by otherwise efficient sewage treatment processes. Treatment only removed these materials, the alkyl benzene sulphonates, to the extent of about 67 per cent. A Standing Committee was set up in 1957 to review the problems. Consisting of industrial and local authority representatives, the Committee publishes an annual report on its deliberations and progress.

The development of the 'soft' detergent was introduced first of all in the Luton area in 1958 and by the end of 1964 about half the domestic detergents used in the country were of this type, i.e. more easily broken down by a sewage-treatment process. This trend continued and manufacturers voluntarily agreed to discontinue the manufacture of the 'hard' detergents for the domestic market. This was completed in 1965, and 90 per cent of the detergents were being removed at efficient sewage works.

In some areas, however, notably on the Rivers Aire and Calder, foaming continues to be a problem. It seems that whereas the domestic 'soft' detergent has reduced the problem considerably, industrial detergents should now be subject to a voluntary undertaking in a similar way.

The Eleventh Report of the Standing Committee says that the concentration of detergent residues in rivers is now showing no sign of improvement and there is a danger of deterioration. The situation could become critical again. It occurs in areas where there is a concentration of firms using detergents, as in the Yorkshire wool towns. The Borough Council of Castleford in Yorkshire has found that in certain wind conditions foam from the River Aire is sometimes blown into the streets.

Water sprays to control foam have been reasonably successful, but the only real solution will be the complete change-over, affecting industry, to soft biodegradable detergents. There has been no evidence of fish being killed as a result of sewage carrying detergent residues, so the problem could be said to be primarily an aesthetic one. Difficulties can, however, arise in that residues may retard the process of sludge digestion; fortunately, it does not inhibit the process.

Agriculture

There are three principal methods of disposal from the traditional type farm.

1. Discharge to the public sewer, in theory, provides the most trouble-free answer; but farm effluent is generally much stronger than crude domestic waste, and the smaller treatment plant is often incapable of dealing with large volumes of farm waste without some form of additional treatment.

2. Discharge to a watercourse must have the approval of the river authority and treatment prior to its discharge will be required.

3. Surface irrigation, subsoil irrigation and spray irrigation are three basic methods by which effluent from farms may be returned to the land. Apart from spray irrigation, the methods depend upon soil permeability and a guarantee that underground water will not be contaminated.

Because of the risk of spreading various disease organisms dangerous to man and animals, precautions should be taken to avoid putting slurry on to land for grazing or on growing crops – particularly if the crops are not to be cooked before consumption. If pasture land is to be used then an interval of six weeks should elapse before the land is grazed.[3]

The disposal of wastes from intensive farming units frequently creates problems. Although it is generally better to handle these wastes in a solid form, economic considerations make it more usual for the excreta to be diluted with water, producing a slurry. As an example, poultry manure from battery houses can amount to 1 ton per 1000 birds per week. Methods of treatment of such a weekly waste may be as follows:[5]

1. Underground slurry tanks which receive the waste matter plus an equal weight of water will have to be pumped out at, say, fortnightly intervals.

2. Discharge to the public sewer is unlikely to be accepted by the local authority as the strength of the effluent could be too great for the smaller type of rural purification works.

3. Spreading the waste directly on the land after removal from the battery house or after removal and mixing with other farm manure.

4. Deep pits may be installed under the slatted floors of the poultry houses. Droppings are mixed with water and air is blown in to aid aerobic digestion. Ten thousand birds will produce 10 tons a week – the problem is pit-emptying and disposal.

5. Drying. The product from a dryer can be used as a fertiliser and it has also been found that mixed with protein it can produce an acceptable and economic animal diet. The drying process is said to kill salmonella organisms and parasites. The product may be sold as an activator for rotting compost for mushroom growers; horticulturists use it on lawns and herbaceous borders and farmers may apply it as a grassland dressing. It has been claimed that the material has an organic content that promotes a luxuriant growth which is more palatable to livestock than vegetation fed solely on chemical fertilisers.

The drying process certainly complies with current thinking that farm wastes should be returned to the land. A wide range of chemicals is used, however, to stimulate animal and bird growth and the persistence of these and other feed additives must be considered when investigating the spreading of manure, as these can enter the soil.

DISPOSAL AND POLLUTION

Types of Pollution

1. Bacteria, viruses and other organisms which can cause disease.

2. Decomposable organic matter, which by absorbing oxygen in the water kills fish, produces offensive smells and gives rise to unsightliness.

3. Inorganic salts not removed by any simple conventional treatment process.

4. Plant nutrients – potash, phosphates, nitrates – which are also largely inorganic salts but which have the added property of increasing weed growth.

5. Oily matter.

6. Specific toxic agents ranging from metallic salts to complex synthetic chemicals.

Human sewage contains matter of the first four classes; industrial wastes any or all of the classes, and drainage from agricultural land can include classes 3, 4 and probably 6.[2]

Disposal Outfalls

At the moment sewage from about 40 million people in England and Wales is drained to treatment works and then discharged to rivers or estuaries.[3]

Inland waters

Discharges may change the chemical quality of the river water and this alters the biology and biochemistry of the water. Cooling water from industry may cause overheating, and disease organisms of human and animal origin can prejudice the quality of a receiving water. Chemical pollution may affect colour, odour, turbidity and create foam and oil films. Organic matter may use up oxygen, suspended solids may settle to form silt or sludge, toxic matter may destroy life, and certain other substances such as phenols and oils may impart a taint to the water which could be detected in the public supply.

There appear to be major differences of opinion about the nature of the substances which transform lower water levels into a lifeless environment. These eutrophising substances may be of phosphorous or nitrogen origin, but others such as vitamins, hormones and other growth-stimulating substances are also suspect. Enrichment by these substances encourages aquatic growth and the proliferation of algae affects the penetration of sunlight with a reduction in the photosynthetic process and oxygen availability. The excess algal growth dies, falling to the bottom of the river, where it rots, causing the oxygen content of the water to fall and so killing other life such as fish which depend on dissolved oxygen. Although the nitrates and phosphorus can be extracted from the sewage effluent, it has been held that this would not significantly improve the situation. Those in support of this opinion believe the contribution from the leaching of agricultural fertilisers is of great importance. But views differ. Fortunately the eutrophication situation seems less serious in Britain than in other parts of the world.

When domestic sewage is discharged to a natural and fresh water, a vast number of the bacterial population contained in the faecal matter die as a result of transfer to an abnormal environment. Each gramme of faeces contains about 1000 million *E. coli* (the most common intestinal organism) but a 99 per cent reduction takes place in about three weeks. The same reduction period applies to many of the pathogenic intestinal organisms. Effluents from treated sewage are not, however, sterile and large numbers of pathogens can be present.

The natural purification effect in a river is greatest in the first two miles from the outfall, and this length really acts as a vast settling tank. Aerobic bacteria will reduce animal or vegetable organic matter to simple organic salts which act as fertilisers for the natural life of the matter. Oxygen in the water is also converted into CO_2 which is absorbed by the vegetation. So the cycle requires a sufficiency of dissolved oxygen for the use of bacteria, and vigorous growth of vegetation to return oxygen to the water. If the cycle is broken by inadequate oxygen then anaerobic bacteria will reduce the organic matter, but this is accompanied by foul-smelling gases and incomplete reduction. The balance is delicate.

The continuous discharge of crude sewage to a watercourse in excess of the water's capacity for self-purification is rapidly followed by the establishment of anaerobic conditions, which leads to the destruction of animal, fish and plant life and to the silting up of the watercourse through the deposition of partially digested organic matter.[6]

Estuaries

For a long time it was thought that the salt present in estuaries had particular powers of purification so that a vast amount of polluted water could be accepted by them. The Tyne, Tees and Mersey estuaries prove how incorrect was that belief. The amount of fresh water, the state of the tidal flow and the geographical formation of the estuary influence the capacity of the estuary to accept effluents.

Because of the tidal cycle an estuary can become polluted above- and downstream of the outfall and it can be some time before the pollution is finally taken out to sea.[6]

A number of estuaries provide supplies of fish and shellfish and severe pollution will, for example, act as a barrier against migratory fish such as the salmon and trout.

The sea

There has been much public anxiety about the effect of sewage pollution in the sea. The sewage from an estimated population of some 6 million in British coastal towns is discharged direct to the sea.[7] The position is accentuated by the increasing use of our coastal waters for recreation, and seasonal population explosions have made many existing partial treatment systems hopelessly inadequate. In some locations aesthetically revolting conditions have been created in which identifiable sewage solids have been found on beaches and in sea bathing areas. Sewage, when discharged to the sea, is diluted and almost wholly eliminated by chemical and biological degradation. The sea itself, although not significantly affected by the discharge, must not be used to give rise to unpleasant local effects.

In 1957 a serious epidemic of poliomyelitis in Britain added to the public's concern about sewage-polluted bathing beaches, and in 1959 the Medical Research Council published a report on the subject.[8] It said that with the possible exception of a few aesthetically disgusting beaches the risks to health of bathing in sewage-contaminated sea water can, for all practical purposes be ignored. No other evidence has been produced to alter that view.

The risks to human health in consuming fish or shellfish taken from sewage-polluted waters are very great, and a number of enteric infections have been associated with shellfish. Although easily contaminated, shellfish can be made safe through their self-cleansing action in purification tanks.

Methods of disposal must be improved in some areas, as dirty beaches and sea bathing areas cannot be accepted as part of our natural environment. Polluted water must be disposed of in the most economical method possible that is consistent with health and amenity requirements and ecological factors. Gross solid matter must be removed and the length and position of the outfall sewer must be determined by local hydrographic conditions – wind direction, tidal movements, wave heights, etc. The Water Pollution Research Laboratory has suggested as a guide that an outfall serving a population less than 10,000 might be taken to a point 400 yards beyond low water mark. In some instances, however, two to three miles might be necessary.

Recently, Commander Cousteau reported to four Council of Europe Assembly's Committees on the shocking state of the seas of the globe. The stage has now been reached, he said, where the ocean can no longer be considered as an endless dustbin. The ocean's self-purifying power is already greatly overtaxed. Cousteau described the conditions found on many different sea-beds and urged the setting up of an independent international pollution board.

RECLAMATION

A scientific group of the World Health Organisation has said that although the re-use of waste water has been practised for many years, particularly in agriculture, it has become increasingly important both as a means of pollution control and as a possible way of increasing supplies for agricultural, industrial and municipal purposes.[9] But the purification of waste water for human consumption involves health risks. For example, not enough is known of the long-term effects of certain of the trace chemicals found in waste water, and there is still much to be learned about the removal of certain microbiological pollution. It is apparent, however, that not enough consideration has been given to the possibility of using reclaimed water for many municipal and domestic purposes other than drinking. It must, however, be biologically safe and adequate provision made to prevent its misuse as drinking water.

The demand for water is increasing by some 2½ per cent per annum. If this rate is maintained it has been said that the whole of Britain's available freshwater resources will be in use within this century.

At several places in this country sewage effluent is being used to make good losses in cooling towers at power stations. Although precautions are taken to prevent algal growths, corrosion and foaming, little additional treatment is necessary. At Santee in California, highly purified sewage effluent is used to supply a series of recreational lakes.

In Israel a number of projects for the agricultural utilisation of waste water were initiated as early as 1948 and through the years the programme has developed. In 1956 the first National Water Plan included the use of waste water as one of the sources of water in developing schemes to meet the needs of the country's agricultural and industrial growth. Israel has become one of the few countries in the world where the reclamation of waste water has become a matter of national policy. Almost 20 per cent of the sewage from urban areas is re-used in some form or other.[10]

At Warrington, Lancashire, millions of gallons of water from the River Mersey are treated each day and sold, at a price considerably less than that of the domestic supply, to industry for use in condenser cooling. The water is also used apparently without complaint in a few low-pressure boilers.

Then in places where a local authority charges for the treatment of trade wastes, and where the formulae for calculating the cost of treatment are based wholly or partly on the volume discharged, water extraction may become economical. Increasing water rates may bring about a radical change in some processes, so that people will design for water economy as they design for fuel economy. Perhaps some industrialists could rely entirely, or almost entirely, on recirculation and regeneration.

The volume of sewage effluent from a town and its industries is not appreciably different from that of the water supplied to it. If the effluent is discharged to an inland watercourse and it is abstracted further downstream then little net loss results. Many discharges are, however, lost, such as those put into estuaries, and clearly reclamation from these offers advantages.[11]

An advanced waste water reclamation scheme at South Lake Tahoe in California has, since 1968, operated to produce an effluent exceeding the stringent requirements of the regulatory agencies. It has created California's newest water resource, Indian Creek Reservoir, which is approved for all water sports; and the releases from the reservoir are used downstream for grazing crops. Drinking water standards do not apply to the direct use of reclaimed water, and research is planned by the United States Bureau of Water Hygiene to investigate the establishment of standards for water originating from heavily polluted sources. With regard to public acceptance, it has been said that public attitudes may change faster than at first might be assumed.[12]

The only plant producing potable water from sewage effluent for direct re-use is in Windhoek, South-West Africa, where a million gallons per day is treated and discharged directly to a potable water reservoir.

The Department of the Environment announced recently that a two-year programme of pilot plant experiments had begun at an abandoned water treatment plant in Essex, to show to what extent typical sewage effluent can be restored for water supply purposes and whether treatment are costs economic. Initially the pilot plant is designed to produce up to 2·5 million gallons of water a day, which is discharged into the River Chelmer, downstream of the Water Company's raw water intakes. The results of the experiments will show whether it is possible for water produced in this way to be used eventually to augment rivers used for water supply, for direct 'second-class' supply to industry, or ultimately to produce potable water from heavily polluted rivers normally considered unsuitable as raw water sources.

From early times it was realised that decaying wastes could improve soil fertility. In India, in the early years of this century, night soil was allowed to decompose under controlled composting conditions to form a humus and so help increase food production. Sir Albert Howard, Imperial Economic Botanist to the Government of India, said: 'Cleaner and healthier villages will go hand in hand with heavier crops.' Various systems were tried which brought considerable improvements in food quantity and quality.[1]

It appears that the first composting system of dealing with municipal waste in this country was developed at Leatherhead in 1936, where the aim was to prevent sludge disposal affecting a tributary of the Thames. Pulverised refuse was put into shallow lagoons and flooded with liquid sludge. The liquid would be drained off and the mass stockpiled and fermented for perhaps six months.

Pulverisation, mixing and fermentation are essential for town waste composting, and the combination of these three was developed by a Danish engineer. In 1954 the first mechanised composting plant to treat domestic wastes was put into operation in Switzerland. This equipment, the Dano Bio-Stabilisation Plant, first appeared in this country in Edinburgh the following year. Many more authorities have installed the plant.

The spraying of liquid sludge on farmland was mentioned when disposal methods were considered. L. D. Hills examines the question 'fertility or pollution' and refers to some seventeen authorities which distribute liquid sludge having no smell and looking like thin tar. He claims that it is more economical for a local authority to give sludge away than to dry, bag and sell it.[13] Much work is being done on the question of sludge as a soil conditioner by a number of bodies such as the Soil Association.

The Working Party on Sewage Disposal said that sewage sludge as a fertiliser has a restricted use, but agreed that it should be encouraged where it is practicable. Perhaps local authorities should be more marketing-minded. Properly digested sludges involve virtually no danger, but those contaminated with toxic materials should not be used on any land. Although there seem to be differences of opinion

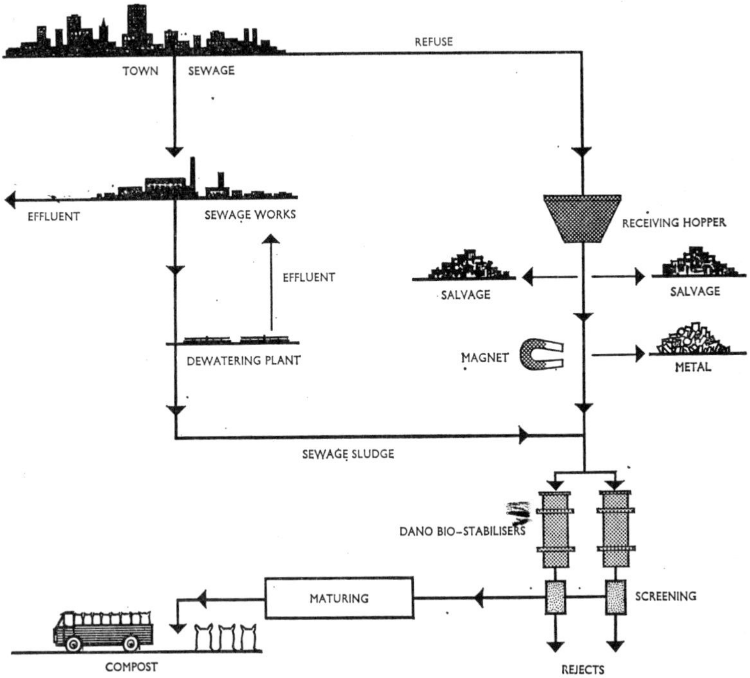

Combined disposal of refuse and sludge can be achieved in a Dano Composting Plant. Composting is a biological process in which organic wastes are decomposed to a humus-like substance. The process requires moisture which can be added in the form of water or sewage sludge. Should the available sludge be in excess of the moisture requirements it can be partially dried on a de-watering machine in order that the whole of the sludge can be processed with the refuse.

The composting process in the bio-stabiliser is controlled and destruction of pathogenic organisms is ensured

on the quantity of nutrients available from the sludge it is undesirable to waste any material which could be beneficial.

Dr Barry Commoner is reported as having put this into perspective when he said that the natural ecological system that can accommodate organic waste is not in the water but in the soil, and no solution to the deterioration of both surface waters and the soil can be achieved until organic waste is returned to the soil.

Hills suggests a complete ban on new outfalls into sea or estuary and no loan sanction for replacement outlets costing more than sewage treatment; no loan sanction for other than heat digestion process plants; no loan sanction for sludge-burning incinerators or dumping vessels, but easy loan sanction for plants assisting in return to soil. Subsidies on the nitrogen and phosphorous artificial fertilisers could be abolished, ending the unfair competition between subsidised fertilisers and home-produced sludge and municipal composting. Clearly this is an aspect of sewage treatment and disposal on which there is much controversy and on which continuing research is needed at the present time.

INNOVATIONS

Instead of using water for conveying sewage through and from the building, an alternative system has been developed in Sweden which is based on two principles. Air is used instead of water and secondly, faecal matter and urine (black water) are separated from all other liquid wastes (grey water). Black water is treated chemically and the grey water by biological or chemical treatment. The main advantage of this scheme appears to be the large saving in water; only a small amount of water is used in the black line, which is self-cleansing on a vacuum-based system.

FINANCIAL IMPLICATIONS

In August 1970, Peter Walker said that capital expenditure in England on sewerage and sewage disposal installations in 1969 amounted to about £110 million. Although the actual amount can vary quite widely it has been said that it costs about 32p a week to deal with the sewage of an average family of four.

River authorities and local authorities are empowered to impose conditions of consent on industrial effluent discharges and in the case of discharges to the public sewer a charge may be imposed to meet receiving and treatment costs. Industry bears a considerable capital and recurring expense in connection with treatment plant constructed by industry on its own premises. Although this figure is not known it is thought to be about £50 million a year but on top of that must be added the charges imposed by local authorities. Local authorities probably bear about £100 million in recurr ng expenditure per annum, and as most large authorities cope with about equal quantities of industrial and domestic effluent a large proportion of this recurring expenditure is met by industry by way of trade effluent charges.[14]

Finance has been a hindrance to improved sewage disposal for a long time. Some treatment works are unsatisfactory by present standards, many are overloaded and there are those which cannot cope adequately with complex trade wastes. Large capital outlay is required and revenue expenses will be equally large.

In October 1970, replying to a debate in the House of Commons on planning and the environment, Peter Walker said that no one would solve the problems of pollution until the polluter had been made to pay the full cost of the pollution he created.

It is technically possible for all the rivers of the country to be converted into distilled water flowing through concrete banks if society wanted this and paid for it. Despite our concern for protecting the environment it is not possible for any country to set aside resources to ban all pollution on principle. Limits have to be defined, the costs assessed of working to that limit and of course what the cost is if that limit line is overstepped. The costs of conservation must be weighed against the costs of non-conservation.

CONCLUSION

Man has been polluting his environment ever since he appeared on earth. No environmental health problem has had greater significance than the disposal of man's wastes, and the accumulation of waste around camping sites undoubtedly was the reason for the ancient nomadic tribes moving to new, clean sites. The disposal of solid and liquid wastes is the problem that faced, and faces now, settled urban communities. One hundred years ago there was tremendous concern in Britain about the pollution of water supplies, rivers and the insanitary conditions of the towns together with the diseases spread by filth and its contamination of food and drink. Today, pollution, for the second time in British history, is recognised as requiring urgent action if man's environment is to be protected and preserved. There are some who would have us believe that all is gloom and doom. But provided we do not take sewerage and sewage disposal for granted, provided we recognise that these really are essential services, then there should be no reason why the scene need be one of despair.

1. J. C. WYLIE (1959) *The Wastes of Civilisation,* London.
2. *Water Pollution Control*, World Health Organisation, Tech. Rpt 318.
3. *Taken for Granted* (1970), Ministry of Housing and Local Government, Report of the Working Party on Sewage Disposal, H.M.S.O.
4. W. D. SCOTT-MONCRIEFF (1909) *Chadwick Lectures on Sanitation, 1907-8*, London.
5. J. W. STEPHENSON (1967) *Treatment and Disposal of Community Wastes*, Association of Public Health Inspectors, **76**, London.
6. J. H. MCCOY (1965) 'Sewage pollution of rivers, estuaries and beaches', *Public Health Inspector*, November.
7. *Notes on Water Pollution* (1969), No. 46. Ministry of Technology.
8. *Contamination of bathing beaches in England and Wales* (1959), Medical Research Council Memo 37, H.M.S.O.
9. *Treatment and Disposal of Wastes*, World Health Organisation, Tech. Rpt 367.
10. *Problems in Community Wastes Management* (1969), World Health Organisation, Public Health Papers 38.
11. *Notes on Water Pollution* (1965), No. 31, Ministry of Technology.
12. F. P. SEBASTIAN (1970) *Repurification and Use of Municipal Waste Water*, Envirotech Corporation, Palo Alto.
13. L. D. HILLS (1970) Fertility or Pollution, *The Ecologist*, **1**, No. 5.
14. *Working with Industry*, Report to the Standing Committee of 'The Countryside in 1970'.

11

SIZE AND GROWTH OF THE HUMAN POPULATION

WILLIAM BRASS

IN 1971 the size of the world population was about 3700 million. Such a number is beyond the grasp of our minds since it is too big to be appreciated within personal experience. Statistics of densities are rather better but still not very illuminating. The world relation of people to land area is twenty-six per square kilometre, about one-twelfth the density of England and Wales and one-twentieth that of South-East England. Whatever our views on the pleasantness of life at these higher densities, the world situation is not obviously a frightening one. Of course, the size of the population is meaningless except in terms of the resources to support it. Some of these resources, such as land area, are limited and known, others are limited but doubtfully known: for example oil reserves or the total supply of solar energy usable in food production; others again depend on possible technical innovations in agriculture or industry which might come if the need was sufficiently strong. As a result there is wide disagreement about how far the present population is from a level which would lead to dangerous biological and economic consequences.

Rather than starting from such complex and controversial questions, it is easier to consider the changes that are taking place in population size, the growth-rate, its trends and consequences. An understanding of population problems requires an appreciation of time-scales in several senses. A rate of growth of 1 per cent per year means a doubling of population in seventy years and a multiplication by 145 times in 500 years. It is worth noting that this is roughly the present pace of increase in Europe, the slowest growing of the major regions. At this rate the population of England and Wales, now just under 50 million, would rise to over 7000 million in five centuries. If the trend of increase per year were only 0·1 per cent, a negligible figure on our current standards of assessment, there would be a doubling in 700 years and a 145-fold rise in 5000 years. On a biological time-scale of human development the latter period is not long; over the past five millennia the rate of population growth has been slower than the 0·1 per cent per annum used for illustration. If we are to continue to live on this planet the average growth-rate of the population over any substantial interval must be near zero.

There are other scales which influence the assessment of population changes. One is the length of human life. Decisions by parents about births now determine numbers and age-structure directly up to the date these children die, the majority fifty, sixty and seventy years ahead but also, indirectly, much further forward through the children's children. A high proportion of the young becomes a large number in the reproductive period for the next generation, keeping the births at a substantial level even if fertility falls. The effects are carried on for upwards of a century. In contrast the speed of technological development is altering social, economic and natural conditions on a scale of years. It is in the latter terms that we tend to think ahead and act accordingly. Human beings have so far proved incapable of giving weight to the consequences of what we do on the long time-scales required. These are the basic factors which make the adjustment of the population to the environment so intractable a problem.

In 1971 the rate of growth of the world population was about 2 per cent per year, compared with 0·5 per cent in 1750-1900 and 0·8 per cent in 1900-1950. The difference between the rich one-third of peoples (Europe, North America, Australasia and Japan), and the remaining poor, is large. The people in the rich countries have increased in number at a rate which has not deviated much from 1 per cent per annum during well over a century; the growth in the poor countries has shot up from a low rate to 2·2 per cent per year or more over the past fifty years. Despite arguments about the precise importance of different factors it is clear, on a broad view, why this has happened. In the rich countries, mortality fell comparatively slowly with improved standards of living and medical technology, but fertility came down also only slightly after, leaving the natural increase of births minus deaths at a fairly constant rate. In the poor regions the impact of better conditions, of food distribution and public health was later and sharper. Although on average mortality is still high there has been little, if any, overall decrease in fertility, which remains at a level substantially above that from which the decline in the rich countries started.

The considerations above lead to two clear conclusions. The first is that the population growth in both the rich and the poor countries is far above the order of size which is supportable for any moderate period of time on a biological scale. In the five-century interval used for illustration, the present rate would give a twenty-thousand-fold increase in the world population. Even the most optimistic assessments of the earth's capacity for sustaining human life are well below that. The second conclusion is that the excessive growth is not new but has existed for at least two centuries. The earlier imbalance between births and deaths, limited to the more prosperous areas of Europe and North America, has now spread to the whole world and at the same time has reached an extreme so outside the scope of our previous experience as to be almost beyond comprehension. Nevertheless, we are essentially still in the same crisis which Malthus wrote about at the beginning of the nineteenth century. In the rich countries the fall in the birth-rate blunted the impact of the mortality changes; it has not yet, whatever the future prospects, reached the low level which would ensure the necessary near-stability of the population size over long periods of time.

The sharp surge upwards in growth which provoked the invention of the evocative terms 'population explosion' and 'the new flood' came suddenly. Nevertheless, the response of professional population scientists to the threat was slower than can be excused on the grounds of novelty or the uncertainty of the trend data. One reason for this was the comforting promise of 'natural' stable equilibrium in the Transition Theory. The implication of the theory was that rising standards of living would cause a falling death-rate and higher growth. Following shortly after, the birth-rate would decrease because of the social changes associated with the rising standards and the removal of the need to counteract the high proportion of deaths in infancy. A new balance, with low mortality and fertility giving zero or small growth-rate, would result. The extent to which this was intended as a description of what had happened in the richer countries, providing a greater understanding of possibilities for the future, as compared with a rigorous law, is doubtful. But too many accepted that by some automatic route, as the poor countries went through the development process, increased education and opportunities for female employment, longer survival of children and so on would bring the birth-rate down to meet the death-rate.

The complacency has in the main been replaced by pessimism, active or passive according to temperament. The springs of the mood are several. The rich areas persist in a high growth-rate despite the transition which appeared to be complete. Recent work on trends of fertility in Europe, in cooperative studies centred at the Princeton Office of Population Research, has brought out the complexity of the timing, speed and characterisation of change in relation to social and economic factors. We are now less sure about the dominant influences and therefore about prophesying the future. There is no agreement as to how beneficial different rates of population growth are for economic advance (and clearly the assessment will not be the same in the varied circumstances of different countries). Strong arguments support the view however that the very rapid growth, accompanied by high dependency ratios, of the poor regions imposes a heavy penalty on development, at least in terms of the income per person. The burden may be carried where other conditions are particularly favourable and increasing population size brings offsetting benefits. For the bulk of peoples in the poor regions there is a lack of balance between the increase in numbers and the pace at which physical and human resources can be exploited. There is progress but it is slow. The real fear is that development will be so hindered by population increases that it will never reach the level which will stimulate a self-correcting lowering of fertility.

It is obvious that if the world population continues to grow at the present rate we will outrun and destroy the capacity of the earth to support human life – food, energy and space will be exhausted. Long before the limits were approached there would be the dangers of a deteriorating environment through pollution and perhaps of mental disturbance leading to aggression, war and sterility such as are found in controlled, although artificial, experiments with some other animals. The erosion of natural amenities which add to the pleasures of life would occur much earlier; some would claim that these effects are already serious.

The disagreement is about how long it will take for the more damaging consequences to operate and about the value we should place on the less utilitarian and quantitative factors – natural beauty, wildlife and space – as opposed to economic advance. In terms of food alone there is the enormous discrepancy between those like the Paddocks and Borgstrom, who claim that the present population size is about the limit that can comfortably be sustained, and Malin, who estimates that the earth could support several billion people, that is, perhaps one thousand times the number living now. It is worth noting, despite the repetition, that even this total would be reached in 350 years with present growth. A realisation of the factors which impose restrictions is much easier than forecasting the innovations which could overcome them. Coale has illustrated the problem by pointing out how, in the later nineteenth century, the production of fodder for transport animals might reasonably have been put forward as a serious limitation to the possible growth of the United States population. These are legitimate differences in assessment and attitude. But unless we believe that sheer quantity of life has a value transcending all else (and a few people do) we must regard the rate of population increase as a matter of concern.

Many scientists, particularly those whose primary field of study is biology, such as Ehrlich and Hardin, see the concern as of overwhelming urgency. They are so impressed with the potential consequences of unrestrained growth and the immediate dangers (to put the mildest interpretation on their statements) that they demand extreme measures to reduce birth-rates. Demographers have tended to be more cautious, or perhaps more cowardly, because of the failure of past forecasts. As representatives, Coale in the United States and Glass in Britain can be cited. Both have pointed out oversimplifications and contradictions in the outline scene presented by the prophets of disaster. The proposed solutions and recommendations for swift action to reduce birth-rates are also treated with great reservations because of their lack of realism and ignorance of experience.

One of the inherent contradictions in the simple picture has become widely familiar outside specialist groups in the past year or two. To what extent is the rapid using-up of world resources due to population increase and to what extent to economic development and more sophisticated ways of living? Energy consumption can be taken as a crude but simple and illuminating index of a major element in resource exhaustion. It is increasing at a rate of about 5 per cent per year or two and a half times as fast as the population. The richest section of the world, North America and Western Europe, now contains about one-sixth of the people but consumes nearly 60 per cent of the energy utilised. The discrepancy is not narrowing but gaping ever wider. Over the past ten years, only one-ninth of the population rise was in North America and Western Europe but these areas accounted for more than half the increase in energy usage. Other indications that the relation between over-exploitation of resources and population is not a simple, direct one come from a consideration of population densities. More than 300 persons live per square kilometre in England and Wales, Belgium and the Netherlands but the level in the Channel Islands is nearly twice that. Luxembourg and Burundi in Central Africa have about the same population density, rather less than half that of England and Wales. On the other hand the United States and Australia, both of which have serious pollution problems, are respectively inhabited by only 22 persons and 2 persons to the square kilometre. Such elementary statistics are sufficient to show that the influence of how people live is much more dominating than the relation of numbers to land area.

Although many would accept that increasing consumption was a factor – perhaps the major factor – leading to ecological imbalance and destruction, they would argue that population growth had a significant influence. A reduction in the rate would, therefore, be valuable. Less publicised but as intractable contradictions appear when the implications of the aims are examined more deeply. In the rich countries the pressures for a population policy to encourage slower growth and stabilisation of numbers come from demands which are largely non-economic, at least in any immediate sense. A claim that a reduced birth-rate would cause a faster advance in consumption is opposed to the ecological and conservation ends which are the mainsprings of the movement. But the poor countries which have established family planning programmes to reduce birth- and hence population growth-rates have done so explicitly to forward economic development. The aim has been to relieve the constant strain on capital resources imposed by the provision of goods, services and employment for the extra population. The margin would then be used for productive investment to raise the level of living per person – and, in fact, the total national income – faster. The policy of lowering population growth is, therefore, one of increasing consumption. In view of the huge gap between standards of living in the rich and the poor countries any suggestion that the latter should have other aims in a population policy is disingenuous and certain to be treated as imperialist exploitation. Even the idea that the wealthier areas of the world might conserve resources by restricting consumption has not the simple validity that seems apparent. Coale has pointed out that the development plans of many poor countries rely heavily on the production and export of raw materials and commodities which can only be absorbed if the rich economies continue to expand.

The purpose of drawing attention to these discrepancies is not to be wholly negative or to deny possibilities of planned action. It is to raise doubts about the adequacy of simple slogans, particularly those which imply that some other group has only to change its ways for the problems to be solved. The effect of reducing population growth on economic development and use of resources, at least in the short run, is far from obvious. Neither are the implications of restricting consumption in the rich countries. There is an unfortunate tendency for solutions to be polarised, for scapegoats to be chosen, when the important and difficult questions are in the relations between population and social-economic change.

Contradictions of a different kind appear when we examine the predictions of the disastrous effects of population growth against actual trends. The evils forecast by Malthus in the early nineteenth century did not occur, partly because falls in the birth-rate kept the population increase to more modest proportions, partly because he underestimated the impact of technological innovation. Perhaps also he had his time-scale wrong, and the main consequences are still to come. Of course the failure of the more extreme prophecies of the past is not evidence to justify complacency about the future. It would be equally silly to ignore the measures of what is happening. Ehrlich, for example, sees the immediate outcome of the rapid population growth as increased death-rates due to malnutrition and contamination of the environment, as agriculture fails to expand at the necessary pace but contributes to the destruction of the ecology in the struggle to do so. But, in fact, the trend of food output per head has been upwards over the recent period on any valid method of analysis, although by a small amount as against aspirations. It is true that the population growth-rate has continually been increasing but so far agricultural production has been able to match the rise.

The contrast between the pessimism of the forecast and present movements is even more striking in the case of deaths. For, in both the rich and the poor countries, mortality is still falling rapidly on any sensible scale of measurement, that is, taking into account what has already been achieved in the most advanced areas. Only for middle-aged men in the wealthiest countries and for certain of the poorest and slowest developing populations, for example in parts of Africa, is the trend retarded or reversed. No convincing case can be made that these anomalies are directly due to population growth and, therefore, significant pointers to the future for the world as a whole. As knowledge and understanding of the process of mortality decline (particularly in developing countries recently and in historical Europe) has extended, it has become increasingly clear that the part played by medical technology, despite its importance, has not by itself been decisive. Although details are still obscure, the studies have shown the crucial influence of rising standards of living, operating through improved nutrition, sanitation, child-care practices as a result of better education, and so on. The fact of continuing falls in death-rates provides one of the strongest arguments for the belief that we are still some distance from the manifestation of the more severe of the predicted effects of the population flood.

Nearly every positive technological achievement – whether to increase food production, to give man an advantage over his biological competitors, or directly to improve his health and fitness – has some negative, undesirable side-effects. There are long lists of examples ranging from the introduction of measles to Australia when boats could travel there more quickly than the incubation time of the infection, through the spread of the parasitic disease schistosomiasis with the extension of favourable conditions for the snail host by irrigation, to the possible mercury methyl poisoning from the fungicides applied to increase yield of 'green revolution' crops. The necessity of specifying side-effects, investigating their nature and realising their dangers, monitoring and minimising them, should not overwhelm judgement about the advantages of a new technology. Of course, the dangers can be avoided by demanding sufficiently 'certain' guarantees that all adverse effects can be controlled. This ignores the evils which might be eliminated or reduced by adopting the discoveries. These remarks are platitudes, only justified in this context by the many accounts which concentrate on the side-effects without giving the positive features. In particular, few attempts to arrive at a quantitative assessment are made. There is no convincing evidence to attack the conclusion that the net balance of the influence of technological change on mortality is still strongly favourable.

Calculations of the enormous population sizes that would result from unrestrained growth and the catastrophic consequences are legitimate as a warning, but they are a diagram and not a reasonable forecast. As I see it the probabilities are of a different kind. With population increases outrunning the capacity for economic, social and resource development, pressures will build up, as they are beginning to do now, in particular countries with differing time-scales, characteristics and constraints. They will force modifications in the way of life of the community and in the economy, leading eventually to reduced fertility when the weight becomes sufficiently heavy. The justification for the belief in this type of evolution comes mainly from the lower birth-rates in more primitve communities subject to particular population burdens, for example desert nomads or island groups in the Pacific and Africa, and from some recent falls in fertility. One of the most striking and interesting of the latter, because it can be traced accurately and in detail, is occurring on the island of Mauritius. A rapid population increase – due to the remarkable drop in mortality following disease control measures in the late 1940s – led to obvious signs of economic strains. Since 1965 there has been a dramatic fall in fertility amounting to about 40 per cent by 1970 and extending to all the component communities (Hindu, Muslim, Creole and Chinese). The compactness and relative homogeneity of the community may be the explanation of the speed of events. The occurrence of the process in different countries will be dominated by changes in society and technology which we can hardly foresee. Reduction of population growth is one element in an interrelated set of responses. We cannot set it aside in a tidy compartment of its own; and the argument that it is the trigger that can more easily be operated on to effect a desirable complex of developments has yet to be proven.

The present tendencies do not seem to me to imply that the population sizes over the next thirty years or so will have disastrous effects. Although the suggestion and the previous discussion do not add up to a forecast of the doom warning kind, they are certainly not optimistic. Population growth has a powerful momentum; even a heavy brake on fertility over the next ten or twenty years will not prevent the numbers of people multiplying by a substantial factor, since the parents of the next generation have already been born in expanded cohorts. The prediction of the manner of life our descendants would prefer is likely to be a good deal less certain than a population projection, whatever its deficiencies. It is not for us to impose views on them. Few living now would happily accept the ideal conditions which our ancestors of two or three hundred years ago would have chosen for us – two acres and a cow – even in a green and pleasant England. Nevertheless, it is our responsibility to prevent our successors from being placed in difficulties which can only be solved by bitter remedies or, more mildly, where their freedom of choice of living conditions is greatly restricted. I see population policy as an attempt to preserve scope for a flexibility which is being eroded by the extreme speed of expansion. These grounds are sufficiently powerful to justify strong action to reduce birth-rates, whatever the assessment of the length of time before exhaustion and destruction of resources become a serious threat.

Much of the recent drive for rigorous population control measures has come from biologists and conservationists, particularly in the United States, who are strongly aware of possible dangers. The battle is being fought under a variety of banners, one of the most flamboyant being that of ZPG, 'Zero Population Growth'. A rapid approach to this state is advocated. Unfortunately, equal attention has not been paid to the difficulties and adverse consequences of the means suggested for achieving it, mainly by state incentives (or disincentives) and coercion. The British demographer David Glass has described some of these activities as 'offensive and unrealistic hysteria'. Without necessarily adopting the phrase as a general description, it seems fair to point out that experience over the past ten years has shown that enthusiasm is no substitute for careful analysis of the needs and problems of particular countries, leading to integrated developments over a broad range in conformity with the social and cultural constraints. Lacking this approach, the enthusiasm can hinder rather than help.

The studies of Frejka and others have shown in detail that a rapid fall to zero growth in populations which have been increasing at a moderate to fast rate would imply an unbalanced and fluctuating age-structure with serious economic disadvantages. Essentially, this occurs because of the long time-scale of human life and the divergence between the initial age composition and that which would conform with the mortality conditions and a constant population size. The research highlights also the complicated fertility variations which would be necessary to ensure rapid stabilisation and, therefore, draws attention to the fact that the refinements of control required are far beyond our present powers of social engineering.

More immediately dangerous are the large range of proposals

for extreme forms of birth limitation. These give the impression that simple, quick solutions are possible and divert attention from the slow, difficult process of changing social and economic conditions, and modifying attitudes and opinions, which is necessary. Although such proposals are often put forward in a partly speculative manner, their number and the seriousness with which they are taken is symptomatic of a desperate search for painless measures and avoidance of thought about major alterations in society. Berelson has taken a hard, cold look at the schemes in 'Beyond family planning'. Among them are such extremes as universal sterilisation at puberty with government licences for reversal; mass use of fertility control agents in water or food; large compulsory rises in the age at marriage; promotion of easily dissolved types of childless marriage; and savage financial penalties on large families, such as refusal of free education beyond the first two children. Berelson gives six criteria for judging the present value of proposals: (*a*) scientific readiness; (*b*) political viability; (*c*) administrative feasibility; (*d*) economic capability; (*e*) ethical acceptability; (*f*) presumed effectiveness. The phrases may not glitter with a fine cutting edge, but they are cogent. Before them the types of suggestion given above are reduced to their proper status as playful exercises. More moderate schemes do not survive the examination much better because increased feasibility is inversely related to effectiveness, but some may fit in as part of a range of measures which could have results in the long term.

The prospects of stabilising population sizes relatively soon in the rich countries and possibly, in the more distant future, in the poor ones, presuming that prosperity continues to increase, is now much discussed. Many surveys have shown that, on the average, parents state that given satisfactory conditions (which are of course relative) they want to have numbers of children well above the level needed for a constant or very slowly growing population size. In several European countries, with the greater efficiency of birth control, mean family sizes are now larger in the wealthier and better educated groups than the overall average. There is thus a real possibility that as the planning of family size becomes more certain and the level of living improves, there will be a further upward pressure towards population growth. It would be foolishly optimistic to believe that parents' desire for children will automatically adjust to an optimum balance. If a direct association of income with family size becomes established along with too high a birth-rate, the obvious policy would be one of financial penalties for 'excess' children. There is good support for the view, however, that these would have to be heavy to achieve much effect. The dilemma is that with the present organisation of society and the parents' freedom of decision, children would suffer for the irresponsibility of their forefathers, contrary to social justice.

Although the examination of these themes and attempts to design ways in which the main drawbacks can be overcome are legitimate and may promote better understanding of the nature of the problems, I find them unconvincing as a guide to action. In population planning all we can hope to do with our present knowledge and powers is to aim roughly in the right direction and that is towards reduced growth. There is still wide scope for doing this by making methods of family planning, suited to particular societies and individuals, better known and freely available. In the poorer countries there are reasonable grounds for the belief that a combination of easier access to efficient methods of preventing births – and more information about them – with social-economic developments such as extended education, increased participation of women in the labour force, and urbanisation, will result in lower birth-rates. There are signs of modifications in attitudes to the place of women and children which may lead in the right direction. The increasing independence and influence of the young and the pressure for women's rights are examples, though it would be naïve, in view of past history, to predict the outcome in terms of birth-rates. In Britain some professional groups, notably women doctors married to men doctors, have remarkably high average family sizes despite late marriage. Probably the most important contribution to the long-term solution of population growth problems would be the development of a stronger appreciation of corporate responsibility. Only when individual decisions about births are related to the needs of larger communities and perhaps, ultimately, the world as a whole, will it be possible to solve some of the major dilemmas. But we do not know how these attitudes can be established and what part governments and other organisations should take.

This paper has been primarily concerned with the difficulties of arriving at a balanced judgement about the dangers and disadvantages of the trends in world population and also with the contradictions and inadequacies of proposals for modifying these trends. There has, deliberately, been no attempt to pick out the path which will most effectively and conveniently take us where we want to go, although some possible directions have been indicated. Decisions about family size are not determined by single, superficial, easily influenced factors but by the essential structure of a society. Although we have some understanding of the nature of the determinants and relations we are still ignorant about the weights and interactions of the components. The classification of 'futurology' as a separate subject may be a tactical error if it prevents social scientists from exercising a proper concern about the implications of their own work, but there are important general principles. Herman Kahn has said that a major problem of the future will not be the concentration of authority in the hands of a small number of persons but the frightening power of countless individuals to make effective decisions. The population problem will only be contained if we learn how to equate individual choice of family size with the general good. It would be deception to pretend that we have any knowledge of how to succeed.

B. BERELSON (1969) 'Beyond family planning', *Science*, **163**, 533-43.

G. BORGSTROM (1967) *The Hungry Planet*, Collier-Macmillan, London.

A. J. COALE (1970) 'Man and his environment', *Science*, **170**, 132-6.

P. R. AND A. H. EHRLICH (1970) *Population, resources and environment: issues in human ecology*, W. H. Freeman, San Francisco.

T. FREJKA (1968) 'Reflections on the demographic conditions needed to establish a U.S. stationary population growth', *Population Studies*, **22**, 379-397.

D. V. GLASS (1970) 'World population trends and controls', *Proc. roy. Soc. Med.*, **63**, 1172-6.

K. M. MALIN (1967) 'Food resources of the earth', *Proceedings of the World Population Conference*, **3**, 385-90, United Nations, New York.

W. AND P. PADDOCK (1967) *Famine-1975! America's decision: who will survive*, Little, Brown, Boston.

12

CONSERVATION AND WILDLIFE

MAX NICHOLSON

COMING in half-way through this outstandingly comprehensive series of discourses, I plan to review first the wider aspects of conservation, its meaning and origins, its function and its role within the general context; and then to give some account of the current activities and situation of the world conservation movement as it relates to wildlife in the wide sense, which includes plants as well as animals and their natural environment. Then, in conclusion, I will try to review the basic concepts which have emerged from our work and our thought; to indicate their repercussions upon the great debate which is now under way concerning man's place on earth and in the universe in the light of what we are coming to know about his nature and potential, and about the errors in his course hitherto.

Although conservation of water, of soils, and of wildlife hunted for game goes back to prehistoric times, the concept as we know it today is new. Unlike all other animals man has acquired a capacity to break out of the otherwise universal system of ecological balance and constraints, by evolving mind and by learning tool-making. These two great new departures have triggered off an ever-growing instability in the relation of man to his environment which today has burst at last into consciousness as it builds up to the ultimate level of compound hazard. The obsessive urge to exploit man's tool-making capacity has distorted the evolution hitherto of the noösphere, that precious and intangible veil of higher intellectual and spiritual essence, defined by Teilhard de Chardin, which floats lightly above the biosphere, which in turn brings to life the latent promise of the atmosphere, the hydrosphere and the lithosphere. Before man became rampant on the earth, natural processes had evolved to a remarkable equilibrium between these four. Man's contribution, by adding the noösphere and the technosphere, has so far been to start upsetting the global applecart by failing to reconcile these two with each other, or the pair of them with the biosphere and its underlying layers.

Fig. 1 represents man's environment, inner and outer. You see here that I have tried to reconcile the quite different meanings the

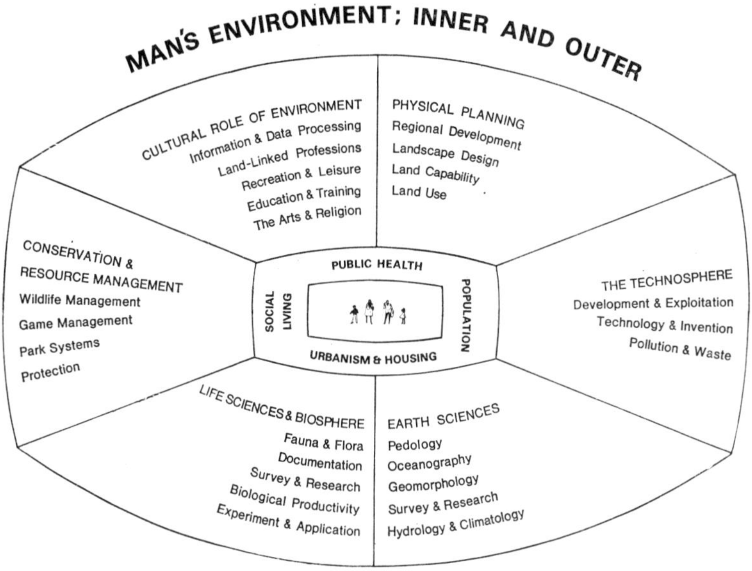

Fig. 1

word 'environment' has from the points of view of, say, an architect and a public health officer. Inner environment is what you see in the middle. You see the family, and intimately connected with this is public health, population, social living, urbanism and housing. We here are in an environment in that sense, and when we go outside we are still in this environment of urbanism.

That is not the environment in the sense which I shall be mainly discussing. I am talking about the outer environment, which I have divided into six blocks. Going up from the bottom you have the *life sciences and biosphere*, and the *earth sciences* counterpart. That is the scientific infrastructure of everything we know and do about the environment.

Next, you have *conservation and resource management*, which here I have simply listed as wildlife management, game management, park systems protection, but could well include agriculture and forestry and fisheries, which are really applied ecology. The farmers in the neolithic period did not realise they were applied ecologists; still, that is what agriculture is, and gradually we are catching up with the scientific basis of the exploitation of the land and primary production.

On the right-hand side lies the *technosphere*. This is the whole system which man has evolved for cropping, for extracting materials, really for parasitising the biosphere, the lithosphere and the hydrosphere, and for processing what he takes out of it in ways which yield some economic production, some marketable products, but also yield by-products or waste products which go back into the biosphere as shown in Fig. 2.

At the top are two rather more stratospheric sectors which include *physical planning*: regional development, landscape design, land capability, land use, and regional planning of the environment as a whole. That is where we apply our knowledge and our power over the environment in rather generalised ways at a higher level, distinct from what the farmer does actually on the soil. The cultural role of environment, which I suppose is especially relevant to us, I have divided into information and data processing, and land-linked professions, such as surveying and land management and, of course, landscape architecture, and recreation and leisure, which involve an enormous number of open-air activities; and education and training and the arts and religion.

Fig. 1 serves to show that when we speak of environment we are speaking of a conglomeration. I am basically concerned with the *life sciences* and *conservation*, but willy-nilly I will have to touch on the others, because we are more and more involved in what has been called the altogetherness of everything.

I now come to the dynamics of the system. You have the biosphere which starts from the natural areas and the way they work in terms of the ecological relationships, in terms of biological productivity. But the object of Fig. 2 is to show the two systems, nature's, which we call the biosphere, and man's, which we call the technosphere. In the left-hand bottom corner are the natural areas – highlands, low-lying lands, estuaries, lakes, rivers, oceans, atmosphere; that is, the residue of natural environment, which of course once accounted for 100 per cent of the earth's surface and is now a shrinking part of it. These, unfortunately for themselves, contain a lot of what we call natural resources, the prey for the technosphere. But these natural

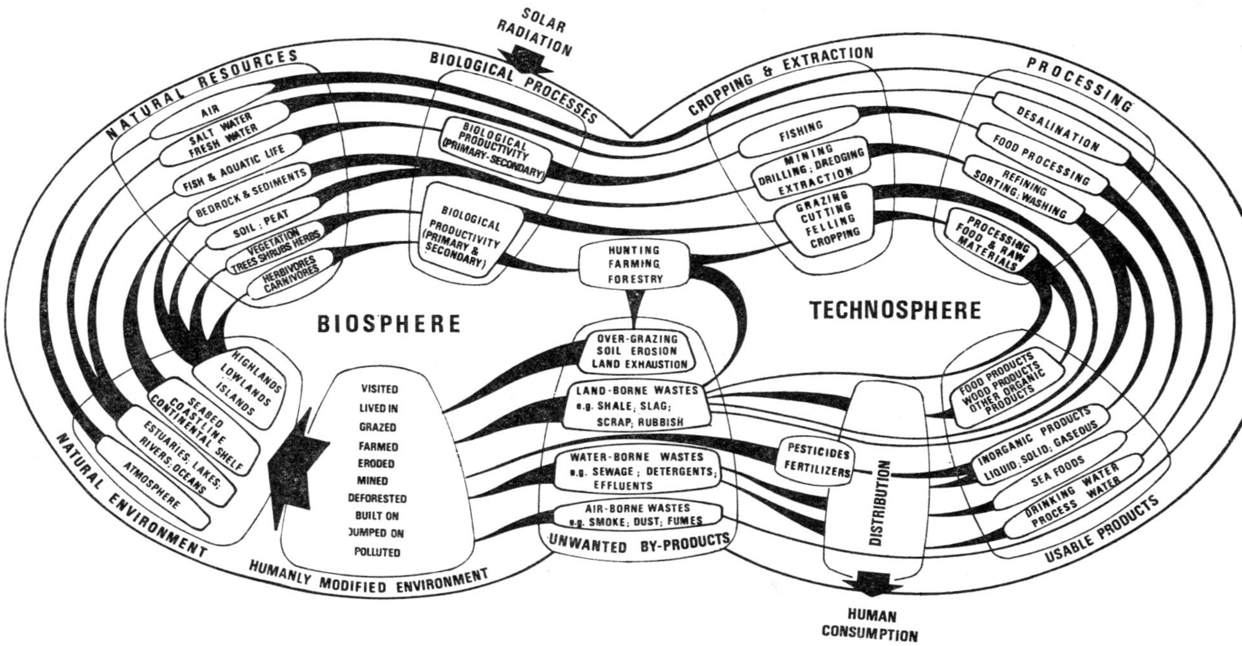
SOLAR RADIATION
NATURAL RESOURCES
AIR
SALT WATER
FRESH WATER
FISH & AQUATIC LIFE
BEDROCK & SEDIMENTS
SOIL : PEAT
VEGETATION TREES SHRUBS HERBS
HERBIVORES CARNIVORES
BIOLOGICAL PROCESSES
BIOLOGICAL PRODUCTIVITY (PRIMARY-SECONDARY)
BIOLOGICAL PRODUCTIVITY (PRIMARY & SECONDARY)
CROPPING & EXTRACTION
FISHING
MINING DRILLING; DREDGING EXTRACTION
GRAZING CUTTING FELLING CROPPING
PROCESSING
DESALINATION
FOOD PROCESSING
REFINING SORTING; WASHING
PROCESSING FOOD & RAW MATERIALS
HUNTING FARMING FORESTRY
BIOSPHERE
TECHNOSPHERE
OVER-GRAZING SOIL EROSION LAND EXHAUSTION
LAND-BORNE WASTES e.g. SHALE; SLAG; SCRAP; RUBBISH
WATER-BORNE WASTES e.g. SEWAGE; DETERGENTS; EFFLUENTS
AIR-BORNE WASTES e.g. SMOKE; DUST; FUMES
UNWANTED BY-PRODUCTS
PESTICIDES FERTILIZERS
DISTRIBUTION
FOOD PRODUCTS WOOD PRODUCTS OTHER ORGANIC PRODUCTS
INORGANIC PRODUCTS LIQUID; SOLID; GASEOUS
SEA FOODS
DRINKING WATER PROCESS WATER
USABLE PRODUCTS
HUMAN CONSUMPTION
VISITED
LIVED IN
GRAZED
FARMED
ERODED
MINED
DEFORESTED
BUILT ON
DUMPED ON
POLLUTED
HUMANLY MODIFIED ENVIRONMENT
HIGHLANDS LOWLANDS ISLANDS
SEABED COASTLINE CONTINENTAL SHELF
ESTUARIES; LAKES; RIVERS; OCEANS
ATMOSPHERE
NATURAL ENVIRONMENT

Fig. 2

resources from the standpoint of the natural system are processed by the input of solar energy and by the chemistry of plants and so on into a most elaborate productive mechanism which can yield a very high level of biological productivity. In fact, it is only perhaps in sugar-cane that man is able to attain a higher level of biological productivity. But of course man, by superseding the diversified natural area with a mono-cultural crop, whether maize or rice or Corsican pine, can produce a higher proportion of materials which are valuable to the economy.

In the area of the technosphere are the immediate cropping and extraction from the biosphere, the processing in terms of food and raw materials; the production of usable products and finally distribution. At that point the flow goes theoretically out of the system into human consumption. But of course what is supposedly consumed, as we know to our cost, is not really consumed. It goes back as refuse, scrap and waste, and you have all these unwanted by-products, including the effects on the soil and erosion, the effects of overgrazing, the effects of exhaustion of the land – all this impact back on the biosphere from the technosphere. As a result the humanly modified environment is visited, lived in, grazed, farmed, eroded, mined, deforested, built upon, dumped on and polluted. If we could show this in film form we would show the right-hand sphere growing and growing and the left one diminishing as the life is extracted from it by the disproportionate growth of the technosphere. This is an over-simplified diagram, but it makes the point that these are dynamic systems and that when we talk about man and nature it does not follow that man has much more control, certainly in the short term, over the technosphere than over nature. The technosphere is a system which has grown to a point where it has attained a momentum of its own. People like economists who assume that we are in control of the technosphere are really, more often than not, deluding themselves, as we see from the out-turn of their prognostications and interventions.

Conservation has to be a hybrid activity. It has a scientific component in ecology and the earth sciences. It has a technological component in applied park management, the management of forests, the protection and management of wildlife, and so on. It has an ethical element because all these questions, these decisions on management, raise ethical questions of conscience, of trusteeship for the future. How far are we entitled, in the interests of adding 1 per cent of G.N.P., to leave our unfortunate grandchildren in a state where they will have to take not successive increases but successive cuts in their standard of living? A lot of computer exercises have recently been done at the Massachusetts Institute of Technology[1] on a variety of assumptions concerning the availability of natural resources, population growth, pollution and quality of living. Every one of these, although they are very different, gives the result that you, whether you realise it or not, are now living in the midst of the golden age. The West has never had it so good. Some of the parameters on certain assumptions result in a downturn in the next five years. On other assumptions some of them result in a gradual downturn over a longer period. All of them show that the 'twenties and 'thirties of the next century will be so unpleasant that I am glad I will not be alive then. We are using up world resources on a scale which is quite beyond the sustained yield capacity of the biosphere; there is no getting round that. The expectations and the plans of the politicians and the economists will require us very quickly in the next fifteen years to add to our resources two other planets about the same size as this, but neither of those planets could have as much sea or ice on it; they would both have to be more conveniently arranged from the point of view of the economists and the engineers, in order to fulfil the expectations currently being voiced by the great majority of the economists and politicians on earth.

This hybrid nature of conservation is, I think, the explanation of its formidable current dynamic. It results from a fusion which is occurring between the four elements: the scientific, technological, ethical and political, releasing untold energy and by-passing traditional creeds and institutions. This is a kind of chain reaction. In terms of social engineering this synthesis may well prove to match or surpass the discovery of nuclear power. Because of course nothing is so irresistible as an idea whose time has come. Conservation may well prove the means of splitting the cultural atom and of reintegrating human culture in ways which would have been unthinkable even ten years ago.

Up to ten years ago, conservation was regarded as just one part of knowledge and action, of quite minor status. There have been all kinds of historical accidents in the history of conservation. That history or prehistory is much longer than most people think. First of all in the areas of the great rivers of the Middle East and the Indus valley it was found possible very early on, almost still in prehistory, by harnessing these rivers and by distributing and allocating their waters, to develop agriculture and provide for a very much larger population than under any other system. This led to the necessity for taming the rivers, for farming out their waters, and to some quite unexpected by-products, one of which was the invention of government: not perhaps a very happy result, but it came from the need for some system to control the use of the waters of the rivers. And of course on the heels of that came mathematics and therefore science, and also allied to this came the basis for a priesthood and for organised religions. And so this hydraulic civilisation really caused quite a number of problems which we have still to solve. One of them was urbanism. That civilisation made it possible and indeed necessary for people to live in large cities. And one of the extraordinary things for which we are getting more and more evidence every year, is how very closely urbanism followed pastoralism and agriculture. It is even argued that there may well have been cities in the world before there were villages. At any rate, the city developed very quickly as soon as there was any basis for feeding it.

Another historical accident for which we are paying a very heavy price is that there were two outstanding small peoples in prehistory and in early history: the Greeks and Jews. The Greeks had a wonderful capacity for the handling of ideas, for developing language and so on, but from the point of view of conservation the Greeks were atrocious. With their colonising habit, as soon as they were unable to support an increase of population in some original city, they founded daughter cities which they went to with their goats, stripped the forests, denuded the water supplies and so on, all round the Mediterranean. In a very short time, even by 300 B.C., they had treated their country so badly that it has not recovered yet. Indeed it is still gradually getting worse. So, from the point of view of the environment, the ancient Greeks for all their high civilisation are great criminals. And so also are the Jews. I am talking now about the Jews of the classical period, because they produced a religion which exaggerated the claims of man to dominance over nature. There are many ways of reading the various religious writings and the prophecies, but the interpretation that was in fact adopted painted man as the master of nature, and gave him a charter to multiply and replenish the earth. It thus gave him a charter to ruin nature, and we are only just beginning to realise how harmful that was.

On the other hand, some of the hunting aristocracies of the early dynasties, particularly in Mesopotamia, in Egypt, in Persia and so on, realised very early on that if people destroyed wildlife indiscriminately, there just would not be any. In the Middle East by about 5000 B.C. deer, for example, became so scarce, as a result of over-killing, that the rulers took them under control, and deer were preserved in what we would now call game reserves. After that, the rulers also introduced non-native trees. They made nature reserves, botanic gardens and zoos, at a surprisingly early date, because the destructive effects of man were so serious that the rulers at least realised that this could not be tolerated if anything was to remain. But of course they conserved these things in the interests of a very small privileged group.

Now many centuries later, during the Industrial Revolution, we had in Britain another outburst of what we would now call conservation, due to the cholera outbreaks and the resulting fears among the middle classes. I have been attacked for saying this, but anybody who looks at the records will find that it is so. Our earliest comprehensive environmental legislation and administration were due to the realisation by the middle classes that if disease, particularly cholera, broke out as a result of polluted water supplies, festering refuse and so on, it would not stop short at the working classes, but would go right through society. And so in the 1840s there was a very keen interest in what we now call the conservation of the environment in terms of prevention of pollution. Because they did not use the particular jargon we have become used to we do not recognise how very close this was to some of the things we are worrying about and doing now, in terms of air and water pollution and so on. It was then, of course, called hygiene.

Then there was also the great movement in favour of national parks and wildlife conservation. Although it built up quite a head of enthusiasm, it was so remote from political and economic issues that for a long time it had a life of its own almost as a backwater.

Natural resources development of course attracted much greater attention from the big interests, particularly in the United States where there were great natural resources in the hands of a federal government ready to be handed out to applicants. And therefore the American conservation movement, which started so promisingly with Emerson and Thoreau, was sidetracked into a struggle between exploiting industry and commerce on the one hand, and people who wanted to save something of wildlife and wilderness on the other.

I think very few people realise how modern in their approach, as we look at it in 1971, Emerson and Thoreau were. Emerson, for instance, wrote: 'The reason why the world lacks unity and lies broken in heaps is because man is disunited with himself through failing to look at the world with new eyes.' Thoreau is largely remembered for having contemplated a large pond – Walden – and written a book on it. But he also wrote a tract on civil disobedience which greatly influenced Gandhi. It was just a historical accident that a hundred years ago this movement, which had very much wider implications, was started in the United States by Emerson and Thoreau, and followed up by others such as G. P. Marsh. Of course Darwin had a great influence in a less direct way. The movement in the United States somehow fizzled out about eighty years ago, although Theodore Roosevelt did a noble job in trying to contest the crude type of exploitation of the natural environment. Even with his great authority and prestige, he was not successful in really building up a broad-based appreciation of the relation between the ecology and conservation of wildlife and nature and the environmental problem of civilised man.

Of all the possible growing points, it was, however, the wildlife and wilderness group that (after a long time itself in the wilderness) finally flowered into a full-blown intellectual and ethical appreciation of the structure of the environmental challenge. It took the better part of a hundred years to do that. The doctrines of ecology and conservation were too unpalatable for the then establishment, and were ignored by the left-wing radicals and anarchists. There was one conspicuous and rather curious exception to this. A hundred years ago Engels was writing about the price to be paid for this senseless exploitation in terms which would read very well today. Engels, unlike Marx, perceived the limitations imposed by the resources of the planet, but of course Engels did not win that particular power game, and so what he said about it may be highly relevant, but is not very influential.

I come now to the present situation in regard to the conservation of wildlife, of nature and its bearing on the wider issues. In 1948 at Fontainebleau there was formed a body then called the International Union for the Protection of Nature. This was created by people who had a sentimental, or perhaps one may say a prophetic, interest in the importance of this field, but who were very much a minority group and were not effectively linked up with the professional sciences.

At a meeting in Copenhagen in 1954 there was a kind of revolution, by which the scientists took over the leading role, and the name was changed in 1956 to the International Union for the Conservation of Nature Resources. That was largely under American inspiration. We found then that not only was the word conservation unknown in Britain and Europe but there was very strong resistance even to mentioning it. It was virtually banned on the BBC and by the Press, and in order to launch it we had to lay on a special non-event: the New Forest Commemoration Walk, fifty years after the walk by Theodore Roosevelt and Edward Grey. This walk through the New Forest compelled the broadcasting authorities and the Press to quote the word conservation, and that day – 10 June 1960 – was the first occasion on which the word conservation was even printed in its modern sense in the British Press. And it took quite a struggle to get it printed. At that time the official and unofficial national and international bodies concerned with wildlife conservation laid on a whole series of initiatives. We had meetings on the importance of the coast, which led up to the great exercise Neptune and the attempt to save as much as can be saved of the coasts of Britain, although the question of saving the coasts of Europe – particularly the Mediterranean coasts – from the British and others is something which remains to be tackled.

Again, in 1959, we started the Council for Nature, which was an umbrella body for all the voluntary movements. We gave it two new arms. One was the Conservation Corps, where for the first time we got a lot of young people to clear unwanted scrub, make paths through natural areas so that people could visit them, provide educational facilities, and so on. This is still going on and it has given energetic young people something they can actually do with their hands, in parties, to help in conservation. We also started an intelligence unit which for the first time fed information to the Press and broadcasting (this I must say was very handsomely supported by the BBC). We were able to collect from innumerable sources a great deal of news and put it in a suitable form to the Press. Many people take for granted now the enormous flow of items of information about conservation. It took a lot of organising, because we had to bridge the gap between Fleet Street journalists and people working up and down the country in remote areas. This was very effective; the Press played very well and there is now an enormous amount of publicity. If you analyse almost any day's newspaper you will now find a great deal of news about conservation and ecology.

We were also able to develop the beginnings of professional nature conservation. We started with universities – and they took some persuading. Conservation courses for ecologists, for people who were going to apply ecology in conservation, such as the one at University College London, began in 1960. Also we got together the nucleus of the Naturalists' Trusts. There are now Naturalists' Trusts in every county in England, and also for all of Wales and Scotland. This brought in many valuable people who were not really naturalists, but who had an interest in the future of their county and were often more effective and knowledgeable than most of the naturalists. They were therefore able to exercise a considerable influence on what went on, and to reason with County Councils and other authorities in a way which has made a decisive difference to the treatment of the environment. Also in 1961 the World Wildlife Fund was started, and it is rather interesting to recall that in the first ten weeks or so we raised £46,000 of which £10,000 came from the late Jack Cotton and some £36,000 from readers of the *Daily Mirror* in sums of shilling postal orders upwards. The World Wildlife Fund has now of course raised millions, and has a very considerable influence on the conservation of wildlife all over the world. There are fourteen affiliated bodies.

Again, in 1961, we were told by the pundits that as soon as the European governments went out of Africa, the poachers would swarm in, there would be no national parks, and all the animals would be shot. We decided to talk to the Africans and we managed to assemble fifty-five at Arusha in Tanganyika; quite a large number of whom were, as we had guessed, soon included in the new African governments. I think it is true to say, particularly of East Africa, that since the European colonial governments were displaced, conservation has never looked back. The African governments have done much better both in quality and quantity. There are more and better-run national parks in Africa now than there were under the European governments. The only partial exception to this is the Congo, for although the Congo government has given extraordinarily good support, the previous Belgian administration, under the inspiration of one man, Victor van Straelen, did make an extraordinarily good scientific effort which it has not yet been possible to replace. I think that is perhaps the only case where one can say there has been some set-back, although even there the parks themselves have been maintained.

Again, we had in November 1962 a small meeting in the Camargue and we made a list of all the wetlands in Europe and North Africa which were important as staging posts for migrating wildfowl and so on. We wanted also to involve the botanists, but as so often happens the ornithologists had to do about 90 per cent of the initial work. As a result of that we got governmental action on a widespread scale, and this passion for draining marshes, often only to let them lapse again into ruined wetlands a few years afterwards, has been, if not stopped, at least slowed down.

In July 1962 at Seattle, we had the first World National Parks Conference. Those running national parks had hitherto regarded themselves as voices in the wilderness in their own country. They had had no other contact with people in the next country who were fighting the same battle. Thanks largely to Harold Coolidge, who is now the President of the International Union, it was possible to get together representatives from about fifty countries at Seattle, and since then the National Parks Administrations of the world have worked together in the spirit of a world trusteeship. They are going to meet in 1972 to celebrate the centenary of the Yellowstone Park at Jackson Lodge in Idaho.

In 1962 we had also the beginnings of the International Biological Programme. When in the 'fifties it was decided to replace the old polar years by an international Geophysical Year, enormous resources were whistled up by physicists, astronomers, radiophysicists, etc., and a very successful world programme was mounted. Not unnaturally a number of biologists were rather pained at this confirmation – it was only a confirmation – that biology, since being the queen of the sciences under Darwin and Huxley, had gone down and down. They also wanted to mount some kind of World Year.

But when they went over the whole of biology – genetics and molecular biology and so on – they found that the only subject in biology which made sense for a world programme was the ecological field. This was a painful discovery for quite a number of biologists whose interests lay in other fields, but the best of them swallowed their disappointment and backed the International Biological Programme. It has been very badly supported financially, but now at last has about sixty countries behind it, nominally at least, and is producing remarkable programmed results in terms of biological productivity, even in terms of human adaptability. One section is even studying the uniqueness of different human groups which may become extinct, as the animals in the Red Book (which I shall mention later) may become extinct in the near future. They are measuring human capability for standing up to high altitudes, to high and low temperatures and other extreme conditions, especially where there may be some genetic factor involved.

We were also in the early 'sixties working hard on the educational problem in Britain, and the report, *Science Out of Doors*, came from that study group. We worked on the teacher-training colleges, particularly on the question of replacing the old-fashioned nature study by a more modern concept of ecology and of the role that ecology could play, not just in teaching people about the countryside, but in teaching people to think in terms of dynamic patterns. The natural sequences go over much longer periods than the Treasury is accustomed to think of in budgeting our fate, and ecology gives people an apparatus in their minds which could help them on many other subjects.

Again at that time we had National Nature Week in May 1963. The Duke of Edinburgh was appalled at the state of disarray in which he found the conservation movement, and he initiated the 'Countryside in 1970' conferences which have been successful in bringing together most of the bodies interested in this; not only conservationists but industry, government departments, local authorities, farmers and so on. Although a number of people may be impatient about the results, no other country in the world has made so much progress through infiltrating different groups which had goodwill, or at least potential goodwill, towards conservation, but just did not know what it meant or what they could do about it. We got tremendous dividends from getting together with them and from producing a more sophisticated appreciation of environment, for example in large sectors of British industry.

After the launching of IBP, there was a first meeting in 1964 of the Council of Europe committee of experts. Looking at the original papers I find that in 1964 they said the working party's policy was to create an active sense of responsibility among Europeans for their environment. Now, in 1971, having finished European Conservation Year, we can say not only that the working party had a good policy but that their efforts have been instrumental in giving it a degree of fulfilment which would be envied by many politicians and by other groups which have tried to persuade people to feel responsibility for other good causes.

I would like to give you a few examples of the kind of work that has been done in relation to wildlife. I am a member of the International Commission on National Parks and ten years ago we persuaded the United Nations to pass a resolution calling for a world survey – a kind of Domesday Book – of what national parks there were, where they were, what was in them and how well they were run; whether they were being given enough support by the legislature, whether they had enough money and manpower, and what were their problems. In the newly revised version of this survey there are now over 1200 areas admitted to this register, many others being denied admission unless they conform to certain standards. Naturally the standards could be and should be raised in some cases, but we have in this United Nations list an instrument of recognition, of persuasion, and also a sanction against the misuse of the term 'National Park' where the area is not fully and properly supported by the government concerned.

In those early 'sixties we had too many people writing in from all over the world on all kinds of emergencies about which we were not adequately informed. There were fire alarms being rung all over the place and the fire brigade did not know where to go, or which were the false alarms. We therefore compiled the so-called Red Book, the Survival List, in which we now have up-to-date details of virtually every animal and an increasing number of plants which are in some recognisable danger of extinction. We now know pretty well where the remains of these species are, what state they are in and what their problems are. There is a kind of network of the conservation movement at all levels which is very effective. Not much happens that we do not hear about, if it is really a matter of life and death to conservation. We generally have means of intervening – not of course always successfully, but we are increasingly listened to.

In East Africa we had a revolution in wildlife management which was largely brought about by the American Fulbright scholars who went out there during the 'fifties and showed how to replace the purely anecdotal and amateurish management of game by scientifically based methods. There was an illuminating story about in East Africa at that time. One of the old-time trustee boards had a recommendation that they bring in an ecologist to a certain national park. One of the older members objected and after a great deal of discussion he said that if they must bring in an ecologist, why couldn't they bring in a pair so that they might breed. It turned out he thought an ecologist was some sort of antelope. The Director appointed a young ecologist who had recently married and had the great satisfaction a year after of sending this gentleman a telegram: 'Ecologists have bred'. We have come a long way from that. People now know what an ecologist is, and those who go to or see films about the East African national parks soon see what a big reward we have got for putting these on a scientific basis.

I am the convener of the conservation section of the International Biological Programme. There we are conducting a very ambitious exercise called the Check Sheet Survey, which brings in material about scientifically important sites throughout the world. We have about two years to run on it and we are computerising the information. When enough has been put into the data banks we will be able to find out how many different types of ecological community there are on the earth, how many of these are included in some protected natural area, which ones are not protected, where are the best examples of these, and how to protect them. I am slightly impatient and think it is going far too slowly, but at least we have made a considerable start with global environmental monitoring in this sense.

Another body called Scope is concerned with the other aspect of environmental monitoring, of finding out how much pollution there is, how much DDT is floating about in the air, how much mercury is getting into the ocean, and what the levels are. We will eventually, we hope, get the full world-wide system set up in time for the 1972 Stockholm conference of the United Nations. We hope that just as a climatologist can tell you what the rainfall is or what the hours of sunshine are in different parts of the world, we will have a network of stations which will be able to report and sound the alarm if there is any sudden increase in certain types of pollution or if any of the species indicated within the environment register some change. For example, the peregrine falcon suddenly dropped from 650 breeding pairs in Britain thirty years ago to less than 60 in 1962. This means something. In that case it meant that toxic chemicals on the land were being consumed by the prey species and were making it impossible for the peregrines to breed, because so much toxicity was concentrated at the top end of the food chain that their eggs became infertile and the eggshells were too thin. Through the work of Monks Wood, one of the prototypes of the new type of ecological station, we were able not only to find out what was happening on the land but to propose remedies and get them agreed to by the farmers and the chemical industry. We now know that whereas in 1962 the peregrine was down to 10 per cent of its former breeding numbers, it has recovered to 55 per cent. So we monitor by what is happening on the ground that our diagnosis was correct and that the remedies are being successfully carried out. We are getting a really scientific basis for the monitoring of the environment.

We also have in the International Biological Programme a series of biome studies upon the forests, the deserts and so on. We are now looking at these great regions of the world as a whole and we are getting a growing network of international ecological stations. One of the first was the Darwin Station in the Galapagos, set up in 1959. We now have stations in Serengeti in East Africa, one on Aldabra which was snatched from the jaws of the Ministry of Defence with the aid of a devaluation provided thoughtfully by the Treasury at the critical moment; also stations in West Africa. One is being formed in the Gir Forest in India, one in Malaya in the Pasoh Forest and another in the Canadian Arctic. We are getting towards a point where every part of the world will have some station where ecologists of different nations can go and work out what is happening in these biomes.

We also made a start with what Mr MacNamara of the World Bank calls ecological validation. Last year the World Bank hired its first ecologist. I am told he is doing very well, and rather to the surprise of the bankers and economists his advice has not only proved ecologically good but has not led to the troublesome practical consequences and difficulties which the economists told the bank it would have.

We are of course continually fighting destructive projects and forces all over the world. One of the saddest has been the mass destruction of the whale population, which in its shame and horror can only be compared perhaps with the destruction of the buffalo or bison in North America a hundred years ago. Owing to the selfish slaughter imposed by a few nations on the whale stocks of the world several species of this wise and remarkable animal have been vastly reduced, fortunately to such an extent that it is ceasing to pay commercially to hunt them. The main hope is that in God's good time they may build up again.

I think I have said enough to show that we have not been idle.

People who think that concern for the environment is something which has suddenly happened are wide of the mark. It is because of what was done, above all in the 1959-64 period, that things are at last beginning to happen now. That is almost seven years, about the minimum time-lag in which in this imperfect world you can get much to happen.

We are now building up a trained force of ecologists and conservationists, which is effective within its limits. On the other side, of course, it is a question of the build-up of the forces making for the destruction of nature. And if you look at the galloping population explosion, the enormous increase of pollution, the great growth of half-baked economics and technology which are leading to the senseless destruction of so many irreplaceable assets in the environment, and the worship of the golden calf of growth of the Gross National Product – which I am glad to see is now becoming repudiated by such leading economists as Kenneth Galbraith – it would be very rash to say that all our efforts and all our successes would add up even to keeping pace with the growing impact of the forces on the other side. Indeed, as I said earlier, the computer in its rather hard-hearted and impersonal way indicates the opposite. The computer indicates that the forces of doom are still in the ascendant.

We are forced then ever to widen the front. We have to remember that ecology has a dual role. Ecology, as we know, is the study of plants and animals in relation to their environment and to one another. But it is also more than that: it is the main intellectual discipline and tool which enables us to hope that human evolution can be mutated, can be shifted on to a new course, so that man will cease to knock hell out of the environment on which his own future depends.

We have seen events which are heartening, like Earth Day in the United States; we have seen the European Conservation Year; these are very encouraging, though they would be even more so had they happened in 1955 rather than in 1970. Time is getting very late now. And the question I would like to leave you with is the question on which I wrote an article in *Le Monde*. I said: Where are the savants? Where are the artists? Why is it that in all this great struggle which is so decisive for mankind – not only for its existence but for all the values of mankind – where are the leaders of literature, where are the painters, where are the sculptors, what are they doing? What did you do in the Great War, Daddy? We conservationists, who are fighting a very stiff battle, not without success and with great determination, we would like to see some more support from the ranks of the upholders of culture. Could there not be – sometime on this earth, before it vanishes – just one high culture that does not make a slum of its environment as the Greeks did, and as so many other cultures have done, including our own? Could there not be a culture which really promotes the harmony of man and the environment, as well as the harmony between man and man – and the two are very closely related. Could not these things go together? Could not the people who regard themselves as, and to some extent are subsidised as, the upholders of culture, could not they join in this cause which surely has a certain cultural relevance?

Having put that question, I would like to close with a rephrase of Nelson's signal at Trafalgar: Nature expects that every man this day will do his duty.

1. For the computer exercise at M.I.T. on projecting world resources, see Professor J. W. Forrester (1971) *World Dynamics*, Cambridge, Mass.

13

FOOD

MICHAEL ALLABY

WE are discussing survival. The subject of this series of papers is the survival of civilisation as we know it, perhaps the survival of man as a species. We are considering the limitations imposed on our society by natural laws which we cannot evade and we ignore at our peril.

Clearly, one of the prime requirements for the survival of any living organism is a supply of food. If our numbers are increasing, then somewhere there must come a time when we meet the barrier of the planet's capacity to feed us. The earth is sometimes likened to a spaceship: all its natural cycles are closed and it receives from outside only the solar energy that powers it, and this is a constant.

There can be no doubt that the 'population explosion' is happening. Indeed, to a large extent it has happened already. It took 200,000 years for the world population to reach a thousand million, 100 years to add the second thousand million, thirty years to add the third thousand million and the fourth thousand million will be added in fourteen years.[1] Man is the only creature that is able to modify its environment and each environmental improvement that has been made – the discovery of fire, the discovery of agriculture, the industrial revolution – has resulted in an increase in our numbers. Looked at in this way it would seem that the aim of each technological advance we have made has been to increase our numbers. The final revolution was achieved by medical science, which has introduced a measure of death control. Many who would have died from infectious disease before reaching the reproductive period of their lives now survive. We have introduced death control without a parallel introduction of birth control; and given the conditions in which so many of the additional human beings have to live, there can be little doubt that the advances made this century in medical research have added very greatly to the sum total of human misery.

The world's population is now doubling every thirty-five years or so. Paul Ehrlich[2] has calculated the eventual effect of this rate of growth. In 900 years, he says, there will be a million billion (10^{18}) people, or 1700 per square mile. In 2000 to 3000 years the people would weigh more than the earth. In 3000 to 4000 years the mass of humans would equal the size of a sphere with the same diameter as the earth's orbit around the sun. In 5000 years the entire visible universe would be people, expanding outwards at the speed of light. The ultimate big bang, you might say.

Obviously it will not happen. It is dangerous even to make predictions beyond the end of this century because there are so many factors that might intervene. A change in the ratio of the sexes would affect profoundly the rate of population growth or decline.

It seems unlikely, however, that the present rate of growth will be checked before the end of this century and this means we must allow for a doubling of world population by the year 2000. In 1969 the world population growth rate was 1·9 per cent for the third successive year.[3]

The population explosion is not distributed evenly. In 1965 the economically developed countries of Europe, the USSR, North America and Japan had somewhat more than 1000 million inhabitants. A further 800 millions lived in the communist countries of Asia. Some 1500 millions lived in the less developed countries of the third world. By 1985 the population of the rich countries will probably have increased by 25 per cent, while that of the poor countries will have increased by 60 per cent. Thus, of every 100 additional human beings born between 1965 and 1985, 85 will live in the poor countries.[4] This increase in population will call for an 80 per cent increase in food supplies by 1985, assuming that the *per caput* income in the poor countries does not rise. If it does, and if the FAO's calculations of its increase are accurate, then the demand for food will increase by 140 per cent.[5] Dr Norman E. Borlaug, winner of the 1970 Nobel Peace Prize for his work in developing hybrid wheats, sent a message to the FAO 25th Anniversary Conference in Rome in November 1970, in which he warned that the monster of rapidly increasing population could destroy the world.

If we allow, then, that world population is doubling every thirty-five years and that 85 per cent of this increase is taking place in countries of the third world, can they be fed? In my view they can be, for a strictly limited period, provided the primary problem, that of population growth, is tackled and solved. In his conclusion to a symposium on population and food supply, Sir Joseph Hutchinson, FRS, said:

> Population growth at anything like the current rate cannot be supported for many generations. . . . There can be no disagreement with the view that our first obligation is to provide the food and other biological resources for those already born, or whose arrival we can foresee. In the longer term, however, it should be accepted that agricultural production cannot be multiplied indefinitely. It is no more than common prudence to plan for the stabilisation of human populations before the point is reached that food production can no longer keep pace with human multiplication, and readjustment by catastrophe becomes inevitable.[6]

What are the theoretical limitations of population with regard to food supply? Colin Clark, former Director of the Agricultural Economics Research Institute at Oxford, has calculated that the world could support a population of 45,000 million.[7] Looked at in terms of ecological energetics, Deevey has calculated that theoretically, population could increase by thirty or forty times, but to do so man would have to replace all other herbivores, and utilise all the world's vegetation. No land could be spared for non-agricultural use and people would have to inhabit the polar regions and artificial islands 'scummed over with 10 inches of Chlorella culture'.[8] All this is theory. What is certain is that other limiting factors would prevent our numbers from ever reaching such proportions. I mention them only to indicate that the limiting factor in population growth may not be food production.

The international organisation set up to solve the problem of food production and distribution is the Food and Agriculture Organisation of the United Nations. In 1963 the FAO held its First World Food Congress in Rome and as a result of that congress, work began on what is now called the Provisional Indicative World Plan for Agricultural Development (IWP). The IWP was published in August 1969 and was debated at the Second World Food Congress, held in The Hague in June 1970.

The IWP postulates a population increase of 2·6 per cent per year, which, combined with the increased income it also assumes, will call for an increase in food supply of 3·9 per cent per year. From 1956 to 1966 food production rose by 2·7 per cent per year.[4] The latest figures available, for 1969, indicate that for the first time in twelve years there was no increase in overall world food production. The population growth has been revised to 2·7 per cent per year and with the exception of the Far East, food output in the developing countries has fallen still further behind population growth.[9] The world figures are slightly misleading, because they include a drop in production in the developed countries. In fact, production in some of the developing countries did increase, but not enough. In the one exceptional area, the Far East, there was an increase of 4 per cent, which is a little lower than that in previous years, but for the first time production seems to be overtaking population. In Latin America, on the other hand, production rose by an average of only 1 per cent over the 1968 figure, while the population grew by 2·9 per cent. In Africa as a whole production remained at about the 1968 level; there was an increase of about 1 per cent in the Near East, where the population is increasing by 2·6 per cent per year; total output in Eastern Europe and the USSR was down by 5 per cent, total production remained static in Australia and New Zealand, the United States and Western Europe, while Canada produced 5 per cent more than in 1968.[9]

The IWP calculates that to meet the difference between production and demand by importing from the countries with surpluses, the developing countries would have a food import bill of $26,000 million by 1985, and that is assuming that prices did not rise above their 1962 level.[10] Since the countries concerned found considerable difficulty in meeting their $3000 million food bill in 1962, the IWP concludes that any substantial increase in food availability must be achieved within the developing countries themselves.

The FAO has reasoned that increases in food production must begin with an increase in cereal production. It is the cereal crops that provide the staple foods and the feedstuffs for livestock. They are psychologically important, too. Even we call bread 'the staff of life'.

Cereal production may be increased in one of two ways. The first is to bring new, 'virgin' land into cultivation. The IWP rejects this approach.[11] To bring new land under the plough would divert investment which could be spent on improving and intensifying the farming systems already in existence. In fact, there may be no tillable land left. Over the planet as a whole, 40 per cent of the land area is desert, wasteland or permanent human habitation; 20 per cent is inaccessible forest which it is difficult to reach for present-day forestry production. There is 13 per cent of accessible forest, which is itself quite inadequate for our needs and which cannot be considered as available for food production. If then we add in the total area that is being farmed already, we are left with some 950 million acres of marginal land from which food might be produced. At present-day production levels, the annual increase in world population requires an additional 125 million acres per year. Thus, if the world food problem were to be tackled by expanding production, at existing levels, into the marginal land, we would run out of such land by the late 1970s.[12]

The FAO has opted for the intensification of production on existing farms. It concentrates on cereals, but recognises that the major need is not for an increase in carbohydrates but in protein. The *per caput* protein requirement varies from country to country, but averages 48·4 g per person per day.[13] In the developing countries, this is supplied mainly from vegetable sources. Whereas in this country, where daily *per caput* consumption of protein is 87·5 g, 53·8 is provided by animal protein,[14] in Peru, the daily protein consumption is 54·1 g, of which 19·9 g is animal protein.[15] In Libya people eat 63·7 g of protein a day, of which 14·7 is of animal origin.[16] In India, in 1963, the IWP base year, protein consumption was 50·1 g per person per day, of which 6·4 were of animal protein; by 1966 these figures had fallen to 45·4 and 5·4 respectively.[17] This is what the world food problem is about.

The simplest solution to closing the protein gap might be to introduce new, high-protein cereals. Even quite a small increase in the protein content of rice could improve the protein/calorie balance and eliminate much of the protein deficiency in Asia.[18] Other high-protein crops might also be introduced, such as soya, and then, with a secure, high-protein cereal base, livestock might be brought in to increase the availability of animal protein.[19] There is a school of thought here that argues that it is more efficient for man to utilise vegetable protein than to re-process it through animals. A kind of ecological rule of thumb says that each stage in the energy cycle utilises about 10 per cent of the energy available to it. Thus, green plants capture something like 10 per cent of available sunlight, and animals, in converting plant protein into animal protein, capture about 10 per cent of the energy in the plant. This reduces the solar energy available to carnivores to about 1 per cent. These figures vary a little, but the reasoning is sound so far as it goes. If man were to live on an exclusively vegetable diet, instead of a partly animal diet, then it should be possible to increase the protein available from animal sources by a factor of ten. In practice, however, there are limits to man's adaptibility to a wholly herbivorous diet and there are large areas of land that are suitable only for grazing animals and from which it is possible to harvest protein at little cost. The trouble is that we cannot digest cellulose, which means that most vegetable protein is not available to us directly. The difficulty has been overcome by synthesising protein from cellulose on an industrial scale. If this limitation is removed and man can make digestible almost any plant, then it has been calculated that the most efficient source of food will be natural ecosystems, with their own climax vegetations and their own diversity, helped a little, perhaps, to increase their natural productivity.[20] The calculation is based on ecological energetics. A great deal of research work has been done on the synthesising of protein by growing yeasts on a number of nutrient bases, and some of the products are on the market already. These synthetic and simulated foods may have a part to play in gaining time, but they are not cheap. To provide synthetic food for the world's additional population in one year, more than 70 million persons, would require an annual investment of at least $15,000 million.[21]

Even if this were feasible on a major scale, have we solved the problem? Are we to devour our natural habitat? In any case, is this the most efficient way of converting vegetable protein into digestible food? The oceans are rich in crustacean zooplankton called krill. We might be able to harvest the krill and convert them to a palatable food, but would we ever be as good at it as the blue whale? The blue whale mother weighs 75 to 100 tons and converts 2 to 2·5 tons of krill a day into milk for her suckling baby, which grows at the rate of 170 to 200 lb a day.[22]

It would make more sense to produce protein food additives to increase the protein content of existing diets, but there is nothing new in this. The Chinese have used soya for this purpose for thousands of years, and people of many other cultures have discovered similar additives. We run a grave risk of trying to teach our grandmothers to suck eggs.

The IWP aims to increase cereal production. The method is deceptively simple. It depends on a series of new, high-yielding hybrid cereal plants.

Traditional varieties of cereals are not sufficiently responsive to inputs of fertiliser. They are long-stemmed and if the ear becomes heavier, which is desirable, the plant is likely to be flattened, to 'lodge', by wind or heavy rain. This makes it impossible to harvest. The new varieties are short-stemmed, so reducing the risk of lodging. They are also quick-maturing, which means that up to three crops a year may be taken from the same land. The new 'miracle' rice is called IR8. It was developed in the Philippines and its performance, although this varies from country to country, has given a yield of 10,000 lb per acre in the Quezon Province of the Philippines, as compared to 1330 lb for the local variety.[23] This is exceptional, of course, but if increases of anything approaching this figure can be achieved throughout the third world, the food problem is solved. Always provided, of course, that the population problem is solved, also.

The introduction of the new varieties has been called 'The Green Revolution'. At a press conference in The Hague on 23 June 1970, FAO's Secretary-General A. H. Boerma said he had not invented the name 'Green Revolution', he was not happy with it and he would prefer to see it dropped. The sad fact is that the Green Revolution has turned sour. The first snag had been the social-economic-political one of providing the essential structure within the developing countries themselves to ensure that the profits from increased yields are distributed equitably. If they serve only to enrich already wealthy landowners, they will meet with fierce opposition from the workers and those political organisations and trade unions that represent them. Largely for these reasons the Green Revolution has barely begun in Latin America.

The second snag, also a political one, concerns the attitude of the rich countries to the poor ones. If the new cereals are to succeed they will require high inputs of fertiliser, they will need insecticides, fungicides and herbicides and they will call for improved irrigation systems. It is the policy of FAO to encourage the developed countries to make these inputs, or their capital equivalent, available. This has not happened. The 1 per cent of GNP that Lester Pearson recommends developed countries to give in aid is no more than a dream.

If the inputs were available, how successful would they be likely to be? and anyway, how large are the inputs?

The first requirement is for improved irrigation. At the present time, according to WHO surveys, only some 500 million people in the entire world enjoy the luxury of tap water. Over 90 per cent of the populations of the developing countries are actually short of water. The Aswan Dam is hailed as a triumph of engineering, which undoubtedly it is. It will create one of the largest artificial lakes in the world, and it will augment the cultivable land of Egypt by 15 per cent. During the time it has taken to build it, Egypt's population has increased by 35 per cent.[24] At the same time the dam increases the spread of diseases transmitted by aquatic organisms that used to decline in numbers during the dry season. Bilharzia, now more usually known as schistosomiasis, is on the increase. This is the fifth Aswan Dam and it will lose by evaporation water equivalent in volume each year to the entire lake held by the dam it replaces.[25] As a direct result of building the dam, and so cutting off the annual floodwater, the salinity of the eastern Mediterranean has increased and the fish population is declining.[26] This affects Egypt and Israel particularly.

All in all it is extremely unlikely that the fresh water needed for the irrigation of the new varieties exists, and it is fairly certain that in years to come major projects such as the Aswan Dam will be regarded as catastrophes.

If there is doubt about the availability of water, there is just as much doubt about the availability of fertiliser. IR8, the new rice, requires 70 to 90 lb of fertiliser per acre.[27] If two crops are grown in a year, this means 140 to 180 lb, and three crops, which are considered possible, will need 210 to 270 lb. Fertiliser production is increasing each year, and so is its consumption in the developing countries, but in 1967-68 the average consumption per acre of arable land in developing countries was 13 lb per acre (12 kg/ha). The average consumption in Western Europe during the same period was around 168 lb per acre (153 kg/ha).[28] So, although the recommended fertiliser consumption is not high by our standards, it nevertheless represents an increased consumption in the third world of between five and twenty times.

Where is the fertiliser to come from? By 1966 the developing countries were producing 50 per cent of their own fertiliser,[29] but at 1966 consumption levels. Perhaps the reluctance of the developed countries to make available the finance to buy in fertiliser in the kind of amounts required might be explained in part by the fertiliser shortage such purchases could cause at home.

The effectiveness of fertilisers depends to a very large extent on the structure of the soil. In Britain we are fortunate in having a mild climate and several centuries of careful husbandry, which have given us some very robust soils that will stand up to heavy fertiliser applications. Even so, troubles are looming ahead. There is incontrovertible evidence that over-use of nitrogenous fertiliser is harmful to the soil and to the nutritive value of the crop.[30] Although these effects have been observed only at very high application rates, it is also known that fertilisers have an addictive effect if they are used as the main nutrient source. Thus the maximum of 90 lb per acre may be expected to increase, while adverse effects may begin to appear at much lower application levels on soils poorer than our own. Eroded soils need organic matter to build up a good structure. Without this, neither fertilisers nor irrigation can work efficiently.

To some extent the introduction of a new species into any area is likely to cause ecological problems as the ecosystem adapts itself to receive them. It does seem, however, that the new hybrids are particularly vulnerable to pests and to disease. This may be due in part to the intensity with which they are grown, or it may be a genetic weakness in highly sophisticated plants bred selectively for particular qualities. Whatever the reason, there will need to be an increase in the use of pesticides.[31] At the present time 20 per cent of the world's total pesticide production is used in developing countries, on 70 per cent of the world's farm land.[32] Again, where is the increase to come from?

There are two points that spring to mind in connection with the use of agrochemicals generally. Fertilisers and pesticides are closely bound in with the petrochemical industry. Current estimates are that the world's resources of petroleum will be exhausted within the next thirty-five years or so. What happens then? The second point is that the theory on which agrochemicals are based is itself inherently unsound. At one time it was believed that the total nutrient requirement of a crop could be met by synthetic soluble salts that would dissolve when it rained and be taken up by the plant roots. We know now that this is a gross over-simplification and that the soil micropopulation is involved in making nutrients available to plants. Thus the effectiveness of fertilisers depends on the soil microorganisms. These are associated with the soil's organic matter, which also gives the soil its structure. Thus a reduction in organic matter at once affects nutrient availability. At the same time, the addition of concentrated doses of chemicals will itself alter the ecology of the soil organisms in a way which on the one hand reduces the capacity of the soil to make nutrients available naturally and on the other hand tends to break down the soil's structure by reducing the organic content. All too often, what has happened is that a useful tool has become a crutch and fertilisers, which used wisely are a valuable aid to the good farmer, have made it easier for the bad farmer to stay in business.

In the case of pesticides, the pollution caused by the persistent organochlorines is notorious. More serious, however, may be the response of the pest insects to insecticides and of weeds to herbicides. After each application of an insecticide there are a few individual insects that survive, either because their outer skin is too thick for the pesticide to penetrate or because they have metabolic pathways by which these substances are de-toxified. These individuals form the nucleus of the breeding colony which is immune to the pesticide in question. Frank Wilson, director of the Sirex Biological Control Unit, has said that there are now some 250 species of farm pests that are so resistant that pesticides cannot be used against them. Although pesticides have not been used to such a large extent in agriculture in the third world, they have been used in disease control programmes, and the likelihood is that their residues are distributed widely in the environment in these countries. In July 1970 Professor James Busvine of the London School of Hygiene and Tropical Medicine informed a meeting of the FAO Working Party on Pest Resistance to Pesticides, of which he is a member, that he knew of 600 cases of pest resistance involving over 100 different types of pest, 'and these only represent the cases we have verified'.

The development of resistant strains of a pest is called loss of biological efficiency. It is a natural response to the introduction of toxic materials into the creature's environment and it is extremely well documented. A classic example occurred in a part of Queensland, Australia. *Boophilus annulatus microplus*, a cattle tick, was introduced to Australia in about 1872. It spread fairly rapidly and about fifty years ago farmers began to try to control it by dipping or spraying their animals, using arsenite of soda. This was only partly successful and some resistance appeared. Then DDT was introduced, but eight years ago DDT dips were banned because residues remaining in the produce rendered the meat unacceptable for export. So they introduced organophosphorus compounds, which are more toxic than the organochlorines, but which break down more quickly, so leaving no residues. Five years ago the problem grew worse. Farmers were having to dip their animals more regularly, and more resistant strains appeared. The Queensland Government introduced a control programme which required farmers to dip animals frequently in extra-strong solutions. By late 1969 they were dipping at ten-day intervals at double strength. When last I heard from Queensland the farmers were achieving only about 40 per cent kills and the pests were becoming immune to the pesticides almost as fast as they could be introduced. I don't know whether there will be a satisfactory solution to the Queensland ticks; but if there is, it will certainly involve abandoning all insecticides, probably for some time.

The FAO is becoming increasingly concerned about the effects on health of pesticide use. In May 1971, there is to be a seminar on the safe and effective utilisation of pesticides in South America. Not surprisingly, part of the objective is to accelerate the growth of the agrochemical industry in Latin America. The seminar is sponsored by eleven pesticide manufacturers and the chairman of the committee which has made all the arrangements for it is J. I. Hendrie, head of the Agricultural Division of Shell. The FAO also announced in October 1970 that $2 million have been allocated to establish a Pesticide Research Centre for the developing countries and also a similar centre for Integrated Pest Control.

There is yet one more drawback to the new hybrid cereals. They require 'a continued flow of suitable new varieties, resistant to the major pests and diseases, and capable of high yields in response to the application of modern farming technology. This implies both a multi-disciplinary breeding and research programme to produce and test the varieties; and a well-organised multiplication and distribution programme to ensure that quality seed is available to the farmers in adequate quantity.'[33] This seems to mean a steady supply of new seed. The reason is probably that the hybrids are genetically unstable and that they will revert to the old varieties from which they were developed if they are grown year after year from seed kept back by the farmer. Is their success due, in part at any rate, to the hybrid vigour that is a phenomenon well known to plant breeders, but which can be maintained only by periodical repetition of the cross?

It seems, therefore, that the Green Revolution is doomed in advance if it is based solely on (*a*) hybrid cereals that require water which is not available; (*b*) fertilisers which are not available and which could probably not be used at optimum efficiency on poor, unstable soils; and (*c*) pesticides that are not available and to which those pests that are not resistant already will develop resistance.

As though this were not enough, there is consumer resistance to

IR8. It becomes soggy when it is cooked and has chalky spots.[34] Also, its protein content is low, 5 to 7 per cent, compared with 7 to 9 per cent in the traditional varieties.[35] Where it has been introduced the price of the traditional varieties has increased.

The new cereals are a perfect example of what Nigel Calder has called a 'technological fix'. We are told that new varieties are being developed that will double or treble food production in the developing countries and so we can all relax and forget about the world food problem. I do not believe this to be the view of the FAO, but the IWP does lay great emphasis on the new varieties.

The mistake is to attempt a short-term solution to a long-term problem. In fact, there are two problems. The first is that there are people who have too little to eat. The second is that there are countries that need to be able to develop economies, based on agriculture, strong enough to support themselves.

In the short term, food is available. The developed countries over-produce to such an extent that the countries of the EEC are collecting stockpiles of produce for which there is no market. British farmers have been demonstrating in the streets because of the fall in their income, due in the main to over-production. In America farmers are paid not to produce. Food from the developed countries could be diverted to the third world to tide it over.

In the middle and long term, more could be done to reduce wastage. In India, the protein available amounts to 71·5 g per person per day, whereas that consumed is around 51 g.[36] One authority has calculated a wastage of food grain in India in 1964 as 47·3 per cent of the harvest.[37] In Nigeria 46 per cent of sorghum is lost and 41 per cent of the cowpea harvest; in Sierra Leone 41 per cent of the rice crop and 14 per cent of the maize; in tropical Africa 30 per cent of all crops.[36] Not only is food wasted, but other food is contaminated and contributes to the spread of disease.

Wastage could be reduced by relatively simple measures. A 4-inch high parapet all around a warehouse will keep out rodents. Sacks can be treated to repel insects. Better drying of grain prevents moulds and better storage bins can be constructed from plastics at low cost.[37] A halving of the total food wasted in this way would increase the amount of food available by up to 20 per cent.

Land reform might achieve substantial increases. This is particularly true in Latin America, where the tendency is for the peasant to produce most of the foodstuffs for domestic consumption, but to do so on small areas of the poorest land. The best land belongs to large estate owners and its productivity is low. In Chile, for example, 40·8 per cent of all agricultural families are peasants, yet they own only 7·4 per cent of the farm land from which they produce 20 per cent of the country's total agricultural output. In Brazil 23·5 per cent are peasants owning 6·5 per cent of the land, but producing 21·3 per cent of total output.[38] In all of these countries there are landless peasants: 49·7 per cent in Chile, 61·9 per cent of the agricultural population in Brazil.[39] A land reform that enabled them to work as peasants might produce significant increases.

A soundly based agriculture will require animals, both to provide manure and to provide animal protein. The IWP suggests intensive units on European lines.[40] Some authorities hold that there may be a place for intensive systems in some developing countries, particularly close to large urban areas. K. E. Hunt, Director of the Institute of Agrarian Affairs at Oxford, believes they may have a part to play, though probably not a major one.[41] Dr N. A. Mujumdar of Zambia and F. D. T. Good, a distinguished veterinarian with experience in Zambia and Kenya, both feel intensive rearing of livestock indoors is not relevant to the needs of these countries at any rate.[42]

The aim should be to increase food production in developing countries by improving soil structure, preventing further erosion and improving on existing methods of husbandry, but within their own context. It will be a slow process, not very dramatic perhaps, but safer and more assured of success than grandiose schemes with names that suggest instant answers. The process will be slow, but it will also be somewhat cheaper than the Green Revolution.

At the present time the outlook is gloomy. In June 1970 the FAO held its Second World Food Congress at which some of the difficulties, mainly social, economic and political, that the Green Revolution had encountered, were debated by eight commissions and a large number of plenary sessions. One plenary session was devoted to population control. It proceeded smoothly enough until Professor Jose de Castro of Brazil launched a violent attack on the whole concept of population planning. He spoke of genocide. He was cheered warmly and it became apparent that he was supported by many of the Latin American and African delegates.

That was in June. In October the FAO issued a series of background papers to mark the occasion of its 25th anniversary. One of them[43] began with this paragraph:

The world's nutrition authorities are worried. For the past twenty-five years they have been trying to bring people more and better food through the Food and Agriculture Organisation of the United Nations. But in spite of their efforts, the protein gap in developing countries is increasing. By 1985 the world is expected to be 3·6 million tons short of animal protein – more than the amount consumed in 1962 in the Common Market countries or in Black Africa, Latin America and the Near East together.

The paper goes on to point out that in 1969, for the first time in twelve years, world food production fell because of a cut-back in the developed countries.

The problems in the developed, industrialised, rich countries of Western Europe and North America are the reverse of those in the poor, developing countries. British farming will serve as an example, although it is not necessarily typical of farming in other countries in every respect. Generally the principle remains the same: that agriculture has come to be regarded as an industry. The economic framework within which our farmers operate is devised and applied by the central government on the advice of the civil service, not many of whom are actually farmers themselves. On paper, in Whitehall, our agricultural policies make a great deal of sense. They aim to produce the maximum quantity of food at the lowest possible price. Surely there can be no objection to this? If we are agreed that the aim is desirable, then how shall we set about attaining it? The snappy answer is the so-called agricultural revolution. Men are replaced by machines and chemicals, processes are speeded up and automated and production is maximised by the heavy use of fertilisers. The average fertiliser consumption in Western Europe is 153 kg/ha, as compared to 64 kg/ha in North America and 3 kg/ha in Africa.[28] British farming is the most highly mechanised in the world. There are now almost as many tractors on our farms as there are men. Only some 3 per cent of the population is employed in agriculture, which is the lowest figure in the world. We may expect, therefore, that British farming will be the most efficient in the world and the most highly productive.

It is here that some confusion sets in, because there are two kinds of productivity: productivity per man and productivity per acre. When tables of these two kinds of productivity are compared interesting facts emerge. The countries with the highest productivity per man are New Zealand, Australia, the United States, Canada, Belgium and the United Kingdom, in that order. The most highly productive per acre are Taiwan, the United Arab Republic, the Netherlands, Belgium, Japan and Denmark. In terms of productivity per acre, Britain ranks fifteenth, the United States twenty-ninth and Australia fifty-first. If efficiency is to be measured in terms of productivity per acre, or actual gross food output, then Korea and Ceylon are more efficient than we are.[44]

Let us not be too disheartened, for the output of food from our farms has been increasing steadily since the war. In 1968-69 we produced 3·1 million tons of wheat, 5 million tons of barley, 893,000 tons of beef, 2648 million gallons of milk and 1045 million eggs, not counting those kept back for hatching.[45] In 1946 the average yield of wheat was 19·1 cwt per acre: in 1968-69 it was 28·2 cwt. The barley yield has risen from an average 17·8 cwt per acre in 1946 to 27·4 cwt in 1968-69. Output of all other farm produce has grown in proportion. Meanwhile the price to the consumer, although it has risen, is still lower than it would be were farming not subsidised. We have our cheap food, and we produce about half of what we consume.

Yet there is a price. Agricultural wages are low, far lower than those paid in industry, and the farm worker's living standard in terms of housing, education, public transport and even feeding are lower than the town-dweller's. Small wonder that the countryman leaves to make tractors in the nearest factory. This human price causes the debilitation of rural communities and a vicious spiral is created. It no longer pays to run a bus to this village or to that because too few people use it. The service is cut and the few people remaining in the village are cut off and, sooner or later, they move away, because the range of goods the village shop stocks also decreases, the village school may close and the children have to travel to the next village or to the nearest town. This is the way communities die and it is happening. But it is not the whole of the price. It is not even the most important part of it.

In the interest of efficiency, livestock has been taken from the land and reared in intensive units. This has meant that the land they once grazed can be sown to a more nutritious crop than grass, which is then taken to the animal. By restrictions on the animal's movement, energy is conserved and by the feeding of concentrated food, growth rate is accelerated. It so happens that in Britain the eastern side of the country, generally speaking, has the climate and the soils suitable for cereal growing, while the western side of the country has gone in for the intensive livestock units. The extent to which this has happened is illustrated by the fact that in 1964-65 a total of 6·7 million acres of farmland was growing grass and 5 million acres were growing barley, almost all for cattle feed. In 1968-69, 5·7 million acres were growing grass and 5·9 million acres growing barley.[46] Thus, in the space of four years, the total area of grassland has been reduced by a million acres and the area growing barley has increased by 900,000 acres. Never before in British history has such a large proportion of our land been devoted to the production of a single crop. In the interests of barley growing, hedges are disappearing at the rate of some 5000 miles a year and large areas of the countryside are becoming prairie.

Should we mind this? After all, the countryside we like to think of as traditional was man-made. The hedges we are grubbing up were planted by men, many of them not long ago.

Unfortunately, side-effects are beginning to appear. The intensive units are finding it difficult to dispose of their effluent. In the days of mixed farming this would have gone back to the land to return some of the nutrients extracted by cropping and as organic matter to maintain soil structure. As it is, it has ceased to be a raw material and has become a waste product, a liability. The cost to the farmer of treating the effluent from his farm to the minimum standard acceptable for discharge into a river is very high indeed, and many farmers may go out of business as the laws relating to the discharge of pollutants into rivers are enforced more strictly. At the same time, the land to which this organic matter should be returned is losing its structure. As it does so it becomes increasingly difficult for the nutrient salts to be made available to the plant, and so more and more fertiliser must be added to achieve the same result. At one time an organic matter content of 8 per cent in the top soil was considered desirable for arable land. In many areas it is now down below 3 per cent and in some cases it may be much lower. Meanwhile, evidence is accumulating to show the harmful effects on plants and therefore ultimately on animal and human health, and on the soil as well, of repeated heavy applications of nitrogenous fertiliser.[30]

The creation of very large fields growing the same crop year after year leads to a build-up of pests and diseases specific to that crop. These are controlled by chemicals which become less and less effective as resistant strains develop.

Each year in parts of the country where the soil is light, there are dust storms. Yields have begun to decline and it looks as though the years of increase are over and production has passed its peak. Weed, pest and disease problems are worse than they have ever been.

Pesticides may be likened in many ways to antibiotics. These are used in farming, too. Again, resistance to them has increased to such an extent that there have been outbreaks of enteric disease among humans that did not respond to antibiotic treatment because the salmonella organisms associated with the illness were immune to the drugs used. In such a situation antibiotics may be actually harmful, for they may destroy beneficial organisms while leaving the pathogens unharmed. Again, the documentation of the development of this resistance and, most disturbing of all, of the transfer of this resistance intra- and interspecifically is extensive. When large numbers of animals are housed in close proximity the danger of epidemic disease is very real. For this reason antibiotics have been used prophylactically. They have also been added to feeds as a matter of routine because, in ways not yet fully understood, very small doses stimulate growth. It is these two uses that have been criticised most severely, and the Swann Committee has recommended that they cease to be used in these ways. But without at least the prophylactic use can intensive livestock husbandry coninue?

When one criticises intensive livestock husbandry, so-called 'factory farming', one is met with the argument that with so many mouths to feed in the world we must swallow our scruples and produce high-quality protein by any means possible. To this there are two answers. The first is to point out that the trade in intensively reared animal products takes place exclusively among the rich countries. We export no broiler chickens to India. The second answer is to state the percentage of the total protein production of the developing countries that is absorbed by the rich countries as additional feed for their livestock. In 1964 to 1966 the Peruvian-Chilean fishmeal export deprived South America of more protein than that contained in the total South American production of meat, and almost twice that of the milk output. The 1966-68 average has increased this delivery to 1·5 million metric tons.[47] The Peruvian catches alone would suffice to raise the nutritional standard with respect to protein for the undernourished on the entire South American continent to southern European level.[48] The fishmeal from Africa would be enough to reduce by 50 per cent the protein shortage on that continent.[48] Thus it seems that the contribution made by

Western European intensive livestock husbandry to the world food problem is to take food from the undernourished and give it to the overfed.

What future is there for British farming? That depends on the steps that are taken now to remedy the ills that have appeared. If there is a trend back towards mixed farming, with a larger total area sown to grass or herbal leys and grazed, then the structure of the soil will recover and the problem of effluent disposal will be solved. There must be a reduction in the total quantities of nitrogen fertiliser used, particularly in lowland areas where surpluses drain into water that may be required for domestic use. There must be a return to rotational cropping and an increase in the diversity of species in any given area. This will help to control pest and disease problems. What is required, in fact, is a higher standard of farming.

Agriculture is not an industry in the same way that manufacturing industry is an industry. The differences are very fundamental. It is harmful to think of farming as an industry at all. Manufacturing industry begins with an inert, mineral, non-renewable resource which it subjects to a series of processes ending with the finished commodity. There is, in theory, no limit to the degree of acceleration of the operation as a whole, beyond that of the ultimate availability of the raw material. It is, if you like, a straight linear process. Agriculture, on the other hand, is based on the renewability of its basic resource, the soil. This makes it a cyclical process in which everything removed from the land must be recycled back to it. If we regard it as a linear process, again there is no theoretical limit to the extent to which it can be accelerated and production maximised beyond the ultimate availability of the raw material. But in the case of farming the soil is liable to become exhausted in a much shorter space of time than that required to exhaust a mineral resource. If we can think in terms of optimum, rather than maximum production, and if we can remember that the aim of farming is to produce the optimum amount of food consistent with the maintenance of the fertility of the soil, in order to sustain the population in a state of good health, then and only then will our agriculture be built on a firm base.

We are talking about survival. We are here to explore the immediate future. When Professor J. R. Bellerby was asked to organise a seminar on factory farming which was to take place during one of the annual meetings of the British Association for the Advancement of Science, he asked the then president, Dame Kathleen Lonsdale, what the Association had in mind. She replied: 'The process of arriving at the truth by the ascertainment of facts.'

If we examine the statistics compiled by the FAO we may conclude that there will be world famine, possibly within the next fifteen years, and that as a result of this famine there will be unleashed the dogs of war. If we examine the statistics compiled by our own Ministry of Agriculture, we may conclude that our own ability to sustain the level of production that we have achieved over the past decade is in question. If we examine world food resources as a whole, and if we include the potential production of those countries that have deliberately cut back production, we may find that in fact there is enough for all if it were distributed more equitably.

The world food problem is not an agricultural problem, but a political and economic one. It can be solved. The problems of British agriculture are not agricultural in nature, but political and economic. They too can be solved. The real problem is that of population. Unless and until that problem is solved and the human population of this planet is established at a level the planet can support indefinitely – and this figure is calculable – then solutions to any of the other problems that face us today can at best be postponements. At worst they may make the solution to the main problem more difficult.

1. SIR A. S. PARKES (1969) 'Human fertility and population growth' in *Population and Food Supply*, ed. Hutchinson, Cambridge.
2. DR PAUL EHRLICH (1970) *Famine 1975: Fact or Fallacy?*, New Haven.
3. United Nations Demographic Year Book (1970).
4. *Provisional Indicative World Plan for Agricultural Development* (1969) FAO, Rome, 3, 57, para. 258. (*IWP*.)
5. *IWP*, **1**, 12, para. 14.
6. SIR JOSEPH HUTCHINSON ed. (1969) *Population and Food Supply*, Cambridge. p. 137.
7. COLIN CLARK (1963) 'Agricultural productivity in relation to population' in *Man and His Future*, CIBA Symposium, ed. Gordon Wolstenholme, London. pp. 23ff.
8. EDWARD S. DEEVEY Jr (1960) 'The human population' in *Scientific American*, September.
9. *The State of Food and Agriculture 1970* (preliminary version), FAO, Rome.
10. *IWP*, **3**, 57, para. 259.

11. *IWP*, **3**, 13, para. 56; and 18, para. 71.
12. GEORG BORGSTROM (1969) *Too Many*, London, pp. 298-300.
13. H. PARPIA (1969) 'Waste and the protein gap' in *Ceres*, FAO, Rome, Sept./Oct. 2.5.20.
14. *The State of Food and Agriculture 1969*, FAO, Rome. Annex table 2G, p. 151.
15. *Ibid.*, Annex table 8G, p. 189.
16. *Ibid.*, Annex table 9G, p. 196.
17. *Ibid.*, Annex table 7G, p. 181.
18. *IWP*, **3**, 24, para. 144.
19. *IWP*, **3**, 35, para. 151.
20. DR JOHN PHILLIPSON (1970) *Ecological Energetics*, London, p. 5.
21. GEORG BORGSTROM (1969) *op. cit.*, p. 24.
22. *Ibid.*, p. 276.
23. HUBERTUS ZU LOWENSTEIN (1969) 'The story of a sophisticated breed' in *Ceres*, FAO, Rome, Jan./Feb. 2.1.44.
24. GEORG BORGSTROM (1969) *op. cit.*, p. 188.
25. *Ibid.*, p. 196.
26. *Arab World* (1970) **26** (new series), Summer, p. 19.
27. HUBERTUS ZU LOWENSTEIN (1969) *op. cit.*
28. *The State of Food and Agriculture 1969*, FAO, Rome, Table 1-14, p. 27.
29. *IWP*, **1**, 196, Table 7.
30. A. H. WALTERS (1970) 'Nitrates in soil, plant and animal' in *Journal of the Soil Association*, July. 16.3.149.
31. *IWP*, **1**, 209, para. 113.
32. *IWP*, **1**, 209, para. 111.
33. *IWP*, **1**, 103, para. 80 (ii).
34. HUBERTUS ZU LOWENSTEIN (1969) *op. cit.*
35. GEORG BORGSTROM (1969) *op. cit.*, p. 49.
36. H. PARPIA (1969) 'Waste and the protein gap' in *Ceres*, FAO, Rome, Sept./Oct. 2.5.20.
37. A. RAMSAY TAINSH (1965) 'Waste not want not' in *Journal of the Soil Association*, April. 13.6.479.
38. ANDREW PEARSE (1969) 'Subsistence farming is far from dead' in *Ceres*, FAO, Rome, Jul./Aug. 2.4.33.
39. *IWP*, **3**, 54, paras 242-244.
40. *IWP*, **3**, 58, para. 151.
41. K. E. HUNT (1970) 'Indoor livestock systems in areas of food deficiency' in *Factory Farming*, ed. J. R. Bellerby. Br. Ass. for the Advancement of Science, p. 83.
42. N. A. MUJUMDAR 'Zambia's livestock sector' and F. D. T. GOOD 'Livestock systems in Africa' *Ibid.*, pp. 92 and 96.
43. FAO Release, Rome, Ann/8/70.

44. *Smaller Farmlands Can Yield More* (1969) FAO, Rome, p. 9.
45. *Output and Utilisation of Farm Produce in the U.K.* 1964/5 to 1968/9 (1970) H.M.S.O., Table 1, p. 4.
46. *Ibid.*, Tables 5 and 10.
47. GEORG BORGSTROM (1969) *op. cit.*, p. 236.
48. *Ibid.*, p. 237.

COMMENTS ON MICHAEL ALLABY: 'FOOD'

C. D. SUTTON

There is much in Mr Allaby's paper, particularly on the problems of feeding the expanding populations of the developing countries, with which I heartily agree. However, on the whole I take a much more optimistic viewpoint and two specific instances are worthy of comment.

The 'Green Revolution', according to Mr Allaby, is doomed in advance because he presumes shortages of water, fertilisers and effective pesticides, plus consumer resistance to the palatability of IR8. All these have caused difficulties in the past, and will in some locations and times cause similar problems in the future. But overall, I am completely sure that they are difficulties easily surmountable by present technology.

New high-yielding varieties of increased palatability have already been bred and are in use, e.g. IR20 and IR22. The rate of installation of tube wells in both India and Pakistan has increased phenomenally now that they are economically justified. Similarly, there is no foreseeable limit to the amount of fertiliser that can be produced, either in the developed or developing areas, provided there is a market for its use. Indeed, Western Europe has recently had a glut of fertiliser due to a general over-estimate of the rate of increase in demand from the Far East.

The problems of the 'Green Revolution' are, however, very real. It was born in the famine in Bihar in 1966-67, when cereal prices throughout the Far East were inflated to panic levels. It now must survive, out of the limelight, with its necessary inputs competing with many other calls on limited national resources. The major problems are thus political and economic, not technical as Mr Allaby supposes.

The second major area of disagreement is on British agriculture. Mr Allaby deplores its achievements in ranking sixth in productivity per man and fifteenth in productivity per acre. He omits to point out that, Belgium apart, all the countries with a higher output per man have an extensive type of agriculture, not at all comparable to our intensive land use; or that countries with a higher output per acre are primarily those with climates suitable for two and sometimes three crops per year! Looked at in this light, there is little need for concern about the productivity of this country's agriculture.

Nor is it correct to imply that the structure of British soils is being drastically or irrevocably impaired. The recent MAFF report 'Modern Farming and the Soil' showed that current concern originated in the abnormally wet seasons of autumn 1968 and spring 1969. Use of heavy machinery or very high stocking rates under these conditions resulted in much structure damage which was not fully rectified until the dry conditions of 1970. The Report stresses the importance of drainage and of ley farming on soils of inherently poor structure. Its recommendations can be summed up as saying that from economic necessity farmers have mechanised and intensified arable agriculture to the point where those on the more marginal land were caught on the wrong foot by two abnormal seasons. Until there is a technological advance in cultivation equipment, such that it does not cause compaction, it is obviously necessary for those farmers to balance the economics of increasing the proportion of grass in the rotation against possible crop loss in freak wet seasons.

Finally, it is worth stressing that it is my conviction that very many of the responsible scientists who are deeply involved in helping to solve the problem of feeding the world's population would interpret many more of Mr Allaby's facts in a different way. Indeed, I am certain that many would challenge the validity of some of the 'facts' themselves.

14

PROBLEMS OF OCEAN RESOURCES: STRATEGIC AND ECONOMIC ASPECTS

FAROOQ HUSSAIN

MODERN industrial society has requirements of material physical resources which its scientific and technological expertise sets out to meet. Scientists are becoming increasingly conscious of the physical and biological significance of the presence of oceans on the planet, and the possible consequences of interfering destructively with their ecological processes. The socio-economic pressures of technocratic society create the need for extending exploitable resources on the earth through which nations compete for their security and influence over others. The need for new solutions within the contemporary value system has given rise to the development of oceanology. Ocean sciences at present contribute to the development of commercial exploitation together with the militarisation of the oceans. In this context the future use of ocean resources depends wholly on political necessity and economic means.

As land-based strategic armament has achieved a totally futile dimension and become increasingly vulnerable to detection by satellite reconnaissance, to the greater accuracy of attacking missiles, and to the deployment of MIRVs (multiple independently targetable re-entry vehicles), the attraction of the relatively invulnerable nuclear ballistic missile submarine has increased. The Polaris/Poseidon missile submarine is a supremely complex system, limited in its capacity to remain submerged only by the amount of food it can carry for its crew. The nuclear-powered engines are carefully silenced so as to make them indistinguishable from surrounding noise at low speeds. Most operational systems are duplicated to the extent that the newer American nuclear ballistic missile submarines even have two reactors. The crew require quarantine before missions and live in a sterile atmosphere in the submarine to prevent the spread of contagious disease.

The development of the ballistic missile submarine has led to a great deal of research and development into anti-submarine warfare (ASW) techniques. Once a ballistic missile submarine has submerged, it is virtually undetectable at distances beyond 3000 feet from its position, because electromagnetic radiations of even the lowest frequencies are rapidly attenuated in the ocean. Normal detection systems such as radar are consequently of little use. At present the most probably effective ASW technique is the use of a complex coordinated network of ocean bottom detection sensors, nuclear attack submarines, satellites, and aircraft. The oceans will soon contain a vast amount of various ASW detection devices belonging to, of course, both NATO and Warsaw Pact countries. The obsolescence of some of these systems can be readily predicted in the short term.

In spite of this extensive development in ASW systems, ballistic missile submarines are likely to remain largely invulnerable for a number of years. Submarine-launched ballistic missiles (SLBM) must be kept within range of their targets for the maximum possible period in order to be fully effective. The range of the missile limits the parts of the ocean which the submarine may occupy, and also defines a specific area for ASW systems. In order to overcome this limitation a long-range undersea missile system, Poseidon, with a range of 8000-10,000 kilometres (approximately twice that of the Polaris system) has been developed and will replace the present one by the mid-seventies. This increase in range of the missile increases the area of ocean which the ballistic missile submarine may roam by ten times, while retaining the capability of delivering their missiles to their targets. In fact the missiles would be capable of reaching their targets as soon as the submarines leave their home base. Thus the submarine can operate from coastal waters or even the inland lakes of the United States; naturally this increases further the invulnerability of the system.

Along with the development of increasingly sophisticated submarines in the United States there is a project for a deep submergence search and rescue vessel (DSSRV) which was initiated after the U.S.S. *Thresher* accident. This kind of project, developed with a great deal of consideration for the lives of submariners, is valuable only to the extent that it may prove useful. Regrettably, most accidents to submarines do not leave them with an intact hull from which the crew may be rescued. Owing to the extreme ambient pressure at depth, any significant damage leads to the entire hull being crushed. This has been the experience so far with nuclear attack submarines lost at sea. Furthermore an accident to a nuclear ballistic missile submarine would cause serious radioactive contamination of that part of the ocean, and since these submarines give no indication of their whereabouts at any time during their mission they are extremely difficult to locate quickly.

Projects like DSSRV do not fulfil their original role, but largely provide corporations whose earnings are firmly rooted in defence contracts a means of extending their scientific and technological capability. There is a tragic vicious circle between industrial corporations and requirements for national security, based solely on the economic profitability of working defence contracts. The military rely on the ingenuity of science and technology to create the means of destruction; the industrial corporations rely on the military to purchase these ideas and techniques. These simple dynamics underlie the strategic arms races carried on by world powers at the same time as 'talks' to call a halt to the whole futile process. Herbert Marcuse has written in the preface to *One-dimensional Man*:

> Does not the threat of an atomic catastrophe which could wipe out the human race also serve to protect the very forces which perpetuate this danger? The efforts to prevent such a catastrophe overshadow the search for potential causes in contemporary industrial society. These causes remain unidentified, unexposed, unattacked by the public because they recede before the all too obvious threat from without – to the West from the East, to the East from the West. Equally obvious is the need for being prepared for living on the brink for facing the challenge. We submit to the peaceful production of the means of destruction, which deforms the defenders and that which they defend.

Commercial exploitation of ocean resources, naturally, is in the hands of the giant industrial corporations. The presence of significant oil deposits on the continental shelf has recently led to considerable research into methods to extract it successfully. Different corporations are competing with half-developed concepts and techniques for the most profitable short-term utilisation of these oil deposits. Regrettably, such endeavours are inextricably wound up with contemporary socio-political attitudes and influences. Solutions to those processes which are largely responsible for the blatant and detrimental exploitation of the third world, pollution of the environment, and production of the means of total destruction are claimed by those organisations, corporate or political, who are actually responsible for their creation. These solutions never reach the fundamental sources of the problems involved and the information offered by these 'potential' solutions can only hope, at very best, to appease the minds of those who are prepared to accept that they were made in good faith.

The mineral resources of the ocean have increased in importance during the last five years mostly for purely economic reasons: the increasing scarcity on the land of equivalent mineral resources on which industrial society is dependent for its material processes.

Heavy metal deposits with significant proportions of iron, zinc and copper occur in the quaternary sediments on and immediately below the ocean floor. Also widely distributed are nodules of manganese and phosphorite; the manganese nodules contain significant percentages of nickel, copper, titanium and cobalt. In some coastal and continental shelf regions, deposits of diamonds, zircon, rutile, monazite and cassiterite in particles are of considerable economic value. Below the ocean floor there may be found ores, rock salt, sulphur, coal, and important oil and gas deposits. In the Red Sea there are brine 'fountains' rising from the deep ocean which are rich in extractable minerals, particularly rare metals.

For quite some time mineral raw materials have been extracted from the sea water (which can be considered by itself as an important resource) and from the continental shelf. These minerals are mainly oil, natural gas, sulphur, salt, and sands from *placer* (particulate) deposits. The techniques for mining and extracting these resources are comparable in principle to those used in the normal land-based operations. An approximate survey of the deposits is made by means of gravimetric, magnetic and seismic measurements, and more precise information on the quality of the deposit is obtained from core samples taken by drilling. Research and development undertaken in the exploration and exploitation of ocean resources uses a high potential of scientific and technological expertise and involves with it a high rate of entrepreneurial risks.

The indirect and direct exploration/exploitation of ocean resources involves the use of satellite reconnaissance systems, aerial survey, ships and surface buoys, submersibles and submergence hardware systems, all of which are heavily dependent on efficient electronic data processing. The development of engineering systems for the utilisation of ocean mineral resources is at present limited to modifications of land techniques to undersea environments. The very sophisticated technological problems that are presented in the development of submergence hardware for the exploration and exploitation of ocean resources mean that these systems can only be successfully developed and operated by large corporations, usually with substantial government backing.

The purposeful use of the 'living' resources of the oceans will similarly require a more sophisticated technology than is available at present. According to the findings of the Indicative World Plan (IWP) world fishery production has tripled since 1948, from less than 20 million tons to more than 60 million tons in 1968, or an annual rate of 7 per cent during the last decade. Over the same period the production of no other basic commodity has increased at anything approaching this rate, which emphasises the potential role fisheries may play to meet the demand of the world population for animal protein.

There are both biological and economic reasons for supposing that in the next two decades the world fish-catch will not increase as fast as in the immediate past, and last year the world fish-catch decreased to some extent for the first time. The increase of world fishery production is undoubtedly attributable to scientific and technological progress and to the construction of large distant-water fishing fleets.

The largest proportion of the increased volume of fisheries production has been in the catching of clupeoid fishes and other large-volume low-priced species like herring and anchovies, for the manufacture of fishmeal and oil. Currently 40 per cent of the world harvest is being used for fishmeal and oil whereas in 1958 about 85 per cent of the total catch had been used directly for human consumption. Demersal fish stocks are probably the most fully exploited groups in terms of their total potential. The IWP working group on Marine Resource Appraisal concluded that there are no large demersal fish stocks left unexploited in the north-east Atlantic, the north-east Pacific and, partly, in the north-west Atlantic. With the rapid expansion of trawl fisheries in the north-east Pacific it is unreasonable to expect any general increase in production of demersal fish in the northern hemisphere. There are under-utilised demersal stocks in the southern hemisphere but their potential for biological reasons is not as great as that of the northern hemisphere. Furthermore, nearly 70 per cent of the world continental shelf lies in the northern hemisphere, which is already heavily exploited. By contrast pelagic fish stocks have the largest potential for increased production, though as with demersal fish their utilisation is at present most intensive in the northern hemisphere. The potential for growth is the greatest in the southern hemisphere.

Estimates of magnitude of the ocean's potential vary considerably according to scientific and technological capabilities assumed, and the economic and political presumptions implicit in such predictions. A fishery production in the order of 100 to 150 million tons would seem to be a realistic estimate. That corresponds to a doubling of the present world landings and would probably meet a projected demand for fish based on extrapolations of world population. However, a doubling will hardly be sufficient within the following decade. If the oceans are to be an important source of high-quality protein there must be more effective methods of utilisation. Large increases in ocean food production will most probably come from a shifting of utilisation from luxury products most esteemed for human food towards the lower trophic levels. Methods of using this raw material for foods for direct human consumption need to be found, because the potential of these organisms in the lower food chain is extremely large.

A consequence of the increased utilisation of the 'living' resources of the oceans is that marine populations are becoming fully exploited. It is readily conceivable that overfishing, and/or problems of jurisdiction arising from that, could seriously affect the growth of world fisheries. The number of stocks requiring some form of management is steadily increasing, and in order to get the most sensible use of these resources there is an urgent need for the international regulation of world fishing.

In the attempt to increase the use of the ocean's living resources the risk of detrimentally overloading the ecosystems is extremely important. In the case of some species a lack of positive control would lead directly to extinction (e.g. whaling, salmon). This question is an economic as well as a biological one: reproduction, growth and competition between species are affected by the catch. Although many of these problems have been recognised for many years and have become subject to international agreements regulating minimum size of fish caught, mesh size of trawl, etc., they are still pertinent problems desperately needing new solutions.

The limitations of national jurisdiction pose problems for the potential establishment of an international regime for the exploration and exploitation of the oceans. The mechanics of international regimes – their initial organisation, legality, policing, and distribution of wealth – are obviously a formidable political problem in which, quite naturally, those nations with most at stake and with the strongest influence are attempting to mould a system which is acceptable overall. Equally obvious is that the political dichotomy of the East and West, involving strategic and economic interests of both parties (not only the super-powers but also nations associated by defence treaty) makes a mockery of the United Nations General Assembly resolution of 21 December 1967 (No. 2340) that the use of the world ocean resources should be made in the interests of mankind.

The dividing-line between the legal regime of the high seas, which are open to the common use of all nations, and the legal regime of territorial waters, which are subject to the exclusive use of the coastal state (without prejudice to the innocent passage of shipping), has become invalidated through the extension of the coastal states' jurisdiction over the continental shelf. By virtue of the continental shelf doctrine that is now part of general law, the coastal state exercises exclusive sovereign rights over the ocean floor and its subsoil in the areas adjacent to its coast for the purpose of exploration and exploitation of its natural resources (predominantly mineral and non-living resources). The outer limits of a nation's continental shelf remain undetermined with respect to its delineation *vis-à-vis* neighbouring states (cf. the problems of equidistance lines, judgement of the International Court of Justice of 29 February 1969), but in particular with respect to its seaward extension.

The continental shelf convention of 29 April 1958, which has been ratified only by a few of the states, determines the outer limit of the national continental shelf boundary at the depth of the 200 metre isobath. However, there is a provision that the outer limits move deeper where the super-adjacent waters permit the exploitation of resources. That this kind of boundary will be continually extended with the advances of technology is a recognised part of international law. However, only those nations which have ratified the convention can rely upon each other for the delineation of a moving frontier of the continental shelf.

The recognition of a moving continental shelf frontier is a direct contradiction of the general consensus of international conferences and symposia that the resources of the world's oceans should be made for the benefit of all mankind (viz. the resolutions of the UN

General Assembly No. 2467 [XIII] of 21 December 1968 and No. 2602 [XXIV] of 16 December 1969). In addition the convention determining the moving frontier principle leaves completely in doubt whether exploitability is meant in the technical, economic, abstract or concrete sense.

The legal regime of the high seas applies to the deep ocean floor and its subsoil and means that it may not be appropriated or subjected to national sovereignty, but should be open to all nations for their common use (cf. Article 2 of the Convention on the High Seas, 29 April 1958). Whether this convention allows or prohibits private exploitation of the natural resources is not clear. Essentially the articles of the convention were developed for the purposes of fisheries, the laying of submarine telecommunication cables, and in general any other use which does not interfere with the similar use of others. The development of technology to extract mineral resources from the ocean floor inevitably implies an exclusive use. The main purpose of legal prohibition of the national appropriation of any part of the high seas was to prevent just this. Consequently, the present assumption that private commercial exploitation of the ocean's resources is a free for all is inherently contradictory to the aims and intentions of the convention.

The industrial exploitation of the natural resources of the oceans for the benefit of the world community would presuppose the establishment of some form of international regime (in the light of the general consensus expressed through the various conventions). The actual situation bears little relationship to the original ideals, which are steadily distorted by the political/economic process, sometimes with subtlety, though more often blatantly under a crude and superficial disguise.

The extent and potential of ocean resources provides *impressive statistical* values, though their utilisation is almost entirely by modern industrial society for its own advantage. Patterns for future development are largely based on traditional values and methods. The political problems and economic processes have smoke-screened the real issues of ecology and industrial and military exploitation, and created a new pseudo-science of oceanology out of the rather pedestrian oceanography that previously existed.

The superiority of the scientific solution is a dialectic in itself, which seems in the case of oceanography only to receive adequate ventilation in the Mickey Mouse activities of international conferences and symposia, where the consensus of opinion becomes distorted and manipulated through the mass media to serve the ideology of the *status quo*. New solutions from these sources have very little validity in that they are either impossible to realise within the contemporary socio-political system, or are economically unacceptable to the organisations who would carry them out.

Neither pure science nor technology will ever solve the problems of a world political and economic system which, through reasons of self-perpetuation, requires a progressive erosion of those human values which they claim to protect.

R. CLARKE (1971) 'Militarisation of the oceans', *The Science of War and Peace*, London.

J. D. COSTLOW (1971) *Fertility of the Sea*, London.

DAVID DAVIS MEMORIAL INSTITUTE OF INTERNATIONAL STUDIES (1969) *Ocean Pollution—A Survey and Suggestion for Control*, M. M. Sibthorpe, Ed.

Water Pollution as a World Problem—Legal, Scientific and Political Aspects (1971) London.

F. E. FIRTH (1970) *Encyclopaedia of Marine Resources*, New York.

FISHERIES OCEANOGRAPHY (1971) Ilno Hela, Taivo Laevastu. Fishing News (Books); London.

D. HOOD ed. (1971) *Impingement of Man on the Oceans*, New York

INSTITUTE FOR STRATEGIC STUDIES (Periodical publications) *Strategic Survey, The Military Balance*, September; London.

T. LOFTAS (1969) *The Last Resource*, London.

R. VAISSIÈRE (1969) *L'Homme et le Monde Sous-marin*, Paris.

15

INDUSTRIAL POLLUTION OF AIR AND WATER

ARTHUR G. BOURNE

THE title of this paper presupposes that industry pollutes (whatever that might mean) the atmospheric and hydrological regimes of the planet Earth. These two systems are intimately associated both with each other and with the other factors that form the environment. It could be argued that industry is itself an essential factor in the environment and as far as mankind is concerned this is true.

There are two ways of viewing the problem and we should consider both of them carefully, because whichever we decide on will be critical to the kind of conclusions we draw. The first way is to view the environment as an evolving physico-chemical system in which man's activities form a part. The alternative is to view the problem in terms of the health, wealth and happiness of mankind. These two approaches are not necessarily the same or compatible.

The second view is attractive inasmuch as it is of immediate concern, but it can lead to a too subjective view of the problem. The first, on the other hand, might prove that events are outside our control and that the fate of our species is already set and that we can do nothing to avoid whatever is in store for us. But to be aware is to be forewarned. All in all, I believe it is more useful to look at the problems of industrial-environmental interaction in the first way, if only because it provides a certain detachment and avoids a too anthropocentric view of the world.

The method we choose will have to enable us to consider the environment as a whole and to provide us with a means of studying it on a large enough scale for us to grasp the mechanics of the system. For essentially what we need is an understanding of the atmosphere and hydrology of the earth. When we have this we will be a long way to understanding the planetary environment as a whole.

In this paper I am going to try to examine those major factors that govern the nature of our environment and to see whether man's activities have any effect, and, if the answer is yes, to see how much he is affecting it, and to try to discover trends.

The first requirement is to establish what we mean by industry and perhaps, more importantly, what we mean by pollution. By industry, or rather industrial processes – that is what we are considering in the context of this paper – I mean all those activities that man performs outside his own physiological regime, when he takes the material resources of the planet and with energy converts them into new or different forms, which in the conventional understanding of natural processes are considered outside the realm of nature. Pollution is more difficult to define. For what is considered pollution one day may not be considered so the next. However, I am going to take it to mean anything that degrades or reduces the vitality of the environment.

Having taken these two definitions as our base, we must now learn what we can about the parts that constitute the environment. If we were to examine Earth from space, much as we examine Mars or Venus, we would be struck by the fact that 70 per cent of the planet's surface is covered by water. Water in the form of vapour or condensing vapour would also be seen at different levels in the gaseous envelope that forms the planet's atmosphere. This atmosphere would also be notable for its composition, which is unique among the planetary atmospheres of the solar system, for it consists largely of two gases – nitrogen and the highly reactive gas, oxygen.

The gaseous atmosphere and the liquid hydrosphere dominate and are responsible for much of the activity on the surface of the earth; the relatively small land surfaces are inert by comparison. Changes that take millennia are the rule with the solid earth. Some changes, mostly of local importance, do occur at a faster rate, but they are symptoms of the slower changes that are continually going on in the crust. However, this is too superficial a view, for as we shall see later the crustal materials are continually being moved by the atmosphere and hydrosphere. A more noticeable movement on the solid surface would be the seasonal variations in colour due to changes in the biosphere – the advance and retreat of vegetation as the seasons progress.

But above all we would observe that the atmosphere and hydrosphere are in constant motion driving each other on and deriving their energy from the star at the centre of the planetary system to which the earth belongs, and it is from this quite ordinary star, the sun, that all the activities that we are going to consider obtained their energy – at least until very recently, with the introduction of nuclear power.

Thus there are three physical factors determining the activities on the surface of the planet – the atmosphere, the hydrosphere and the solid crust, or lithosphere. The slowest mover in this system is the last of these three, and we can safely presume that it is the rate of change in this that governs the rate of change of the environment as a whole. All the major environmental factors are inter-related; there is a flow of energy through the system which is responsible for the changes in the environment.

This energy arrives at the earth's surface in the form of sunlight, but not all of the radiation gets down to the actual surface of the planet. The atmosphere acts as a protective layer and moderates the amount of radiation reaching sea level. In the upper layers of the atmosphere the oxygen and ozone molecules absorb the ultra-violet portion of the radiation, thus protecting the biosphere from its damaging effects. As the rest of the radiation passes down through the atmosphere, part of it is absorbed by the water vapour, part is reflected back by clouds and dust particles and is lost to space (earthshine), while the remainder, about 50 per cent, is absorbed as heat by the land and ocean surfaces (Fig. 1).

Without the atmosphere and the oceans almost all the radiation would be immediately re-radiated back into space. It is the ability of the oceans, the atmosphere (particularly the water vapour and carbon dioxide) and to a lesser degree the land surface to 'store' this energy as heat, that prevents this happening.

Instead a complicated heat 'machine' has evolved which uses the heat energy to power the winds and ocean currents, thereby ensuring that the heat is distributed over the surface of the globe, and to drive the hydrological cycle. Ultimately of course all the radiation received from the sun does find its way back into space, otherwise the earth would have become by now a hot, lifeless planet, but on the other hand, the 'holding' of the heat and its circulation ensures that the planet does not become too cold. The efficiency of this heat engine is surprisingly poor – it may be less than 1 per cent but it is sufficient to power the environment. I will come to its relationship with the biosphere later; for the moment we must see how it energises the earth's hydrological cycle.

Most of the earth's water supply, as one would expect, is contained in the oceans; only about 3 per cent of the total water mass is found as fresh water on the continents and three-quarters of this is locked up in the polar ice-caps and glaciers. Although the amount of water in the atmosphere is minute it is vital to the heat machine.

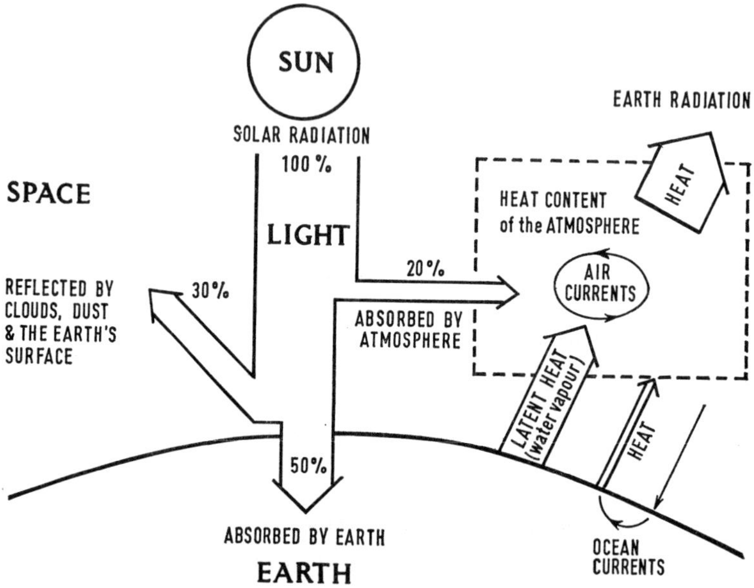

Fig. 1

The water, or hydrological, cycle (Fig. 2) operates in essentials like a large distillation apparatus. The sun's energy is used to heat the water on the ground and on the surface of the oceans to form water vapour. This then rises up to the cooler layers of the atmosphere where it condenses and in time is precipitated in the form of rain, hail and snow on to the land or back into the oceans. Eventually even the portion that falls on the land finds its way to the oceans, where it is reheated and the process repeated, and so a cycling of water is guaranteed.

This movement of water and the changes of state to which it is subject with variations in temperature are responsible for soil formation and the fertility of the seas. The breakdown of crustal materials by the action of water makes possible the transformations of the land surface. Water transports the materials in suspension from the place of origin to the place of rest, usually estuaries, the bed of the shallow seas or the ocean floor. What might be the top of a mountain range in one era may form the ocean floor in another, and conversely the sediments on the sea bottom may one day be thrust into the air by some geological event to form a mountain range. This crustal cycle is a slow but continuous process.

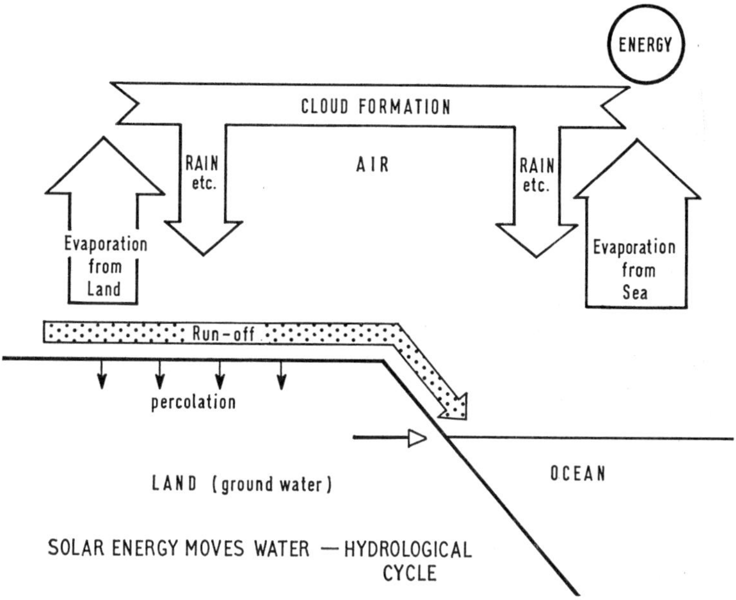

Fig. 2

Over long periods of time the interaction between atmosphere, hydrosphere and lithosphere ensures that an equilibrium is maintained in the environment. The amounts of water, oxygen and carbon dioxide, for instance, remain remarkably constant. A reduction in solar energy would be met by a lowering of the other activities until a new equilibrium was reached; but changes do occur. The primitive earth was a very different place from what we find today, for example, it had a reducing atmosphere of hydrogen, methane and ammonia. It took a long time for it to change to the oxidising one we have now and that change was brought about by a new factor that appeared on the planet some 2000 million years ago. This factor was a system which could utilise the solar energy to build up its own structure and reproduce others like itself. This was the beginning of the biosphere.

The evolution of the oxidising atmosphere and the biosphere are closely related – a relationship recorded in the geological history of the planet. Green plants produce oxygen by a process called photosynthesis, in which they manufacture complex 'organic' materials from water, carbon dioxide and simple mineral compounds with the aid of sunlight. This photosynthetic process can account for all the oxygen in the atmosphere and almost all the 'fossil' oxygen found in the geological strata. It has been conjectured that when the level of oxygen in the atmosphere reached 1 per cent of the present-day level, it provided sufficient oxygen and ozone to filter out most of the damaging ultra-violet radiation and enabled the phytoplankton (microscopic plants) to survive in the upper sunlit layers of the primitive seas.

In time early plants such as these were able to produce the surplus of oxygen which has made possible the wide variety of organisms which have existed on the earth. Thus the dependence of the biosphere on photosynthesis was established very early on in its creation. Further, the continuance of the oxidising atmosphere and therefore life is dependent on the survival of green plants.

The biosphere has been able to expand or contract according to the energy available at various times during the earth's history. It has been able to fill a variety of habitats within the environment and always to find a balance in the energy exchange system. We have seen how the sun's energy drives this environmental system, but its relationship to the biosphere is particularly important to our study. The energy is first fixed by the plants which use it in their photosynthetic processes; it is then dissipated as heat in their respiration and that of their consumers, the herbivores and the predatory animals that live on the herbivores, and ultimately by the organisms of decay. The biosphere has spread itself over the entire globe, a new prime factor to join the forces activated by solar energy. Like the other systems the biosphere tends to equilibrium, and this single factor which first changed the atmosphere to suit itself was to have a profound effect on the future *rate* of change in the environment.

Some two million years ago out of the biosphere a new organism appeared, struggled, and emerged as a geomorphic and geochemical factor in its own right – man. In his earlier period man was in equilibrium with his environment. He was not only dependent upon it for the energy and materials of his own survival but he was also vulnerable to its changes. Gradually, however, he learnt to bring more and more of it under control and this has enabled him to attain his present position of dominance over every other living species. It requires only the most casual survey of the environment to see what man has achieved in the comparatively short time he has been upon the earth: it took the primitive plants millions of years to change the atmosphere but it has taken man very much less than half a million years to change significantly the face of the earth. Man has already altered the biosphere to such an extent that thousands of millions of his kind can be supported by the environment. This has been achieved through the practice of agriculture and the release of solar energy stored in wood and fossil fuels.

Before man discovered how to domesticate crops and animals his numbers were controlled by the carrying capacity of the land. Under natural conditions the photosynthetic cover of the land surface could support about ten million human beings, and yet at the present time, although only about 10 per cent of the earth's land surface is under cultivation, it forms the primary support of over 3500 millions. Over 5 per cent of the total energy passing through the biosphere is used by this single species and it is no wonder that changes have occurred with the growth of the human population.

The changes in the biosphere brought about by man's agriculture are by far the most impressive for which any species has been responsible, but these changes, which are irreversible, have brought with them heavy penalties, penalties of deserts, barren islands and wet wastelands. Today the productivity of the agricultural land can only be sustained by the continued use of fertilisers and through the protection afforded by pesticides. This new regime is being maintained at enormous expense in environmental terms.

Whereas nature's system is prolific and invests in diversity, man's method is based on selectivity. As he developed his monocultural ecosystems, only very adaptable biological species, especially those that live preferentially on plants cultivated by man, could survive. In so doing they are competing with man for food and therefore he has to find some means of destroying them, hence the use of pesticides. But the more he throws pesticides and antibiotics at his competitors the more are they surviving: already what were once extremely successful pesticides are losing their effectiveness because of the evolution of resistant strains of pests. And in destroying the pests man has eliminated many beneficial organisms.

Man's increase has depended on a reshunting of the solar energy.

It is made possible too by the taking apart of certain molecules and the recombining of them into forms which are not found in nature and with which nature cannot cope. In other words, instead of being part of the profit and loss in the environmental system, these substances persist and accumulate as waste. The give-and-take between man and his habitat has broken down. Man has become a prime factor for change, every bit as important as the other factors, and perhaps most important of all he acts as a catalyst – the changes he is responsible for are swift.

We have reached a point now at which we can assess man's role in the environment. Through his agriculture he has altered the biosphere – but what of the atmosphere and hydrosphere? Has he changed these significantly? The answer to this is that we do not know, for whatever effect he is having, or will have, will take time to show itself. The reason for this lies in the rate of flow of the various components of the environment through the system. For instance, it takes about two million years for all the earth's water to pass through the biosphere, about 2000 years for the oxygen and 300 years for the carbon dioxide. We do know, however, that the atmosphere, hydrosphere and lithosphere are interdependent and we can, therefore, safely assume that man has set in motion forces that will eventually lead to changes in them.

We must now look at the effects industrial man has had and is having on the environment; and compared with his agricultural practices the effects of his industrial activities are almost instantaneous. In the mere 200 years since the Industrial Revolution, there has been a rapid acceleration in man's 'conquest' of the environment, and we must now examine what the cost of this is and may be in the future in environmental terms.

Man's industrial processes depend on energy and until very recently this has been obtained from the sun, in the form of wind or water power, and more particularly from fossil fuels. The energy cycle involved in the combustion of fossil fuels began millions of years ago when the solar energy was trapped by the plants of the young earth. A small fraction of these were buried under conditions that prevented complete oxidation and in time their bodies underwent chemical changes that transformed them into coal, oil and other fuels. When these are burned they release their store of energy but only part of this is employed usefully in industrial processes. Most of the energy is lost to the atmosphere as heat together with the by-products of combustion: carbon dioxide, carbon monoxide, oxides of sulphur, hydrocarbons, nitrogen oxides, water vapour and solid particles. To find out how this release of energy can affect the environment, we will have to look once again at the major environmental factors.

Of the atmospheric constituents, oxygen, carbon dioxide and nitrogen are essential to life. The production of molecular oxygen seems to be beyond the means of man to tamper with, and the chance of a single species interfering with the oxygen cycle on a sufficiently large scale would appear to be remote – until we are reminded of the effect that the primitive plants had on the atmosphere in the past and the quickening in the rate of change which man's activities generate. The current consumption of oxygen is staggering: each of the 3500 million human beings uses 7 lb of molecular oxygen every day. In addition, the burning of the huge amounts of fuel needed to provide this population with heat and to drive the machinery producing its material requirements, plus the exposure of oxidisable materials, such as iron, are contributing to the debit side of the oxygen account. On the other side of the balance sheet the recruitment of oxygen from the globe's plant cover is being reduced by the destruction of the world's forests and other photosynthetic areas of the land and sea. The productivity of the remaining green plants might be sufficient for our needs, and shifts in the balance may enable this to go on for some time, but it must have a limit. It is evident that we cannot go on indefinitely.

A major difficulty in studying this problem is the size of the system. As with all the large-scale environmental factors we do not have sufficient knowledge about the profit and loss in any terms that are meaningful, and herein lies a danger. We would not be able to detect any adverse trends on a global scale until they had gone some way in their development, by which time it would probably be beyond our capability to do anything about it. This destruction of the earth's plant cover is bound to bring about climatic changes – in fact it has already done so in some areas – for not only is it essential in the oxygen cycle but it is also important to the hydrological and carbon dioxide cycles. The biosphere depends on plants to absorb large amounts of carbon dioxide from the air. All living things, including the plants, need oxygen for their internal processes and they all have to get rid of their waste products, among them carbon dioxide.

When animals and plants expel carbon dioxide it becomes freely available in the environment and during the daylight hours it is readily taken up by the green plants. The photosynthetic processes of the biosphere need far more carbon dioxide than the plants can produce through their own respiration. There is therefore a direct exchange of gases between plants and animals. With the advent of industry and the massive human population there has been a noticeable increase in the amount of carbon dioxide in the atmosphere. During the last 100 years it has risen from some 290 parts per million to 320 parts per million (ppm), and more than a fifth of this rise has occurred during the last ten years. It is easy to visualise that high concentrations of carbon dioxide could occur locally in a given habitat, for instance, in a heavily built-up urban area, and that this might give rise to bad health and a lowering of efficiency. But it is difficult to imagine what the effects might be on a global scale and even more difficult to assess the damage that might accrue. If we look at our energy system again we can see that one effect of increasing carbon dioxide would be to prevent the normal radiation of heat back into space, and thus an increase in the earth's surface and atmospheric temperatures could result.

This effect of carbon dioxide is often referred to as the 'greenhouse effect' because glass in a greenhouse behaves in a similar way to carbon dioxide in the atmosphere. If this were to happen and the ambient temperature were to rise, it might be sufficient to melt the ice-sheets of the polar regions. In all these systems, as we have seen, there is a balancing effect and in this case energy comes in in one form and is re-radiated out in another, maintaining the energy balance. Likewise there is an equilibrium between the gases in the atmosphere and therefore if there is a change in any one of these, some balancing mechanism must come into play to restore the equilibrium, albeit a new one. Thus if the carbon dioxide in the atmosphere is increasing, the equilibrium must be changing. The total increase in carbon dioxide in the atmosphere in fact accounts for only a little more than a third of the carbon dioxide released from fossil fuels, and therefore there must be some compensatory factor which is keeping the increase down. Most of the excess carbon dioxide is absorbed in the oceans but it has been suggested that a not insignificant fraction may be going into increasing the total productivity of the vegetation, for plants have been shown to grow faster in atmospheres rich in carbon dioxide. This would have the effect of increasing the oxygen available, offsetting to some extent the loss of oxygen caused by man's activities and compensating for some of the increasing carbon dioxide. However, we do not know whether this is the case; all we can say is that the carbon dioxide is increasing and therefore the gaseous equilibrium must be in a period of transition.

The most rapid processes of adjustment in the environmental reservoirs take decades before new equilibria can be established. On the other hand, as we have said, man's actions are catalytic. He is speeding up his consumption of fossil fuels and this means that the carbon dioxide in the atmosphere will continue to increase. By the end of the century it will have reached 400 ppm and we can only guess at what will happen in 100, 500 or 1000 years from now. New ecological regimes might develop which may even exclude man and the more complex life forms.

To return for a moment to the thermal problem. Far from there being a build-up in temperature during this period of increase in carbon dioxide, there has been a drop of something like 0·3°C. Whether or not this change is due to natural causes or whether it is another symptom of pollution is not known. Fluctuations in temperature have been a common occurrence throughout the planet's history. Only long-term studies will provide the information necessary, but there might well be a clue in the fact that the rate of change has been rapid and has paralleled the rise in industry.

This latest cooling may be due to the presence of particulates in suspension in the atmosphere. Dust is a natural constituent of the atmosphere, the particles usually consisting of salt, sand and volcanic ash – the latter being particularly prevalent during and just after eruptions. If to these natural emissions are added the particulates from man's activities, the industrial processes and the agricultural chemicals, then we have a very effective method of reducing the solar energy reaching the earth's surface, which could cool the planet. It has been estimated that a decrease in the atmospheric transparency of as little as 3 to 4 per cent would produce a drop in temperature of about 0·4°C. The particulates also act as nuclei around which moisture can condense, which means that an increase in the global cloud cover could be produced. An increase in this of only 1 per cent would lower the earth's temperature by 0·8°C, three times the drop measured in the last twenty years. Normally about 31 per cent of the earth's surface is covered in low clouds. If these were to increase by 6 per cent the planet's temperature would drop by 4°C, which would bring us very near to conditions approaching those of the Ice Ages. Regardless of whether man-made particulates are having any significant effect on the world's atmosphere, they are certainly the cause of a great deal of suffering to mankind. Soot and other solid particles block or irritate the delicate lung tissue, lowering its efficiency and putting great stress on the respiratory system and the heart. In addition tarry matter in suspension in the air irritates the skin, the nasal passages and the eye. It also clogs up the stomata (small pores) in the leaves of plants and kills them.

The sulphur dioxide, carbon monoxide and nitrogen oxides also produced by the burning of fossil fuels are another major threat to the environment and certainly to human health. There is a growing mass of evidence to suggest that they may in themselves produce disease in man, animals and plants; but there is no doubt that they aggravate and sometimes trigger off diseases lying dormant in a population. Bronchitis is aggravated by both sulphur dioxide and particulates, so much so that in recent years as much as 40 million working days have been lost through it in Britain, and it still drains the British economy of some £28 million a year. There is also a correlation between areas with high pollution levels and the incidence of rheumatism, arthritis and lung cancer.

Sulphur dioxide, a heavy, pungent and poisonous gas, is the most widespread of the gaseous pollutants. In the United Kingdom the quantity emitted each year has increased from four million tons in 1938 to six million tons in 1967 and it is still increasing. In the atmosphere sulphur dioxide combines with water and oxygen to form sulphuric acid which eats into stonework, metalwork and fabrics. The cost of this damage in Britain has been estimated at about £1 million a day and in the United States at $5 million a day. Sulphur dioxide also aggravates bronchitic conditions, and even exposures to low levels can cause shallow, rapid breathing and increases in the pulse rate. As sulphuric acid, it penetrates deep into the lungs and destroys the tissue. It also seems that the gas can be a contributory cause of birth defects. It prevents plants from closing their stomata, thus aiding its own penetration into their metabolism, which eventually leads to their death.

However, particulates and sulphur oxides form a relatively small percentage of the total amount of pollutants pumped into the atmospheric machine. In the United States for instance they form 27 per cent of the annual total of 200 million tons. Of the remainder no less than 47 per cent is the invisible, odourless but lethal gas carbon monoxide.

The prime producer of this substance is the motor car. It only needs the level of carbon monoxide to be maintained at 1 per cent for half an hour for it to be lethal. On average, car exhaust gases contain 3·5 per cent of carbon monoxide, but this goes up to around 7 per cent when the engine is idling. The levels of concentration of the gas in the air close to traffic can be as much as 25 ppm, six times the accepted maximum allowable concentration for an eight-hour exposure, and 10 ppm over this period is sufficient to retard mental reactions. Carbon monoxide combines readily with the haemoglobin molecule in the blood and thus deprives the body, and especially the brain, of oxygen. And while we are considering the brain, it is sobering to remember that another constituent of motor car exhausts, lead, is highly dangerous to the brain and the nervous system. Lead is added to petrol usually as a mixture of tetraethyl and tetramethyl lead in quantities up to 4·8 ml per gallon. This mixture is added to prevent 'knock'. The motor car is also the greatest producer of organic waste products in the form of hydrocarbons. These can react under the action of sunlight to form photochemical oxidants. These include ozone, nitrogen dioxide, aldehydes and acrolein, and when present in the air, they can irritate the eyes and lungs and damage plants. Combined with solid and liquid particles they produce the familiar photochemical smog of Los Angeles.

The pollution of the earth's atmosphere is now an established fact and nowhere on the surface of the planet is free from it. Locally it may be more intense here and there, but inevitably the atmospheric machine will ensure its wide distribution. In time it will undoubtedly cause widespread changes in the atmosphere, even to the extent of altering its composition. Atmospheric pollution is already causing damage to man, his artifacts and the biosphere.

Earlier I talked of the relationship between the atmosphere and the planetary water system. We should expect, therefore, that pollutants in the atmosphere will find their way into the water cycle, and this is in fact the case. Some of the complex and persistent man-made molecules have been found thousands of miles from their source, for instance DDT from Africa has been found in the Bay of Bengal. The same substance has also been found in the tissues of penguins and fish in the Antarctic and the whales of the Arctic Ocean; these could only have been carried there by the atmosphere. A further observation is the increase in the lead content of the surface waters of the Pacific since the advent of the motor car.

In the case of fresh water, although the amount of water on the earth has remained more or less constant for as long as man has been on the planet, the usable amount, which must be shared by an increasing human population, is dwindling because of misuse, waste and pollution; the result is a growing shortage.

It is ironic that the freshwater shortage will be felt most of all and have its greatest effect in the highly industrialised countries. For it is in these that more and more fresh water is needed, not only for life itself but also for the industries which keep these nations in the forefront. The requirement for the United States alone, at present the most advanced industrial nation in the world, will be doubled by 1980 and trebled by the end of the century. Parts of the United Kingdom, particularly the south-east and London areas, will be short of water by the end of the seventies. Even if the world's population levelled out, the demand for industry would continue to increase so long as our economic system is geared to a philosophy of growth. In such a situation the problems of pollution and wastage assume serious proportions.

In our survey of the environment we saw how the water cycle begins in the oceans and how it moves through the atmosphere as rain, snow and hail. The proportion falling over the land that is not evaporated runs down the rivers back to the oceans or percolates into the soil and in some areas into the rock strata and there forms the groundwater. Of the water that falls on to the urban areas most of it is lost through evaporation or run-off down the drainage systems where it is frequently contaminated with sewage. Although sewage is not within the scope of this paper we cannot ignore it entirely because in our times human and animal excreta are not entirely natural. The use of drugs, particularly those containing hormones in both animal and human foods and as medicinal preparations, has made sewage a dangerous component in the hydrosphere. The cycling of water through the biosphere aids the distribution of these substances throughout the environment, and their accumulation is a potential hazard to the biosphere, as well as to human health.

To the no longer natural effluents of man and his animals we have to add the effluents of industry. Some rivers would not even flow in dry weather if it were not for industrial effluents and it has been estimated that these and sewage make up as much as 50 per cent of some rivers in the United Kingdom. One of the greatest threats to the biosphere is the carriage by the freshwater system of the enormous quantities of nitrates and phosphates washed off from agricultural land. These chemicals so enrich the rivers and lakes that there is a rise in biological productivity, and this has resulted in a population imbalance and wholesale destruction of localised biological systems. This phenomenon is called eutrophication. Under natural conditions, a lake may reach this stage after the course of thousands of years of accumulation of nutrients, but man's activities have once again proved themselves to be catalytic. It has been estimated that man has prematurely aged Lake Erie in North America by about 15,000 years.

The problem of nitrates in water is not however just a matter of eutrophication. It is also a matter of public health. Nitrate levels of above 20 ppm in tap water can produce toxic effects and even death to children under two years of age, a sobering thought when we consider that 15 ppm have already been recorded in several parts of the British Isles.

Nitrogen is an essential component of the biosphere, and although 78 per cent of the atmosphere consists of the gas, it is unavailable until fixed by bacteria, atmospheric or industrial processes. In a natural regime a balance is maintained between the nitrogen fixed by the soil organisms and that released by denitrifying bacteria. In the last century when little was known about the organisms that fix nitrogen, scientists feared that the nitrogen of the soil would eventually be depleted by the newly discovered denitrifying bacteria and a cry went out for nitrates. The distribution of nitrogen in the environment is not completely understood even today. The only reliable data are the amount of the gas in the atmosphere and the rate being fixed by industrial processes. These industrial processes may be making available to terrestrial plants more nitrogen than that being returned to the atmosphere by denitrifying bacteria in the soil. Doubtless much of this nitrogen eventually ends up in the oceans. It seems probable therefore that nitrogen is building up in the environment and there is a fair amount of evidence to substantiate this. There are indications that in its 'fixed' form nitrogen is finding its way into the biosphere at the rate of some 92 million metric tons every year, while only 83 million tons a year are being returned to the atmosphere by denitrification. The difference between these two figures, 9 million tons, may represent the rate of accumulation of 'fixed' nitrogen in the biosphere. The long-term consequences of this accumulation are obscure, but they could lead to the eutrophication of all the freshwater systems and even the oceans.

The addition of other chemical substances, whether deliberately or accidentally, aggravates the problem. The heavy metals such as lead, mercury and cadmium, and man-made substances such as DDT and PCBs (polychlorinated biphenyls) are particularly dangerous; they are accumulated in the natural food webs and have been responsible in recent years for the wholesale destruction of wildlife.

Millions of tons of pollutants enter the world's hydrological cycle each year. It is not surprising therefore that during the 'sixties there was a rash of catastrophic kills of marine and freshwater organisms. With so many pollutants entering a water system it is to be expected that they will react with each other and produce even more dangerous substances. To the factory discharges we must add the seepage from rubbish dumps, spoil heaps and mineworkings, a much neglected aspect but one that is likely to give trouble in the future. The combination of all these pollutants makes it very difficult to know exactly what is in the water, and although standard tests have been designed and are regularly carried out for the most obvious pollutants, many can slip through. Even the most efficient sewage and water cleansing treatment cannot get rid of the invisible chlorinated hydrocarbons and many of the other persistent chemicals. They are entering the biosphere and accumulating within individual organisms, including man.

Pollution by heat is particularly important in the rivers and lakes. An increase of as little as 4°C can speed up most of the biological processes, 5 to 10°C can have adverse physiological effects and can cause a redistribution of the flora and fauna. Sewage fungus, for instance, flourishes at high temperatures and can rapidly absorb all the available oxygen. In stretches of rivers where deoxygenation through pollution is already severe and the organisms are at the limit of their tolerance, thermal pollution can tip the scales to produce anaerobic conditions. The Rhine is already called the 'sewer of Europe', but the problems of that river will be much greater if the plan to build forty nuclear power stations along its banks is realised. Thermal pollution from power plants and industry can also affect the biological productivity of estuaries and coastal regions.

The discharge of radioactive materials from nuclear power stations is for the present a minor problem compared with the others. The greater danger will present itself to the generation living when the wastes now being 'stored' in the oceans leak out and enter the biosphere. For this generation and for many that follow, the radioactive material already in the atmosphere, hydrosphere and biosphere from the detonation of thermonuclear devices is already of sufficient magnitude to damage the individual organisms and undermine their genetic integrity.

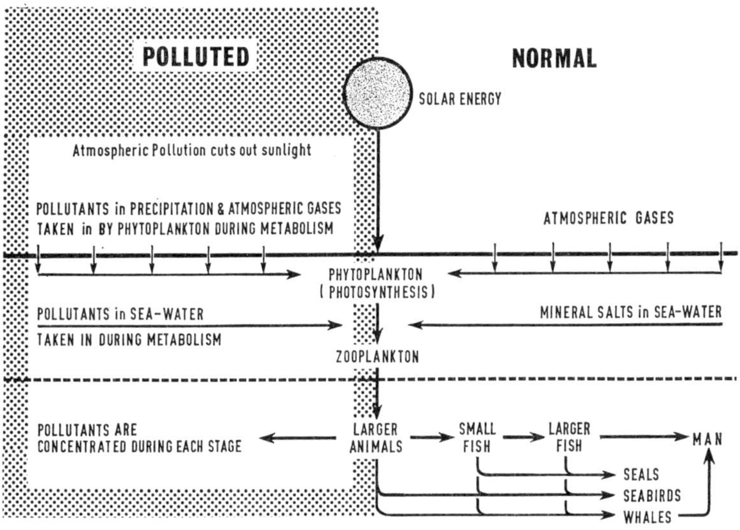

Fig. 3

In the oceans, vast as they are, the problem is just as acute as in the fresh water, and here we suffer from a shortage of data. What we need to know is whether the prime converters of solar energy, the phytoplankton, are being damaged. If these were to be destroyed, not only would we lose the biological productivity of the sea but also a very high proportion of our oxygen supply. Oil pollution of the oceans is increasing daily, and it has been suggested that a film of oil covering the seas may be formed; if this were to happen, it would prevent the exchange of gases at the sea's surface and lower the solar energy reaching the phytoplankton. Fortunately for us the oceans are in constant motion and it is unlikely that such a film would ever be created, but there are so many unknowns that there is no room for complacency. In any case, of far more importance are the unseen pollutants, for example the persistent hydrocarbons being absorbed in the food chains (Fig. 3).

Water is vital to life and industry. The scale on which man can alter the environment when he interferes with the natural water regime is enormous, and yet it seems that when he is planning water schemes or siting industrial plants, the economic and technical questions are the only ones to be considered.

Environmental quality is the concern of mankind, because man has the ability to change his habitat and probably the environment as a whole too. When we look at the large environmental systems of the planet earth, we can see a pattern beginning to emerge. Man has the potential to change the atmosphere back to a non-oxidising one, and maybe this is part of the overall evolutionary tale. But here we are running into philosophical questions.

Whatever the final outcome, at the moment few people doubt the precariousness of the situation in which man finds himself today. One thing is certain – the environment will establish a new balance, but whether man will be included in the new regime is questionable.

We have to suppose that our species will inhabit the planet for thousands of years to come, and we can presume that its technological ability will increase so that in some far distant time it will be able to perform the miracles that we can only dream about. We must find a way out of our present difficulties and as a first step we must ensure that our population is geared to the planet's resources and not the other way round.

16

MAN'S EXPOSURE TO RADIATION

E. ERIC POCHIN

RADIATION was one of the first of the modern environmental contaminants to arouse a general public anxiety, and for very understandable reasons. Here was an unfamiliar menace, an apparently new addition to the environment, and one which had been disastrous on a huge scale to the people of Hiroshima and Nagasaki, world-wide in its distribution with fallout, and unexpectedly varied in the ways in which it was carried into the body by a range of radioactive isotopes. It was an agent that was unseen and unfelt, capable of causing cancer – and causing it twenty or thirty years later – and of harming the germ cells of the race in ways which might continue to be expressed for many generations to come. It would have been astonishing if the situation had not caused anxiety, and irresponsible if it had not led to detailed investigation and assessment.

As a present, and potentially increasing, feature of our environment, radiation exposure clearly needs the most careful assessment; and as a factor which could influence human ecology, our added and artificial exposure to radiation must be seen in relation to the amount of the normal and natural radiation exposure to which the race has always been exposed. How much have we increased, and are we increasing, our normal exposure by increments from various sources?

The need is, then, firstly, to discuss the ways in which the body cells or organs are being exposed to radiation, and the amounts of radiation received from every such source; and, secondly, to indicate the types of harm that such exposure may cause, and to try to assess the frequency with which injuries may result from any given exposure.

SOURCES OF IONISING RADIATION

What concerns us is the whole range of the radiations which cause ionisation in tissues, and the injuries that can result from the energy that is released in the cells in consequence of this ionisation. Such effects are not produced by the visible, the ultra-violet or the infra-red parts of the spectrum of electromagnetic radiations, nor by those at radiofrequencies. They do result, however, at the higher frequencies

Table 1

RADIATIONS *Causing ionisation*	*Not ionising*
Electromagnetic	
X-rays	Visible infra-red and ultra-violet
Gamma radiation	At radiofrequencies
Particulate	
Neutrons	
Electrons (beta radiation)	
Helium nuclei (alpha radiation)	
Etc.	

of X-rays or gamma radiation, and they are caused by the so-called particulate radiations, whether the particles in the beam are neutrons, electrons (in beta radiation) or helium nuclei (in alpha radiation). We are dealing therefore with all such ionising radiations, whether received from the sun or outer space, from reactors, from X-ray or other equipment, or from nuclear fuel and waste products from atomic fission. We are also concerned with all radioactive materials, since various of these types of radiation are given off from all such materials in the course of their radioactive decay.

This list may sound formidable. Our present problem is greatly simplified, however, at least in principle, by the fact that our estimate of the harm done to any particular body tissue by radiation can be based simply upon the total amount of energy delivered to that tissue by any of these forms of radiation, and it does not matter which particular type of radiation is responsible.

This statement is broadly, but not exactly, true. Energy deposited by alpha radiation and by neutrons is rather more damaging than equal amounts of energy from other types of radiation, but allowance is readily made for this in the estimates of exposure to radiation. Also, energy delivered during a short time is often more damaging than an equal amount delivered over a longer period, and some consideration must be given to 'dose rate' and to the spacing in time of contributions to the total dose. And for some effects, no harm is produced unless the amount of energy delivered to the tissue exceeds a certain 'threshold' amount in a given time period. Broadly, however, we need only estimate the energy delivered to the body, or to different body tissues, by all of the various sources of ionising radiation, whether, for example, that energy reaches the cells of the body from outer space in cosmic radiation, from natural radioactive materials present in rocks below the ground, or from radioactive isotopes of the common chemical elements which have entered the body and have become incorporated in bone like Strontium 90, in the thyroid gland like Iodine 131, or throughout body cells like Caesium 137 or the naturally occurring Potassium 40 (where the numbers indicate the atomic weight of the particular isotope of the chemical element named). So, what matters essentially is the amount of energy delivered to the body tissues by ionising radiation, not the way it gets there.

NATURAL RADIATION EXPOSURE

We can start with the natural sources of radiation to which the race has always been exposed. Here it is easy to draw up a balance sheet of the radiation doses – of the energy delivered – by different natural sources.[1] The total is fairly constant throughout most of the world, and has probably remained fairly constant over many millennia. We are, and have always been, irradiated by cosmic rays, by radiation

Table 2

Radiation from natural sources (annual genetic dose, in millirem)	
Cosmic radiation	35
Terrestrial	50
Internal	27
Total	112

from the earth, and by naturally occurring radioactive isotopes that become incorporated in body tissues. These three sources are of roughly equal importance, cosmic radiation contributing about one-third of the total, terrestrial radiation a little under a half, and normal body radioactivity about one-quarter.

These figures apply for most of the world population. The cosmic ray dose is somewhat lower at the equator than at middle latitudes, but only by about 10 per cent. The variations with longitude are slight. The rate increases with altitude, doubling for every 5000 ft, so that the small populations living at great heights receive rather heavier cosmic radiation, although the total from all natural sources is only about doubled for communities living at the altitudes of Tibet or the Andes.

Similarly the radiation received from terrestrial sources is much the same for most of the world's population, although rather lower on clay soils, and rather higher on granite by a factor of 2 or 3; lowest of all at sea; and highest of all over the areas of monazite sand in south-east Brazil and south-west India, where the radioactive thorium in the sands can give an average dose to the resident population of from five to 10 times normal.

And for the third natural source, from radioisotopes incorporated in the body, the rates must be very constant since the main contributor is a small radioactive component of all normal body potassium, and the concentrations of potassium in body tissues are rather accurately controlled by body processes. Traces of other elements contribute: naturally occurring radium, polonium, and radioactive rubidium, and small amounts of Carbon 14 produced in the atmosphere from ordinary carbon by the action of cosmic radiation, but the doses that they produce are trivial. In quoting these doses, and in comparing amounts of radiation received from other sources, I will keep to a single unit of radiation dose – the rem (or the millirem, which is simply the thousandth part of a rem). This is basically just a measure of the amount of energy delivered to the tissues by the radiation, but one which makes allowance for the rather greater damaging effect of neutrons and alpha radiation.

For most of the world's population, therefore, the body tissues are irradiated at a rate of about 100 millirems, that is, one-tenth of a rem, per year, although in a few localities the rate may be twice or, occasionally, several times this value.

This then is our baseline, a criterion of the normal although not necessarily of the harmless, but a criterion which is I think the relevant one for our present ecological purpose, so that we can assess, in a strictly quantitative fashion, what things we are doing to increase this normal level of irradiation, and by how much we are in fact increasing it.

The level is now increased by a number of additional and artificial sources with which I will deal in turn: irradiation in medical diagnosis and treatment, exposure from fallout, from radioactive waste disposal, from work in nuclear energy establishments and from the industrial use of radioactive sources. And we must look particularly at the contribution that the irradiation of individuals makes towards the average radiation of the population as a whole, as this is what is of particular genetic and ecological significance. Because quite obviously we must be concerned not merely with the proper radiation protection of the individuals or the small groups of people particularly exposed because of their work or other special circumstances but also with the size and number of such groups and their levels of exposure, and therefore the total contribution to any radiation-induced disabilities throughout the population, and the increased irradiation of the germ plasm of the race as a whole.

MEDICAL USES OF RADIATION

We may take first the irradiation of patients in medical work, both from diagnostic X-rays and during radiotherapy. The exposures of individuals will of course vary enormously, from less than one-tenth of a rem to a small part of the body in many diagnostic X-rays, to some thousands of rems throughout a volume of tissues requiring treatment by X-rays, and the safety of such exposures must be viewed in relation to the value of the information or of the treatment they are expected to give. The total exposure of genetic significance from medical radiology, however, as averaged through the whole population, has been soundly sampled and assessed in Britain[2] and now in a number of other countries.[3] From the whole of diagnostic radiology the contribution is about 14 millirem per year. From radiotherapy, the figure is less – 5 millirem per year, the far higher individual doses being offset by the fewer individuals involved and the greater age of most of those treated, the contributions of genetic significance being correspondingly much less. From the use of radioactive isotopes, both in the diagnostic methods in which they are proving to be of great value and in therapy, the contribution is much less again, about 1/5 millirem a year, since the necessary information or therapeutic effects can often be secured with very limited general radiation exposure.

Table 3

Medical irradiation
(mean annual UK genetic dose, in millirem)

Diagnostic X-rays	14
Therapeutic X-rays	5
Radioisotopes	0·2
Total	19

(i.e. adds 17% to natural annual genetic dose)

In total, therefore, the whole of medical radiology adds rather less than 20 per cent to the natural exposure of the population, as regards irradiation of germinal tissues. Or if estimated in regard to mean exposure of the bone marrow, thinking of the possible induction of leukaemia, the figure is somewhat higher,[4] increasing the natural level by about a half.

Table 4

Medical irradiation
(Mean annual UK bone marrow dose, in millirem)

Diagnostic X-rays	32
Therapeutic X-rays	12
Radioisotopes	2
Total	46

(i.e. adds 43% to natural annual bone marrow dose)

FALLOUT

In the case of fallout, the estimation is perhaps rather more complex but has been carefully and fully done by a scientific committee which was set up by the General Assembly of the United Nations in 1955 to produce a factual assessment of the types and amount of radiation received by the world population and its likely effects, as a result of the various forms of exposure that fallout has entailed. This committee, of scientists from fifteen very different nations, has worked quite hard and harmoniously, and has I think produced good objective estimates of world radiation levels from fallout and from other sources, and of the possible consequences.[5] I have the feeling, personally, that the United Nations might very usefully initiate similar small groups of authorities from different nations to keep under review a number of other environmental contaminants of possible ecological importance. This possibility might well be reviewed at the 'Conference on the Environment' in 1972 in Stockholm that is being organised by the United Nations.

In looking at the estimates of radiation exposure from fallout, I may re-emphasise the fact that what matters biologically is the total radiation delivered to body tissues, not the particular ways in which the radiation gets there. What hurts is the energy deposited in the cell, not the particular type of radiation or radioactive isotope which brings it there. In the analysis, it is of course vital to examine the formation of these various isotopes in nuclear fission, their diminution by radioactive decay in the upper atmosphere before they are ever deposited on the ground, and their routes of concentration into articles of food and subsequently in certain body tissues, whether in bone for strontium, in the thyroid gland for iodine or in the body tissues generally for caesium. These steps need individual and quantitative assessment for the various circumstances of weapon testing and for the diverse diets of the world, as do the variations of fallout with latitude and with weather conditions, and the way the type of soil or the mode of agriculture affects the incorporation of its constituents into different articles of diet. In the outcome, however, it is the total radiation dose to the bone, the marrow, the thyroid or the germinal tissues which is needed as the basis for assessment of harm. And for this the figures can be simply stated.[6] The total radiation doses that will finally have been delivered to human tissues, by all tests conducted until 1968, will average between 250 and 450 millirem, varying somewhat according to the particular body organ or tissue for which the estimate is made; and tests since 1968 add only slightly – probably by about 4 per cent – to these figures. Let me be sure that I have put this point clearly. These are the total doses that will finally have been delivered to people by all the fission products and other radioactive materials produced by all tests to date, when these materials have finally fallen to the earth's surface, entered the food and the body, and undergone full radioactive decay, to the extent that they do so, within the body. It is the total dose to which we are committed by all tests.

I express these as the total doses rather than as an annual rate since, happily, massive weapon testing was largely confined to a period of eight years and is not a continuing annual process. But if

Table 5

Radiation from fallout
(From all tests before 1968; world average for all radiation received or to be received; millirem)

	Fallout total	*Natural per year*	*Equiv. years of nat. radn.*
Genetic	247	112	2·2 years
Bone	434	150	2·9 years
Marrow	307	108	2·8 years

these figures are compared with the annual rates of natural radiation, it is evident that eight years of heavy testing committed the world to the equivalent of between two and three years of natural radiation. The total varies a little, but not greatly, between the northern and

Table 6

Radiation from fallout
(Equivalent in years of natural radiation)

	World average	*Northern temperate zone*	*Southern temperate zone*
Genetic	2·2	2·5	1·8 years
Bone	2·9	3·0	1·9 years
Marrow	2·8	3·1	2·0 years

southern hemisphere, our northern temperate zone being about 10 per cent higher than the world average. So if the fallout radiation of genetic importance is quoted in relation to the natural radiation received in thirty years, the average length of one generation's childbearing, the natural radiation dose to the germ cells of the generation will have been increased by 8 per cent by all tests. In fact, no one generation will sustain more than a 4 per cent increase, since over half of the dose is delivered at an extremely low dose rate from a long-lived form of carbon, Carbon 14, which is formed in the atmosphere by neutrons released during the nuclear fusion processes. A very small proportionate increase, therefore, will be sustained by many generations to come.

So the biological severity of fallout lies I think not just in the magnitude of the increased radiation dose commitment, which after all is comparable to that derived from a few years' stay in a granite district, or from the protraction of this dose in time, or from the unfamiliar radioisotopes which deliver the dose, since it is essentially the dose rather than its mode of delivery that matters. The more disturbing fact is that this quite limited additional radiation is worldwide.

I do not, of course, need to emphasise that we are looking here at the radiation exposure from weapon tests which are so conducted that no irradiation of people results from the immense releases of gamma and neutron radiation which occur at, and immediately after the explosion of the weapon, and which caused the deaths from radiation in Hiroshima and Nagasaki. Moreover, it has usually been the case, although as you know not always, that no fallout of the resultant radioactive materials on to people has occurred until these fission products have been carried in the atmosphere some hundreds of miles from the site of the explosion. In consequence of this, and of the time that has therefore elapsed since the detonation, a large proportion of the fission products has already undergone radioactive decay to harmless and non-radioactive chemical elements before they reach any human populations in fallout. In addition, in the most powerful tests the main mass of radioactive material was carried so high into the atmosphere by the heat produced, that only the products with the longest half-lives of radioactive decay were still actively present by the time the material finally settled to earth some years later. The exposures from weapon tests, with which we are concerned in the present context, are of course therefore, although worldwide, vastly less than if the same weapons were ever used in warfare.

OTHER SOURCES

So far, therefore, the position is that the radiation rate to the population as a whole, of a little over 100 millirem per year from natural causes, is increased by an added rate of about 20 millirem per year from radiological examinations and treatments, and by a rate from fallout from all past tests which now has fallen to a few millirem per year, but corresponding to a total for past and future years of about 250 millirem – the doses here being those of genetically significant radiation.

Table 7

Population radiation exposure
(mean annual genetic dose in millirem)

Natural	
From natural sources (in some places 200, occasionally to 600)	about 110
Additional	
From medical radiology (UK)	about 20
From fallout (tests to 1968)	
If all in one generation, 8	
Actual present generation, Southern, 1; Northern, 4	world av., 3
From occupational exposures	about 1
From all other sources	about 2
Total additional, +25% of natural rate	

These are the main contributions to population exposure. To these must be added figures which at present are much smaller and seem likely to remain so, resulting from a variety of exposures of individual groups within the population. We must return to the individual's exposures, but from the standpoint of the ecological impact, the total contribution from all of these is limited, contributing less than 3 millirem per year to the genetic total.[7]

Radiation received by those working in X-ray departments, in nuclear power production processes, and in all industrial uses of radioisotopes and radiation is likely to involve a population average of rather under 1 millirem.[7] Further small population doses arise from radioactive waste disposal, from use of luminous watches and other devices, and to a trivial extent from television sets, flights at high altitude, contained radioactivity in some building materials, and a number of such miscellaneous sources. Taken together, these add to our total exposure by at most 2 per cent which may seem, and indeed must be, of small impact ecologically. What is clearly important, however, is not merely that the size of this total exposure from various sources shall be kept under review, but that no type of significant radiation exposure which contributes to this total shall be incurred unnecessarily, and also of course that no individual or group of individuals shall be unduly exposed. The ecology of the race demands a low population average, but the protection of the individual requires also a proper control of local and personal exposure. And here we are immediately involved not merely with the types of harm that undue exposure may cause but in an attempt to estimate the frequency with which such injuries are likely to be caused by a given exposure of individuals.

HARMFULNESS OF RADIATION

This is clearly an extremely difficult point on which to obtain exact or even approximate figures, despite the very great amount of experimental work that has been done on the subject, and the increasing number of epidemiological studies on the observed effects of such human exposures to radiation as have occurred. It has long been clear that certain types of leukaemia might be caused by radiation, and that many other forms of cancer were occasionally induced by high exposures. It is known that other, non-malignant, causes of death are induced or accelerated in animals, although the evidence for such effects or for their relative importance in man remains equivocal. It is evident that the function of many body organs or tissues is impaired after local exposure to high doses – of hundreds or thousands of rems – but that at lower doses no impairment is detectable, either because of the great reserve capacity of most organs or because of their known powers of repair. For example, high doses to the lens of the eye may impair vision by formation of cataract, but lower doses do not.[8, 9] Our major problem, in assessing numerically the level of risk from the much lower levels of radiation with which we are concerned, is difficult on either a direct or an indirect basis. Directly, it might be hoped that the health statistics of areas of high natural background radiation would show the importance of such exposures, and studies are being made in Kerala in southern India. Existing health statistics however are poor, and the detection of what are likely to be small proportionate increases in naturally occurring diseases will necessarily involve careful study of large and static populations over long periods, and comparison with adjacent populations having similar diet, culture and environment, except as regards the radiation exposure from the ground they live on. This is a tall order; and it seems doubtful whether the sizes of the population concerned, although large, would even so be large enough to do more than exclude an unexpectedly great effect of radiation at these dose levels.

The indirect assessment is no easier. Such quantitative data as we have on the frequency of harmful effects in man comes in the main from doses of hundreds of rems – and we wish to infer the likely frequency from exposure to single rems or hundredths of a rem: you will remember that natural radiation gives about a tenth of a rem per year, medical sources an average of a fifth of this natural rate, and all other artificial sources a third of the medical. So we are asking for information at very low levels.

In trying to infer the likely harmfulness of low doses from that observed at high doses, the most naïve basis is to assume that the frequency of injury is directly proportional to the size of the dose, and that very low doses just involve a proportionately low risk of harm. And for protection purposes, this is I think an assumption that we have to make, to be on the safe side, unless this possibility, of a simple proportionality for all effects, can be excluded. It is however the most pessimistic assumption that can be made, and may over-estimate enormously the element of hazard involved in low exposures. For in fact it is known that if the dose, or if the rate of delivery of the dose, is low, a variety of repair processes in the body may restore normality and prevent the development of damage, in a way that does not occur with high doses and dose rates when the repair mechanisms may be saturated and overwhelmed. Even in the induction of genetic mutations, it has been shown that some form of recovery occurs, a given dose producing fewer mutations if delivered slowly than when delivered fast. Moreover, more mutations are observed in the offspring of irradiated mice when conception occurs soon after the irradiation than when it occurs later, when the mutagenic effects of the radiation appear to have been in some way corrected.[10, 11]

You will appreciate how much it matters that the harm per unit dose may be less when the total dose is small than when it is large. In the first place, it is possible that the harm is in fact zero when the dose is small enough for its effects, and all its effects, to be repaired. This condition of a threshold level below which damage does not occur is certainly true for some radiation effects, and may be true for many, although it can certainly not be assumed as a basis for protection, with perhaps the one exception of the causation of cataracts in the lens of the eye.

Secondly, however, and even if the frequency of harm does vary with the size of dose even to the lowest dose levels, there is no conclusive evidence that this frequency is more likely to be directly proportional to the size of the dose than, for example, to the square of the dose size, which seems to be nearer the truth for several effects studied, including chromosomal translocations. And this matters considerably, since all of our basic epidemiological evidence is derived from the exposed populations of Hiroshima and Nagasaki, from radiation-treated patients, from uranium miners, or from luminisers handling radioactive paints under previously bad conditions, situations where doses up to some hundreds of rems were received by the body or by particular parts of the body. If the estimates so obtained suggest that 100 rem to the whole body might produce a fatal malignancy in a few per cent of people irradiated at this level,[12] then one-tenth of a rem (the annual natural radiation) would cause such malignancies in a few people per hundred thousand if effects are directly proportional to size of dose, but only in a few per hundred million if the frequency is in fact proportional to the square of the dose.

RADIATION PROTECTION CRITERIA

Radiation protection standards must still be based on the possibility – if you like, on the most pessimistic assumption – that the frequency of harmful effects is linearly proportional to the size of the dose, without threshold, repair, or effects of dose rate, down to the lowest doses. This may in fact be a gross over-estimate of risk, even though for safety's sake we must use it for planning for the time being and perhaps for many years to come. The strikingly good health records of the atomic energy industries do indeed seem to indicate that protection criteria ensure a high degree of safety against radiation-induced disease.

The planning of radiation protection must, however, continue to be based on cautious criteria for a number of reasons. Firstly, of course, some of the diseases, and indeed most of any malignancies that may be induced by radiation exposure, will only be detected after many years, so that one cannot confirm the actual safety of the precautions on any simple year-by-year test of experience, although it is by now possible to confirm this on two decades of such experience for atomic energy workers and on three or four decades of health statistics amongst medical radiologists and radiographers, in whom the incidence of leukaemia has fallen to a normal value since adoption of modern radiation measurements and protection methods.[13, 14]

This direct experience is only now becoming available, however, for a purely statistical reason also. Even with the substantial numbers of people who are occupationally exposed to radiation, reaching tens of thousands in a number of countries, any excess rate of leukaemia or of malignancies as a whole would in fact have been unwarrantably high if it had been statistically detectable at all hitherto in terms of the numbers of people and the time periods involved.

This immediately brings up the key question: how safe is safe – how low should the risk be for any necessary occupational exposure to radiation? Ideally of course the goal should be zero, in these as in all other occupations, and it is indeed basic to all protection measures, and in the recommendations of the International Commission on Radiological Protection,[7] that any unnecessary radiation exposures should be prevented and avoided as far as it is practicable to do so. But this does not let us off the hook. If some exposure is unavoidable in the course of the work, and if even the smallest exposures may involve some element of risk, how small should that exposure, how low should that risk, be kept? What, numerically, is an acceptable risk?

Let us agree first that this is not a question purely for the scientist or the radiobiologist to decide. It is, or should be, one involving informed and responsible public opinion, obviously including those concerned, as indeed it should for the safety of all occupations. Ideally, the job of the radiobiologist is to say that, if you set the limit of annual radiation exposure at a certain value, or if you achieve an average exposure of less than, say, 1 rem per year in those who are occupationally exposed, then the maximum toll of illnesses or deaths would be at the following rates for various diseases, for various types of mutations, for cataract. Or, if the dose limit is halved or doubled, then the following rates instead. Now choose: where should the limit be set?

This, I am sure, is ultimately the right role of the scientist, to set out clearly and numerically such hazards as are involved at different dose levels, so that they can be properly assessed in the perspective of occupational hazards generally, and of working requirements in the particular industries concerned; and to hope for a sound and responsible decision as to the levels of restriction and of safety that are appropriate. And this is the type of decison, with the balancing of incommensurables and imponderable factors, that the sensible and practical man, and his more or less sensible and practical representatives, are highly competent to do, and in fact do every day of the week, but which the scientist is by training and by inclination bad at doing, when the equation is not a neat one of ergs and grams, but a loose one of risks and needs and fears.

This I am sure is the objective, and I think it is valuable that such estimates of radiation hazards as can at present be made with any confidence, are being published and reviewed in the scientific literature[8, 12, 15, 16] and are being widely discussed. There is still, however, so much difficulty in evaluating the evidence, the implications of linearity or otherwise of the dose-response relationship, of repair processes and tumour induction, of the influence of dose rate, of the expression and elimination of genetic mutations and chromosome aberrations, of the effectiveness of alpha radiations, of intense local irradiation, of partial irradiation of the body or of organs, and so on: there are still so many interpretative problems on this essentially radiological level that an easy numerical statement of radiation risk per rem cannot yet be made without detailed qualifications as to dose level, tissues involved, and assumptions in evaluating frequency and degree of harm. What can be done, however, and is done, is to estimate the maximum likely frequency of harm, and particularly of any fatal disease, and ensure that limits are so set that the maximum likely frequency of any deaths due to the occupational exposure is at any rate low compared with the rate of fatalities in other occupations of recognised safety.

Now, is this the right criterion? Is this what we, the public, would feel was sound; or if not, what else? Granted the aim is zero risk, in this as in any occupation, and the aim must always be to minimise any unnecessary exposure. Granted also that there is all the difference in the world between the unfortunate occurrence of a certain fatal accident rate in one industry and the planning of exposure levels which would allow such a death rate in another – or is there really such a difference? What we need to ensure is that, at the end of the century, looking back, the overall risks have been those of a normal safe occupation, and this is at least in part a numerical question of frequency and types of harm.

So again, how safe is a safe occupation? And for that matter how informed, numerically, are we on the relative safety or hazard even of existing occupations of conventional types? Is it in fact generally known that, even within the dozen or so manufacturing occupations reported annually by the Chief Inspector of Factories, the fatality rate for the safest is, year by year, about one-fiftieth that for the highest in the list, and this in turn is less than a fifth of some other regular occupations?[17] This of course is nothing new. We all know that some occupations involve only a slight risk, and others an appreciable risk of fatal accident. What are naturally less familiar are the numerical levels and their differences, and the constancy of these differences year by year, despite some improvements in safety generally. The deaths are accidental but the range of risks is constant.

This gives no criterion of what is acceptable, since no industrial risk is acceptable if it can practicably be reduced; but it does give a criterion of what is in fact accepted, under circumstances in which all efforts are made to minimise exposure but where some exposure is unavoidable. And it does seem likely that present criteria of radiation dose limitation will, even on the maximum estimates for hazard based on direct proportionality of dose and effect, ensure that the safety of these occupations is comparable with, for example, those of light manufacturing processes, and less than those of trawling, or mining, or heavy industry. The present occupational radiation limit of 5 rem per year, as a maximum or ceiling which must not be exceeded[7], in fact of course ensures that average annual exposures both of individuals and of the group as a whole are considerably below this ceiling, with actual averages in the latter case of well below 1 rem per year. These rates are likely, even on the most anxious estimates of radiation hazard, to correspond to a minor rather than a major occupational risk, and to give these activities at least the safety of the light industries which have a few accidental deaths per year per hundred thousand workers, rather than entailing the greater present hazard of heavy industries and occupations with a few deaths annually per ten thousand workers. And the emergence of health statistics in both medical and industrial occupations involving radiation exposure is beginning to give direct confirmation of the effective safety in this sense of present protection criteria.

I should add, here, that occupational dose limits are recommended internationally, and largely adopted in practice, not only for situations in which the whole body is irradiated but also when only single organs or tissues of the body are irradiated.[7] This may occur for example when radioactive dust may be inhaled and deposited in the lung, or when radioiodine is taken into the body from the air, milk or food, and then becomes concentrated selectively in the thyroid gland as a result of normal body processes. The problem of assessing, in the necessary strict and numerical fashion, the sensitivity to injury of the different human tissues or organs if irradiated singly, as compared with irradiation of the whole body, is inevitably a difficult one, but one on which considerable progress is being made. My own impression, in the light of this work, is that the occupational dose limits for single tissues such as thyroid, bone or lung are at least as safe, and probably rather more cautious, more restrictive, than those for the whole body exposure, and should also ensure adequate protection when observed. It is striking, however, that in the one industrial situation in which it is still often found impracticable to achieve the recommended protection criteria, namely in uranium mining, a clear excess of lung cancer incidence is readily demonstrable.[18]

EXPOSURE OF MEMBERS OF THE PUBLIC

We have looked at the average exposure for the population as a whole, and seen that the mean annual genetic exposure from natural sources is usually of about 0·1 rem per year, and has been increased by about 25 per cent from the total of all man-made additions to this rate. We have looked at those whose work involves some necessary radiation exposure, where the existing dose limitation of 5 rem per year in practice implies an annual occupational average of under 1 rem per year. We must now look finally at the sources of radiation which may cause exposure of individuals or groups of people within the general population, and the limitations that should apply to their exposure. A long list of sources has been evaluated, many proving trivial, some appreciable, and some needing really careful control. Television sets, of correct design and initial voltage adjustment, involve trivial exposure for any viewing position, distance or length of time; luminous watches give significant but ordinarily small local doses and even these are being lowered by marking with radioactive material of low energy and penetration. Shoe fitting 'pedoscopes' may give doses which are not trivial, with exposures of the order of half a rem to the foot in each five seconds viewing time and certainly they are not devices for children to have fun with, or indeed to be used at all in the absence of clear need for their help. With a variety of luminous dials, static electricity eliminators, thickness gauges and similar devices, no real dose problem arises with proper design and usage. Some building materials, particularly from stone or materials of volcanic origin, may contain enough radioactivity to double the normal radiation levels as measured within the house, just as these levels may be doubled when one lives in districts of volcanic rock. Some foods, for example the Brazil nut, naturally contain alpha-emitting elements derived from the soils in which they grow[19, 20] but do not form a sufficient component of a normal diet to affect the body radioactivity to appreciable extent. The pigment in some ceramics may contain uranium and be, rather weakly, radioactive. I understand that luminous fishing floats have been used to fish the evening rise, but here the real risk is to the fish.

All these, and other such miscellaneous uses, involve only trivial doses if properly designed and used, but in a few instances the usage may be crucial and, with some industrial sources, requires as exact and careful control as for X-ray tubes in radiological departments; and the control may be harder to ensure on the building site. You may have heard of the disaster a number of years ago in Mexico, when a ten-year-old boy found a small, shining, attractive metal object in a container on a construction site, which he took home in his pocket and kept at home in a cupboard.[21] This was in fact a 5-curie radiocobalt source used for X-raying castings for cracks in the metal. It was only traced to his household and recovered when he had been admitted to hospital for radiation burns. Within the next six months both he and three of the four other members of his family had died from radiation effects.

So, despite the safety of such sources when properly used, or when contained within their housing, it is essential to recognise the potential lethality of the more powerful ones when improperly used or carried. The proper precautions are as necessary and straightforward as for dynamite in the quarry, but it is essential that these simple, silent sources be recognised as 'dynamite', and be just as strictly secured.

An equally strict control is, and needs to be, maintained upon the environmental conditions which may involve any groups or sectors of the general population in added radiation exposure. The recommendations of the International Commission, which are widely adopted in countries throughout the world, are that no single group of members of the general public should receive any radiation exposure, additional to that from natural sources and from their medical care, exceeding in total one-tenth of that which applies for occupational exposure.[7] This limit, of 0·5 rem per year as the total for any such special exposures from environmental or other factors, is I think rightly set at a considerably lower level than for occupational exposure, for a number of reasons: the members of the general public include children, they are not individually monitored for dose received, they will have their own occupations with any separate element of hazard that these occupations may imply, and they have not themselves accepted an activity involving radiation exposure. It could, I am sure, be argued as to whether the reduction, from the occupational limit to that for any small group of the general public, should be by 5, or 10 or 20. In practice, of course, the use of a limit for any such exposure implies that the actual exposure will ordinarily be a lot less than this limit, in the sense that if a room has a ceiling one tends to live below the ceiling, and most such exposures will thus in fact be within the variations of natural background radiation. Also, the figure is the limit for all additional exposures, not for each of several sources which might impinge upon the same small group of people. It is against this criterion that any discharge of radioactive materials into sea, rivers or air is controlled, having regard to the selective concentration of any radioisotope that may be taken up into seaweed or fish or other materials. On a similar basis, one must look at the exposures likely at the altitudes at which Concorde should fly[22] since at 60,000 ft there is little shielding from cosmic radiation by the overlying atmosphere. At such altitudes the rate of cosmic radiation may be 1 or 2 millirem per hour, depending on latitude, as compared with 2 or 3 millirem per month at ground level. For the crew, flying say 500 hours per year at altitude, the annual exposure would thus be of 0·5 or 1 rem per year if all the 500 hours were on routes far from the equator (where the rates are less), so this total could somewhat exceed the conventional limit for members of the general public (at 0·5 rem/year), although not approaching that adopted for occupational exposure (5 rem/year). Or, for a passenger commuting weekly to New York, and so with about 200 hours per year at altitude, the public limit would be approached but not exceeded by this source. In either case, however, a monitor in flight is planned as an important necessity, to detect the occasional occurrence of higher radiation levels from developing solar flares, since exposure rates may mount rapidly in such conditions to levels of some tenths of a rem per hour or more, and might occasionally require descent to lower and more protected altitudes.

THE FUTURE OF THE ENVIRONMENT

Of necessity I have presented and discussed a lot of numbers, since numbers are the essence of the problem. Some radiation we have always had. This level we have, on average, in the genetic and ecological context, increased by about 20 per cent for medical purposes, and by a further 7 per cent on other grounds. The medical total seems as likely to fall owing to greater efficiency of techniques, as to rise from wider use of radiological methods. Of the remainder, the fallout rate will continue to fall unless any extensive atmospheric testing is resumed, and the occupational contribution seems unlikely ever to add more than a few per cent. If the present restrictions are maintained on the limits of exposure of members of the public, and with proper surveillance of sources and techniques of radioactive containment, so that substantial proportions of the total population are not so exposed, the average exposure of the population as a whole from artificial sources should certainly not rise in proportion to the future increase in nuclear power production and radioisotope techniques. Ecologically, our radiation environment is not at present much changed, and I think it should not be greatly altered within this century if we maintain our protection criteria and continue our practice of containment. And for the longer future, we can hope for an increasingly clear and objective assessment of the biological cost of any increases in radiation exposure, and an increasingly clear opinion as to whether the value of a procedure justifies the biological cost that it entails. I hope that this type of evaluation will be strongly developed, both for radiation and for other types of environmental contamination.

I think that the long and detailed studies that have been made of the whole range of harmful effects of radiation, and the attempts to reflect this information in practical and quantitative guidance as to safe limits for occupational and population exposure, do carry some moral in regard to other physical, chemical or psychological pollutants of our environment. It was in some ways an absurdly ambitious, although necessary, attempt – to try to predict and calculate for radiation the effects and the hazards of an essentially new set of occupational and environmental factors, even before these factors had had time to express their effects at these dose levels. But this, ideally, is what should and must be done for each new environmental contaminant of which the harm, if any, may take many years to express itself, or to become detectable.

If the extent and significance of man's exposure to radiation can now be objectively assessed, this is because our anxieties on the subject have led to careful, prolonged and quantitative study of the amounts of exposure and the possible type and extent of the resultant hazard. It is only by similar assessment of many other pollutants of the public or the working environment that we can hope to evaluate the harm that they may be causing to the community. One of the values of radiation study and radiation protection criteria may be as a model, however imperfect, for the examination and control of other potential hazards.

1. *Report of United Nations Scientific Committee on the Effects of Atomic Radiation* (1966), General Assembly XXI, Suppl. 14.
2. *2nd Report of the Ministry of Health Committee on Radiological Hazards to Patients* (1960), H.M.S.O., London.
3. *Report of United Nations Scientific Committee on the Effects of Atomic Radiation* (1962), G.A. XVII, Suppl. 16.
4. *Final Report of the Ministry of Health Committee on Radiological Hazards to Patients* (1966), H.M.S.O., London.
5. *Reports of United Nations Scientific Committee on the Effects of Atomic Radiation* (1958), G.A. XIII, Suppl. 17; (1962), G.A. XVII, Suppl. 16; (1964), G.A. XIX, Suppl. 14; (1966), G.A. XXI, Suppl. 14; (1969), G.A. XXIV, Suppl. 13.
6. *Report of United Nations Scientific Committee on the Effects of Atomic Radiation* (1969), G.A. XXIV, Suppl. 13.
7. *Recommendations of the International Commission on Radiological Protection*, Publication 9 (1966), Pergamon, Oxford.
8. *Report of the International Commission on Radiological Protection on Radiosensitivity and Spatial Distribution of Dose*, Publication 14 (1969), Pergamon, Oxford.
9. G. R. MERRIAM AND E. F. FOCHT (1957) 'A clinical study on radiation cataracts and the relationship to dose,' *Amer. J. Roentgenol.*, **77**, 759.
10. W. L. RUSSELL (1965) 'Effect of the interval between irradiation and conception on mutation frequency in female mice', *Proc. Nat. Acad. Sci.*, **54**, 1552.

11. W. L. RUSSELL, L. B. RUSSELL AND E. M. KELLY (1958) 'Radiation dose rate and mutation frequency', *Science*, **128**, 1546.
12. E. E. POCHIN (1970) 'The development of the quantitative bases for radiation protection', *Brit. J. Radiol.*, **43**, 155.
13. W. M. COURT BROWN AND R. DOLL (1958) 'Expectation of life and mortality from cancer among British radiologists', *Brit. med. J.*, **ii**, 181.
14. S. WARREN AND O. M. LOMBARD (1966) 'New data on the effects of ionizing radiation on radiologists', *Arch. Environ. Hlth.*, **13**, 415.
15. *Report of International Commission on Radiological Protection on the Evaluation of Risks from Radiation*, Publication 8 (1966), Pergamon, Oxford.
16. 'Radiation-induced Cancer', *Proceedings of WHO/IAEA Symposium, Athens, 1969*, IAEA, Vienna.
17. E. E. POCHIN (1965) 'Occupational safety and risk in relation to radiation exposure' in *Strahlenschutz in Forschung und Praxis*, Verlag Rombach, Freiburg in Breisgau. Band 5, p. 173.
18. F. E. LUNDIN, J. W. LLOYD, E. M. SMITH, V. E. ARCHER AND D. A. HOLADAY (1969) 'Mortality of uranium miners in relation to radiation exposure, hard-rock mining and cigarette smoking, 1950 through Sept. 1967', *Hlth. Phys.*, **16**, 571.
19. R. C. TURNER, J. M. RADLEY AND W. V. MAYNEORD (1958) 'The naturally occurring α-ray activity of foods', *Hlth. Phys.*, **1**, 268.
20. E. PENNA-FRANCA, M. FISZMAN, N. LOBAO, C. COSTA-RIBEIRO, H. TRINDADE, P. L. DOS SANTOS, AND D. BATISTA (1968) 'Radio-activity of Brazil nuts', *Hlth. Phys.*, **14**, 95.
21. *Revista Medica, Suplemento* 1, **III**, 1964. (Instituto Mexicano del Seguro Social.)
22. 'Radiobiological aspects of the supersonic transport. A report of the ICRP Task Group on the Biological Effects of High-Energy Radiations', *Hlth. Phys.*, **12**, 209, 1966.

17

THE POLITICS OF ECOLOGY

DONALD GOULD

To talk about the politics of ecology is almost a contradiction in terms, for although, in deference to fashion, the leaders of the richer nations now find it prudent to proclaim a belief in the need to protect the world from the greed and excrement of industrial man, in fact, our legislators loathe dealing with environmental problems.

There are two chief causes for this dangerous indifference towards a task which should clearly be a chief concern of people who have put themselves up as fit to regulate the affairs of their fellow-men. The first is plain ignorance. The second is the politician's precarious hold on power. This insecurity, which threatens dictators just as much as those who rule by consent, means that the politician is almost totally concerned with manipulating the immediate business of each passing day, and will gratefully put aside anything that can possibly be stuffed into his always bulging 'pending' file.

That there *is* ignorance among our legislators about the physical nature of the world we live in is sadly evident. One of the most dramatic revelations of this blithe disregard which politicians show toward nuts and bolts and brass tacks was made quite casually by the late Lord Attlee in the book *Twilight of Empire*. He was referring, sixteen years after the event, to the time when he, as British Prime Minister, had given his approval to President Truman's decision to drop an atom bomb on Hiroshima.

> We knew nothing whatever at that time about the genetic effects of an atomic explosion. I knew nothing about fall-out and all the rest of what emerged after Hiroshima.
>
> As far as I know, President Truman and Winston Churchill knew nothing of these things either. . . . Whether the scientists directly concerned knew or guessed, I do not know. But if they did, then so far as I am aware they said nothing of it to those who had made the decision.

It is almost incredible that what was arguably the gravest political decision in modern history could have been taken in ignorance of one of its grim and inevitable consequences, for the relevant information had been common knowledge for decades.

As far back as 1919 a German biologist had observed damage to chromosomes in the cells of grasshoppers exposed to X-rays, and so established the fact that radiation does fundamental mischief to the machinery of living things. This clearly crucial finding led to the rapid development of a whole new specialty – radiobiology – and by 1927 Hermann Muller, a fellow citizen of President Truman, had achieved the next great advance in our understanding of these matters by demonstrating that X-rays cause mutations in the germ cells of fruit flies. In other words, radiation produces genetic damage which may be passed on to future generations, and which may cause faults ranging from mental deficiency to a strong susceptibility to cancer. Muller's observations also led to the use of X-rays as a tool for inducing high mutation rates experimentally, and so, for example, greatly increasing the rate at which new strains of wheat could be produced, and therefore greatly increasing the chances of breeding better plants – hardier or more fruitful. Such was the richness and importance of the research to which Muller's original work gave rise, that he was given a Nobel Prize in 1946 – one year after the Hiroshima decision had been taken.

This was the background against which the educated, experienced and intelligent Clement Attlee had found it possible to sustain a blessed innocence concerning the true obscenity of the weapon which he partly fathered on mankind.

His ignorance (and presumably Churchill and Truman *were* equally uninformed) appears all the more disturbing in view of the fact that the Manhattan Project had involved the active cooperation of a high proportion of the most knowledgeable and prescient scientists in the Western hemisphere, so that there was no lack of men to whom the politicians might have turned, with total confidence, for a full briefing on the certain and probable physical consequences of the deed planned.

It is clear, therefore, that even the most capable and worldly-wise of politicians are quite content to reach decisions which they know will have a fierce impact upon a great many people, and which involve the use of powerful and untried instruments of science, without feeling the need to spend a little time face to face with the experts who have planned and made the whole thing possible, just in order to cross-question, and to be sure that no relevant technical considerations have been ignored during the process of reaching a political judgement. The Hiroshima affair is perhaps an uncommonly dramatic example of this dismal truth, but is in no other way atypical.

A good contemporary counterpart is provided by Concorde. There is real reason for believing that by filling the stratosphere with supersonic jets we may bring about a permanent change in the earth's climate of a nature which will almost certainly be unpleasant. The daily injection into this layer in our sky of tons of water vapour from burnt fossil fuels could, for example, produce a permanent haze, so that bright sunshine becomes a forgotten delight. And the addition of quantities of carbon dioxide to this space could alter the balance of heat exchange between this planet and the cosmos. Solar energy reaches the earth as ultra-violet radiation which readily penetrates carbon dioxide gas. The energy leaves the earth as infra-red radiation, to which carbon dioxide is much more opaque. The present temperature of the earth is stable because, at this temperature, the energy that can escape into space in the form of infra-red rays just balances the energy that reaches us as ultra-violet radiation. If the escape of infra-red rays should become more difficult, the earth would need to become hotter before a fresh balance was struck between the input and output of solar energy. Perhaps the polar ice caps would melt, raising the level of the oceans, and flooding most of the major cities of the world. In any case, a rise in the earth's temperature would cause a major disruption of the whole ecology, so that the prairie farmers of (say) Canada would have to turn to growing rice; and the Greater London Council would have to spend large sums each year on controlling the malarial mosquito; and Scottish lairds would need to find keen parrot-hunters, willing to pay for shooting rights over the tropical highland rain forests covering their estates.

It is true that some scientists dispute the idea that high-flying jets would indeed have any significant effect upon the upper atmosphere, but the possibility is there, and a good many entirely sober-minded and well-informed scientists believe the risk is real, and if the pessimists are right, then by the time we know the truth of the matter it will be too late.

But the point is that the politicians, in their squabbles over SSTs – whether to build or not to build – entirely ignore this moderately long-term risk, although it is by far the nastiest potential consequence of this particular technological folly.

In this instance there is even less excuse for pleading ignorance than there was for the men of the bomb, for not only are there ample experts ready and able to advise: this time the technical and environmental problems involved have been spelt out in the plainest possible language, time and again, in popular books, on television, and in the Press. But the politicians have a remarkable capacity for remaining blind and deaf to facts they do not want to recognise. This, of course, is an even more dangerous proclivity than the disinclination to seek out the truth, since it means that the people who take the decisions cannot even be persuaded to notice the arguments of those who *can* see, and *are* concerned for, the ineluctable consequences of the manner in which we are using our awesome and growing technical powers. Indeed, it seems highly unlikely that even the men of the bomb were in truth never told of the existence of radiation hazards, or of fallout. Some reference to these pertinent details must have been made in the talks they held, and the documents they read, concerning the Manhattan Project. It seems far more likely that while they *were* told of these vitally relevant matters, they remained oblivious to their meaning, perhaps because, if admitted into conscious thought, their significance would have added intolerable weight to the already heavy burden of decision.

Now, all this may seem to argue a belief that politicians are either cynical opportunists, or dunderheads, or both. True enough, the trade does attract its fair share of villains and pompous asses, yet it is demonstrably a fact that those who reach positions of real influence and power are more often than not men and women of better than average ability, some are among the intellectual grandees of their generation, and (in some countries, at least) many are truly concerned to make the world a better place. Why, then, are they commonly so inept in their attitudes toward science, and their handling of the things of science?

I suggest that this is in the nature of the beast. There must, after all, be some good explanations for the fact that most legislatures contain numbers of lawyers, and journalists, and economists, and businessmen, and soldiers and trade union officials, but only the very rare chemist, or engineer, or molecular biologist, or architect, or master joiner. In other words, the political life seems to attract men who are essentially concerned with the manipulation of man-made systems, institutions and ideas, but it holds small charm for the sort of people who find their satisfaction in the manipulation and understanding of things possessed of a physical reality. To the politician the law of tort may indeed seem more real and more relevant to daily life than the law of gravity; and certainly to any service minister, the law of supply and demand will appear far more important to the conduct of human affairs than the third law of thermodynamics.

Abstract concepts and ethical systems and behavioural conventions do indeed possess a functional reality, and it is man's good luck to own a brain capable of creating this realm of ideas as an additional dimension to life on earth. But there is grave danger in the delusion that ideas are the stuff of some superior and perpetual order of reality, so that in a substantial sense they free men from the tyranny of the physical laws which govern the material world.

I suspect that the conventional political mind is of a kind that fosters this delusion, which is, after all, no more than an unformalised expression of religious faith – and religion is a common enough indulgence. But the delusion is dangerous, and may prove fatal, if it persuades politicians that a brave philosophy or noble purpose can in any way substitute for the most urgent and respectful care for the material structure of our world.

If I am right, and if the representative politician is temperamentally unsuited to the task of assessing and handling physical problems, then we are in deep trouble, for there is now the most urgent need for man's manipulations of the physical world to be placed under firm and enlightened political control. But if the politicians won't acknowledge this need, nothing will be done.

Whether or not the men and women in government are the wrong kind of people to manage a world in which technology is king, there are several practical reasons why the traditional political systems within which they work prevent environmental problems from receiving the attention they deserve.

In the first place governments must respond briskly to the unbroken succession of extraordinary happenings that interrupt normal life at home and abroad from day to day. They must also unendingly supply decisions on problems raised by the routine business of the state. They are also constantly under pressure from trade unions and mothers' unions, agents of the rich and friends of the poor, hawks and doves, prudes and libertines, to take some instant action in some urgent cause. On top of all this their members must always be issuing statements, and delivering speeches, and debating issues in order to demonstrate their presence on the bridge. In other words, every member of any government can always fill in every hour of the day coping with instant issues. But by and large the rape of the earth by industrial man is not an instant issue. It is more often a steady process of corruption, not markedly increased from one day to the next. It doesn't stir people to pester their elected representatives. It earns no time in the politician's frantic day. The problems it raises can usually be shelved. And they are.

Secondly, the reduction of pollution, or the conservation of resources, means, in the short term, spending money or losing income. In the long term such measures always pay off. But in money matters politicians tend to care only for the moment. Their financial horizon is mostly bounded by the estimates for the current year and the budget next ahead, and they never have as much cash as they would like for their most cherished projects, such as ABMs, or ferrying heroes to the moon, or building desperately unwanted supersonic passenger planes. So once again, the claims of a dying but unprotesting environment are put back in the queue in favour of more glamorous items on the shopping list, or more insistent creditors.

And if there is a reluctance to spend public money on the care and maintenance of the natural world, there is an almost equal reluctance to force individual industries to pay the price of keeping their contributions to the littering and poisoning of the earth as small as may be. This is because all politicians still believe in the disastrous myth that material welfare can only be maintained in the wake of an expanding economy. There must be a continuing rise in the gross national product. For a country like Britain, of course, this means that every year it must make more and export more. But in order to raise exports in the face of cut-throat competition, everything possible must be done to keep down prices. Manufacturers cannot be asked to meet over-costly standards, either in the matter of the excrement from their factories, or in the matter of the ecological innocence of the goods they sell.

A few months before the last British Labour Government fell from power, Harold Wilson named a member of his cabinet, Anthony Crosland, as minister with special responsibility for the environment (in addition, of course to his principal role as Secretary of State for Local Government and Planning). Here is an extract from an interview with the then new 'Mr Environment', as the *Sunday Times* called him when they printed the piece in January 1970:

> Take the question of cleaner car engines. Here, as often with pollution, there is a genuine problem of international competition. It may be simple in a country as rich and self-sufficient as the United States, but for any single one of the European countries – most of them with large motor-car industries – to go right out in advance of their competitors on things which would increase the cost of their cars would be extraordinarily altruistic. . . .

Now there is, of course, a problem here for those who are caught up in the frantic struggle for customers that stems from the doctrine of an ever enlarging GNP. But I am not, at the moment, concerned with the folly of that clearly suicidal policy (what happens when – for a start – the zinc runs out?). What I am concerned with is the language used by Mr Crosland. He implies that building cleaner car engines is some kind of extravagant and self-indulgent piece of pharisaic posturing which is all very well for 'a country as rich and self-sufficient as the United States' if it pleases the citizens to fling their money around in that rather vulgar fashion. He ignores the fact that the Americans, who are second to none in their enthusiasm for the quick buck, were forced to lay out the small extra money needed to make their cars less poisonous (thus making them slightly less competitive abroad) because their cities, where most of the cars are bunched, were fast becoming uninhabitable. Los Angeles, with its bright sun that works on exhaust fumes to produce a permanent smog of tear gas over the entire city and suburban spread, was the most dramatically affected area, but other cities, all across the continent, were beginning to be an abomination. Even Ford and General Motors saw that a cleaner car made sense, because their existing products seemed poised to kill a high proportion of the customers. Now what has already happened in the United States will shortly happen in Europe, unless something is done to stop it. Crosland ignores the fact.

But worse is to come, for Mr Crosland then states his belief that any European country which might decide to avoid the Los Angeles experience, by making less noxious but slightly pricier cars than its neighbours, would be 'extraordinarily altruistic'.

This phrase perfectly reveals a view that so many politicians take of people who worry about the natural world, regarding them as some kind of woolly-minded sentimentalists, fussing over field-mice and baby seals, but out of touch with the truly important issues (such as pre-tax profits) of a real and earnest life. Of course, so long as this remains the attitude of governments, there is no hope at all that the warnings of scientists will be heard.

The final circumstance which inhibits politicians from either acknowledging or attempting to correct the self-destructive habits of man is the fact that many of these habits are dear to their practitioners, and any attempt to break them would be horribly unpopular, and politicians – even tyrants – cannot afford too much unpopularity. It is understandable, for instance, that politicians should be shy of going on record about the greatest pollution problem of all – pollution of the world by people.

In a few places, like India, the leaders have attempted to encourage the citizens not to breed so readily, and have backed up exhortations with inducements like the gift of a transistor radio to volunteers for vasectomy.

But in other countries, including Britain, governments have refused even to offer advice about family sizes, or to say what numbers the country might best support (despite the fact that careful estimates exist), fearing to be accused of intolerable interference in the most private affairs of the people. In few countries has thought been given to possible means of enforcing limitations on family size by taxation, say, or compulsory contraception.

Similarly, no politician has attempted to spell out the unpopular truth that the world is fast running short of natural resources, so that, even if governments get around to doing something fairly tough and firm about the population problem, we shall still have to start thinking of ways of enjoying life without quite so many manufactured aids, and without squandering quite so much energy on needless bright lights, and half-empty jet planes, and the synthesis of unnecessary, if nice, new materials.

It will, of course, be argued that a lot has, in fact, been done through political action, and on the initiative of politicians, to halt and reverse damaging assaults upon the environment. But in almost every case it will be found that action only followed a situation so dramatic or intolerable that it could not be ignored.

America passed laws requiring that her cars be made less poisonous only when city air had already become physically distressing.

The Thames in London has been cleaned up, but 8000 miles of English rivers beyond sniffing range of Westminster remain corrupt, because they are used as sewers.

The air in London has been cleaned up, but only because the famous smog of 1952 killed tough beef cattle, brought into the city from the country for the annual Smithfield Show, and this was enough to shock some action out of legislators who had accepted the fact that for decades, 300-400 tons of soot had been falling on each square mile of London every year, and that thousands of the old and ill had died each year, before their time, because of the choking gas we Londoners used for air.

It apparently takes a sharp and painful personal experience to persuade a politician to apply his authority to the care and conservation of some small part of the natural world.

President Nixon, speaking in the closing days of 1969, said: 'the 1970s absolutely must be the years when America pays its debt to the past by reclaiming the purity of its air, its waters and our living environment. It is literally now or never. . . .' A few days later he asked Congress for £90 million to clean up the nation's water – less than one-third of the then estimated cost of tackling Britain's far smaller river pollution problem.

President Nixon has also recently created an Environmental Council to advise him on the physical state of the nation. In addition the Council has the task of receiving reports from any government department planning some enterprise, and these reports set out what the environmental impact might be, and suggest, perhaps, alternative schemes. So the council has, at least in theory, a function clearly *vital* to any rational management of a nation – it has the chance of assessing how one major project may interact with another. There is no such mechanism in Britain.

But the Environmental Council is, it appears, a toothless fox, which can advise away to its heart's content, and be sure of upsetting no one, and from the record of its first year's work it has, sadly, all the appearance of a placebo.

In Britain a permanent Royal Commission now keeps a reassuring official eye on environmental problems. The Commission's first report, published in February 1971, contained such robust stuff as this glorious conjugation of trenchant observations: 'there is need to accelerate the trend towards the use of less persistent pesticides; valuable manure from intensive farming is wasted.'

And in addition Mr Heath has done better than his predecessor, and instead of just saddling an already busy colleague with 'special responsibility for the environment', he has made a whole new ministry – a Department of the Environment. This Department, among other things, looks after ports, British Council libraries in foreign parts, the railways, sport, the Channel Tunnel, and ancient monuments.

To be fair, Peter Walker, now Secretary of State for the Environment and in charge of that rag-bag of a ministry, has said that he would like to spend £700 million over the next five years improving sewage works, and cleaning up our rivers. He has also promised to act on the Royal Commission's advice that something should be done about the fouling of coastal waters. He may or may not get the money, but a cynic might reflect that cleaning up the rivers is the cheapest and easiest way of finding some of the huge extra quantity of clean water that industry will want within the next few years. And a cynic might also reflect that the country's coastal fisheries are big business.

None the less, a little is being done, and at least now the politicians proudly display the word 'environment' on their banners, even if they do simply use it as a bright new label on the same old pot. Whether these small beginnings will ever develop into the massive and urgent international exercise that must be mounted if the corruption of our planet is to be halted and reversed is altogether another question. I have sketched out my reasons for thinking any such crusade unlikely, and for fearing that ecology will never become a serious political issue.

There is, however, one small cause for satisfaction; for if I am right, at least there won't be any politicians left to write their memoirs and complain that the wretched sicentists never told them what was going on.

18

THE REAL SIGNIFICANCE OF CBW

STEVEN ROSE

CBW is chemical and biological warfare. Over the past four years CBW has become a bogey word almost on a par with nuclear weapons. Not only have the military expenditures on CBW rocketed through the 1960s, and vast research and development programmes been shown to exist both in government research establishments and linked to the campuses of many universities in Britain and the United States, but one form of CBW has actually been used – and its use is on a continuously increasing scale – in Vietnam. At the same time, the more lurid aspects of the weapons themselves – the number of hundreds of millions to be killed with an ounce of botulinus or V-agent – have made scary headlines, and, of course, the whole CBW issue, with its overtones of poisoning the environment, has become linked into the wave of concern which has swept the United States, and to a lesser extent Britain, concerning the 'ecosystem'. Which is, I suppose, why a discussion of CBW has been included at all in a series on ecology. What I want to establish by this paper is that CBW at one level – the more spectacular Doomwatch sort of level – is not much more of a problem (or a non-problem) than any of the other ecological hazards which are alleged to beset us, whilst at another level, the *reality* of the use of chemical agents in Vietnam, and for that matter Belfast or Paris or Berkeley, California – is a great deal more serious than they are.

Much is often made of the accidental hazards associated with scientific and technical advance. My point is that the real hazards are not accidental but *deliberate*. They concern the actual, specific and intended applications of the techniques of science and technology for the achievement of aims associated, not with human welfare, but with its reverse. CBW is a casebook example of such application, and the study of its real significance can be of considerable value.

BIOLOGICAL WEAPONS

First, though, we may dismiss a red herring, that of BW. The folklore of biological weapons ranges from tales of smallpox-infected blankets given by white settlers in the United States to the Indians, through anthrax-infested cows in the First World War, biological 'bombs' made by the Japanese in the Second, and the infected rats allegedly dropped by American planes over Korea in the first of the post-Second World War wars. The myths include the perennial saboteur with his fatal vial dropped into the water supply. The realities include substantial United States, British, West German, Russian and Scandinavian research over the last three decades, plants such as that at Porton in Britain or Fort Detrick in the United States, field trials such as the spraying of bacterial aerosols from ships along the United States seaboard and the experimental infection of Gruinard Island in north-west Scotland with anthrax (it will remain uninhabitable for another one hundred years), and schemes such as the United States 'project Pacific Bird' under the control of the Smithsonian Institution, which was to investigate the migratory habits of birds with a view to the choice of sites for BW tests which would not run the risk of carrying infection back to the United States. Research on every conceivable bacterial and viral-borne illness has been conducted – and some inconceivable ones as well, such as those reported by the ex-Director of Medical Research Establishment Porton, in which a live virus which carries encephalitis in monkeys was injected into terminal leukaemia patients at St Thomas's Hospital in London.

Yet President Nixon in his statement of endorsement of the Geneva Protocol has announced his government's intention unilaterally to abolish BW stockpiles and convert Fort Detrick to peaceful research. The British government, in the same moment as excluding CS from the Protocol, has tabled a draft treaty banning possession and manufacture of BW agents, and the Russians, who till 1971 held out against the separation of C and BW, have now accepted that BW can be banned independently.

Why? Actually, because BW, for all the ballyhoo, is not a sensible weapon; its use makes neither tactical nor strategic sense. Its risks are enormous, and above all its effects are unpredictable. Could it be swift-acting enough to knock out an enemy population without running the risk of an epidemic sweeping the globe and affecting one's own? Or will it be so slow-acting that the enemy will have time to unleash full-scale conventional or nuclear war? In any circumstances in which BW might be feasible, it is a safe bet that the military would prefer nuclear weapons. The United States and British governments have not been convinced of the immorality of BW, but of its inutility. Everything else is public relations. And, now BW is effectively about to be banned for a second time – it already was under the Geneva Protocol of course – the scope for permitting the existing bans against the far more significant chemical weapons to become eroded is that much wider. So, it is to chemical weapons that we can now turn.

CHEMICAL WEAPONS

The large-scale use of CW began in the First World War; initial experimentation by the French was followed by massive developments by the Germans, with techniques perfected by the great organic chemist Haber, also inventor of the large-scale nitrogen fixation process, who was later driven out of Germany because he was a Jew and died broken-hearted in exile. By the end of the war, chlorine, phosgene and mustard-gas had all been used, and there had been casualties running into hundreds of thousands. It was the experience of these weapons which led to the signing of the Protocol in 1925, which is worth quoting in detail.

. . . the undersigned Plenipotentiaries, in the name of their respective Governments,
Whereas the use in war of asphyxiating, poisonous or other gases, and all analogous liquids, materials or devices, has been justly condemned by the general opinion of the civilised world:
and
Whereas the prohibition of such use has been declared in Treaties to which the majority of the Powers of the World are Parties; and
To the end that this prohibition shall be universally accepted as a part of International Law, binding alike the conscience and the practice of nations;
Declare;
That the High Contracting Parties, so far as they are not already Parties to Treaties prohibiting such use, accept this prohibition, agree to extend this prohibition to the use of bacteriological methods of warfare and agree to be bound as between themselves according to the terms of this declaration.

The Protocol was signed by virtually all major powers, though the United States subsequently failed to ratify it, and still has not, despite several declarations over the years to the effect that she is about to.

The developments subsequent to 1925 were slow: chemicals were used by Mussolini against Abyssinia, to a chorus of protest; there were wide fears that they would be used in the Second World War, and research and development in belligerent countries was stepped up. But, always excluding the concentration camps, little happened, except for a major breakthrough in research in Germany when a new class of agent, outdoing all previous types in toxicity, the nerve gases, was developed. These can kill by absorption through the skin in low concentration: a gas mask will not protect. They were stockpiled in quantity by the Germans under the names Sarin, Soman and Tabun. The captured stocks were renamed G-agents and removed after the war to the USA, USSR, and the UK, and a new era of R and D commenced. It is perhaps worth giving a description of the toxic effects of the nerve gases at this point:

> The symptoms of nerve-gas poisoning are diverse and spectacular. In a comparatively inactive man an exposure to sarin of 15 mg-min/m^3 dims the vision, the eyes hurt and become hard to focus. This may last for a week or more. At 40 mg-min/m^3, the chest feels tight, breathing is difficult, there is coughing, drooling at the mouth, nausea, heartburn, and a twitching of the muscles. At 55, there is a strangling tightness and aching of the chest, vomiting, cramps, tremors, and involuntary defaecation and urination. At 70, severe convulsions will set in followed closely by collapse, paralysis, and death.[1]

The next breakthrough in the development of more toxic agents was British and occurred during the early 1950s, based on the discovery at ICI of a highly toxic class of substances related to the G-agents, during research on organophosphorus insecticides. The good news was relayed to Porton, and so the V-agents were developed, perhaps thirty to fifty times as toxic as the G-agents. This makes them amongst the most poisonous chemicals known to man, surpassed to my knowledge only by bacterial agents and toxins, and one very poisonous substance, dioxin, to which we shall have occasion to return.

Since that time both G-agents and V-agents have been manufactured, in small quantities at plants like that at Nancekuke in Cornwall, or in much larger ones in the United States. They have been stockpiled, tested at places like the joint Canadian-British testing ground at Suffield in Alberta or at the Dugway ground in the United States, where several thousand sheep died in an accident in 1968. They have been packed into missile warheads based in underground caves, as at Denver, Colorado, or disposed of by being dumped at sea, as by the US army in the Caribbean recently, or as with their – fortunately frustrated – much more ambitious proposal to take 12,000 tons of gas through the United States by train to dump in the Atlantic.

But once again, in my view the present threat is not that presented by the nerve gases – at least not against largely urban populations like that of Britain. In any condition where an enemy might use nerve gas, he might as well use high explosives or, if he was really engaged in major conflict and prepared to risk all, nuclear weapons. Attacks by one army against another with nerve gas are also relatively improbable; the protective clothing needed by the attackers is both cumbersome and relatively ineffective – the Porton-produced protective clothing has to be discarded and changed every twelve hours or so if it is to retain its effectiveness. Realistically, the use in war of the nerve gases by one industrialised nation against another seems improbable, but its use by an industrialised nation against a non-industrialised one – as with the United States in Vietnam, for example, seems much more possible. So at last we can come to the meat of the issue: the actual weapons used in the one place where CBW is now being waged – Vietnam.

VIETNAM–THE CASE OF CS

Concurrently with the British development of the V-agents, another, potentially more significant development was under way, that of a replacement for the old tear-gas, which had been used for decades, chloracetophenone, known as CN. CN had a number of disadvantages: it was unstable and could not be stored readily; it liquefied easily and was not suitable for use in the tropics; tolerance to its effects built up rapidly, so that a victim once exposed and recovered was less likely to suffer so much next time. It was also, for a supposed crowd-dispersing agent, relatively toxic. Obviously for all these reasons a replacement was desirable, and in 1956 the British Ministry of Defence directed the Chemical Defence Experimental Establishment at Porton to examine, at high priority, the possibility of alternatives. They came up with orthochlorobenzylidene malononitrile, originally synthesised in the 1920s in the United States by two researchers, Corson and Staughton, and code-named for them CS.

CS suffered from none of the disadvantages of CN; it was stable, affected several physiological systems at once, nose, throat, eyes and stomach, and hence tolerance to its effects seemed less likely. And it was no more toxic. Production began at Nancekuke in the early 1960s, though only 4-6 tons a year were produced, transported to a firm called Schermuleys in Dorking, and there packed into the Porton-patented grenades. As well as CS grenades being exported to many countries, the information as to its manufacture found its way, by way of something called the Quadripartite Agreement, an information-sharing system between Britain, the USA, Australia and Canada, to the United States.

There production started in earnest, with the spur of the Vietnam war. By 1965, CS, along with CN and the more toxic arsenical DM, were in use in Vietnam. CS rapidly replaced the others in favour: by 1970, 9 million pounds of CS had been used, enough to cover the whole of South Vietnam 1·3 times over. CS production was a major industry; it was even being made in South Vietnam itself. What is more, escalation was not merely in scale of use but type of weaponry. By 1969 the US Army Training Circular (my copy is, I fear, marked 'Return to the Pentagon Library') listed no less than eighteen different types of device with which to dispense CS. Grenades, bombs, including canisters packed in cluster bomb units which can be assembled into 'liquorice-allsorts'-type packages along with fragmentation weapons and defoliants; liquid dispensations for spraying from helicopters; missiles and shells, and finally the 'mighty mite', a device like a rat-catcher's, for blowing CS, fed at a rapid rate into a hopper at the top of the machine, into the caves and tunnels used as shelters by the Vietnamese. The escalation has not merely been in types of dispenser but in quality of CS used as well. A new formulation, CS2, has a different particle size and is bonded for durability on to siliconised particles which may retain their potency for long periods of time.

War has always been a spur to technological innovation. There is no question, of course, but that, as used in Vietnam, CS kills. It kills because it is applied at high concentrations in confined areas, and because it is used as an adjunct to conventional weapons, for flushing

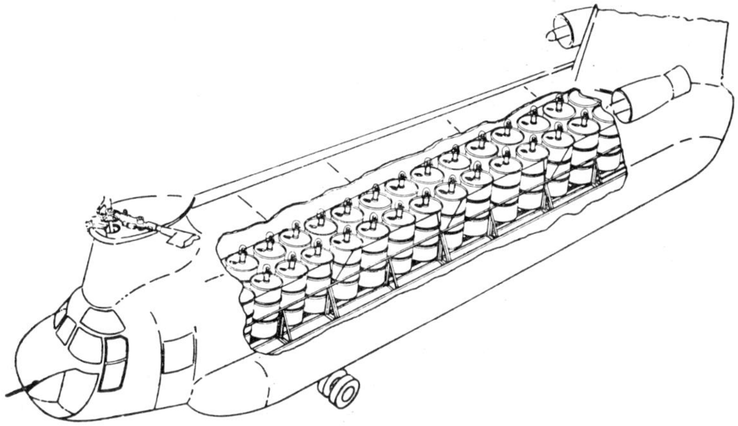

Fig. 1. Helicopter load of CS – from the US Army Training Circular

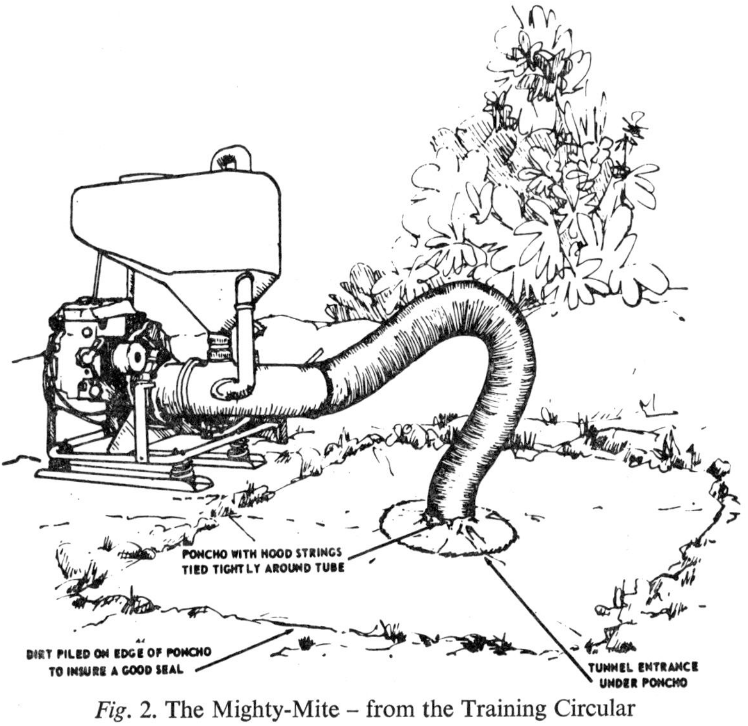

Fig. 2. The Mighty-Mite – from the Training Circular

people out of caves or shelters, for instance, and into the range of explosives or fragmentation bombs. These roles are described frankly in the Training Circular: 'the use of the agent,' it concludes 'is limited only by the imagination of the field commander.'

Dr Vennema, a doctor in a civilian tuberculosis hospital in 1967, put it differently:

During the last three years I have examined and treated dozens of patients, men, women and children, who had been exposed to a type of war gas, the name of which I do not know. The type of gas used makes one quite sick when one touches the patient, or inhales the breath from their lungs. After contact with them for more than three minutes one has to leave the room in order not to get ill.

The patient usually gives a history of having been hiding in a cave or tunnel or bunker or shelter into which a canister of gas was thrown in order to force them to leave their hiding place. Those patients that have come to my attention were very ill with signs and symptoms of gas poisoning similar to those that I have seen in veterans from the First World War treated at Queen Mary Veterans Hospital in Montreal. The only difference between the cases was that these Vietnamese patients were more acutely ill and when getting over their acute stage presented a similar picture to that of the war veterans.

Patients are feverish, semi-comatose, severely short of breath, vomit, are restless and irritable. Most of their physical signs are in the respiratory and circulatory systems. Both lungs exhibit rales throughout, severe bronchial spasm, heart rate is usually very high and all of the patients had pulmonary oedema. In most cases active treatment for pulmonary oedema and complicating pneumonia was helpful and they survived. Those that survived developed a chronic bronchitic type of picture complicated by infections.

The mortality rate in adults is about 10%, while the mortality rate in children is about 90%. I have only kept accurate records of the number of such cases that I have seen since last June. Since then I have seen 7 cases of which:
there was 1 child of 6 years of age who died.
,, ,, 1 ,, ,, 15 years of age who survived.
,, ,, 1 lady of approx. 40 years of age who died.
,, were 4 other adults who survived. . . .

THE DEFOLIANTS

Another aspect of CW, now become conventional warfare, is the use of defoliants. This was another British 'first', pioneered in Malaya to clear jungle tracks against the threat of ambushes and indeed, several herbicides now used extensively in agriculture were originally developed as potential weaponry. In Vietnam the agents used are predominantly the organochloride phenoxyacids, 2,4-D and 2,4,5-T, the arsenical cacodylic acid, and picloram, which functions as a soil sterilisant. Originally claimed to be used exclusively to destroy the NLF's jungle cover, they were soon admitted to be part of a massive American campaign of crop destruction as well. The scale of the escalation is indicated by Fig. 3. By 1969 more than 5·5 million

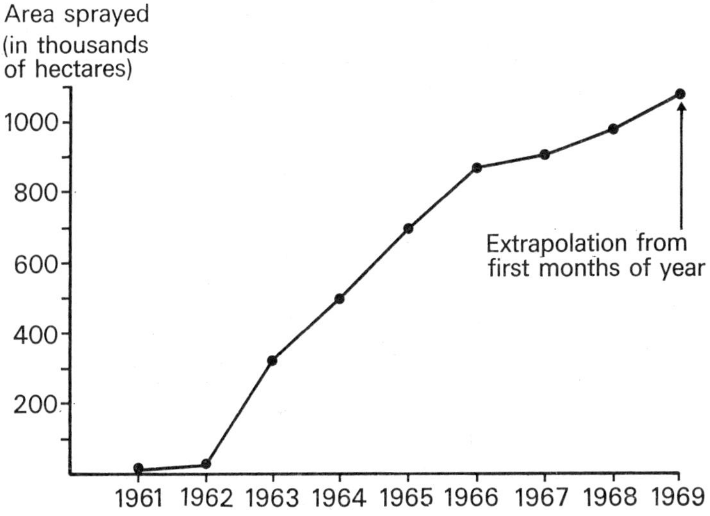

Use of Herbicides by the Americans in Vietnam

Fig. 3

acres of forest and cropland had been sprayed with more than 15 million gallons of herbicide, and the use had extended to Laos and Cambodia as well. According to a study commissioned by the American Association for the Advancement of Science, large areas of mangrove swamps, perhaps 50 per cent of the total, which is crucial to the maintenance of the elaborate ecology of the Mekong Delta region has been, perhaps permanently, destroyed. Twenty per cent of the total area of hardwood forest, once a major source of income for the Vietnamese, has been sprayed, and the areas concerned are rapidly being invaded by bamboo. It may be anything from twenty to one hundred years before the area recovers. Rubber production has plummeted, and South Vietnam has become a net importer rather than exporter of rice. Sterilisation is likely to affect the crop-producing soil in some regions for many years. Indeed, some have argued that there is a danger of a permanent, irreversible change in the soil structure of the defoliated areas, a process known as laterisation, which bakes the soil into a hard, impervious rock-like composition.

Meanwhile, there are direct effects as well upon the human population. One such effect of course – and the deliberate aim of the crop destruction campaign – is starvation, which as has been pointed out many times, is a weapon of war which of its nature singles out for severest treatment the weak, babies, the aged or sick, rather than the fighting men. But there are other effects too, both more immediate and long term, for it is now abundantly clear that the defoliants are toxic substances.

For a long time this was denied by US military spokesmen, who claimed that they were just like the herbicide sprays used in agriculture. But they neglected to add that the defoliants in Vietnam, instead of being diluted manyfold before use, were sprayed undiluted on to the heads of the population below. Also they neglected to point out that many areas – and people – have been sprayed time and again. During our visit to Hanoi in December of 1970, to investigate the effects of the defoliants, we spoke with people who had been sprayed as many as eight times, and often with complex mixtures of chemicals. Clearly this alters completely the toxicological picture.

But even the 'pure' herbicides have proved to be less than ideal. Early in 1970 news began to leak out concerning industrial accidents in Britain, Germany and the United States in which a highly toxic impurity, dioxin, accumulated during manufacture of 2,4,5-T. Dioxin is very stable and more poisonous than any of the known nerve gases. A laboratory study of teratogenic effects of 2,4,5-T in the United States showed that it caused birth deformities in mice. The deformities were ascribed to the dioxin impurity in the particular sample of 2,4,5-T analysed, but before long pure 2,4,5-T, and for good measure 2,4-D as well, were implicated as being themselves teratogenic and their use banned in the United States. Incidentally, they have *not* yet been banned in Britain and numbers of agricultural and Forestry Commission workers are presumably still at risk.[2]

Although the use of the principal 2,4,5-T-containing defoliant, 'orange', was restricted in Vietnam early in 1970, later in that year it was still in use – apparently approved by local field commanders despite official US orders. Meanwhile it was estimated by the botanist Arthur Galston in the United States that the doses already taken up by Vietnamese women in sprayed areas might well put their infants at risk. Reports began to appear of large numbers of stillbirths and birth deformities in South Vietnam hospitals, and a security clamp on data on deformities was imposed by the Saigon regime. These effects are notoriously hard to quantify, particularly in a nation at war and with a population in a poor nutritional state: none the less Meselson in the AAAS study collected some evidence on such deformities in the South, and in the North we saw the deformed babies of three mothers who had been sprayed while pregnant. This is no more than circumstantial clinical evidence, and in collaboration with the Vietnamese we have embarked on a more scientific survey of the effects of the defoliants, which we will publish in due course.[3] But it has, even so, been enough to push the United States government towards a restriction of this type of warfare. It is worth making the point that the effects of the defoliants are experienced by generations as yet unborn, and are such as to cause permanent harm to the environment; thus they are analogous to the long-term genetic hazards of radioactive fallout.[4]

THE POINT OF IT ALL

It is this hazard which makes the problem of CBW of particular ecological significance and human horror, of course. But if we are going to react in any other way than simply regarding this as one of the inevitable horrors of war, it is necessary to ask: why? Why CS and the defoliants, and not, for instance, nerve gases or BW?

The answer, so far as Vietnam is concerned, lies in the tactical and strategic role of such weapons. In assessing the defoliation campaign, we should be conscious of this role. It is not mindless atrocity, any more than the use of fragmentation weapons in the North, including the newest types in which the metal pellets are replaced by plastic—invisible to X-rays and hence not possible to localise and remove – is mindless atrocity. All the scientific and technological innovations of the Vietnam war are linked to some strategic analysis. In the case of the fragmentation weapons, perhaps this may be to maim, rather than kill, as many as possible, so as to tie up scarce economic and manpower resources in medical care. We may compliment our scientific colleagues in the United States on their resourcefulness in the development of such a weapon! Defoliation, and the use of CS, with which, to judge by our preliminary study in Hanoi, it seems to be very frequently coupled, is linked to the Vietnamisation of the war. Deny the peasantry its crops, and it will be forced to move into Saigon-held areas; the effectiveness of the campaign can be seen from the fact that 14 per cent of the villages of South Vietnam have been regrouped in concentration areas and strategic hamlets – though whether this is simply replacing the war in the jungle with a war in the cities, as both Western journalists in South Vietnam and the North Vietnamese suggest, remains to be seen. The point is that both CS and the defoliants are weapons which are precisely tailored to the needs of anti-guerrilla warfare. They are particularly suited to being applied by a highly mechanised, protected and mobile force against a relatively simply equipped, less mechanised and less mobile force which has the trust or open support of the civilian population in which it moves. If this description fits precisely the situation of the guerrillas in the rural peasantry of South Vietnam, let us look further.

For a helicopter gunship, similar to those which have seen service in Vietnam, circled the campus at Berkeley, California, in 1969, dropping CS on the heads of the students beneath. A war technology developed in Vietnam had come full circle, home to the American people. And not surprisingly, for the situations of the rural guerrilla amongst the peasants and the urban guerrilla amongst the city streets are very comparable. In neither case is high-explosive or conventional weaponry alone an adequate weapon. Hence the use of CS in Berkeley, Mace in Chicago and CS again in Paris, Londonderry and Belfast. Solidarity between the urban guerrilla of the city streets of the West, and the NLF fighters of Vietnam is often expressed; in this case there is also a parallelism of the weapons technology used against them.

What I have been trying to show is that in the escalation of CBW, certain weapons have been used because they fill certain tactical and strategic needs of the industrial-military complex. Lurid tales of mass disaster aside, particular technologies have had to develop in response to these military demands; it is not the accidental but the deliberate evolution of such technologies which is a facet of our time and over which we need to assert social control.

CBW is but an example of such technologies, and a good study to make. Yet people are often confused and argue that in some sense CS, for instance, is at the least more humane than horrible. Even the great Marxist biologist J. B. S. Haldane fell into that trap back in the 1920s (admittedly before he became a Marxist!). Yet in fact the field experience of the real use of chemical weapons, in war and civil conflict, shows them applied not as a substitute for, but in *addition* to conventional weaponry, aiding it, making it more effective.

I am often asked what I would substitute, say, for CS, in civil conflict. My answer is that I do not think that I am in the business of aiding governments improve their technologies of repression. If a government needs CS, then it is time it was changed. Instead, it acts on the famous Brechtian advice, 'The government has lost the confidence of the people; it needs to elect a new people'. CS and the other chemical agents are instruments of collective repression and punishment, which most directly adversely affect those least likely to be participating in the struggle – the children, sick or old. And they are never used alone: they are but additional weapons of escalation.

I do not wish to suggest that if we could make the British and United States governments change their mind about CS and the defoliants, and accept UN Secretary-General U Thant's view that they are banned under the Geneva Protocol, all would be well. Nor do I wish to suggest that science and technology are the *source* of the brutalities of the American war in Vietnam, or of class, race and religious war at home. There are other ways of destroying rice, and others of killing other human beings deliberately, with forethought, savagery and joy, than this.

What I do want to maintain is that science and technology are presently in the service of the military-industrial complex, of the ruling class groups of the United States and the United Kingdom, and in their hands are being used deliberately to destroy human welfare. The enemy we must face is not science, despite what some contemporary fashionable prophets of doom say, but the social order which science and technology serve.[5] Science must be placed at the service of the people. This, indeed, was the motto of the scientists of North Vietnam, from whom we learned so much in our stay.

1. Quoted from J. P. ROBINSON in S. Rose ed. (1968), *CBW*, London.
2. Committee of Commerce of U.S. Senate, 91-60 (1970), Government Printing Office, Washington.

3. ROSE, H. and ROSE, S. *Science* (1972), in press.

4. It should be noted that the use of the defoliants has now been extended to the war by the Portuguese against the freedom fighters in Angola. It is probable that the source of the defoliants used by the Portuguese is American.

5. Steven and Hilary Rose are the authors of two Penguin paperbacks on the general uses of science and technology: *Science and Society* (1969) and *Ideology and the Natural Sciences* (forthcoming).

19

ECOLOGY AND THE COMPUTER

PETER CASTRUCCIO

THIS lecture will concern some of the problems we are undergoing in the area of ecology in the United States. Particularly, towards the end of the paper, I will discuss some of the tools we are attempting to develop today, particularly thanks to the efforts of NASA.

I think we are all familiar with what the problem of ecology is and how it arises. In a nutshell, we can look at it this way. When a region of the world is still virgin, as North America was 400 years ago, people are few, the land is vast, the resources are large, we enter an era known as the era of exploration. We have no ecological problems then. As time goes on, population grows, but resources remain constant. We find that the human groups attempt to exploit to the maximum the resources of the region. This we can call the era of exploitation. It began in the United States approximately in the early nineteenth century. The resources that are exploited are of course the agricultural resources, mining, rivers, etc. As these resources are exploited more and more, and as the population continues to grow we begin to notice a phenomenon – well known in engineering terms – which is the phenomenon of coupling between human activities. Activity A begins to couple with activity B. This is what gives rise to the problems of ecology. Let me explain a little better what this coupling means.

You can consider a human enterprise as occupying a certain span of resources: water, land, air, etc., and exploiting these resources to a certain degree of intensity. As long as the span-intensity domains of enterprise A and enterprise B are separate, there is no problem. The problem arises when there is overlap between the enterprises' resource span-intensity domains: it is the areas of overlap which cause the ecological problem. The definition of these domains in somewhat hard terms is a matter of concern today. An example of this is electrical power plants, which several years ago – no more than ten to fifteen years ago in the United States – generated electricity by burning fossil fuels without concern with what the outgoing gases were going to do. As a matter of fact, they weren't doing much because the air resource was vast. As the generation of electricity and the concurrent burning of coal increased beyond a certain limit, beyond the dissipation capacity of the atmosphere, this gaseous efflux began coupling with other enterprises. For example, with shirt makers – they did not make them white any more. Or, another example, with just the enterprise of living: breathing became more difficult.

The far-fetched but very significant ecological consequences of this, I think, will be the following: if we consider, as a function of time, the trend of the measure of all good things that we have used since Adam Smith – namely the Gross National Product – we note that portions of the GNP will be devoted to evading the ill-effects of coupling, which we call pollution. The portion of GNP so devoted is non-productive. Like the $16 per kilowatt-hour required to install an SO_2 filter in an electric coal-burning plant: it produces nothing in return. To be productive, the $16 should be spent in more furnaces or improving the burning process. Thus a larger and larger segment of the GNP of the world will be devoted to such non-productive uses in developed nations. In developing nations this need not yet be the case. Developing nations can continue in the standard manner until they too suffer the problems of coupling, either through their own doing or from interference from developed nations. This may well become a powerful force for closing the economic gap between developed and developing nations.

If we do not seek early remedies for the problem – and fortunately we do – this drop in real GNP could become very drastic as we go on. The cure may become very expensive.

We have had warnings and examples in the past which we did not heed. The Oklahoma dust-bowl is a well-known phenomenon which occurred out West, due to over-exploitation of the land. Lake Erie is another well-known phenomenon, which was caused not by industrial pollution but by excess nutrients leached from agricultural fertilising. This warning we had about seven or eight years ago. We did not heed it. We did not realise that from these isolated warnings we would rapidly grow into a situation wherein the problem became of national dimensions.

The Aswan Dam, planned in the late 'forties and constructed in the 'fifties, is another example of why in the United States no major enterprise, public or private, will be allowed henceforth without a thorough ecological study of its consequences.

This dam was supposed to produce enough electricity, and furnish enough irrigation water, to change drastically the economy of Egypt. And yet today the United Nations are significantly concerned about its ecological impact. Before the dam, the river carried silt, which deposited up to an inch and a half at the delta and made the one and only excellent fertiliser. After the dam, this will not happen any more. Will the crops grow the same way without this fertiliser? Evidence says no. The naïve remedial suggestion is to import additional fertiliser, or construct fertiliser plants in the country. As we all know, it is not as simple as that: there is the whole problem of educating the farmers to use it. This is a typical example of a major work performed without ecological preplanning.

A final example, whose consequences again could have been forecasted (so I say with the advantage of hind-sight) is DDT. This chemical was heralded at the end of the 'forties as the potential saviour of developing nations. It was going to eradicate malaria; it was going to increase the crop yield. We all know what happened to it: it is banned or severely restricted in most developed countries of the world.

I think there are no major technological problems in ecology. I think that technology can cope with the environmental problems. The real problem is really twofold. Number one: money; number two: establishment of the objectives. I would like to present a specific example as an illustration of just these two problems. You remember the large hue and cry which occurred about three years ago, resulting in about 3000 pages of Congressional testimony, on the question of thermal pollution.

What causes the problem of thermal pollution? We all know that it is caused by the fact that certain types of industry need to cool certain portions of their production cycle. The total cooling requirement for US industry in 1969 was 13 'Potomacs'. (Electric power requires 11 Potomacs; the remainder is accounted for by the metal, oil and fertiliser industries.) A Potomac is a unit of heat equivalent to the heat required to bring the River Potomac from its normal temperature to boiling-point. It was necessary to coin this unit because the zeros were too many to be expressed in BTUs or calories.

Now if one extrapolates to the year 2000, which is not far away, one finds that the US cooling requirement will reach 100 Potomacs, for the electric industry alone. The world will need between 300 and 400 Potomacs. This extrapolation is based on the assumption that the future growth of electric power demand will be the same as that of the last twenty years. This was a good assumption last year. Now suddenly last month Con Edison in New York announced that it was not going to advertise any more for increased consumption of electric power. I believe this is only a symptom of what is to come. Which means that the growth coefficient of electric power production will not be as large. In any event, by the year 2000 we can assume that we will need 300 Potomacs to cool the global electric power production.

Now, from the 3000 pages of Congressional testimony there emerges the fact that there are three basic methods of cooling, with many sub-variants. The first one is the closed-cycle method wherein the heat of the hot water is transferred to the atmosphere by means of fans. Ecologically it is the cleanest. Even the heat equivalent of those 300 Potomacs that we saw before, dumped into the atmosphere, appears to be insufficient to cause damage. However, the cost of this method is very high. The capital investment required for this method of cooling for the entire US industry in the year 2000 amounts to about $200 *per capita* based upon the US 2000 population. This is an average of $800 per family, which the country would have to pay, not for the purpose of obtaining electricity but for the privilege of cooling in an ecologically clean manner. $68 billion just for cooling is equivalent to what the Department of Defence spends per year! In addition, the recurring cost of using this method is equivalent to about $20 *per capita* per year, or about $80 equivalent per family.

The second method, which is much cheaper, both in capital investment and in yearly recurring cost, uses the heat of evaporation of water (about 600 calories per kilogram) by evaporating some of the circulating hot water. The typical rate of evaporation from a one-megawatt electric plant (a reasonably large, but not huge, size) is about 25,000 gallons per minute. The problem with this method is that it causes significant ecological disturbances, depending upon geography and season, because all this evaporated water causes problems like fog, condensation, artificial snow and so forth. Suffice it to say that if this method were used throughout the United States' industry in the year 2000 it would cause the evaporation of about thirty Potomacs per day, and that's a lot of water in the atmosphere.

That is why the trend of the electric companies is to use the third method, which is by far the cheapest – about 10 per cent of the first method both in capital investment and in running cost. It consists simply of pumping water into the plant, and pumping it out again after cooling. The plant needs to be located near a moving body of water, such as a river, or an estuary whose water moves with the tides. This is, however, the method that causes all the hue and cry and the fear of ecological disturbances. Infra-red photography is the technique used to detect the increase in temperature. Is this a real problem?

The first concern is the effect upon the marine or aquatic life. Fig. 1 shows species of marine inhabitants of the Chesapeake Bay. The pale grey bars show the area of optimality for the individual of each species. The dark grey bars indicate the limits of lethality of the individual. This means that if one subjects an individual specimen to that level of temperature for a prolonged period of time – two to three weeks – it will die. The black bars are the limits of lethality for the species, namely the temperature at which the larvae cease to survive. From Fig. 1 we can see two things. Firstly, that the balance is quite fine-tuned; not much additional temperature is needed to really upset things. This balance has been worked out in several megacenturies of evolution: it is not easily modified. Second, if we make it too hot we favour the algae and harm the fish life. This in turn has a feedback effect known as eutrophication, which aggravates the problem further because as the algae grow they consume oxygen, which is subtracted from the fish.

However, is the impact on fish life the only problem? Certainly it is not so for the Chesapeake Bay, and I suspect it is not so for most inland and coastal waters. The Chesapeake Bay turns out to be the repository for the dumping of industrial and municipal waste for a population of about 10 million: most of this waste is untreated. In the water exist bacteria which break down this waste. Fig. 2 shows the curve of biological activity of one species of these bacteria. The curve shows the capability to break down waste. One notices that the bacteria, like algae or fish, prefer a certain temperature. If it is too cold or too hot they diminish their activity.

At this point, a first dichotomy begins to arise. You have a body of water with fish, but you also want to keep it biologically clean

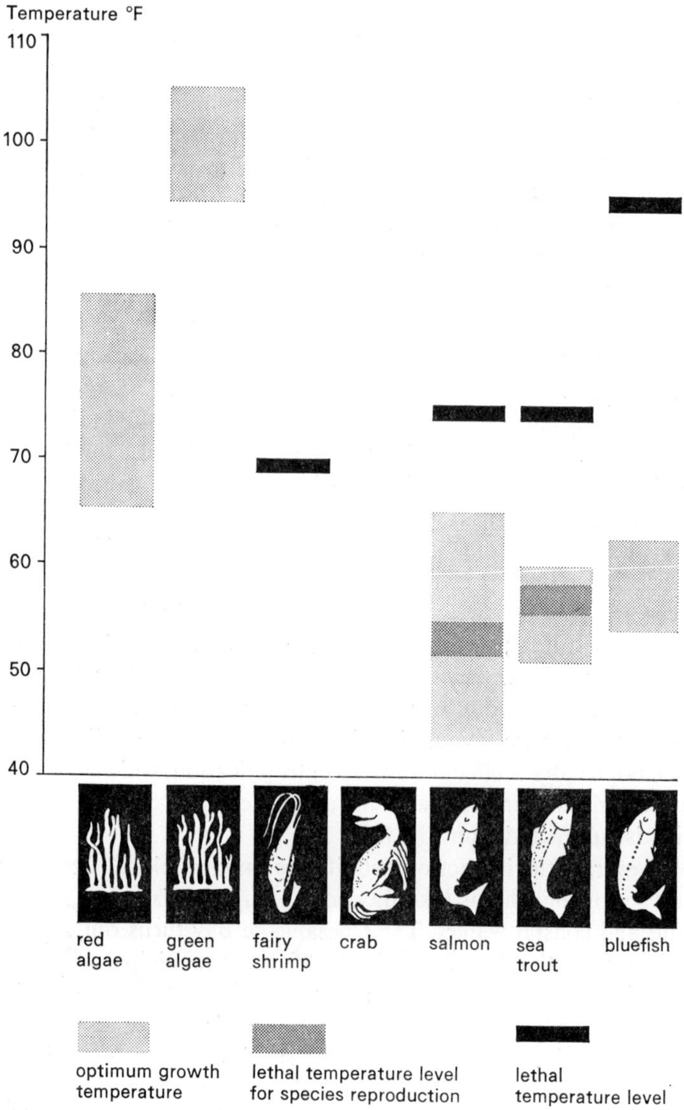

Fig. 1. How much heat

because you have all this waste dumping into it. Which one do you prefer? Keep it cold, and have the fish prosper, or warm it a little, and keep the bacteria working to break down the waste? However, the problem is much vaster yet than fish and waste. Let us consider Chesapeake Bay from the standard of economic values. I am not

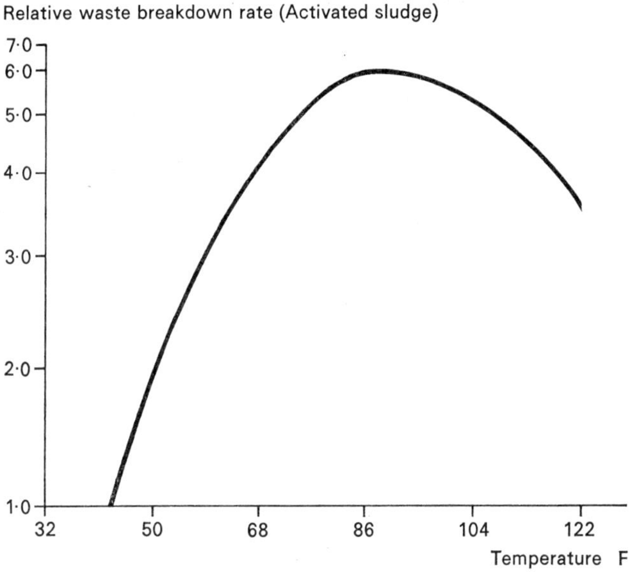

Fig. 2. Heat is bacteria

saying that this is the only standard: it is the only one we can measure right now. From the economic viewpoint, we find that the total value of the fish catch – which is what people were really worried about – is about $40 million per year (the value after the fish are processed). The value of the recreation activities is higher, about $43 million per year. The vertical axis represents pounds per hour for a given concentration of bacteria, and the horizontal axis represents temperature.

The yearly product of the industry which is directly related to the Bay – of those industries that need that water either for cooling or transportation or for other reasons – is approximately twenty times larger yet than the fish catch ($800 million). The value of the real estate that surrounds the Bay, whose value is being threatened now by its dirty aspect, is about $1500 million. And so the question which faces the legislators and planners is not just whether to preserve the fish but rather how to balance all these thing together. For example, one course of action could be to continue in their year-2000 growth plan which calls for about double the industrial product, and for more jobs, more industries – without regard for environmental problems. The problem underlying this course of action is: if we add another $700 million to the industrial product, can we afford to lose the $40 million fishing revenue? From a purely economic standpoint there is no question that we can. Another course of action would be to clean the environment at the detriment of more industry and more jobs. What is the legislator's choice at this point? Would you rather have more industry and not spend any money to clean the environment? Or would you rather make it completely clean by not accepting any more industry – and this means you will have less jobs, and your growth programme will not be fulfilled? Or would you opt for the third alternative, namely to have both in some measure – and spend the necessary money? The answer you get is: we'd like both options; plenty of industry and lots of fish, but we don't want to spend any money! Of course, this attitude is going to change – but it is the problem right now, and it is not a technological problem.

And just to complete the story, the studies made for the Chesapeake Bay found that there exist so-called four major growth inhibitors, factors that are eroding the value and liveability of the Bay: 1. *Shore erosion*; 2. *Sedimentation*; 3. *Fertiliser pesticide leaching*; 4. *Waste disposal* (sewage, industrial discharge, dredging). As regards thermal pollution, the question, in the context of what was shown before, is: what is the effect of the additional heating that must be generated to produce electric power? Six nuclear electric power plants are planned between now and 1980, estimated to add 13 Potomacs of waste near to the present total of 15 Potomacs of heat dissipated. So the question is: if you put these plants in and their effect mixes with the other four growth inhibitors, what is the total effect on your total problem?

The essential problem then becomes one of establishing goals. In the specific case just presented the goals have to be established by the legislature. The goals take the form of what kind of outputs are preferred with what kind of mix. For example: full industrialisation and full fishing capabilities and full recreation, or lesser degrees of some of them. Once these are established the technological problem is to find out what are the key inputs – not in terms of a million things, but generally no more than ten perhaps – in other words, to find what significantly affects the outputs. Having done this, the problem then becomes one of establishing a relationship between inputs and outputs: the totality of these relationships is what we call a model. A model is simply a written, or computerised, relationship between certain inputs and certain outputs. This is where the role of the computer will one of these days become very significant, because the relationships are fairly complicated, they are manifold and they are hard to put on paper. Many are heuristic, many are non-linear, so it is necessary to put them in something more versatile than a sheet of paper and this is where we use the computer. What we do observe – and we have seen it in air pollution pretty clearly – is that the evolution of ecological management is really a four-phase process. This example relates to air pollution but the trends are the same for water, and for other ecological processes. This four-phase process goes something like this. Phase 1 is the collection of data; information is the most costly thing today. For example, how often does a particular pollutant pollute the environment? What is its day-to-day variation? What other simultaneous causes affect the pollution? Is it clean every Thursday? Is it dirty every Friday? – this kind of thing. Phase 2 is the correlation of these data in order to begin working out some relationships: such as, what do these data mean with respect to others? This is where the computer comes in. Phase 3, after we have developed the relationships, is the creation of the model. Now we possess a reasonable way to predict; obviously the model is absolutely no good unless it can predict. For example, there are at least four or five models of the stock market wherein one can plug in the whole past history of stock fluctuation and one can tell in theory within a certain accuracy what should have happened. The trouble is none of these models really predict what is going to happen tomorrow, they only confirm or disprove the past. That does not do us any good in the stock market; it does not do us any good in ecology. Phase 4, many years away yet, after the model is developed, is the creation of a closed-cycle control loop. Under this regime, we will have devices – sensors – which pick up the information, which is then processed through an automatic system, and the system can figure out and give certain commands and change things so that conditions keep in balance. At present, in most ecological problems we are still in Phase 1: the collection of data.

The big problem we are having is the problem of money, since the collection of data is an expensive proposition. This is why some of the latest information-collection tools proposed are the tools of aerial sensing, and eventually some day of sensing from space.

This is how the process works for aerial or space sensing. Let me illustrate with an example applied to one of the major ecological problems of today – the problem of water resources. This is a big problem. The consumption of water today is no less than six tons *per capita* per day in the United States; less, but still quite high, elsewhere. As shown in Fig. 3, the reason why we need so much

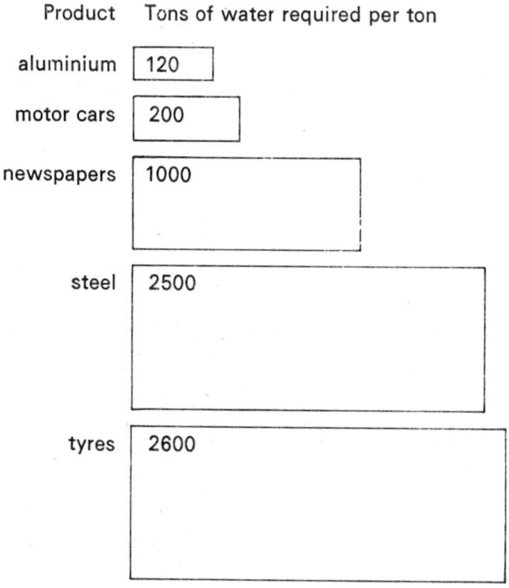

Fig. 3. Water requirements for selected industrial products

water in industrial countries is that industrial products need many tons of water per ton of product. And this would still not be so bad if the industries were to limit themselves to using the water and returning itc lean; however, when they pollute it the additional quantity of water required as a solvent increases the numbers of Fig. 3 anywhere from seven to perhaps twenty times. This is why the United States consumes 6 tons *per capita* compared with the developing countries' 0·7 tons.

Now, how much water is available? It turns out that even with modern technology, practically the only water available is the water that falls from the sky by precipitation. The average precipitation on the dry area of the earth is 850 mm per year. If one multiplies 850 mm times the total area, which is 125 million square kilometres, one gets so many cubic feet or cubic metres of water. Of that water, on the average approximately three-quarters evaporates before it is utilised, so that the theoretical efficiency is about 25 per cent. But not all of that 25 per cent is used. A lot of it flows in the streams and is never used. As a gross figure for the United States, the coefficient of utilisation of rain water is only about 7½ per cent.

Now if you take the 6 tons of water consumed *per capita* per day in the United States, extrapolate its growth to the year 2000, and extrapolate the growth of the other nations, which is probably going to be even faster, and calculate the number of people there will be in the year 2000 on the earth – about 6 to 7 hundred million, depending on the estimate – you come out with a total demand. If you then match it to the total availability of rain water, with an efficiency of 7½ per cent – assuming everybody will get this very high efficiency in A.D. 2000 – you will find you do not have enough water. A significant recirculation cycle will have to be used, or we will have to increase the efficiency of 7½ per cent as close as possible to the theoretical 25 per cent. If we make this calculation assuming 5 per cent efficiency – which is pretty good for the world at large – we find that the available water will have to be recirculated about every 300-400 hours.

There is a lot of work going on to find other sources of water. So far, however, there is nothing economically valid. 97 per cent of the world's water is salty, and the best price today at which water can be desalinised in very large quantities is approximately $1 per thousand gallons. A price at which a city is willing to buy is perhaps half of this, whereas the price for agricultural water is of the order of 5 cents a thousand, and the price for industrial water is 10 or at the most 20 cents. So we are way out of reach so far. The question of desalinisation is a very interesting one, requiring much effort, but it cannot be done economically yet.

Of the 3 per cent of remaining water, about 95 per cent is locked in glaciers and in polar caps – mostly polar caps. A study was made to determine the economics of taking something like a super-tanker and sending it to the Arctic to collect ice – it was found that the transportation rates are too high, it cannot be done economically. Much of the remaining water – which, we must not forget, is really recharged from the sky – is located deep below the surface. It turns out that the cost of drilling and of the electricity to pump is still beyond the price levels mentioned before. Therefore, at the moment, and until a technological breakthrough is effected, we are confined to utilising only the rain water, also known as surface fresh water, which is about one ten thousandth of 1 per cent of the total water available on earth. So be it, at least for the near future: let us see what we can do to utilise it more efficiently.

The problem boils down to watershed management – watershed being that area in which rain collects. Everybody lives in a watershed of one kind or another. The watershed is a system in which the input is stochastic. We do not know, that is to say, when or how much rain will fall. We can take a fifty-year history, we can draw historical curves: maximum probabilities in April, less in May and March and so forth. However, we don't really know with precision how much rain will fall next month. On the other hand, the watershed has highly deterministic *requirements.* A watershed whose water eventually collects in a river has to provide a large number of consumers with power based upon certain schedules; municipalities with water, also against a schedule; has to supply irrigation water, and perhaps recreation water. The consumption schedules are relatively fixed, the input is random; the problem is: how do we match the two?

For several years now the ESSA, Environmental Science Services Administration, has developed a model – a set of relationships – to predict as a function of rainfall how much water will be available in a watershed. This model today is considered the best available in practice. The primary reason why it could stand improvement is economic. Let us see why.

The ESSA model has three functions. First, it tries to correlate how much rain falls down with how much water will flow out – that is the utilisation coefficient I was mentioning before as being roughly 25 per cent average – case by case, it might be 25 per cent, 30 per cent, 18 per cent, because it varies from season to season. The second function is to predict the time behaviour of this water flow. If all the water comes down very rapidly we are going to have a high crest and therefore floods. If it comes slowly then we have a smoother curve and no floods. This technique is called the hydrograph. The third function is to combine the first two parts to give the overall prediction. ESSA has built eleven modifications of this basic model, which run on the 1130 computer. Eleven watersheds – eleven computers.

Now briefly as to how ESSA does it. The first piece of the model is called the 'correlation between rainfall and runoff': rainfall being what comes down from the sky, and runoff being the water which is eventually yielded by the watershed. This model is based upon four inputs. First is the *quantity* of rain that comes down at any given time. Second is the *duration* of the rainfall. It makes a big difference to the runoff whether we have an inch of rain in two hours or in two days. Third is the *season* of the year: they have looked up the records for the last fifty years – where available – and they perform correlations between them. For example, if every October runoff never surpasses a certain amount, or it never lies below a certain value, it is reasonable to assume that history will roughly repeat itself. (Not always, of course.) The fourth input is related to the *humidity*, because dry soil absorbs water faster and therefore yields less output from a given rain, whereas wet soil tends to become more impermeable and therefore with wet soil a given amount of rain yields more runoff. They do not go actually in the field and measure how wet it is because it takes too many people and too much money. But they have developed a computation of something called the Antecedent Precipitation Index, which is based on the rainfall of the preceding period of time: with this Index, they roughly calculate the soil humidity.

The gathering of these data requires instrumentation which is costly. As of a few years ago they had an agreement with farmers whereby they used to pay $3 a season for the farmer to phone in some of this information. This gives an idea of what are the real world constraints upon the system.

The second piece of the model consists of the construction of the time-flow curve, which they construct after painstaking, laborious and lengthy measurements. What they construct is the 'unit hydrograph', which is the response of the watershed system to a run off of one inch, assumed constant over the whole watershed area. Once they have constructed this unit hydrograph by well-known mathematical techniques they can 'multiply' this by convolution, by the actual rainfall in time and duration, and obtain the flow-time output.

How are all these data collected? By three basic types of tools. The first is the river gauge which measures the height of the river. Some of the simpler ones are simply sticks with numbers painted upon them. A man comes periodically, reads them, writes the height down on a piece of paper and that's the whole measurement. But nowadays, at least in the United States and Europe, the man gets fairly expensive:

\$2·50 to \$3·00 an hour, plus 7 cents a mile for his car, plus his supplies and everything, so the method is becoming very difficult to use, particularly if you have a situation where the data are collected in a state capital like Annapolis and you are interested in measuring the upper Potomac, which is 120 miles away. In addition, one would like to make this measurement frequently, once a day or more. So the trend is to install automatic stations which include devices to even out the flow so as not to suffer from ripples in the water. Many of them use an analogue reporting: they write continuously on a strip of paper. The man now can come in every ten days or so, tear the paper chart off, bring it back to the central data collection facility such as the state capital: here they look at it and analyse it. The towers of these stations vary from about 8 feet to 15 feet in height; some can even be higher. The cost of such an instrumentation is about \$30,000. You need several in a river, depending upon its length, uniformity and other characteristics.

The second tool is well known to all of us – the rain gauge. It costs about \$300. Some farmers, for a modest fee, used to read them but they no longer do it. So what do you do? You send a man up there to read them – the same problem as before. So you automate them, by attaching them to telephone lines or providing them with radio transmitters. They measure the rainfall.

The third tool measures the speed of the water, because when one computes the flow one has to measure the area of the channel, or river, then find the average velocity, and multiply the two. Because it is a channel flow the speed is not the same throughout all sections: at the bottom it is low, it grows nearer the surface, then it slows down at the surface. So they immerse this device in the river, and it measures the speed of the water by a little propeller. The speed is measured at different points at various sections of the river: the measurements are then tied all together and an average speed is calculated. Of course if the river changes you have to do it all over again. The laboriousness and the time consumption that these instruments entail calls for increased automation.

And so we are looking rather hard for methods to make data collection cheap, because the cheaper we make it the quicker we can solve the problems. This is of course true not only in the field of water resources but also in air pollution, and so forth. How do we accomplish this? This is what NASA is working at, in remote sensing. If we consider the ESSA model we find that it assumes the watershed to be substantially a 'black box'. It does not care what is inside the box. It only measures an input, namely rainfall, and an output, which is how much water comes out from the watershed in how much time. However, the point is that if one understands what is inside the 'black box' one can get a much better insight and a much finer computation. The method being pursued by NASA is to research the potential of aero-photography. Maps are useless, because maps are edited. We need the actual photography. And from aero-photography – by methods which are partially aerial, and partially checkpoints from the ground, but much fewer checkpoints than before – we can divide the watershed into areas of homogeneity, areas which are similar. Take for example parking lots. A parking lot has a runoff coefficient of 0·95 – practically all the rain runs off. A forest can have a runoff coefficient very close to zero. That makes a big difference. We can therefore label an area which is all forest, type 1; an area which is all parking lots, type 2; and so forth. For each such homogeneous area one can create a kind of micromodel whose coefficients are already pretty well known: and then tie them all together and come up with a prediction which can be far more refined than the simple 'black box' model used today.

Just for example, there are three factors which are ignored in the present models and are easily recognisable in the poorest of aerial pictures. The first one is the phenomenon of *interception*: when rain falls, anywhere from a hundredth to two-tenths of an inch remains attached to the plants, depending on the type of plant. Now two-tenths of an inch over a 100 by 100 mile watershed – a very tiny one – amounts to two weeks' flow of the Potomac. This is a lot of water. What we have to do is to recognise how much area is covered by forest, and know the type of forest. If we cannot tell the type of forest from the picture, we can at least send people there and measure a few samples and come up with a pretty good idea of the type. In a large number of cases we can tell the type from observation – not necessarily with photography but at other parts of the radiant spectrum – infra-red, for example. The second factor, is the very important phenomenon of *evapo-transpiration*, which is simply the sweating of the plants that transpire water: this again is a function of the type of plant. We can measure this too from aerial remote sensing. And the third is *infiltration*. Every soil has different characteristics of water absorption. If you know it is a parking lot, you know almost all the water will come out; if you know it is sandy soil, nothing or very little will come out. There are methods, being experimented with, to measure from above the type of soil. We can also measure its vegetation cover, which has been shown by Holtan (Fig. 4) and others to be connected to the absorption coefficient, because certain plants grow better or grow only on certain kinds of soil. So what one can do is to correlate different kinds of vegetation cover with different kinds of infiltration coefficient. The coefficients

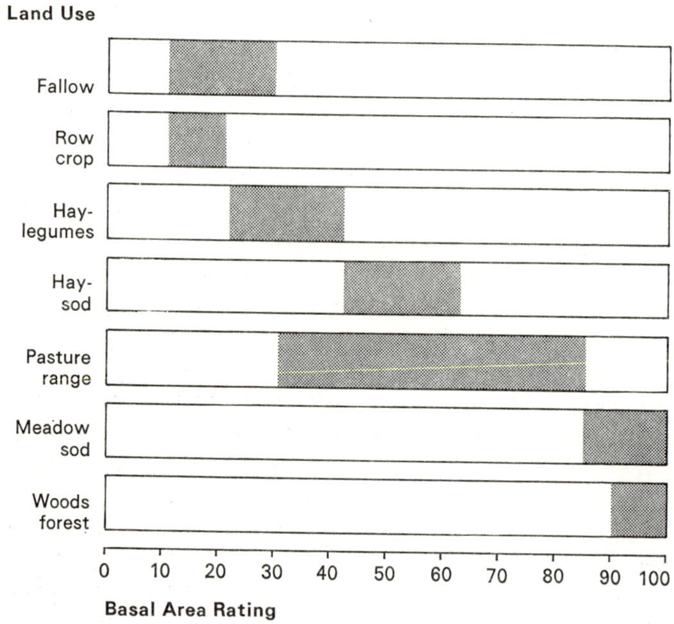

Fig. 4. Holtan's formula.

shown in Fig. 4 are not points – they are not 100 per cent accurate, but this still is much better than having no information at all. The point is that, from observation from above, in a rather cheap way which may turn out to be much less than the cost of doing it by hand as we do now, we can start approaching this very important facet of ecology, the collection of data.

Fig. 5 shows an additional twelve or so parameters where theoretical hydrologists tell us that if they knew them for a particular watershed, they could still further improve its model. All of these parameters are eminently amenable to aerial remote sensing.

I would like to close with one more example of the capabilities of advanced methods of data acquisition in ecology. The particular problem was to determine the *per capita* income – city block by city block – of certain areas of the city. The census performed every ten years gave us these figures, but ten years is a long time these days.

The Office of Economic Opportunity wanted a quick, cheap way of determining how many families were in each city block and what was their income. This was done entirely from aerial pictures plus computers. The way it was done was by observing aerial pictures and determining a certain number – which turned out to be approximately

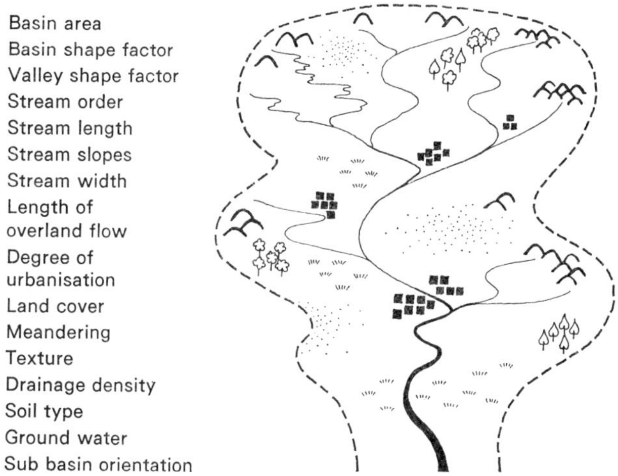

Fig. 5. Some basin characterising parameters.

fifteen – of 'indicators'. These indicators are things like distance from the civic centre; width of the alley; the number of cars per yard of alley (or *vice versa*); the shininess of the roof; the number of garbage cans; and so forth. These indicators were all put together and a programme written for the computer: it turned out that the problem worked, and predicted the *per capita* income with an accuracy which turned out to be no more than 10 per cent off from that of the census. They accomplished this programme at a cost which was estimated at about 1 per cent of what it would have cost by human collection of data. Also, this process can be repeated, if one wants to, every six months or every year, rather than wait out the ten-year interval of the census.

One point about this programme: the original model was constructured based upon the city of Baltimore. Twenty-eight cities were compared with it: it turned out that though a large number of cities accepted the same model, other cities did not. For example, Puerto Rico did not fit at all. This simply means that there are certain 'similar' cities for which certain models are applicable, that for a different type of city we have got to develop a new model. The method cannot just be transposed across dissimilar cities.

20

THE SOCIAL USE AND MISUSE OF TECHNOLOGY

BARRY COMMONER

I SHOULD like to share some of the ideas that my group in St Louis has developed in the last six to twelve months, regarding the origins of the environmental crisis. I do not need to produce any more horror stories about birds covered with oil, DDT in people's bodies and so on. It is known that there are environmental problems. It seems to me that the issue now has become what to do about it. I take the view, which is perhaps old-fashioned, that the historical approach is a valuable way to decide what has got to be done, that is, asking how we got into this mess, in the hope that understanding the past will point to some way out. And so I shall discuss some tentative ideas about the origin of the environmental problems that we face. (I shall restrict my remarks to an area I know something about, the United States; I have relatively few facts and figures about Britain or almost any other country – these are hard enough to get in the United States.)

First, I shall outline the features that characterise the environment, and then ask the question: what has happened to this system that has made it go so bad?

The basic characteristic of the environmental system is that it comprises a thin skin on the globe of the planet. It is a few miles of air, the surface waters and relatively few inches of soil. This is the ecosphere. One might ask 'Well, why choose the skin?' That happens to be the place where living things are found on the globe. In other words it is the habitat of living things. This may seem like a biologist's parochial view of the world. After all, the environment also contains physical and chemical systems and they might be independent of life. As it turns out, they are not; rather, one of the important things about the environmental system and its chemical and physical attributes is that they are largely the products of living things.

For example, before green plants appeared on the surface of the earth there was no oxygen in the atmosphere. The development of photosynthesis changed the chemistry of the air, and, with the development of oxygen, ozone was produced. Ozone in the higher levels of the atmosphere shields the surface of the earth from ultraviolet light. So the physical ambience of the earth's surface – the fact that it is not now subjected to a high level of this light – is a consequence of a *biological* development. In other words, the environment is something which physically and chemically is largely determined by the activity of living things. Then, with the marvellous reciprocity characteristic of living things, they became adapted to the particular environment they had created. So, for example, when oxygen was produced by green plants, it became possible in the course of evolution for organisms that used oxygen to evolve and survive. Moreover, when oxygen, hence ozone, appeared, and the level of ultra-violet radiation on the surface of the earth was cut down, living animals could come out from under their shelter of water, which was all that kept them from being burnt by the ultra-violet light, and could emerge on to the surface of the earth.

In other words, there is an interdigitation of the evolution of life and the physical and chemical attributes of the earth's surface, generating a very complex system.

A major feature of the dynamics of this system is that it is characterised by circular activity. I think it is very important to become sensitive to the significance of the ecological cycle. Let me run through a couple of ecological cycles in order to develop some feeling for them.

Let us take a typical aquatic cycle. Start with a fish swimming in the water. The fish has a lot of water in it and some solid material; much of that solid material is organic – that is, complex molecules containing networks of carbon atoms; and as the fish does its business of metabolising, it produces waste, which is largely organic matter. The waste in turn turns out to be food for other organisms – bacteria, fungi, and so on – which live on organic wastes, converting them to inorganic material. Urea, for example, excreted by the fish, is converted by bacteria into nitrate and carbon dioxide. You can think of these inorganic products – phosphates, nitrates, carbon dioxide – as the waste products of the bacteria that eat the waste produced by the fish. In turn, these inorganic materials are the food of algae, green plants, which synthesise from them organic matter. Then the organic matter in the form of algae provides food for the fish, which brings us right back to the point of departure.

Now the fact that this is a circular progression has some very important consequences. In the first place, the stability of the cycle is self-determined. Let us take a simple analogy. Consider how a ship is kept on course, the way in which her course is stabilised. A cybernetic feed-back cycle is involved. The helmsman watches the compass; the compass-needle moves; the helmsman moves the rudder; and there is a relationship between the rudder and the ship, such that when the rudder moves, the ship's direction changes, and that in turn changes the relative orientation of the compass, which signals the helmsman that he should stop making adjustments. The result is a cycle of events involving the compass, the helmsman, the rudder, the ship and the compass. This is what keeps the ship on course. When any external agitation – the wind, or the helmsman sneezing – changes these interrelationships, the cyclical relationship brings the ship back on course.

The ecological cycle operates similarly. In our fishpond, suppose, for example, by some quirk, the temperature changes so that algae grow rapidly, reducing the level of algal nutrients. With more algae than there were before, the fish will eat more algae, which will cut down the algae while increasing the number of fish. Now, with more fish, more organic waste is produced – which the bacteria convert to inorganic material. Things come back into balance.

That is one characteristic then of a system of this sort. Now a very interesting question is, 'How does it break down?' Any member of an ecological cycle, functioning in its ordinary way, is incapable of causing trouble. For example, if human beings were part of an ecological cycle – say the soil cycle – and we ate the animals that ate the grass and deposited our organic waste on the soil which the cycle converts back into the grass, then it would be impossible for us to stress this system. There would be no way that we could degrade such an environment. We should simply be part of the system.

But once outside of the system, we can degrade it. For example, man is taken off the soil and put into a city, food crops must now be transported to the city, eaten, and converted into sewage, which goes into the aquatic system instead of back to the soil. Now there is more organic matter coming into the aquatic cycle than the cycle itself produces. It is rapidly decayed by bacteria, which in the process, may use up all the oxygen. With no oxygen left, the bacteria die off and the cycle stops. This, an external stress, breaks down the cycle.

There are some very simple principles of ecology that I suppose one could call 'cocktail party' principles – the very simple ideas that allow one to talk about it in layman's language. One is that in a cycle *every separate entity is connected to all the rest.* A second principle is that *everything has to go somewhere.* If you get into an ecological conversation, you can do quite well by simply repeating one question: 'Where does it go?' Someone raises the question about mercury. He says, 'There's mercury in the hearing-aid battery'. And you say, 'Well, that's interesting. Where does it go?' 'Oh, I never thought of that.' 'Well, what happens when the hearing-aid battery wears out?' 'Well, I throw it away.' And you just say, 'Well, where does it go?' 'Into the rubbish.' 'Well, that's interesting. Where does *that* go?' And then finally you discover that it goes to an incinerator which heats up the mercury in the hearing-aid battery and drives it into the air. And then you ask, 'Where does that go?' – and the answer is that it comes down in rain and gets into water where bacteria convert it to methyl mercury, which poisons fish. And so you accomplish quite an ecological *tour de force.*

The third simple law is one that can be borrowed from economics. There is the well-known fable about the Middle East kingdom that discovered oil. The sheikh was suddenly very rich and needed to know what to do with the money. So he ordered his advisers to retire for a year and come back with a set of volumes that embodied all the wisdom of economics – otherwise their heads would be removed. The next year he said, 'No, I can't read ten volumes, I want it all in one volume'. Finally he said, 'You've got to come back with one sentence which contains the total wisdom of economics or you lose your heads.' And they came back with one sentence: '*There is no such thing as a free lunch*'. Now I think that applies quite well to ecological systems. In a cycle you can't get away with anything. There is a limit to the speed with which it can be exploited, the rate at which it runs; *you can't get something for nothing from it.*

Which brings me to the fourth law of ecology: *nature knows best.* I talked to a group of chemists recently and, as I expected, really horrified some of them. Because, you see, a number of chemists think that Dupont knows best. After all, nature never made Nylon or Terylene; nature never made Wisk or Tide. They are all made by man. Of course we are very proud of what man can do, so the whole notion that man does not know best about these things is rather upsetting.

Let me use an analogy. I have a watch. Suppose I were to open the back, shut my eyes and poke a pencil into the works. It is very likely the watch would be spoiled. The question I want to raise is this: isn't it at all *possible* that the watch might be improved? The watch might have been out of adjustment exactly at the point I happened to hit it, and I might, after all, have just done what was needed to bring it back into adjustment. I think you have to admit there is a finite possibility that the watch might be improved by this random hit. But the next question that comes up is: why is this possibility so very small? The reason is that the watchmakers know best. Watchmakers have tried most of the random arrangements of bits and pieces and have discarded many of them because they are not compatible with the system as a whole. In short this watch is a very complex integrated system, with a lot of research and development behind it. And all of the mistakes – most of them – have been tried out, so that the chance of any new random change being an improvement is extremely small.

How does this relate to the present problem? There are perhaps two or three million years of research and development behind biological systems: the entire course of biological evolution. A chief feature of this evolutionary process is that living things produced a number of complex molecules, such as proteins. Proteins are long chains of amino acid units, with perhaps two hundred units in a chain. There are twenty different amino acids that can participate in the chain, and the chemistry is such that any one can be put at any position. A series of different proteins can be made simply by arranging and re-arranging the order of amino acids in the molecule. So we have a 200-place molecule and twenty choices to make for each place. Elsasser has calculated the weight that would be represented by only one molecule of each of the possible proteins that can be compared in this way: it is larger than the weight of the known universe. Clearly biological organisms do not make all the proteins that they *could*; there are very severe restrictions.

This means that when an organic compound is not found in a living system, it is probably not compatible with the rest of that system. I have a sort of fantasy that I think about – that two billion years ago in some corner of the globe some cell took it upon itself to synthesise

DDT and has never been heard from since. In other words, DDT simply was incompatible with the rest of the system. Incidentally there are data to support this notion. Random inherited changes can be brought about in the chemistry of cells by X-rays. The overwhelming proportion of the X-ray-induced mutations are damaging. In other words, most of the new features that are generated in living cells by such means are worse than the original ones; nature knows best.

I have taken a long time to present my own approach to ecology. The problem now is this: the ecosphere was created before man appeared on the earth. Man occupies a very peculiar position. He is both part of an ecological cycle – as a terrestrial animal – and at the same time an organism which wields huge power outside of the ecological cycle. He can get away from the soil, live in the cities, fly in the air, and so on. The question which arises is this: what activities of human beings have led to environmental pollution? Because clearly we are not suffering from any natural catastrophe. Something has gone wrong in what *people do.*

Let us look at the situation in the United States, beginning at the end of the Second World War. If we trace back the data on levels of pollutants, we find that many of them made their first appearance in the mid-1940s. That is, when detergents, photochemical smog, synthetic insecticides and radiation came on the scene. At the same time older pollutants – such as phosphate and nitrate in surface waters and various air pollutants – became much more concentrated than before. The Second World War is a kind of watershed between the scientific revolution that preceded it and the technological revolution which followed it. This explains why we have been looking at changes in the factors that might influence ecological systems in the United States since 1946.

Now what are the factors? First, if human beings are outside of the ecosystem they belong to, wherein they eat food produced in the soil and contribute their waste to the soil, they can constitute an environmental impact or stress. I have mentioned one way in which this might happen, and clearly, the more people are in that situation, the more stress is placed on the environment. So we have to be concerned with the size of the population.

Other important factors represent non-biological activities: for example, the production of power and goods. The amount of production *per capita* – affluence if you like – is another factor that might be influential in the environment; both population and affluence are frequently invoked by ecological speakers. Some say the more people there are, the worse the pollution; that people are polluters. Others speak of an 'effluent society', meaning that effluents arise from our affluence. They point out that the United States represents 6 per cent of the world's population and uses 40-50 per cent of the world's resources. We are very affluent and therefore highly polluting.

There is a third environmental factor: the amount of pollution produced per unit production. A simple formula connects the three factors: the amount of pollutant emitted is the product of the population times the production per unit population (the 'affluence' factor) multiplied by the amount of pollutant emitted per unit production. What this formula does is to divide the amount of pollutant up into three interacting factors: population, affluence and the nature of production technology (which determines the amount of pollution emitted per unit production).

In the United States, most of the pollutants have increased in level by an order of magnitude that is, generally, between 200 per cent and 2000 per cent since 1946. So we are looking for some change in the three relevant factors that give rise to somewhere between twofold and twentyfold changes in pollution intensity. The results are shown in a series of graphs. In these the horizontal axis is always time, beginning in 1946 and extending to 1968. Fig. 1 (bottom curve) shows the changes in the size of the US population in 1946-68, which has gone up about 42 per cent in that period of time. This change is not enough to generate a tenfold increase in pollution level. Is it rather affluence which is to blame? Affluence might be measured by GNP – which has gone up perhaps 50 to 60 per cent. So that too is not big enough to be the cause we seek.

Let us look instead at individual productive activities, that is, particular technologies, and examine them to see how population, affluence and technology may have influenced the emission of pollutants.

Since 1945 there has been a general decline in *per capita* consumption in the United States of carbohydrate, protein and calories. Fat consumption has gone up a little bit. We can simply say that there has been no change in affluence with respect to food. Nevertheless the production of food in the United States now pollutes the environment. Fig. 2 suggests why.

The top curve in Fig. 2 is simply the *per capita* crop production in the U.S., and you see it is unchanged over this period of time. It is measured by a U.S. Department of Agriculture index of the gross biological production. But two things have changed. The curve that is falling (C) is the acreage harvested in the United States, which has gone down significantly. The rising curve (B) is the amount of nitrogen fertiliser used year by year. The total production (A) is

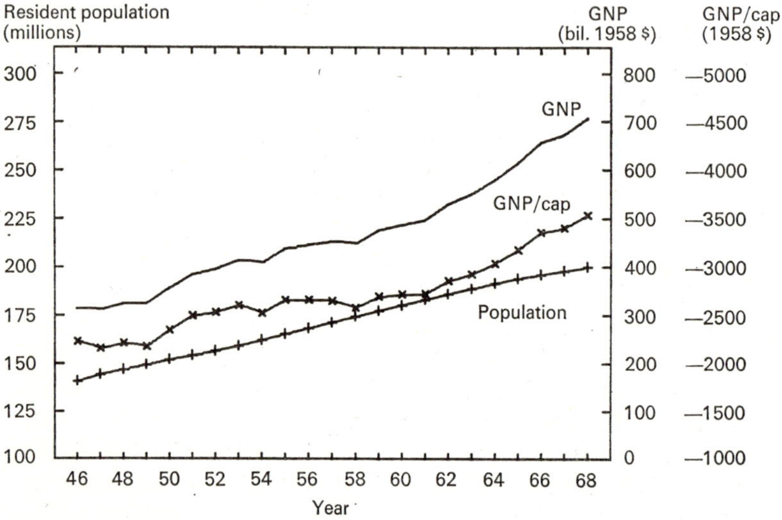

Fig. 1. Changes in population, Gross National Product (reduced to 1958 dollars) and GNP *per capita* for the United States since 1946[1]

rising just about at the rate of the population, so that the *per capita* rate of the production has remained constant. I conclude from this that it is not correct to say that, with respect to food, the United States is more affluent than it was in 1946. Nevertheless, food production is now creating a much more intense stress on the environment than it once did. And the explanation for that is in Fig. 3.

Fig. 3 illustrates a particular situation in Illinois in the corn belt, where corn is grown very intensively; there are two curves here, this time beginning in 1944. The bottom curve is the amount of nitrogen fertiliser used year by year; you see it is a very sharply rising curve. The higher curve is the corn yield in bushels per acre. Now remember that Fig. 2 showed that less and less acreage is used at higher and higher yields per acre in order to get a balanced-out production. And you see that the yield per acre has gone up from about 50 bushels per acre to around 90 in this period of time. But if you look at the two curves you will notice that the yield curve begins to level off, even though the nitrogen curve is rising very sharply. This is because you can push a plant only so far with nitrogen,

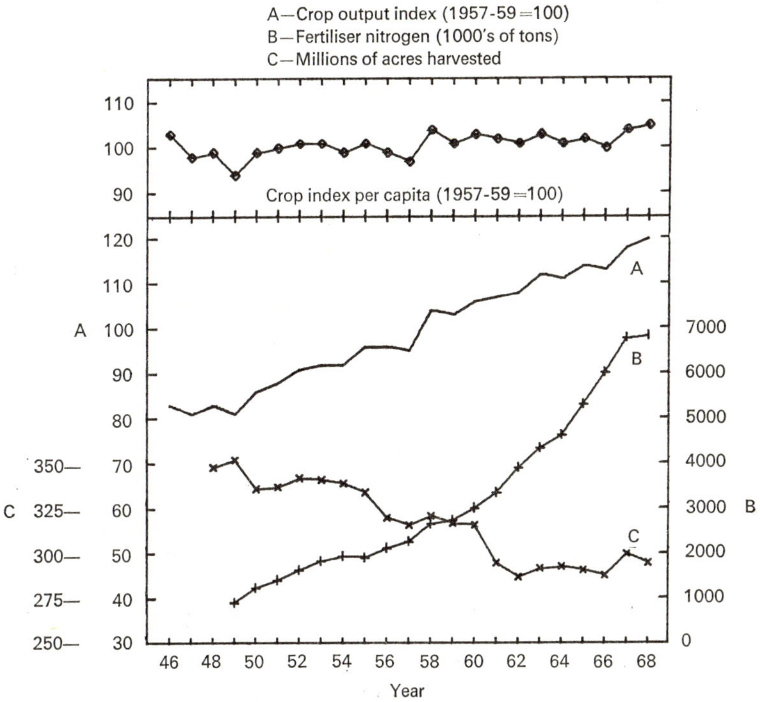

Fig. 2. Changes in total crop output (as determined by USDA Crop Index), in crop output *per capita*, in harvested acreage and in annual use of inorganic nitrogen fertiliser in the United States since 1946[2]

after which it won't take it all up. Let us apply one of the laws of ecology – everything has to go somewhere – and ask the question, what happens to this nitrogen put on the soil if not much of it is taken up into the corn crop? It has to go somewhere, so it goes into the ground and into streams and lakes causing a serious pollution problem. For example in Decatur, Illinois, in March, for the last five or six springs, the nitrate concentration of the drinking water supply of the town exceeds the U.S. Public Health Service limit of

10 ppm. The nitrate itself is not terribly toxic; however, taken into the intestines, particularly by infants, it may be converted to nitrite, which then combines with haemoglobin to form methaemoglobin, a form which will not carry oxygen. This is an often fatal condition known as blue baby or methaemoglobinaemia.

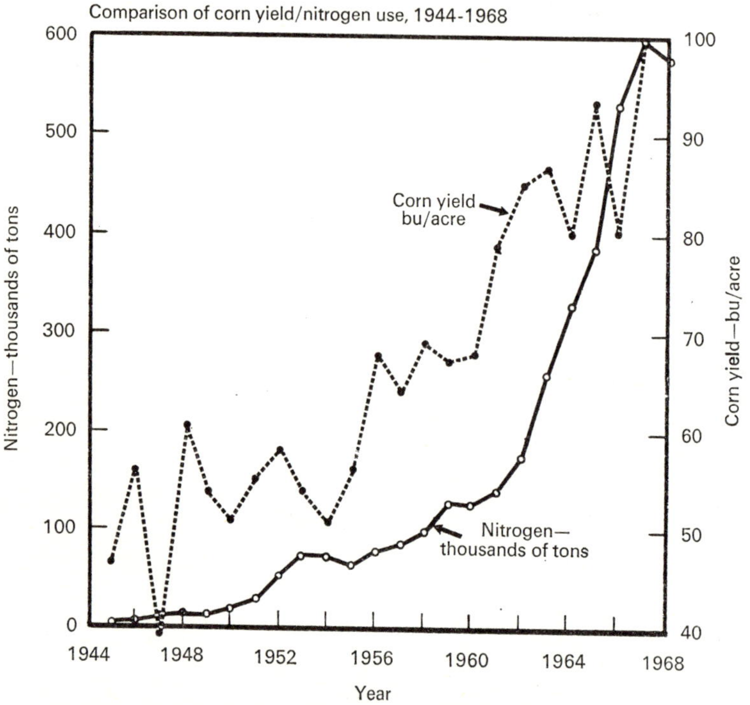

Fig. 3. Corn yield and nitrogen usage for the State of Illinois[3]

The city water supply is the Sangamon river which drains cornfields on the way to Decatur. We now know from very careful experiments that the extra nitrogen that does not go into the cornplant washes into the surface water, causing a pollution problem. In addition to the danger of methaemoglobinaemia, nitrate encourages the overgrowth of algae, which die, releasing an overload of organic matter which in turn breaks down the aquatic cycle.

The root of this problem is a technological change in the means of producing corn; instead of producing it on broad acreage with a low yield per acre, we now produce it on less acreage, at a higher yield – by applying large amounts of fertiliser. Government policy exacerbates this situation: the Land Bank system pays for land that is not put under cultivation in the United States. As the acreage under cultivation has diminished, the ecosystem of the acreage which is being used is being overdriven. Since there is no such thing as a free lunch, we pay for it in water pollution.

The economic consequences are serious. The people who live in Decatur depend economically on the farmer; it is a market town. The city's water pollution problem arises from the economic well-being of the farmer. Economically, the break-even point for corn production in this area is about 75 bushels per acre. In other words, unless the farmer can get yields above that level, he is in economic trouble. The tragic fact is that the Illinois farmer must use fertiliser inefficiently, from a biological point of view, in order to make a profit.

In this situation it is not the increase in population that is culpable, for it only accounts for a 42 per cent rise in demand for food. It is not affluence: we are all eating about the same amount of corn as before. It is the displacement of land by fertiliser.

Fig. 4 provides a numerical calculation of the impact of three factors that affect pollution. The time period is 1949-68 and the

Environmental Impact Index

	Index factors (*a*) *Population* (*1000s*)	(*b*) *Crop production* / *population* (*crop index*/ cap.*)	(*c*) *Fertiliser nitrogen* / *crop production* (*tons crop index**)	*Total index* *Fertiliser nitrogen* (*1000s of tons*)
1949	149,304	$5{\cdot}43 \times 10^{-7}$	11,284	914
1968	199,846	$6{\cdot}00 \times 10^{-7}$	57,008	6841
1968 : 1949	1·34	1·11	5·05	7·48
Percentage increase	34	11	405	648

* The crop output index is an indicator of agricultural productivity with the 1957-59 average = 100.

Fig. 4. Fertiliser nitrogen

population has gone up by a factor of 1·34 between those two years. In column (*b*) is the crop production per unit population, and that has increased by 1·11 – in other words an 11 per cent increase in crop production *per capita* – a negligible increase in affluence. Column (*c*) is the fertiliser nitrogen used per unit crop production, and it has increased from 11,000 tons per production unit to 57,000 tons per production unit; about a five-fold increase. Thus, we are now using about five times as much nitrogen to produce a unit of crop in the United States as we did in the 1940s. Everything has to go somewhere; since the unused nitrogen is not going into the crop, it pollutes the water. Look again at the percentage increase: 34 per cent effective population; 11 per cent affluence; 405 per cent change in technology.

Similar statistics are available on the use of pesticides: 3·7 million pounds of pesticide (all pesticides including the old-fashioned ones) per production unit were used in 1946; 6·1 million pounds of pesticide per production unit in 1968. Population rose 42 per cent and crop production *per capita* 2 per cent within this period. However, we now use more pesticide to produce the same amount of food and fibre than we did; and again the reason is that, as is the case with fertiliser, we are confronted with an ecological backlash – in this case, resistant insects – and have to raise pesticide application levels. Pesticide people say, 'We have to use the pesticide in order to increase production'. In fact we are using more and more pesticide to produce the same amount of material.

Fig. 5 answers the question of cleansers. Are we more affluent in this area? The comparison between detergents and soap depends on how much actual cleanser there is in a box of detergent, and that is not easy to determine. The numbers are somewhat inaccurate, but let us assume that the *per capita* use of cleansers was unchanged during this period of time. As for soap, total production has gone down. Detergent production has risen. There has been a displacement of soap, a natural product, by detergent, a synthetic one.

This prompts me to make a generalisation about natural products which I think is valid. For every organic molecule that a living organism makes, there is an enzyme in some living organism that can break it down. In short, the living system never creates anything without providing for its destruction, so that a characteristic of a natural product is that it can be broken down by some biological activity. When you synthesise an unnatural substance, on the other hand, it is very likely not to be broken down unless it is very similar to some natural product. The first detergents that were made had branched molecules, and the enzymes of the bacteria that break down carbon-chain substances simply would not attack the branch,

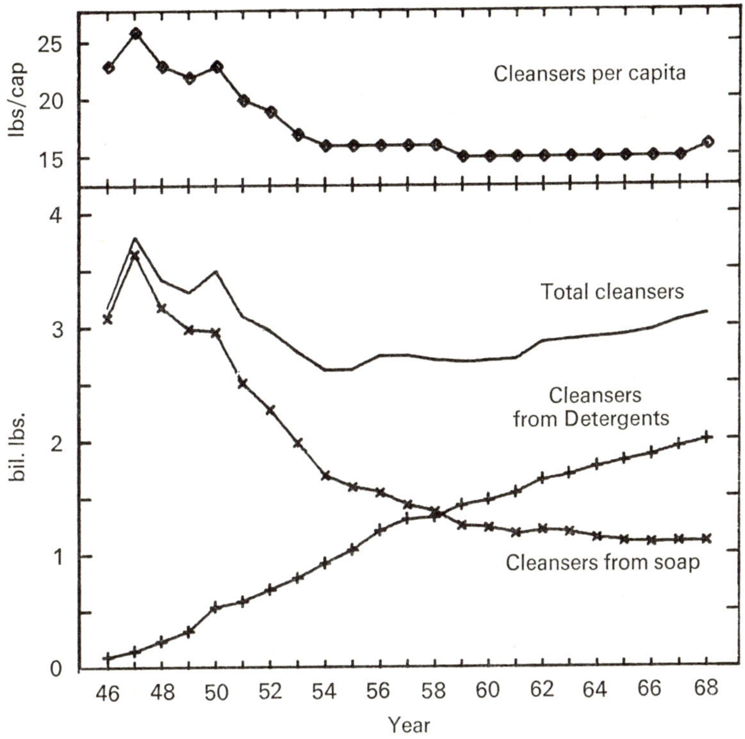

Fig. 5. Total soap and detergent production and *per capita* consumption of total cleansers (soap plus detergent) in the United States since 1946[4]. Detergent data represent actual content of surface-active agent, which is estimated at about 37.5 per cent of the total weight of the marketed detergent

and so the molecules did not break down. These are the so-called non-degradable detergents which, as you know, accumulated in the water supply. Later on they were replaced with degradable detergents (very few people had noticed that the degradable detergent, which is a straight chain molecule, and can be broken down, has at one end a benzene ring. And that benzene ring is very readily converted to phenol, which is toxic). But even degradable detergents have phosphate in them. Phosphate entering surface waters, like nitrate, can stimulate the growth of algae, which can cause a breakdown of the aquatic cycle. So we are confronted here with the ecological consequences of displacing natural fat soap, which is broken down by bacterial decay, by a detergent which has phosphate in it and may not readily be broken down.

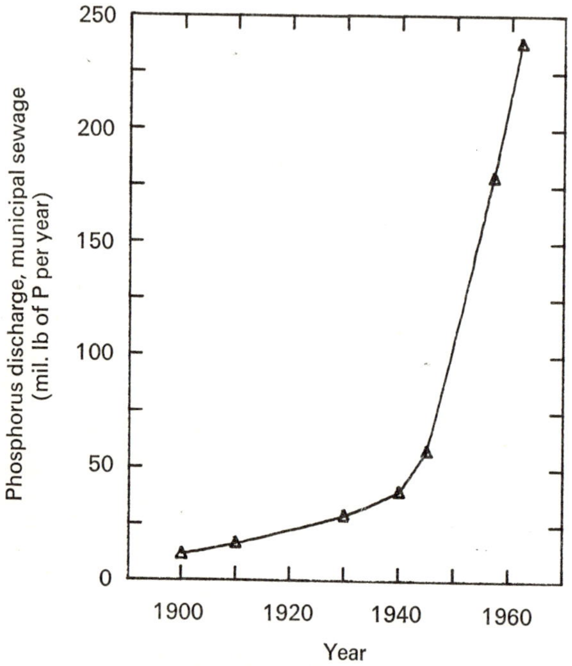

Fig. 6. Phosphorus emitted by United States municipal sewage[5]

Fig. 6 shows the phosphorus emitted by United States municipal sewage systems into surface waters year by year. This curve went up gradually until 1945 and then suddenly took off. The increase can be accounted for pound for pound by the amount of phosphorus in the detergents sold in the United States. (Everything has to go somewhere.)

Fig. 7 is a calculation of the environmental impact index of detergent phosphate. There was a 42 per cent population increase from 1946 to 1968, and the affluence factor (cleansers *per capita*) stayed about the same. The increase in phosphate level per unit cleanser is 1800 per cent. Again it is technology that is chiefly responsible for the impact on the environment: the fact that we now clean with unnatural cleansers containing phosphate.

Fig. 8 gives data on consumption of fibres. The top curve is fibre production *per capita* and there is no real change. We all wear about the same number of threads. There have been all kinds of detailed

Environmental Impact Index

	Index factors (*a*) *Population* (*1000s*)	(*b*) *Cleansers*/population* (*lb/cap*)	(*c*) *Phosphorus/cleansers* (*lb/ton of cleanser*)	*Total impact* ($a \times b \times c$) *Phosphorus from detergents†* (*10⁶ lb*)
1946	140,686	22·66	6·90	11
1968	194,846	15·99	137·34	214
1968 : 1946	1·42	0·69 (1·00)‡	19·90 (13·70)	19·45
Percentage increase 1946-68	42	(0)	(1270)	1845

* Assuming that 35 per cent of detergent weight is active agent.

† Assuming average phosphorus content of detergents = 4 per cent.

‡ Because of uncertainties regarding the content of active agent in detergents, especially soon after their introduction, the apparent reduction in *per capita* use of cleansers is not regarded as significant; the numbers contained in parentheses are based on the assumption that this value does not change significantly.

Fig. 7. Detergent phosphate

fluctuations in fibre use; for example, *per capita* use of suits and dresses has gone down; slacks and blouses have gone up. And the compiler of these data has pointed out to me that there was a remarkable jump in 1966 in the *per capita* consumption of overalls in the United States; he attributes that to the hippies. But this curve is *total* fibre production. We do not use much more, *per capita*, than we did before. However, use of natural fibres (cotton and wool) has gone down somewhat and the increase required to take care of the 42 per cent rise in population is all due to synthetic fibres.

The fact that you now wear a plastic shirt means that the environment is more polluted than it was when you wore a cotton one.

Let me put it this way: cotton represents a complex molecule; it takes energy to put it together. It is made from carbon dioxide and

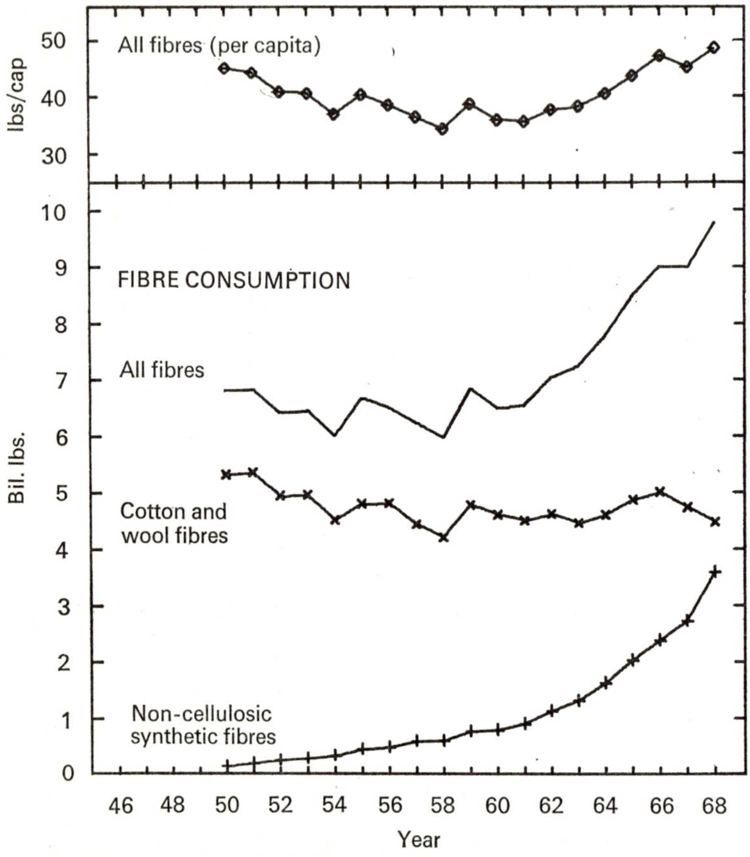

Fig. 8. Natural and synthetic fibre production in the United States since 1946[6]

water, and the energy required to assemble the atoms comes straight from the sun. It is transferred by a complex biochemical reaction which all takes place at ordinary temperatures. The cotton plant does not get hot: it does not smoke, or fume. What it does is to trap the sun's energy in the form of a fibre. That is a nice thing to happen. It is a useful thing: the plant does it free, and by cultivating it a little and burning a little gasoline for the tractor you can get a good deal of free solar energy embodied as cotton fibre. But not satisfied by these benefits, we replace cotton and wool with synthetics.

A synthetic comes from petroleum. In order to make nylon, for example, one has to extract a series of specific compounds from petroleum. That is done by distilling, for example, which needs heat. And when one has the specific compounds, they have to react one with the other, with a lot of fuss and fume. And where is the energy coming from? It comes from burning petroleum, which is in limited supply, whereas solar energy is not. All this is done at high temperatures so that the air is polluted with the various combustion products. We have turned to a process of using energy in an air-polluting way to produce a fibre which we could get quite naturally and quite calmly, free of charge, so to speak, in terms of energy from nature. And although the calculations are not complete, I think that it will turn out that it costs perhaps about ten times as much fuel energy to produce a pound of nylon as it does a pound of cotton. So substitution is again the root of environmental pollution.

Furthermore, no living thing ever synthesised nylon. So there are no enzymes in nature for breaking it down. Therefore, nylon put into the environment accumulates, unless you burn it, and then it pollutes the air. Recently, a British marine laboratory reported an increasing number of tiny nylon fragments from marine cordage turning up in the nets that they use to collect plankton in the ocean. That is not surprising. Let me put it this way: if you were to bury a cotton shirt in the soil and then come back after some weeks you would find that it had been incorporated into the soil. But if you bury a nylon shirt, it will probably still be there when you return. As a matter of fact that is why marine cordage is now made out of nylon. It is not susceptible to attack by moulds, because the moulds don't have the enzymes to attack the nylon.

Fig. 9 shows the consequences of the increase in use of plastics. Curve B shows the production of synthetic organic chemicals; curve C shows the production of chlorine, which is essential to plastics production; and curve A shows mercury used to produce chlorine. Mercury is used because in chlorine production electricity is sent through a brine solution with mercury as an electrode. There has been a vast increase in the use of mercury for this purpose. Any chemical engineering handbook on the mercury electrolysis process will give a table showing all of its characteristics. Down near the

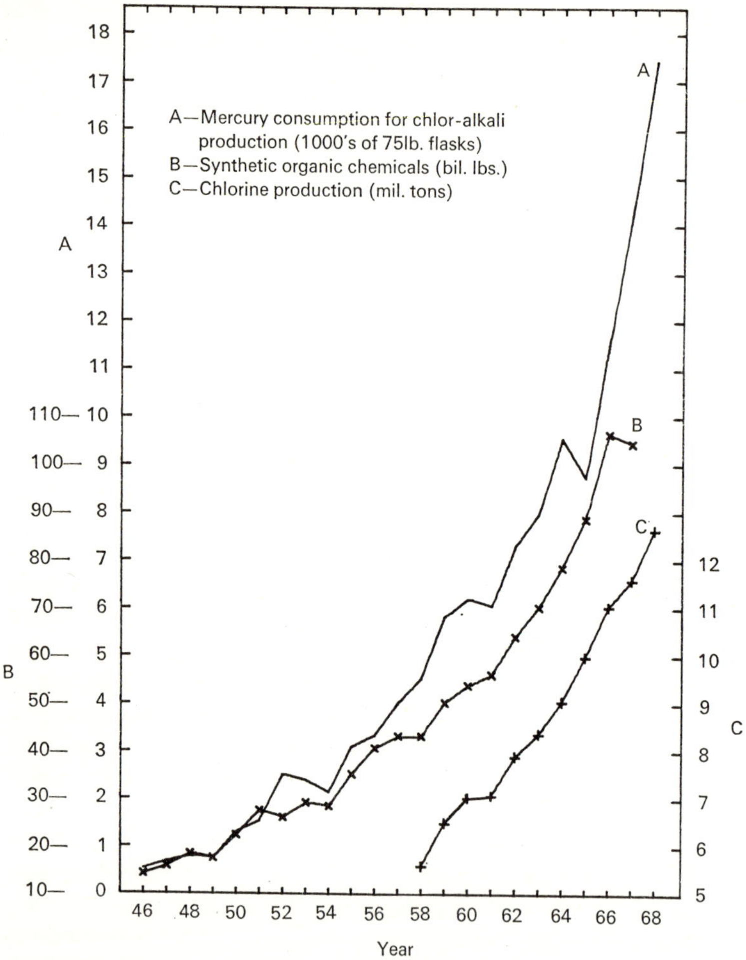

Fig. 9. Changes in annual production of synthetic organic compounds and of chlorine gas, and consumption of mercury for chlorine gas production in the United States since 1946[7]

bottom is a little item called 'Mercury Lost', and the figure is $\frac{2}{10}$ to $\frac{5}{10}$ of a pound of mercury per ton of chlorine produced. Where does it go? It goes into the water with waste and sinks to the bottom. Bacteria work on it there, adding a methyl group to the mercury, which then becomes soluble and is taken up by the fish. This is the cause of most of the mercury problems within the United States.

Some of the mercury also ends up in the alkali which is produced in making chlorine. Where does that go? Some of the alkali is used to make detergents, some is used to make soap, some goes into other products like paper, and with all of it goes a certain amount of mercury. Hence there is mercury in paper. When it is incinerated, mercury is volatilised. According to measurements we have done with a helicopter detection device over incinerators in the Midwest, a large amount of mercury comes out of the stacks. About 80 per cent of the mercury used by industry in the United States is dispersed into the environment, intruding into the environmental system, where its toxic effects become important.

This is one secondary consequence of the displacement of natural products by synthetic ones which has been taking place actively since 1946. Another secondary consequence is that it takes a great deal of power to run this new chemical industry. An important cause of the power shortage in the United States is the use of power to make the synthetic chemicals.

I have some brief words to say about the automobile, and smog. In the United States smog now means a photochemical pollutant formed by the interaction of sunlight with nitrogen oxides; the reaction products then interact with hydrocarbons from automobile exhaust to produce noxious irritating materials. I have plotted in Fig. 10 the characteristics of the average American passenger car, from 1946 onwards. Curve C is horsepower: it goes up and then abruptly drops. That drop represents the introduction of compact cars around 1958. When everyone was happy with compact cars Detroit gradually began making them bigger. They are the same cars, they have the same names, they just got bigger and bigger, so the graph curves up again. Curve B is the compression ratio, and curve A is the gasoline mileage. Now here is a great achievement of Detroit: the gasoline mileage has dropped consistently, except during the compact car period.

Now, when one raises the compression ratio, one raises the combustion temperature in the engine. This intense heat makes the oxygen and nitrogen in the air brought into the cylinder interact chemically, producing nitrogen oxide. I have been able to estimate from these changes in compression ratio the output of nitrogen oxide year by year for the average American car engine. By multiplying through by the number of vehicle miles driven, we can get at the question of the relative importance of the several factors in producing nitrogen oxide, the source of our smog problem.

But, first, Fig. 11 shows lead emissions. Tetraethyl lead is put into the gasoline to counteract the knocking due to the high compression ratio. There is a dip when the compression ratio came down, and then it started up again. Incidentally, the exhaust devices we have are designed to cut down the smog by holding back the waste hydro-

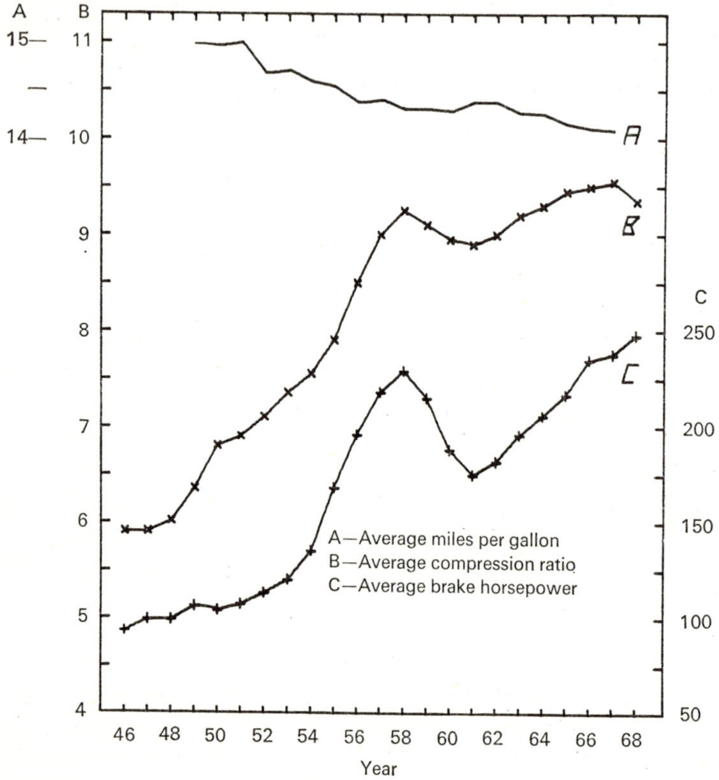

Fig. 10. Average characteristics of passenger car engines produced in the United States since 1946[8]

carbon. There is less smog in Los Angeles now than there was, but there is much more nitrogen oxide. Since everything has to go somewhere, the unreacted nitrogen oxides accumulate. Incidentally, the devices now being proposed for getting rid of the nitrogen oxide will not work, because the lead poisons the catalysts in them. The lead is in the gasoline to stop the high compression, which is what caused the nitrogen oxides in the first place.

Fig. 12 shows the origin of nitrogen oxide. There was a 630 per cent increase in nitrogen oxide emissions between 1946 and 1967, and the major factor again is nitrogen oxides per vehicle mile. There seems to be a pretty serious effect of affluence because we do see more vehicle miles of driving, but that is also explained by a change in technology. In my own town for example we have two-way commuters; whites living in suburbs drive back to the city in the morning to work, and

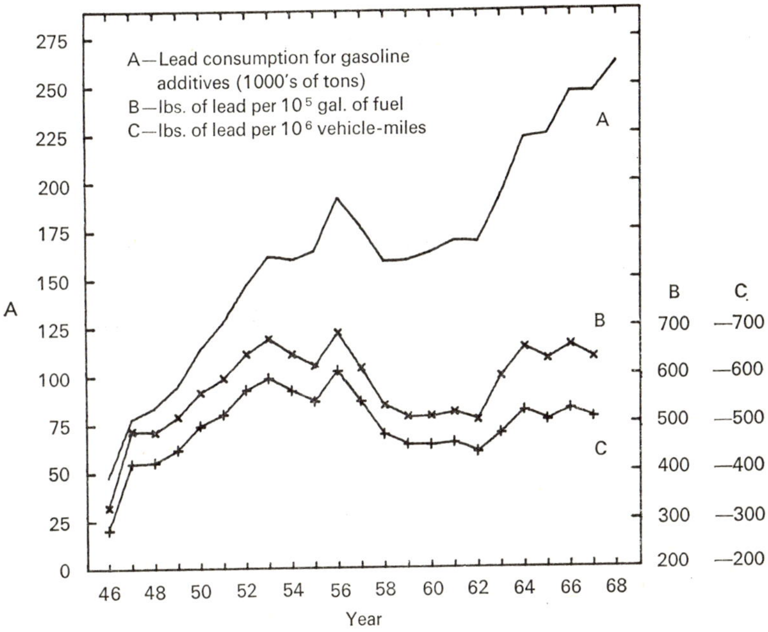

Fig. 11. Lead emissions, from tetraethyl lead in gasoline, in the United States since 1946[9]

blacks who live in the city drive out to the suburbs to work as domestics or in the outlying factories. Now I do not regard that as affluence. I think we would be a lot more affluent if people could live more close to the place where they work. Incidentally, the statistics are very interesting. A black person in the United States, on the average, lives further from his place of work than a white. This is understandable because there are restrictions on where black people can live and where they can work, and the natural result is that they must travel further than whites. So this increase in vehicle miles *per capita* is not to be regarded as increased affluence. It simply reflects a change in the urban technology – of the way that people are distributed.

Vehicle mileage is further accelerated by the freight situation. Although total freighting remains pretty much unchanged, truck freight has encroached more and more upon the domain of rail freight. This has had an important environmental consequence. It takes six times more energy to move a ton a mile by truck than it does by rail, and for every unit of energy something is burnt – polluting the environment. It takes four times more energy to produce the materials

Environmental Impact Index

	Index factors (*a*) *Population* (*1000s*)	(*b*) *Vehicle-miles* / *population*	(*c*) *Nitrogen oxides** / *vehicle-miles*	*Total index* *Nitrogen oxides**
1946	140,686	1982	33·5	10·6
1967	197,849	3962	86·4	77·5
1967 : 1946	1·41	2·00	2·58	7·3
Percentage increase	41	100	158	630

NO_x (ppm) × gasoline consumption (gals. × 10^{-6}). Estimated from product of passenger vehicle gasoline consumption and ppm of NO_x emitted by engines of average compression ratio 5·9 (1946) and 9·5 (1967) under running conditions, at 15-in manifold pressure: 1946, 500 ppm NO_x; 1967, 1200 ppm[10].

Fig. 12. Nitrogen oxides—(Passenger vehicles)

to lay down a mile of road for trucks than it does to lay down a mile of track for the railway. To make matters worse, the road takes a right-of-way of 400 feet, while the track takes only 100 feet. The displacement of railroad freight by truck freight has nothing to do with the increase in population, and we are not more affluent because our freight moves by truck rather than by rail; it is simply a change of technology. And again, as we see over and over again, the new technology puts more of a stress on the environment than the old one.

Fig. 13 concerns beer. I will explain how I decided to investigate this. I did not think much about population and affluence until ecologists such as Paul Ehrlich began to say that the pollution problem is really a people problem; there are too many people, and they are too affluent, and so on. So I asked myself in what way am I affluent? And I decided that one aspect of my affluence is that I habitually drink a bottle of beer with dinner every night. And so I went through the statistics on beer drinking in the United States. The top curve in Fig. 13 shows beer consumption *per capita* in the United States; it is perfectly clear that it has not changed over this

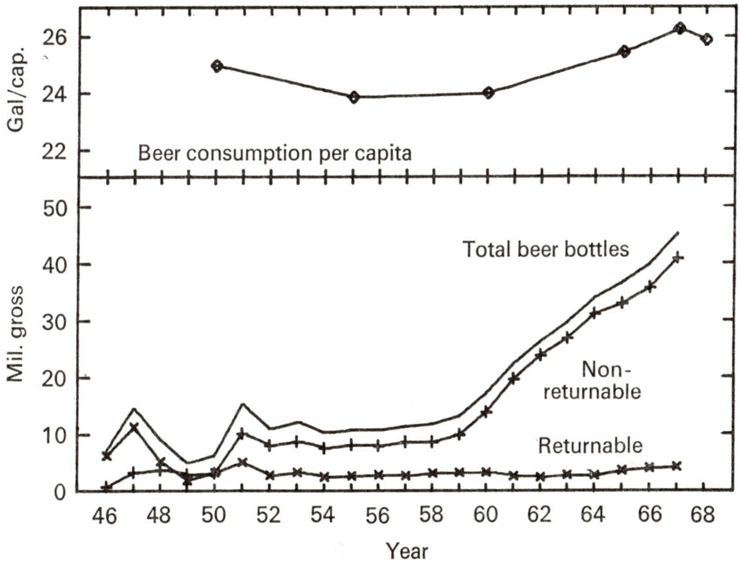

Fig. 13. *Per capita* consumption of beer and production of beer bottles in the United States[11]

period. Everyone drinks on the average 24 to 25 gallons per year. But they now pollute the environment much more than they used to by their drinking. Fig. 13 again shows the beer-bottle production, which has gone up; the reason being that we now use non-returnable bottles. The point is that we now get our beer wrapped up differently, in non-returnable bottles, rather than recyclable returnables. Similarly we are using more aluminium beer cans, which require twice as much electricity to produce as the previously employed steel beer cans, and therefore pollute the environment more.

Fig. 14 shows the impact index for beer bottles. The impact is chiefly due to the technological factor: the beer bottles used per unit beer consumption.

I have summarised in Fig. 15 the changes in the US economy since 1946. The horizontal axis indicates the rate of growth: the rate of annual increase in production *per capita*. At the top are the no-return pop-bottles, which grow at the rate of about 15 per cent per year. At the bottom is work animal horsepower which is shrinking

Environmental Impact Index

	Index factors			*Total index*
	(*a*)	(*b*)	(*c*)	($a \times b \times c$)
	Population (*1000s*)	*Beer consumption/population* (*Gallons/cap*)	*Beer bottles / Beer consumption* (*Bottles/gallon*)	*Beer bottles* (*1000 gross*)
1950	151,868	24·99	0·25	6,540
1967	197,859	26·27	1·26	45,476
1967 : 1950	1·30	1·05	5·08	6·95
Percentage increase 1950-67	30	5	408	595

Fig. 14. Beer bottles

at about 10 per cent per year and will eventually disappear. In the middle there is essentially no change. What has happened in the United States is as follows. Most of the production of basic necessities *per capita* is being maintained at about the same level, but the techniques used for providing for those necessities has shifted (for example, from natural products to unnatural ones) and it turns out that every shift has intensified the impact on the environment.

And here is another interesting fact: those productive activities at the top of the growth curve are also the most profitable. No one makes much money these days investing in railroads; many in the United States are in receivership. We do not make much on growing cotton fibre, or on raising work animals, or making soap. We do make a good deal selling nitrogen fertiliser and detergents and so on. In other words we have shifted the way in which we produce goods in the direction of greater economic return, but, tragically, this has caused a more intensified pollution of the environment.

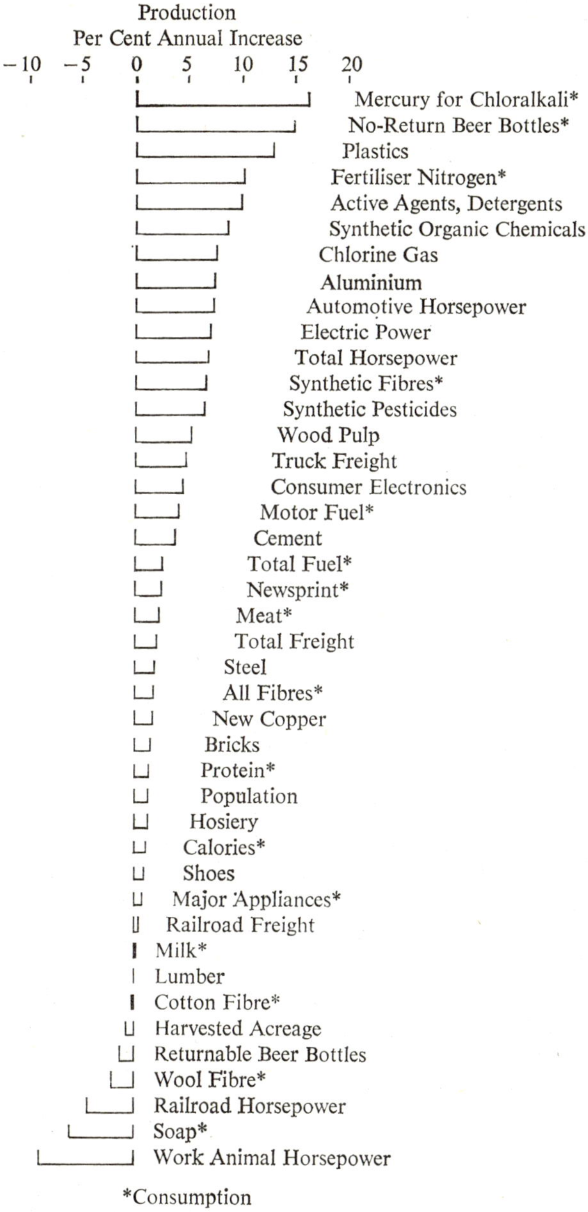

Fig. 15. Annual growth rates of production (or consumption) in the United States[12], see text for method of computation

Am I against technology? The answer is no. Take the present situation as regards sewage. At present a crop is removed from the soil, taken to the city where people are concentrated, converted to sewage which is introduced with surface waters, with or without treatment. This imposes a strain on the aquatic system and a drain on the soil system; introducing fertilisers only makes things worse. But we can get back to zero environmental impact by introducing new technology. The new technology would be a pipeline to conduct sewage from the city back to the land. Man would then be back in the soil cycle. The organic waste would be conducted back to the soil to be converted into humus, taking the strain off the system. The point I am making is that it is not technology *per se* which is harmful but technology which violates the principles of ecology. A technology which replaces a fibre obtained naturally, which you get gratis, without air pollution, with a fibre obtained only by consuming a non-renewable resource and polluting the air, makes no ecological sense. In the same way it makes no sense to use trucks instead of railroads, thereby polluting the air more for the same economic good. The basic cause of environmental pollution, at least in the United States since 1946, appears to be largely the transformation of our productive system in such a way as to intensify the stress on the environment.

We are not going to be able to deal with environmental problems unless we recognise that we are going to have to undo the huge change in our productive system that has taken place since 1946. This means rebuilding our industry. It means building railroads rather than roads. It means using soap made from fats produced by an ecologically sound method rather than detergents. And it is immediately obvious that none of these things are going to happen without first confronting very serious economic, and inevitably political, problems.

So, for example, there is no way that I can see of going back to natural products without confronting the problem of our relations with the Third World, where most such materials originate. The manufacture of synthetic rubber pollutes the environment, whereas natural rubber is made calmly and coolly by rubber plants. The reason why the United States has synthetic rubber plants is partly because the military insist that this is a vital military supply and must be independent of any foreign country. Since this way of thinking leads to an intolerable stress on the environment, then one step towards solving environmental problems is to make sure that military considerations do not control our productive system. It becomes essential that, rather than think of other countries as potential enemies, we consider the world as an ecological whole.

The main message that I want to leave is that the environmental crisis originates in the social misuse of technology, in purposes more closely related to profit than to human welfare. A transformation of our productivity during the Second World War led to general use of environmentally unsuitable technologies. The solution to the problems these unsuitable technologies have caused is a new transformation – this time to technologies that are compatible with the environment.

1. DEPARTMENT OF COMMERCE (1970) *Statistical Abstract of the United States*, US Government Printing Office, Washington, D.C., p. 5 and *ibid.* (1966) *The National Income and Product Accounts of the United States 1929-65*, pp. 4-5.
2. *Agricultural Statistics* (1967), US Government Printing Office, Washington, D.C., pp. 531, 544, 583; *ibid.* (1970), pp. 444, 454, 481.
3. J. H. DAWES *et al.* (1968) *Proc. 24th Ann. Meeting Soil Conservation Society of America*, Fort Collins, Colorado.
4. *Agricultural Statistics* (1970), US Government Printing Office, Washington, D.C., p. 149.
5. L. W. WEINBERGER *et al.* (1966) In Hearings before the Subcommittee on Science, Research and Development of the House Committee on Science and Astronautics, *The Adequacy of Technology for Pollution Abatement*, US Government Printing Office, Washington, D.C., **2**, p. 756.
6. DEPARTMENT OF COMMERCE (1962) *Statistical Abstract of the United States*, p. 198; *ibid.* (1966), p. 789; *ibid.*, p. 713.
7. BUREAU OF THE CENSUS (1911) *Current Industrial Reports, Series M28A Inorganic Chemicals and Gases* and from *Statistical Abstract of the United States, op. cit.*
8. Brake horsepower and compression ratio data are from *Brief Passenger Car Data* (Vols. for 1951 and 1970), Ethyl Corporation. Gasoline consumption data are from *Statistical Abstract of the United States* (1911), *op. cit.*
9. *Minerals Yearbook 1947-1968* and *Statistical Abstract of the United States, op. cit.*, (1900).
10. T. A. HULS and H. A. NICKOL (1968) 'Engine Variables Influence Nitric Oxide Concentration in Exhaust Gas' in *Society of Automotive*

Engineers Journal 76:8, pp. 40-44. *The Effect of Engine Operating Variables on Oxides of Nitrogen.* A report to the Variables Panel of the Group on Composition of Exhaust Gases. CRC, from the General Motors Research Staff, September 25, 1957.

11. *Statistical Abstract of the United States*, *op. cit.* (1951), p. 792; *ibid.* (1955), p. 833; *ibid.* (1970), p. 12.
12. *Ibid.* (1948-70).

INDEX